DR. JANG'S SAT* 800 CHEMISTRY SUBJECT TEST

SIMON JANG

Published in the United States by CreateSpace Publishing, North Charleston, SC.

Jang, Simon.
Dr. Jang's SAT 800 Chemistry Subject Test/ Simon Jang
484p. 28 cm.
1. SAT (Educational test)—Study guides. 2. Chemistry—Examinations—Study guides. 3. Chemistry / Study & Teaching. 4. Study Aids / SAT.
378.166 -dc23

ISBN-10: 1515216411
ISBN-13: 978-1515216414

www.DrJang800.com

Table of Contents

How This Book Can Help You

For more than 10 years, we have taught chemistry extensively in both the high school and private settings. One thing we have noticed throughout our years of teaching is that there is a lack of effective learning material for students of any level studying for the SAT Chemistry subject test. To remedy this, we have produced this book. It contains all the material you need to know to get a great score. Dr. Jang believes that anyone can get an excellent SAT score in chemistry in a short period of time, provided that he or she focuses on the content required for the test and the skills to tackle the questions quickly and efficiently.

Here are some ways this book can help you on the SAT Chemistry subject test and beyond:

Precise But Detailed Content Knowledge

In this book, we divide all of the content knowledge needed for SAT Chemistry subject test into sixteen chapters organized with the following features:

- All the facts that you need to be familiar with are directly listed. In general, high school chemistry consists of 50% understanding concepts and 50% memorizing or familiarizing facts. Of course, when you try to memorize things, being able to reason with the concepts and to understand what you're reading will help you remember them better.

- More content than most SAT chemistry books on the market. This book covers all the material needed to prepare for the SAT Chemistry subject test. This book is a great study guide for your honors and AP chemistry classes.

2000+ Practice Problems and Ten Mock Tests

In addition to a thorough overview of materials, this book provides over 2000 practice problems to reinforce your understanding of the material and pinpoint your weak areas that need improvement. This book contains ten mock tests at the end, more than any other SAT chemistry book on the market.

The ten mock tests closely mimic the actual exam and provide even more practices. By taking these mock exams with a timer under standard test conditions, students will bolster the skill set required for the real test.

Effective Problem Solving Techniques for Every Question

All questions in this book have been answered with detailed key concepts explained on the side, so that you can check your answer and reinforce your weak areas.

SAT Chemistry Diagnostic Test

This book includes a diagnostic test that contains 90 questions on the 56 topics that are covered on the SAT Chemistry subject test. The purpose of the diagnostic test is to allow you to measure your level of proficiency and to identify your weakest areas.

All of the questions in the diagnostic test are on a medium to hard level on the actual subject test. So if you are quite comfortable with most of these questions, you should be able to do well on the SAT Chemistry subject test. If you have no idea how to solve a question, you should make a note to spend additional time studying that topic.

About the Author

Dr. Simon Jang has been teaching in public high schools and in their own private tutoring studios for more than 10 years. He has developed a unique and proven SAT learning system that suits the students' needs and helps them efficiently prepare for the SAT Chemistry subject test. Over the years, his innovative methods and effective teaching materials have benefitted not only his students' scores, but also his students' endeavors in college and beyond.

Dr. Jang received a PhD. in Chemical Engineering from New York Polytechnic University. He worked as a software developer before he became a high school teacher. He has been teaching math, physics, and chemistry in New Jersey public high schools for many years. He has dedicated his spare time to developing innovative methods of teaching high school math, chemistry, and physics in his established tutoring studio.

This book is a product of the effective learning materials developed over years by Dr. Jang to both introduce a new student to the subject and remedy any test-taking weaknesses for the SAT Chemistry subject test.

Acknowledgements

I would like to acknowledge the help and support from my wife, Tiffany, our lovely daughters, Jennifer and Justine, and the countless students over the years who have provided feedback on our system.

I would like to give many thanks to twin sisters Courtney and Bethany Hou (seniors at West Essex High school) as well as Alexander King (freshman at the University of Washington) for spending their summer helping me write and edit this book.

I send special thanks to my parents back in Taiwan for their help and support as well. Without the help of everyone around me, this enormous project would have never even been conceptualized.

And finally, a special acknowledge to you, the reader, for picking up this book and taking a vested interest in the study of Chemistry. It is often a challenging subject, but also a worthwhile one. I wish you the best of luck in your journey into Chemistry with me.

About the SAT Chemistry Subject Test

The **SAT Chemistry subject test** is administered by the College Board. It is a one-hour multiple choice test given to assess high school honors level Chemistry. Students are **NOT allowed to use a calculator on this test.** The only resource a student may use is a periodic table which is provided with the test booklet. This table only provides atomic masses, atomic numbers, and symbols for each element.

This test contains **85** multiple-choices with **three** types of questions: **classification questions, relationship-analysis questions**, and **five-choice standard questions**. Usually, classification questions are the questions numbered 1 to 24. The relationship analysis questions are the next 15 questions, numbered from 101 to 115 and the five-choice standard questions are in the last 46 questions, numbered from 25 to 70.

Relationship-analysis questions consist of two statements, statement I and statement II. You must determine whether each statement is individually true or false. If both of the statements are true, you then must decide if the second statement is the reason for the first statement being true.

All questions have five answer choices. Students receive 1 point for every correct answer, deduct ¼ of a point for each incorrect answer, and deduct 0 point for the questions left blank. College Board then converted this raw score to a scaled score of 200-800.

Anticipated Skills (From the Guidelines of College Board's SAT Chemistry Subject Test)

- Remembering fundamental concepts and specific information, and demonstrating familiarity with terminology
- Understanding the major concepts of chemistry and being able to apply a single principle to unfamiliar and/or practical situations to obtain a qualitative result or solve a quantitative problem
- Organizing and interpreting results from observation and experimentation; drawing conclusions and inferences from experimental data; integrating two or more relationships to solve problems
- Being able to handle simple algebraic relationships, direct and inverse proportions, and exponents and scientific notations when solving word problems

Topics on the Test (From the Guidelines of College Board's SAT Chemistry Subject Test)

Structure of matter (25%)

- Atomic Structure, including experimental evidence of atomic structure, quantum numbers and energy levels (orbitals), electron configurations, and periodic trends
- Molecular Structure, including Lewis structures, three-dimensional molecular shapes, and polarity
- Bonding, including ionic, covalent, and metallic bonds, relationships of bonding to properties and structures, intermolecular forces such as hydrogen bonding, dipole-dipole forces, and dispersion (London) forces

States of matter (16%)

- Gases, including the kinetic molecular theory, gas law relationships, molar volumes, density, and stoichiometry
- Liquids and Solids, including intermolecular forces in liquids and solids, types of solids, phase changes, and phase diagrams
- Solutions, including molarity and percent by mass concentrations, solution preparation and stoichiometry, factors affecting solubility of solids, liquids, and gases, and qualitative aspects of colligative properties

Reaction types (14%)

- Acids and Bases, including Brønsted-Lowry theory, strong and weak acids and bases, pH, titrations, and indicators
- Oxidation-Reduction, including recognition of oxidation-reduction reactions, combustion, oxidation numbers, and use of activity series
- Precipitation, including basic solubility rules

Stoichiometry (14%)

- Mole Concept, including molar mass, Avogadro's number, empirical and molecular formulas
- Chemical Equations, including the balancing of equations, stoichiometric calculations, percent yield, and limiting reactants

Equilibrium and reaction rates (5%)

- Equilibrium Systems, including factors affecting position of equilibrium (LeChâtelier's principle) in gaseous and aqueous systems, equilibrium constants, and equilibrium expressions
- Rates of Reactions, including factors affecting reaction rates, potential energy diagrams, and activation energies

Thermochemistry (6%)

- Including conservation of energy, calorimetry and specific heats, enthalpy (heat) changes associated with phase changes and chemical reactions, heating and cooling curves, and entropy

Descriptive Chemistry (12%)

- Including common elements, nomenclature of ions and compounds, periodic trends in chemical and physical properties of the elements, reactivity of elements and prediction of products of chemical reactions, examples of simple organic compounds, and compounds of environmental concern

Laboratory (8%)

- Including knowledge of laboratory equipment, measurements, procedures, observations, safety, calculations, data analysis, interpretation of graphical data, and drawing conclusions from observations and data

About the Diagnostic Test in This Book

This diagnostic test contains 90 questions on the 56 topics that are covered on the **SAT Chemistry subject test**. The ordering of each topic is consistent with the chapter arrangements in this book. The purpose of the diagnostic test is to allow you to measure your level of proficiency and to identify your weakest areas.

It is important that you take this diagnostic test to find out your weakest areas and then study those areas accordingly. All the questions in the diagnostic test are on a medium to hard level on the actual SAT. So if you quite comfortable with some of these questions, you should be able to do well on the SAT Chemistry subject test in those areas. If you have no idea how to solve a question, you should leave a mark on the question and spend more time studying that area in the future.

SAT Chemistry Diagnostic Test

Matter and Its Properties

1. Which of the following is (are) the substance that can be further simplified by ordinary chemical means?
   I. An element or a compound
   II. A mixture or a compound
   III. An element or a mixture
   a) I only
   b) II only
   c) III only
   d) I, II only
   e) I, II, III

2. All of the following are chemical reactions EXCEPT
   a) combining atoms of elements to form a molecule.
   b) separating the molecules of a mixture.
   c) breaking down compounds into elements.
   d) reacting a compound and an element to form a new compound and element.
   e) the rusting of the metal iron.

Classification of Matter

3. The ingredients of a can of powder in kitchen contain corn starch, sodium bicarbonate, calcium acid phosphate, and sodium aluminum sulfate. Therefore, this powder is a
   a) compound.
   b) mixture.
   c) molecule.
   d) mixture of elements.
   e) pure material.

Atomic Theory

4. Hydrogen can exist as ^{1}H, ^{2}H, and ^{3}H. Which of the following is true?
   a) ^{1}H and ^{2}H both have the same number of neutrons.
   b) Water molecules (H_2O) in which all the hydrogen atoms are ^{1}H are unlikely to have a different boiling point from water molecules in which all of the hydrogen atoms are ^{2}H.
   c) ^{1}H and ^{3}H are likely to have similar radioactive properties.
   d) ^{3}H and ^{3}He possess an identical number of neutrons.
   e) ^{1}H does not possess a neutron.

5. Which of the following regarding the Rutherford experiment is NOT correct?
   a) Most alpha particles passed through the gold foil without being deflected, since the nuclei of the atoms represented such a small portion of the total atomic volume.
   b) Coulomb's law, which states that like charges repel each other, accounts for the deflection of alpha particles passing close to gold atom nuclei.
   c) Most alpha particles passed through the gold foil without being deflected, since the nuclei of the atoms represented such a small

portion of the total atomic mass.

d) Because of the electrons' small masses, they did not deflect the alpha particles.
e) The high charge of the gold nuclei helps to account for their ability to deflect smaller helium nuclei passing close by.

Properties of Light

6. What is the wavelength of light that has a frequency of $4.00 \times 10^{14}\ s^{-1}$? (The speed of light is $3.00 \times 10^{8}\ s^{-1}$.)
   a) 7.5 nm
   b) 1333 nm
   c) 750 nm
   d) $1.33\ cm^{-1}$
   e) 1.2×10^{23} m

The Quantum Model of the Atom

7. Which quantum number describes the shape of an orbital?
   a) n
   b) l
   c) m_l
   d) m_s
   e) s

8. If the set of quantum numbers n = 3, l = 1, m_l = 0, m_s = +1/2 represents the last electron to be added to complete the ground state electron configuration of an element, which of the following could be the symbol for the element?
   a) Na
   b) Si
   c) Th
   d) V
   e) Zn

Electron Configurations

9. Which electron configuration corresponds to that of a noble gas?
   a) $1s^2 2s^2 2p^6 3s^2 3p^6 4s^1$
   b) $1s^2 2s^2 2p^6 3s^2 3p^4$
   c) $1s^2 2s^2 2p^6 3s^2 3p^6$
   d) $1s^2 2s^2 2p^6 3s^1$
   e) 1s 2s 2p 3s 3p

10. If an electron jumps from $1s^2 2s^2 2p^6 3s^2 3p^6 4s^1$ to $1s^2 2s^2 2p^6 3s^2 3p^5 4s^2$, it will
    a) absorb energy.
    b) release energy.
    c) bind to another atom.
    d) stay at the lowest energy level.
    e) undergo no change in energy.

The Periodic Law

11. The elements within each column of the periodic table
    a) have similar valence electron configurations.
    b) have similar atomic radii.
    c) have the same principal quantum number.
    d) will react to form stable elements.
    e) have no similar chemical properties.

12. Which of the following shows Ca^{2+}, Ar, S^{2-}, $C1^-$, and K^+ in order of increasing size from smallest to largest?
    a) Ar, S^{-2}, $C1^-$, K^+, Ca^{2+}
    b) S^{-2}, Cl^-, Ar, K^+, Ca^{2+}
    c) S^{2-}, $C1^-$, Ar, Ca^{2+}, K^+
    d) Ca^{2+}, K^+, Ar, Cl^{-1}, S^{-2}
    e) Ca^{2+}, K^+, Ar, S^{2-}, Cl^-

Blocks and Groups

13. The transition metals are characterized by
    a) completely filled d subshells.
    b) completely filled f subshells.
    c) partially filled d subshells.
    d) partially filled f subshells.
    e) both (a) and (c) are correct.

14. Arrange the following elements in order of decreasing nonmetallic character: Ge, Sn, Pb, and Si.
    a) Pb, Sn, Ge, Si
    b) Ge, Sn, Pb, Si
    c) Si, Ge, Sn, Pb
    d) They all have equal nonmetallic character since they are all in the same column of the periodic table.
    e) None of the above

Introduction to Chemical Bonding

15. This is responsible for the relatively high boiling point of water.
    a) Hydrogen bonding
    b) Ionic bonding
    c) Metallic bonding
    d) Non-polar covalent bonding
    e) Polar covalent bonding

16. When the electrons are shared unequally by two atoms, the bond is said to be
    a) covalent.
    b) polar covalent.
    c) network covalent.
    d) ionic.
    e) metallic.

Lewis Structures

17. According to the formal charges of the Lewis structures, which is the most stable resonance structure for N_2O?
    a) : N≡N=O::
    b) ::N=O=N::
    c) ::N=N=O::
    d) : N≡N−O:::
    e) None of the above

18. Which of the following sets of molecules contains only non-polar species?
    a) BH_3, NH_3, AlH_3
    b) NO_2, CO_2, ClO_2
    c) HCl, HNO_2, $HClO_3$
    d) BH_3, H_2S, BCl_3
    e) BeH_2, BH_3 CH_4

Molecular Geometry

19. Which of these molecules have all atoms lying in the same plane?
    I. CBr_4
    II. PF_5
    III. NH_3
    IV. SO_3
    V. HCN
    a) I and III only
    b) II only
    c) III and V only
    d) IV only
    e) IV and V only

20. The carbon atoms in acetic acid (CH_3COOH) exhibit what type(s) of hybridization?
    I. sp
    II. sp^2
    III. sp^3
    a) I only
    b) II only
    c) I and II only
    d) II and III only
    e) I, II, and III

Intermolecular Forces

21. The concept of "like dissolves like" is illustrated by which of the following?
    a) I_2(s) is more soluble in CCl_4 than in water.
    b) NaCl(s) is more soluble in CCl_4 than NaCl(s) is in water.
    c) $CuSO_4$(s) is more soluble in CCl_4 than $CuSO_4$ is in water.
    d) CCl_4 is soluble in water.
    e) I_2(s) is more soluble in water than I_2(s) is in CCl_4.

Naming Compounds

22. What is the chemical name of H_2SO_3?
    a) Sulfuric acid
    b) Sulfurous acid
    c) Hydrosulfuric acid
    d) Hyposulfuric acid
    e) Hyposulfurous acid

Types of Chemical Reactions

$CH_3CONa + HC1O_4 \rightarrow CH_3CO_2H + NaClO_4$

23. The above reaction is classified as a
    a) double displacement reaction.
    b) combination reaction.
    c) decomposition reaction.
    d) single displacement and decomposition reaction.
    e) combination and decomposition reaction.

Stoichiometry

24. What is the empirical formula for a compound containing 63.8% N and 36.2% O?
    a) N_2O_5
    b) N_2O_3
    c) NO_2
    d) NO
    e) N_2O

25. In the reaction $CaCO_3 + 2HCl \rightarrow H_2O + CO_2 + CaCl_2$, how many grams of $CaCO_3$ (molar mass of 100) are needed to produce 3.00 L of CO_2 at STP?
    a) 13.4
    b) 9.11
    c) 5.89
    d) 300
    e) 7.47

Limiting Reactants and Percent Yield

26. For the following equation, $Fe_2O_3(s) + 3CO(g) \rightarrow 2Fe(s) + 3CO_2(g)$, when 3.0 moles of Fe_2O_3 are allowed to completely react with 56 g CO, approximately how many moles of iron are produced?
    a) 0.7
    b) 1.3
    c) 2.0
    d) 2.7
    e) 6.0

The Kinetic-Molecular Theory of Gases

27. A gas is the least likely to behave ideally under which of the following conditions:

    I. High temperature
    II. Low temperature
    III. Low pressure

    a) I only
    b) II only
    c) I and III only
    d) II and III only
    e) I, II, and III

28. All of the following statements underline the kinetic molecular theory of gases EXCEPT:
    a) Gas molecules have no intermolecular forces.
    b) Gas particles are in random motion.
    c) The collisions between gas particles are elastic.
    d) Gas particles have no volume.
    e) Average kinetic energy is proportional to the temperature (°C) of the gas.

Pressure

29. What will the total pressure be in a 2.50-L flask at 25 °C if it contains 0.016 moles of CO and 0.035 moles of CH_4?
    a) 31.4 mm Hg
    b) 380 mm Hg
    c) 0.041 mm Hg
    d) 935 mm Hg
    e) 1.23 atm

30. At 30 °C, a sample of hydrogen is collected over water ($P_{30°C}$ = 31.82 mm Hg) in a 500-mL flask. The total pressure in the collection flask is 745 mm Hg. What will be the percent of error in the amount of hydrogen reported if the correction for the vapor pressure of water is not made?
    a) 0.0%
    b) +4.5%
    c) −4.5%
    d) +4.3%
    e) −4.3%

The Gas Laws

31. According to Boyle's law, gases will _____ if pressure is reduced.
    I. increase in volume
    II. increase in temperature
    III. increase in average kinetic energy
    IV. increase in effusion rate
    a) I only
    b) II only
    c) III only
    d) IV only
    e) I and II only

32. If a 360 mL sample of helium contains 0.25 moles of gas, how many molecules of chlorine gas would occupy the same volume at the same temperature and pressure?
    a) 1.2×10^{24}
    b) 6.022×10^{23}
    c) 3.01×10^{23}
    d) 1.5×10^{23}
    e) 7.55×10^{22}

Effusion

33. The rate of diffusion of hydrogen gas as compared to that of oxygen gas is
    a) ½ as fast.
    b) the same.
    c) twice as fast.
    d) four times as fast.
    e) eight times as fast.

Properties of Liquids

34. What factor(s) will determine if two liquids are miscible?
    a) Molecular size
    b) Molecular polarity
    c) Density
    d) Both B and C
    e) None of the above

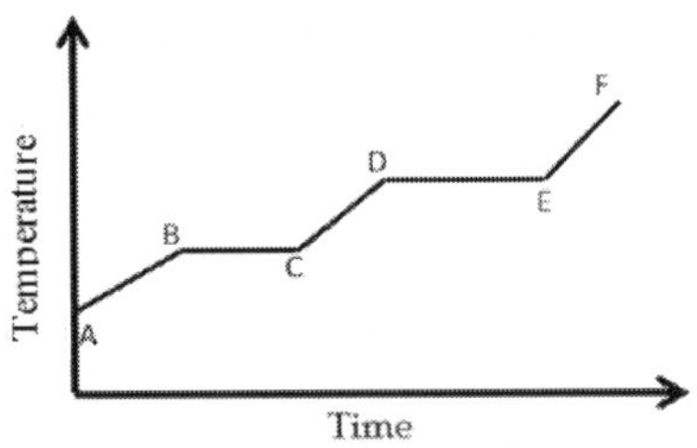

The heating curve of a pure substance

35. Which line segment in the graph above corresponds to a period where the kinetic energy of the liquid is increasing?
    a) AB
    b) BC
    c) CD
    d) DE
    e) EF

Properties of Solids

36. A metallic oxide placed in water will most likely yield
    a) an acid.
    b) a base.
    c) a metallic anhydride.
    d) a basic anhydride.
    e) None of the above

Changes of State

37. The normal boiling point of this substance is approximately

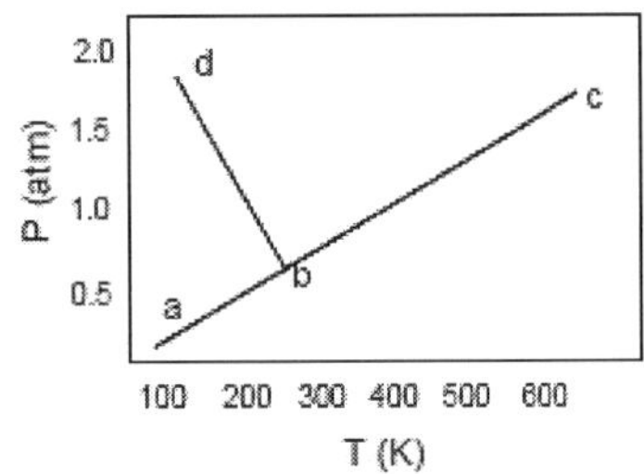

Phase diagram of a pure substance

    a) 100 K
    b) 200 K
    c) 300 K
    d) 400 K
    e) 500 K

38. Put the following compounds in order in terms of increasing melting point: SiH_4, SiO_2, CH_4, NH_3, PH_3.
    a) NH_3, PH_3, CH_4, SiH_4, SiO,
    b) SiO_2, PH_3, NH_3, CH_4, SiH_4
    c) SiH_4, CH_4, NH_3, PH_3, SiO_2
    d) CH_4, SiH_4, PH_3, NH_3, SiO_2
    e) CH_4, SiH_4, SiO_2, NH_3, PH_3

Properties of Water

39. Decomposing water with an electric current will give a hydrogen to oxygen volume ratio of
    a) 1 : 9
    b) 2 : 1
    c) 1 : 2
    d) 1 : 8
    e) None of the above

Types of Mixtures

40. Which of the following is/are TRUE?
    I. Adding a solute will raise the vapor pressure and boiling point of the solvent.
    II. Adding a solute will change in boiling and freezing points of the solvent.
    III. The number of solute particles in a solvent is an important factor in determining the boiling point elevation of the solvent.
    a) I only
    b) II only
    c) I and II only
    d) II and III only
    e) I, II, and III

The Solution Process

41. Which of the following is the most electrically conductive?
    a) Sugar dissolved in water
    b) Salt water
    c) Salt dissolved in an organic solvent
    d) An oil and water mixture
    e) None of the above

Concentration of Solutions

42. To what volume, in mL, must 50.0 mL of 3.50 M H_2SO_4 be diluted to in order to make 2 M H_2SO_4?
    a) 25
    b) 60.1
    c) 87.5
    d) 93.2
    e) 101

Colligative Properties

43. One mole NaCl in 1000 g H_2O will change the boiling point of water to
    a) 100.51 °C
    b) 101.02 °C
    c) 101.53 °C
    d) 101.86 °C
    e) 103.62 °C

Energy and Work

44. Calculate the amount of heat needed to bring 10 g of ice from −45 °C to 110 °C. (The heat of fusion of ice is 80 cal/g and the heat of vaporization of water is 540 cal/g, and the heat capacities of both ice and steam are 0.5 cal/g°C).
    a) 7,325 cal
    b) 7,450 cal
    c) 7.325 kcal
    d) 7.475 kcal
    e) 7.5 kcal

45. A 50 g sample of metal was heated to 100 °C and then dropped into a beaker containing 50 g of water at 25 °C. If the specific heat capacity of the metal is 0.25 cal/g·°C, what is the final temperature of the water?
    a) 27 °C
    b) 40 °C
    c) 60 °C
    d) 86 °C
    e) 90 °C

Enthalpy (ΔH)

46. Given the following thermochemical data:

    $N_2O_4(g) \rightarrow 2NO_2(g)$ ΔH° = +57.93 kJ

    $2NO(g) + O_2(g) \rightarrow 2NO_2(g)$ ΔH° = −113.14 kJ

    Determine the heat of the following reaction:

    $$2NO(g) + O_2(g) \rightarrow N_2O_4(g)$$

    a) 171.07 kJ
    b) −55.21 kJ
    c) −171.07 kJ
    d) +55.21 kJ
    e) −85.54 kJ

47. What is the ΔH of the reaction that forms CO_2 from C and O_2?

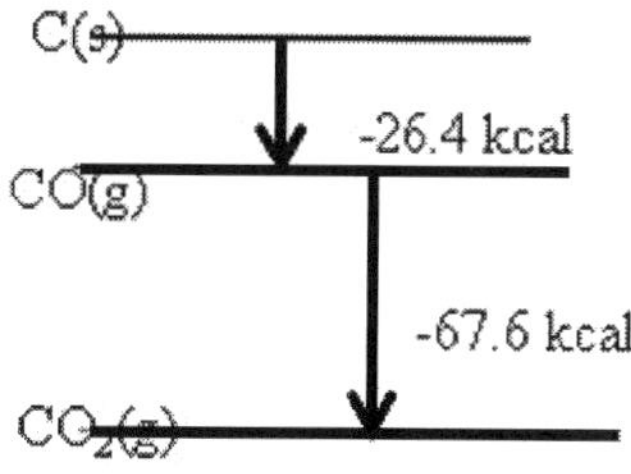

    a) −94.0 kcal
    b) −26.4 kcal
    c) −67.6 kcal
    d) −1.2 kcal
    e) 26.4 kcal

Entropy (ΔS)

48. Which of the following explains the observation that, when KCl is dissolved, water condenses on the outside of the beaker?
   a) ΔH is positive and ΔS is negative.
   b) ΔH is positive and ΔS is positive.
   c) ΔH is negative and ΔS is negative.
   d) ΔH is negative and ΔS is positive.
   e) There is no ΔH and ΔS is negative.

49. Which of the following describes a system that CANNOT be spontaneous?
   a) ΔH is positive and ΔS is negative.
   b) ΔH is positive and ΔS is positive.
   c) ΔH is negative and ΔS is negative.
   d) ΔH is negative and ΔS is positive.
   e) There is no ΔH, and ΔS is positive.

Chemical Reaction Rates

50. According to chemical kinetic theory, a reaction can occur
   a) if the reactants collide with the proper orientation.
   b) if the reactants possess sufficient energy of collision.
   c) if the reactants are able to form a correct transition state.
   d) All of the above

51. All of the following are true statements concerning catalysts EXCEPT
   a) A catalyst will speed up the rate-determining step.
   b) A catalyst will be used up in a reaction.
   c) A catalyst may induce steric strain in a molecule to make it react more readily.
   d) A catalyst will lower the activation energy of a reaction.
   e) A catalyst will change the equilibrium constant.

Rate Laws

52. Nitrogen monoxide and Oxygen are combined in a flask at 25 °C and allowed to react as follows:

$$2NO(g) + O_2(g) \rightarrow 2NO_2(g)$$

The concentrations of the reactants and the initial rates are as listed. Which of the following is the rate law equation for this reaction?

Experiment	$[O_2]$	[NO]	Rate
1	0.02	0.05	0.38
2	0.02	0.1	1.52
3	0.08	0.1	6.08

   a) Rate = $k[O_2]^2[NO]^2$
   b) Rate = $k[NO]^2$
   c) Rate = $k[O_2][NO]^2$
   d) Rate = $k[O_2][NO]$
   e) Rate = $k[O_2]^2$

Reaction Mechanisms

$$2NO(g) + O_2(g) \rightarrow 2NO_2(g)$$

53. The reaction between nitrogen monoxide and oxygen is shown above. One proposed mechanism is the following:

Step 1: $NO(g) + O_2(g) \rightarrow NO_2(g) + O(g)$ (slow)

Step 2: $NO(g) + O(g) \rightarrow NO_2(g)$ (fast)

Which of the following rate expressions best agrees with this possible mechanism?

a) Rate = k [NO] [O]
b) Rate = k [NO] [O_2]
c) Rate = k $[NO]^2$ [O_2]
d) Rate = k [NO] / [O_2]
e) Rate = k [NO]/ [O]

Equilibrium Conditions

54. If $K_{eq} \gg 1$,
   a) the equilibrium mixture will favor the products over the reactants.
   b) the equilibrium mixture will favor the reactants over the products.
   c) the equilibrium mixture will have equal parts reactant and product.
   d) the reaction is irreversible.
   e) None of the above

55. The correct form of the solubility product for silver chromate, Ag_2CrO_4, is
   a) $[Ag^+]^2[CrO_4^{-2}]$
   b) $[Ag^+][CrO_4^{-2}]$
   c) $[Ag^+][CrO_4^{-2}]^2$
   d) $[Ag^+]^2[CrO_4^{-2}]^4$
   e) $[Ag]^2[CrO_4^{-2}]$

Le Chatelier's principle

56. Heat + $2NO_2(g) \leftrightarrow N_2O_4(g)$
   For the above reaction, which change would NOT be effective in increasing the amount of $N_2O_4(g)$ formed?
   a) Decreasing the volume of the reaction vessel
   b) Increasing the reaction temperature
   c) Adding N_2 to increase the pressure
   d) Absorbing $N_2O_4(g)$ with a solid absorbent
   e) Adding more $NO_2(g)$ to the reaction vessel

57. $2NOBr(g) \leftrightarrow 2\ NO(g) + Br_2(g)$ and ΔH = 16.1 kJ/mol. For the reaction above, which of the following will be true if the temperature of the system is decreased and pressure is held constant?
   a) K_{eq} will increase.
   b) The concentration of NO will increase.
   c) The concentration of Br_2 will decrease.
   d) The concentration of NOBr will decrease.
   e) The reaction $2NO(g) + Br_2(g) \leftrightarrow 2NOBr(g)$ will be endothermic.

Solving Equilibrium Problems

58. The weak acid H_2A ionizes in two steps with these equilibrium constants:
   $H_2A \leftrightarrow H^+ + HA^-$ $K_{a1} = 2.3 \times 10^{-4}$
   $HA^- \leftrightarrow H+ + A^{-2}$ $K_{a2} = 4.5 \times 10^{-7}$
   What is the equilibrium constant for the reaction $H_2A \leftrightarrow 2H^+ + A^{2-}$?
   a) 6.8×10^{-11}
   b) 1.0×10^{-10}
   c) 2.3×10^{-4}
   d) 2.0×10^{-3}
   e) 5.1×10^{2}

Properties of Acids and Bases

59. Which of the following has the highest pH?
   a) 0.1 M HCl
   b) 0.200 M $HC_2H_3O_2$
   c) 0.1 M Na_2CO_3
   d) 0.200 M NaCl
   e) 0.500 M $NaC_2H_3O_2$

60. A strip of litmus paper will appear blue when dipped in
    a) HBr(aq)
    b) NH_3(aq)
    c) H_2O(l)
    d) HF(aq)
    e) H_2CO_3(aq)

Acid-Base Theories

61. Which of the following characteristics is associated with Lewis bases?
    a) They react with metal to produce hydrogen gas.
    b) They donate unshared electron pairs.
    c) They always contain the hydroxide ion in their structures.
    d) They taste sour.
    e) They are formed by the reaction of a nonmetal oxide with water.

62. According to the Brønsted-Lowry theory, an acid is a(n)
    a) proton donor.
    b) proton acceptor.
    c) electron donor.
    d) electron acceptor.
    e) H^+ donor.

Acid-Base Reactions

63. In HNO_3(aq) + OH^-(aq) ⇌ H_2O(l) + NO_3^-(aq), which species is the conjugate acid?
    a) HNO_3(aq)
    b) OH^-(aq)
    c) H_2O(l)
    d) NO_3^-(aq)
    e) There is no conjugate acid.

64. When 0.250 moles of NaOH are added to 1.00 L of 0.1 M H_3PO_4, the solution will contain
    a) HPO_4^{-2}
    b) H_2PO^{4-}
    c) $PO4^{-3}$
    d) A and B
    e) A and C

Aqueous Solutions and pH Values

65. What is the pH of a 0.100 M solution of K_2HPO_4? (For H_3PO_4, pK_1 is 2.15, pK_2 is 7.20, and pK_3 is 12.35.)
    a) 1.00
    b) 13.00
    c) 9.78
    d) 6.67
    e) 4.10

Titrations and Determining pH

66. Which of the following sets of materials would make the best buffer solution?
    a) 1 M NaOH(aq), 1 M H_2SO_4(aq)
    b) 1 M CH_3COOH(aq), 1 M $NaCH3COO^-$(aq)
    c) 1 M CH_3COOH(aq), 6 M $Na^+CH3COO^-$(aq)
    d) 1 M CH_3COOH(aq), 1 M NaOH(aq)
    e) 1 M NaOH(aq), 1 M $NaCH3COO^-$(aq)

67. If 50.0 mL of a 0.0134 M HCl solution is mixed with 24.0 mL of a 0.0250 M NaOH solution, what is the pH of the final mixture?
    a) 1.87
    b) 12.40
    c) 5.29
    d) 3.02
    e) 10.98

Oxidation States

68. What is the oxidation number of Mn in $KMnO_4$?
    a) −7
    b) −3
    c) 0
    d) +3
    e) +7

69. For the reaction below, indicate which elements are reduced and which ones are oxidized:
    $2Cu(NO_3)_2 \rightarrow 2CuO + 4NO_2 + O_2$

	Oxidized	Reduced
a)	Nitrogen	Oxygen
b)	Copper	Oxygen
c)	Copper	Nitrogen
d)	Nitrogen	Copper
e)	Oxygen	Nitrogen

Balancing Redox Equations

70. What is the sum of the coefficients of the products for the following reaction?
    $K_2Cr_2O_7 + HCl \rightarrow KCl + CrCl_3 + H_2O + Cl_2$
    a) 10
    b) 12
    c) 13
    d) 14
    e) 28

Oxidizing and Reducing Agents

71. Which of the following lists of reducing agents is ordered in terms of decreasing strength?
    a) Na, Mg, Fe, Ag, Cu
    b) Mg, Na, Fe, Cu, Ag
    c) Ag, Cu, Fe, Mg, Na
    d) Na, Fe, Mg, Cu, Ag
    e) Na, Mg, Fe, Cu, Ag

72. For the reaction $Cu(s) + NO_3^-(aq) + H^+(aq) \rightarrow Cu^{2+}(aq) + NO_2(g) + H_2O(l)$, which of the following takes place?
    a) Cu(s) is oxidized.
    b) H^+ (aq) is oxidized.
    c) Cu(s) is reduced.
    d) H^+ (aq) is reduced.
    e) NO_3^- is oxidized.

Electrochemistry

73. If gold foil was placed in a solution containing Zn^{+2} ions, what would the reaction potential be? The electrode potentials are as listed:

$Zn \rightarrow Zn^{+2} + 2e^-$	$E^o = 0.76$ V
$Au \rightarrow Au^{+3} + 3e^-$	$E^o = -1.42$ V

    a) −1.84 V
    b) −2.18 V
    c) −0.66 V
    d) +2.18 V
    e) +1.34 V

74. In the electrochemical cell shown below, which of the following half-reactions occurs at the anode?

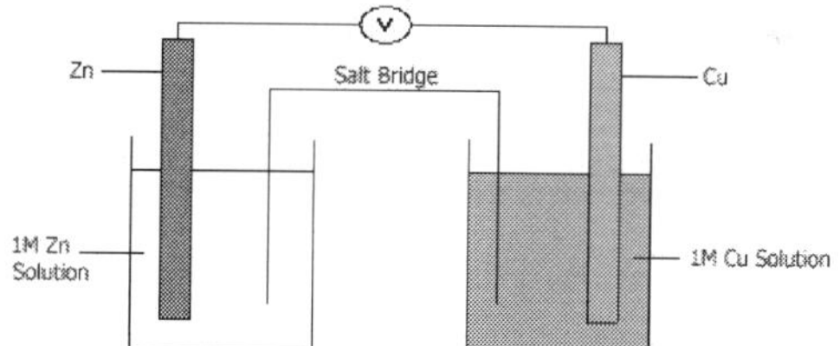

    a) $Cu^{+2} + e^- \rightarrow Cu^+$
    b) $Zn(s) \rightarrow Zn^{+2} + 2e^-$
    c) $Zn^{+2} + 2e^- \rightarrow Zn(s)$
    d) $Cu(s) \rightarrow Cu^{+2} + 2e^-$
    e) $Cu^{+2} + 2e^- \rightarrow Cu(s)$

Allotropes of Carbon

75. The following statements about carbon dioxide are true EXCEPT
    a) It can be produced by a reaction of an acid with $CaCO_3$.
    b) It is used in fire extinguishers.
    c) It dissolves in water at room temperature.
    d) It sublimes rather than melts at 20 °C and 1 atm pressure.
    e) It is a product of photosynthesis in plants.

76. Which of the following statements is true of ethene?
    a) Both carbon atoms are sp^2 hybridized and the molecule is planar.
    b) Both carbon atoms are sp^2 hybridized and all bond angles are approximately 109.5°.
    c) One carbon atom is sp hybridized while the other is sp^2.
    d) Both carbon atoms are sp3 hybridized and all bond angles are approximately 109.5°.
    e) Both carbon atoms are sp hybridized and the molecule is planar.

77. Which of the following is the formula for a noncyclic, saturated hydrocarbon?
    a) C_7H_{12}
    b) C_7H_{14}
    c) C_7H_{16}
    d) C_7H_{18}
    e) C_7H_{12}

Functional Groups

78. Which functional groups are present in the compound below? 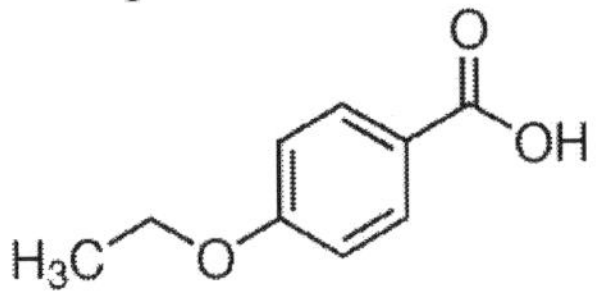
    a) Ester and ether
    b) Ester and amine
    c) Ester and carboxylic acid
    d) Ether and carboxylic acid
    e) Ether and ketone

Organic Reactions

79. Slight oxidation of a primary alcohol results in a(n)
    a) ketone
    b) organic acid
    c) ether
    d) aldehyde
    e) ester

Atomic structure

80. Atoms of ^{235}U and ^{238}U differ in structure by three
    a) electrons
    b) isotopes
    c) neutrons
    d) protons
    e) positron

Nuclear Reactions and Radioactive Decay

81. Which of the following equations represents alpha decay?
    a) $^{116}_{49}In \rightarrow {}^{116}_{50}Sn + X$
    b) $^{234}_{90}TH \rightarrow {}^{234}_{91}Pa + X$
    c) $^{38}_{19}K \rightarrow {}^{38}_{18}Ar + X$
    d) $^{222}_{86}Rn \rightarrow {}^{218}_{84}Po + X$
    e) $^{206}_{82}Pb^{*} \rightarrow {}^{206}_{82}Pb + X$

82. The half-life of a radioactive isotope is 20.0 minutes. What amount of a 1.00-gram sample of this isotope remains after 1.00 hour?
    a) 0.500 g
    b) 0.333 g
    c) 0.250 g
    d) 0.125 g
    e) 0.0625 g

Fission and Fusion

83. Which of the following equations represents nuclear fusion?
    a) ${}^{14}_{6}C \rightarrow {}^{14}_{7}N + {}^{0}_{-1}e$
    b) ${}^{27}_{13}Al + {}^{4}_{2}He \rightarrow {}^{30}_{15}P + {}^{1}_{0}n$
    c) ${}^{235}_{82}U + {}^{1}_{0}n \rightarrow {}^{139}_{56}Ba + {}^{94}_{36}Kr + 3\,{}^{1}_{0}n$
    d) ${}^{2}_{1}H + {}^{3}_{1}H \rightarrow {}^{4}_{2}He + {}^{1}_{0}n$
    e) ${}^{14}_{6}C \rightarrow {}^{14}_{7}N + {}^{0}_{-1}e$

84. Which of the following statements best describes what happens in a fission reaction?
    a) Heavy nuclei split into lighter nuclei.
    b) Light nuclei combine to form heavier nuclei.
    c) Energy is released and less stable elements are formed.
    d) Energy is absorbed and more stable elements are formed.
    e) Heavy nuclei combine with neutrons to form heavier nuclei.

Common Laboratory Equipment

85. A 35.25-mL sample is needed. The best piece of glassware to use is a
    a) burette.
    b) beaker.
    c) graduated cylinder.
    d) volumetric flask.
    e) pipet.

Common Laboratory Techniques

86. Which of the following laboratory techniques does NOT rely on a physical change in the components of a mixture?
    a) Chromatography
    b) Precipitation
    c) Filtering
    d) Distillation
    e) Evaporation

87. A very fine precipitate is best isolated by
    a) distillation.
    b) filtration.
    c) vacuum filtration.
    d) centrifugation.
    e) drying.

Basic Setup of Chemistry Labs

88. Methane is collected by
    a) upward displacement of air.
    b) displacement of water.
    c) downward displacement of air.
    d) displacement of mercury.
    e) filtration.

89. The most common method for determining the molarity of a solution of an acid is
    a) gravimetric analysis (weighing a precipitate.)
    b) titrating with a standard base.
    c) calculating the specific gravity of the acid.
    d) calculating the volume of gas evolved when the solution is reacted with Mg metal.
    e) determining the pH of the acid when the solution reacts with Mg metal.

Analyzing Data

90. A student mixes 10.0 mL of 0.10 M $AgNO_3$ with excess copper metal. The reaction should produce 0.107 gram of silver. However, the student obtains a mass of 0.150 grams of silver. Possible explanations for this yield being > 100% might include
    I. The student did not subtract the mass of the filter paper before recording results.
    II. The student did not thoroughly dry the sample before weighting.
    III. The copper metal did not react completely.
    a) I only
    b) II only
    c) I and II only
    d) I and III only
    e) I, II, and III

SAT Chemistry Diagnostic Test Key

1. B	11. A	21. A	31. A	41. B	51. B	61. B	71.E	81. D
2. B	12. D	22. B	32. D	42. C	52. C	62. A	72.A	82. D
3. B	13. C	23. A	33. D	43. B	53. B	63. C	73.B	83. D
4. E	14. A	24. E	34. B	44. D	54. A	64. E	74.B	84. A
5. C	15. A	25. A	35. C	45. B	55. A	65. C	75.E	85. A
6. C	16. B	26. B	36. B	46. C	56. C	66. B	76.A	86. B
7. B	17. D	27. C	37. D	47. A	57. C	67. D	77.C	87. D
8. B	18. E	28. E	38. D	48. B	58. B	68. E	78.D	88. B
9. C	19. E	29. B	39. B	49. A	59. C	69. E	79.D	89. B
10. A	20. D	30. B	40. D	50. D	60. B	70. D	80.C	90. C

SAT Chemistry Diagnostic Test Answers

1. *Answer: (b)*
   A mixture can be simplified by physical means. A compound can be simplified by chemical means.

2. *Answer: (b)*
   Chemical reactions will produce new substances. Only (b) does not produce a new substance.

3. *Answer: (b)*
   A mixture contains more than one compound.

4. *Answer: (e)*
   Isotopes of hydrogen all have one proton but differing numbers of neutrons.

5. *Answer: (c)*
   The nuclei of the gold atoms represent a major portion of the total atomic mass.

6. *Answer: (c)*
   $c = \lambda v$
   $3 \times 10^8 = 4 \times 10^{14} \cdot \lambda$
   $\lambda = \frac{3 \times 18^8}{4 \times 10^{14}}$
   $\lambda = 7.5 \times 10^{-7} = 750nm$

7. *Answer: (b)*
   The angular momentum quantum number (l) indicates the shape of the orbital.

8. *Answer: (b)*
   The total number of electrons in this element is 2 ($1s^2$) + 8 ($2s^2$) + 4 ($3s^2$ $3p^2$) = 14. Neutral Si atoms have 14 electrons.
   Each orbital can only hold two electrons. The first electron in an orbital will have a spin of +1/2.

9. *Answer: (c)*
   Noble gases have filled p orbitals.

10. *Answer: (a)*
    Energy is always required to make electrons move up higher energy levels.

11. *Answer: (a)*
    Elements of the same family have the same valence electron configurations, which leads to similar chemical properties.

12. *Answer: (d)*
    They all have the same number of electrons so the lower the charge of their nuclei, the larger their size.

13. *Answer: (c)*
    Transition metals have partially filled d orbitals.

14. *Answer: (a)*
    Metallic character increases down a group because losing electrons becomes easier.

15. *Answer: (a)*
    Hydrogen bonding is what causes the high boiling point of water.

16. *Answer: (b)*
    Shared electrons form a covalent bond.

17. *Answer: (d)*
    Only (d) follows the octet rule, with nitrogen having 5 valence electrons.

18. *Answer: (e)*
    (e) is the only one that have an unshared pair of electrons.

19. *Answer: (e)*
    Sp^2 and Sp have co-planar atoms.
    I. CBr_4 sp^3
    II. PF_5 dsp^3
    III. NH_3 sp^3
    IV. SO_3 sp^2
    V. HCN sp

20. *Answer: (d)*
    The carbon atoms of acetic acid (CH_3COOH) have both single and double bonds.

21. *Answer: (a)*
    I_2 is a non-polar molecule. Water is a polar molecule and CCl_4 is a non-polar molecule. Therefore, according to the concept of "like dissolves like, $I_2(s)$ is more soluble in CCl_4 than it is in water.

22. *Answer: (b)*
    H_2SO_4 is sulfuric acid.
    H_2SO_3 is sulfurous acid.
    H_2SO_2 is hyposulfurous acid.

23. *Answer: (a)*
This is a double replacement reaction.
$AB + CD \rightarrow AC + BD$

24. *Answer: (e)*
$N : O = \frac{63.8}{14} : \frac{36.2}{16} = 2 : 1$
There is a 2 to 1 ratio of nitrogen atoms to oxygen atoms, so the compound is N_2O.

25. *Answer: (a)*
$3.00 \text{ L of } CO_2 = \frac{3}{22.4} \text{ moles of } CO_2$
$= \frac{3}{22.4} \text{ moles of } CaCO_3$
$\frac{3}{22.4} \times 100 = 13.4 \text{ g of}$

26. *Answer: (b)*
56 g CO = 2 moles of CO
CO is the limiting reactant.
$CO : Fe = 3 : 2 = 2 : x$
$x = 1.3$ *moles of Fe*

27. *Answer: (c)*
As long as the gas particles are far apart, they will conform to the ideal gas conditions.

28. *Answer: (e)*
Average kinetic energy is proportional to the temperature (K) of the gas.

29. *Answer: (b)*
$PV = nRT$
$\frac{p}{760} \times 2.5 = (0.016 + 0.035) \times 0.082 \times (273+25) = 380 \text{ mm Hg}$

30. *Answer: (b)*
Percent Error $= \frac{31.82}{745} \times 100\% = 4.27\%$ *more than actual amount.*

31. *Answer: (a)*
Boyle's Law: The volume of a fixed mass of gas varies inversely with its pressure at constant temperature.

32. *Answer: (d)*
Two ideal gases at the same volume, pressure and temperature will have the same number of molecules.
$0.25 \times 6.02 \times 10^{23} = 1.51 \times 10^{23}$

33. *Answer: (d)*
Rate of diffusion of oxygen to hydrogen
$= \sqrt{2} : \sqrt{32} = 1 : 4$

34. *Answer: (b)*
Like dissolves like: a polar solute will dissolve better in a polar solvent, and a non-polar solute will dissolve better in a non-polar solvent.

35. *Answer: (c)*
Changing the temperature will change the kinetic energy of the system. CD is a liquid and EF is a gas.

36. *Answer: (b)*
Metallic oxide + Water = Base
Nonmetal oxide + Water = Acid

37. *Answer: (d)*
At 1 atm pressure, a liquid boils at its normal boiling point. The temperature is 400K when pressure is at 1 atm on line bc.

38. *Answer: (d)*
SiO_2 *is a crystalline solid, so it has the highest melting point.* NH_3 *is a polar molecule. Its melting point should be higher than that of non-polar compounds. For non-polar molecules, the higher the molar mass, the higher the melting point.*

39. *Answer: (b)*
$2H_2O \rightarrow 2H_2 + O_2$
$[H_2] : [O_2] = 2 : 1$

40. *Answer: (d)*
Adding a solute lowers the vapor pressure and raises boiling point.

41. *Answer: (b)*
Salt water is the most electrically conductive.

42. *Answer: (c)*
$50 \times 3.5 = x \times 2$
$x = 87.5 \text{ mL}$

43. *Answer: (b)*
One mole of NaCl produces two moles of ions.
$\Delta T_b = 2 \times 0.52 \times \frac{1}{1} = 1.04\ ^\circ C$

44. *Answer: (d)*
Ice at $-45\ ^\circ C \rightarrow$ *Ice at* $0\ ^\circ C \rightarrow$ *Water at* $0\ ^\circ C$
$\rightarrow$ *Water at* $100\ ^\circ C \rightarrow$ *Steam at* $100\ ^\circ C \rightarrow$
Steam at $110\ ^\circ C$
$Q = 10 \times 0.5 \times 45 + 80 \times 10 + 10 \times 1 \times 100 + 10 \times 540 + 10 \times 0.5 \times 10 = 7475 \text{ cal}$
$= 7.475 \text{ Kcal}.$

45. *Answer: (b)*
Assume that there is no heat loss during this process.
Let the final temperature be T.
$Q = 0$
$= 50 \times 0.25 \times (T - 100) + 50 \times 1 \times (T - 25)$
$T = 40\ °C$

46. *Answer: (c)*
Total $\Delta H = \Delta H_{Reaction\ 1} - \Delta H_{Reaction\ 2}$
$= -113.14 - 57.93 = -171.07\ kJ$

47. *Answer: (a)*
ΔH *of the Total Reaction* = ΔH *of Reaction 1* + ΔH *of Reaction 2* = $-26.4 - 67.6$
$= -94$ *Kcal.*

48. *Answer: (b)*
When KCl dissolves in water, the entropy of the system increases, and the system absorbs energy.

49. *Answer: (a)*
A positive ΔH *and negative* ΔS *will result in a positive* ΔG.

50. *Answer: (d)*
All of the choices are true.

51. *Answer: (b)*
A catalyst is not a reactant in a chemical reaction.

52. *Answer: (c)*
Doubling [NO] increases the rate by a factor of 4. Quadrupling $[O_2]$ *increases the rate by 4 as well.*
Rate = $k[O_2][NO]^2$

53. *Answer: (b)*
The first step is the rate determining step.
Rate = $k[NO][O_2]$

54. *Answer: (a)*
The bigger the K_{eq}, *the more the reaction favors the products.*

55. *Answer: (a)*
$Ag_2CrO_4 \rightarrow 2Ag^+ + CrO_4^{-2}$
Pure solids are not a part of the equation that determines the equilibrium constant.

56. *Answer: (c)*
Adding an inert gas will not shift the equilibrium.

57. *Answer: (c)*
When the temperature of a system is decreased, the equilibrium of an endothermic reaction will shift to the left. The concentration of Br_2 *will decrease.*

58. *Answer: (b)*
$H_2A \leftrightarrow H^+ + HA^-$
$+\ HA^- \leftrightarrow H+ + A^{-2}$
$H_2A \leftrightarrow 2H^+ + A^{2-}$
$K = K_{a1} \times K_{a2} = 2.3 \times 10^{-4} \times 4.5 \times 10^{-7}$
$= 1.0 \times 10^{-10}$

59. *Answer: (c)*
The strongest base has the highest pH value. Na_2CO_3 *is the strongest base here.*

60. *Answer: (b)*
Litmus paper will appear blue in a base solution. Only NH_3 *is a base in solution.*

61. *Answer: (b)*
This is the definition of a Lewis base.

62. *Answer: (a)*
A Brønsted-Lowry acid donates protons.

63. *Answer: (c)*
The conjugate acid donates an H^+ *to form* OH^-. *Thus, the conjugate acid is* H_2O.

64. *Answer: (e)*
0.25 moles of NaOH will react with 0.1 moles of H_3PO_4 *past the 2nd equivalence point. Therefore, the solution will contain both* HPO_4^{-2} *and* PO_4^{-3} *at equilibrium conditions.*

65. *Answer: (c)*
At the 2nd equivalence point, the pH is equal to $\frac{pK2+pK3}{2} = 9.78$.

66. *Answer: (b)*
The best buffer solution will contain the same concentration of a weak acid or base and its conjugate salt.

67. *Answer: (d)*
$\frac{50 \times 0.0134 - 24 \times 0.0250}{50+24} = 9 \times 10^{-4}\ M\ H^+$
$pH = -\log(9 \times 10^{-4}) = 3.02$

68. *Answer: (e)*
O: -2
K: +1
Mn: 4(2) – 1 = 7

69. *Answer: (e)*
Cu^{2+} has the same oxidation number.
N changes its oxidation number from +5 to +4 (it is reduced).
O changes its oxidation number from -2 to 0 (it is oxidized).

70. *Answer: (d)*
$K_2Cr_2O_7 + 14HCl \rightarrow 2KCl + 2CrCl_3 + 7H_2O + 3Cl_2$
The sum of the coefficients of the products is $2 + 2 + 7 + 3 = 14$.

71. *Answer: (e)*
The more active the metal, the easier it is to lose electrons, and the higher its strength as a reducing agent.
Na > Mg > Fe > Cu > Ag

72. *Answer: (a)*
Cu(s) is oxidized and NO_3^- is reduced.

73. *Answer: (b)*
$-1.42 - 0.76 = -2.18\,V$

74. *Answer: (b)*
The anode is the electrode where oxidation occurs.
Zn is more active than Cu, so Zn will be oxidized at the anode.

75. *Answer: (e)*
O_2 is a product of photosynthesis in plants.

76. *Answer: (a)*
Ethene has a double bond and both carbon atoms are sp^2 hybridized.

The molecule geometry of sp^2 hybridized compounds is triangular planar.

77. *Answer: (c)*
A noncyclic, saturated hydrocarbon has the formula of C_nH_{2n+2}.

78. *Answer: (d)*
Both $R - O - CH_3$ and $R' - COOH$ are present in the compound.

79. *Answer: (d)*
Slight oxidation of a primary alcohol produces an aldehyde. Further oxidation results in the formation of carboxylic acids.

80. *Answer: (c)*
Isotopes have the same number of protons, but a different number of neutrons.

81. *Answer: (d)*
By balancing the atomic mass and atomic numbers, x is a ^4_2He, an alpha particle.

82. *Answer: (d)*
1 hour is 3 half-lives.
$(\frac{1}{2})^3 \times 1 = 0.125\,g$

83. *Answer: (d)*
Light nuclei fuse together in fusion to form heavier nuclei.

84. *Answer: (a)*
During fusion, heavy nuclei split into mid-weight elements while releasing energy.

85. *Answer: (a)*
Beakers and graduated cylinders are used to measure low precision volumes.

Volumetric flasks and pipettes are used to measure specific volumes such as 1 ml, 10 ml, etc. to a higher precision.

86. *Answer: (b)*
Precipitation is a chemical change.

87. *Answer: (d)*
A very fine particle is very difficult to precipitate using normal processes. Use centrifugation to separate very fine particles.

88. *Answer: (b)*
Methane is insoluble in water. Therefore, displacement of water is used to collect methane gas.

89. *Answer: (b)*
Titration is the most common method used to determine the molarity of acid and base solutions.

90. *Answer: (c)*
I and II will increase the yields of this experiment, whereas III will decrease the yields of this experiment.

Chapter 1 Classification of Matter

I. Matter and Its Properties

Matter is defined as anything that has mass and occupies space (has volume).

Basic Building Blocks of Matter

i. An **atom** is the smallest unit of an element that maintains the properties of that element.

ii. An **element** is a pure substance made of only one kind of atom.

iii. A **compound** is a substance that is made from the atoms of two or more elements that are chemically bonded.

iv. A **molecule** is the smallest unit of an element or compound that retains all of the properties of that element or compound.

Example: For the following, write "E" for element, "C" for compound, and "M" for mixture.

Water	C
Wine	M
Soil	M
Silver	E
Aluminum oxide	C
Hydrogen	E
Carbon dioxide	C
Air	M
Hydrochloric acid	C
Nitrogen	E
Tin	E
Potassium chloride	C

Properties and Changes in Matter

i. **Extensive properties** are dependent on the amount of matter present. Examples of extensive properties are volume, mass, and energy (heat content).

ii. **Intensive properties** are independent of the amount of matter present. Examples include melting point, boiling point, and density.

iii. **Physical properties** are characteristics in a substance that can be observed or measured without changing the identity of the substance.

iv. **Physical changes** are changes in a substance that do not change its chemical makeup. For example, all phase changes are physical changes.

v. **Chemical properties** relate to a substance's ability to undergo changes (ex. being able to combust, oxidize, or neutralize) that transform it into different substances.

vi. **Chemical changes** are changes made to one or more substances when they are converted into different substances through chemical reactions such as combustion, oxidation, or neutralization.

vii. **The law of conservation of energy** states that energy may be absorbed (endothermic) or released (exothermic) in a reaction, but the total energy in an isolated system must stay constant.

Section Practice

1. Which of the following has mass and a definite size and shape?
   a) A liquid
   b) A solid
   c) A gas
   d) A molecule
   e) Matter

Answer: (b)

Only a solid has definite shape and volume.

2. A can of powder in the kitchen has the label "Ingredients: corn starch, sodium bicarbonate, calcium acid phosphate, and sodium aluminum sulfate." This powder is a
   a) compound.
   b) mixture.
   c) molecule.
   d) mixture of elements.
   e) pure materials.

Answer: (b)

A mixture contains more than one compound.

3. A substance that can be further simplified by ordinary chemical means may be which of the following?
   I. An element or a compound
   II. A mixture or a compound
   III. An element or a mixture
   a) I only
   b) II only
   c) III only
   d) I, II only
   e) I, II, III

Answer: (b)

A mixture can be simplified by physical means. A compound can be simplified by chemical means.

4. Which of the following is a physical property of sugar?
   a) It decomposes readily.
   b) Its chemical composition consists of carbon, hydrogen, and oxygen atoms.
   c) It turns black when put in contact with concentrated H_2SO_4.
   d) It may decompose when heated.
   e) It is a white crystalline solid.

Answer: (e)

Being a white crystalline solid is a physical property, not a chemical property.

5. Something that can be observed without changing the chemical identity of a substance is a
   a) physical property.
   b) chemical change.
   c) chemical property.
   d) physical change.
   e) chemical reaction.

Answer: (a)

A physical property is displayed without compromising the chemical identity of the substance.

II. Classification of Matter

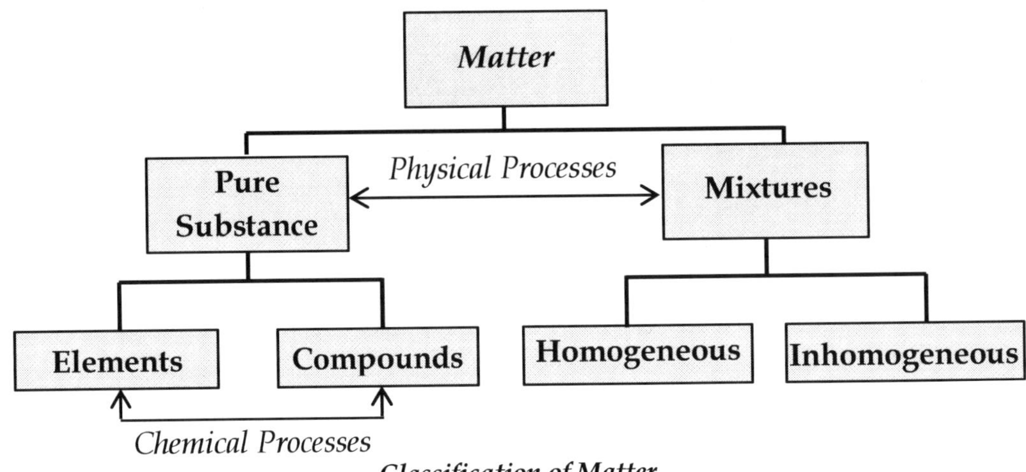

Classification of Matter

Elements are pure chemical substances consisting of a single type of atom.

Elements in the Periodic Table

i. Groups or families of elements are the vertical columns containing elements with similar chemical properties.
ii. Periods of elements are the horizontal rows.

Types of Elements

i. Metals
   1. Are lustrous
   2. are good conductors of heat and electricity
   3. are malleable
   4. are ductile
   5. have high tensile strength

ii. Nonmetals
   1. are frequently gases at room temperature (hydrogen, oxygen) or brittle solids (sulfur, phosphorus).
   2. are poor conductors of heat and electricity.

iii. Metalloids
   1. share some properties with metals and some properties with nonmetals.
   2. are solids at room temperature.
   3. are semiconductors of electricity.

iv. Noble gases
   1. are gaseous members of group 18.
   2. are generally unreactive.

Compounds are pure substances. A compound can be decomposed into two or more compounds or elements by chemical changes.

A mixture is made of different substances in which no chemical reaction is occurring between them. The components of mixtures can be separated through physical means such as filtration, distillation, chromatography, sedimentation, or extraction.

A homogeneous mixture is a mixture that has uniform composition throughout.

A heterogeneous mixture is a mixture that is not uniform in composition. Two types of heterogeneous mixtures are:

i. A **suspension** is a mixture in which the diameters of the solute particles are greater than 1000 nm, or 0.000001 meters. The particles are big enough that they are visible to the naked eye. Sand in water and oil in water are examples of a suspension.

ii. A **colloid** is a mixture in which the diameters of the solute particles are between 2 to 1000 nm; the colloid looks homogeneous to the naked eye. Fog and milk are examples of colloids.

Separation of Mixtures

i. **Filtration** is the process of separating a mixture based upon differences in size, solubility, magnetization, or density.
ii. **Distillation** is the process of separating a mixture based upon differences in boiling point.
iii. **Chromatography** is the process of separating a mixture based upon the movement of particles through a two-phase system.

Calculating the Density of Matter

$$\text{Density} = \frac{\text{Mass}}{\text{Volume}}$$

Example: The density of CCl_4 (carbon tetrachloride) is 1.58 grams per milliliter. What will 100.0 milliliters of $CC1_4$ weigh?

Answer: $\text{Density} = \frac{\text{Mass}}{\text{Volume}}$

$$1.58\frac{\text{g}}{\text{ml}} = \frac{\text{Mass}}{100\ \text{ml}}$$

$$\text{Mass} = 158\ \text{grams}$$

Example: A block of sulfur weighs 227 grams. When it was submerged in a graduated cylinder containing 50.0 milliliters of H_2O, the water level rose to 150.0 milliliters. What is the density (g/mL) of the sulfur?

Answer: $\text{Density} = \frac{\text{Mass}}{\text{Volume}}$

$$\text{Density} = \frac{227}{150-50} = 2.27\ \text{g/ml}$$

Section Practice

1. If a microscope is required in order to differentiate the substances in a mixture, the mixture may be a
   a) homogeneous mixture.
   b) suspension.
   c) colloid.
   d) solution.
   e) None of the above

Answer: (c)

A solution and a homogeneous mixture are the same. Substances in a solution cannot be seen under a microscope.

A suspension is visually heterogeneous and does not require a microscope. A colloid is visually homogeneous but microscopically heterogeneous.

2. Which of the following is a homogeneous mixture?
   a) Milk
   b) Soft drinks
   c) Sand and water
   d) Noodle soup
   e) Pure water

Answer: (b)

Soft drinks are composed of only one phase.

3. A(n) _____ is a material made up of two or more substances that can be separated by physical means.
   a) compound
   b) molecule
   c) element
   d) mixture
   e) atom

Answer: (d)

This is the definition of a mixture.

4. A(n)_____ is a heterogeneous mixture that never settles.
   a) compound
   b) solution
   c) suspension
   d) colloid
   e) alcohol

Answer: (d)

This is the definition of a colloid.

5. A(n) _____ is a substance in which all atoms are the same type.
   a) compound
   b) solution
   c) element
   d) mixture
   e) molecule

Answer: (c)

This is the definition of an element.

6. Which of the following is a chemical change?
   a) Burning a log
   b) Boiling water
   c) Crushing a cookie
   d) Circulating coolant inside a refrigerator
   e) Collecting electricity from a solar panel

Answer: (a)

The burning of a log produces the new substances CO_2 and H_2O.

Chapter 1 Classification of Matter SAT Questions

1. Which of the following measures the mass per unit volume of matter?
   a) Density
   b) A solid
   c) Volume
   d) Weight
   e) Matter

Answer: (a)

2. Which of the following has mass and occupies space?
   a) Density
   b) A solid
   c) Volume
   d) Weight
   e) Matter

Answer: (e)

Matter has mass and occupies space.

3. Which of the following is defined as a measure of the mass times the gravitational force?
   a) Density
   b) Pressure
   c) Volume
   d) Weight
   e) Matter

Answer: (d)

4. Metal solutions are commonly known as
   a) elements.
   b) mixtures.
   c) alloys.
   d) compounds.
   e) liquid metal.

Answer: (c)

5. Which of the following is a colloid?
   a) Vinegar
   b) Water
   c) Oxygen
   d) Smoke
   e) Soda

Answer: (d)

Smoke is a colloid, or a heterogeneous mixture that never settles.

Relationship Analysis Questions

1. −273 degrees Celsius is also known as absolute zero.	C = K + 273	TF
2. A mixture of two different liquids can be separated via distillation.	Different liquids have different boiling points.	TTCE
3. The burning of a piece of paper indicates a physical change.	The chemical properties of paper remain the same after burning.	FF
4. A chemical change involves a change in the composition and molecular structure of the reactants.	In a chemical reaction, bonds are broken, and new substances and bonds are formed.	TTCE
5. Propane can be decomposed chemically.	Propane is a compound that is made up of simpler elements.	TTCE
6. A substance composed of two or more chemically combined elements is called a mixture.	The properties of the constituents of a mixture are retained.	FT
7. The burning of paper is a physical change.	When a chemical change occurs, energy is either gained or lost by the reactants.	FT

Chapter 2 Atomic Structure and Electron Properties

I. Atomic Theory and Structure of the Atom

Discovery of the Atomic Structure

i. John Dalton's Atomic Model

1. All matter is made up of very tiny particles called atoms.
2. Atoms of a given element are identical in size, mass, and other properties. Atoms of different elements differ in size, mass, and other properties.
3. Atoms cannot be subdivided, created, or destroyed.
4. Atoms of different elements combine in simple whole-number ratios to form chemical compounds.

ii. Joseph John Thomson Discovery of the Electron

1. A cathode ray tube produces a ray with a constant **charge to mass** ratio.
2. All cathode rays are composed of identical negatively charged particles (electrons).

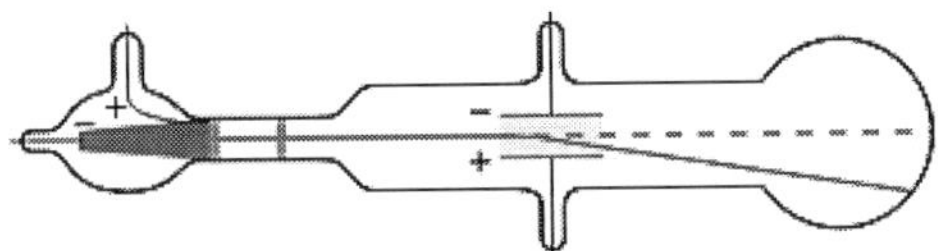

Diagram of J. J. Thomson's Experiment with Cathode Rays

Cathode rays (blue) emitted by the cathode on the left were deflected by an electric field (yellow) in the center. Credit: commons.wikimedia.org

iii. Millikan Oil Drop Experiment

1. Determined the charge and mass of an electron
2. Electron is negatively charged to 1.6×10^{-19} Coulombs.
3. An electron's mass is equal to 9.109×10^{-31}kg.

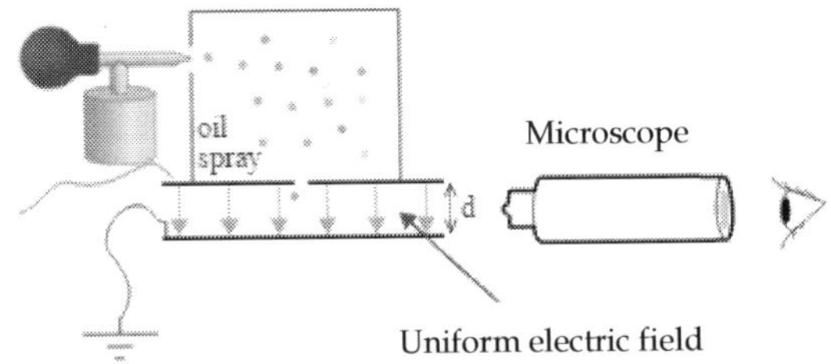

Scheme of Millikan's Oil-drop Experiment

Credit: commons.wikimedia.org

iv. Rutherford Gold Foil Experiment

1. Proved the existence of a nucleus in atoms.
2. Alpha particles (helium nuclei) were fired at a thin sheet of gold.

3. Very few particles were deflected back from the gold sheet.
4. The Rutherford gold foil experiment drew two conclusions: first, the nucleus is very small, dense and positively charged and second, most of the atom is empty space.

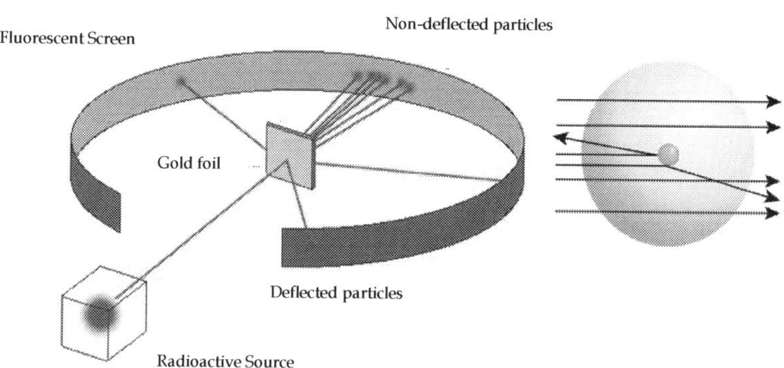

Rutherford Gold Foil Experiment

Some of the particles were deflected, and some at very large angles. Rutherford concluded that the positive charge of the atom must be concentrated into a very small location: the atomic nucleus. Credit: commons.wikimedia.org

Summary of the Modern Atomic Theory

i. All matter is made up of very tiny particles called atoms.
ii. Atoms of the same element are chemically alike.
iii. Individual atoms of an element may not all have the same mass. However, the atoms of an element have a definite average mass that is the characteristic of the element.
iv. Atoms of different elements have different average masses.
v. Atoms are not subdivided, created, or destroyed in chemical reactions.

Atomic Structure

i. Sizes of Atoms
   1. The atomic radius is between 30 and 300 Pico meters (1 pm = 10^{-12} m). Most of the atomic radii are formed by the electron cloud.
   2. The nuclear radius is approximately equal to 0.001 pm. If the atomic nucleus were the size of a marble, a typical atom would be the size of a football stadium.

ii. Structure of the Nucleus
   1. Protons are positively charged particles with a mass of 1.673×10^{-27}kg. The number of protons in the nucleus determines the atom's identity and is called the atomic number.
   2. Neutrons have no charge and a mass of 1.675×10^{-27}kg.
   3. The atomic number is the number of protons in the nucleus of each atom of that element. Atoms are identified by their atomic number.
   4. The periodic table is arranged in the order of increasing atomic number.

iii. **Isotopes**

1. All atoms of the same element have the same number of protons, but may vary in the number of neutrons.
2. Although isotopes have different masses, they do not differ significantly in their chemical behavior.
3. Hydrogen, for example, has the following isotopes: protium ($^{1}_{1}H$), deuterium ($^{2}_{1}H$), and tritium ($^{3}_{1}H$).

iv. **Mass Number**

The mass number is the total number of protons and neutrons in the nucleus of an isotope.

1. The average atomic mass is the weighted average of the atomic masses of the naturally occurring isotopes of that element.
2. The mole is the amount of substance that contains the number of particles in exactly 12 grams of carbon-12. The number of particles in exactly one mole of a pure substance is equal to 6.02×10^{23} (Avogadro's number).

Section Practice

1. An atom of beryllium consists of 4 protons, 5 neutrons, and 4 electrons. The mass number of this atom is
   a) 13.
   b) 9.
   c) 8.
   d) 5.
   e) 4.

Answer: (b)

Atomic mass number is equal to the total number of protons and neutrons.

2. Hydrogen can exist as ^{1}H, ^{2}H, and ^{3}H. Which of the following is true?
   a) ^{1}H and ^{2}H both have identical numbers of neutrons.
   b) Water (H_2O) in which all the hydrogen atoms are ^{1}H is unlikely to have a very different boiling point from water in which all of the hydrogen atoms are ^{2}H.
   c) ^{1}H and ^{3}H are likely to have similar radioactive properties.
   d) ^{3}H and ^{3}He possess an identical number of neutrons.
   e) ^{1}H does not possess a neutron.

Answer: (e)

The isotopes of hydrogen have one proton and different numbers of neutrons.

3. Neutral atoms of F (fluorine) have the same number of electrons as
   a) B^{3-}.
   b) N^{+}.
   c) Ne^{-}.
   d) Na^{+}.
   e) Mg^{3+}.

Answer: (e)

F has 9 electrons. Mg^{3+} has 12 − 3 = 9 electrons.

4. Which of the following is an incorrect association?
   a) Mendeleev – periodic table
   b) Faraday – electrolytic cells
   c) Millikan – charge of electrons
   d) Rutherford – photoelectric effect
   e) They are all correct.

Answer: (d)

Rutherford is associated with the gold foil experiment and the structure of the nucleus.

5. An orbital may never be occupied by
   a) 1 electron.
   b) 2 electrons.
   c) 3 electrons.
   d) 0 electrons.
   e) All of the above are possible.

Answer: (c)

An orbital can be occupied by 0 to 2 electrons.

6. Which of the following regarding the Rutherford experiment is NOT correct?
   a) Most alpha particles passed through the gold foil without being deflected since the nuclei of the gold atoms represent such a small portion of the total atomic volume.
   b) Coulomb's law, which states that like charges repel each other, accounts for the deflection of alpha particles passing close to gold nuclei.
   c) Most alpha particles passed through the gold foil without being deflected since the nuclei of the gold atoms represent such a small portion of the total atomic mass.
   d) Because of the electrons' small masses, they did not deflect the alpha particles.
   e) The high charge of the gold nuclei helps to account for their ability to deflect smaller helium nuclei passing close by.

Answer: (c)

Nuclei of the gold atoms represent a major portion of the total atomic mass.

7. An element consists of three isotopes in the relative abundances given below. What is the atomic mass of this element?

Abundance (%)	Mass (amu)
30.00	20.00
50.00	21.00
20.00	22.00

a) 20.90
b) 21.00
c) 21.90
d) 22.00
e) 22.10

Answer: (a)

Atomic Mass = $20 \times .3 + 21 \times .5 + 22 \times .2 = 20.9$ *amu*

8. You have just discovered a new, fundamental particle of nature. When measuring its mass, you obtain the following data for five samples:

4.72×10^{-34} gram
9.44×10^{-34} gram
1.180×10^{-33} gram
1.652×10^{-33} gram
7.08×10^{-34} gram

If you make the same assumptions that Millikan did, what is the maximum mass of the new particle?

a) 4.72×10^{-34} g
b) 1.18×10^{-34} g
c) 9.44×10^{-34} g
d) 2.36×10^{-34} g
e) 9.91×10^{-34} g

Answer: (d)

The GCD (greatest common factor) of the five samples is 2.36×10^{-34}.

II. Properties of Light

Electromagnetic Radiation, or EM radiation, is the form of energy that moves through space as waves at the speed of light.

$$c \text{ (Speed of the light in m/sec)} = \lambda \nu$$
$$E \text{ (Energy of the light in J)} = h\nu$$

ν: Frequency (1/s). λ: Wavelength (m). h: Plank constant $= 6.627 \times 10^{-34}$ J

Types of EM (electromagnetic) waves as shown in the table below:

Wavelength(m)	10^{-12}	10^{-10}	10^{-8}	4 to $7\text{x}10^{-7}$	10^{-4}	10^{-2}	1	10^2	10^4
	Gamma	X-rays	UV	Visible	IR	Microwaves	Radiowaves		
							FM	short	AM

Light and Energy

i. Wave-Particle duality of light
   Light travels through space as waves and can also be thought of as a stream of particles.

ii. The energy of a photon is directly proportional to the frequency of radiation.

$$E\text{(energy of the light in J)} = h\nu$$
h: Plank constant $= 6.627 \times 10^{-34}$ J. ν: Frequency (1/s)

iii. The photoelectric effect occurs when light shines on a metal surface and sometimes electrons are emitted.

iv. A quantum is the minimum amount of energy that can be lost or gained by an atom due to electrons being emitted or captured.

Example: Determine the frequency of a quantum of blue light that has a wavelength of 492 nm.

Answer: $c = \lambda\nu$

$3 \times 108 = 492 \times 10^{-9} \times \nu$

$\nu = 6.1 \times 10^{14}$ Hz

Example: Calculate the wavelength (in nm) of a photon of green light that has a frequency of 5.5×10^{14} Hz.

Answer: $c = \lambda\nu$

$3 \times 10^8 = \lambda \times 5.5 \times 10^{14}$

$\lambda = 5.45 \times 10^{-7}$ m $= 545$ nm

Example: Determine the energy of a photon of light that has a wavelength of 435 nm.

Answer: E (Energy) $= h\nu = h \times \frac{c}{\lambda}$

$$= \frac{6.626 \times 10^{-34} \times 3 \times 10^{8}}{435 \times 10^{-9}}$$

$$= 4.57 \times 10^{-19}\ \mathrm{J}$$

Section Practice

1. With respect to the electromagnetic spectrum, which of the following is NOT correct?
    a) Electromagnetic radiation of wavelength 700 nm falls in the red region of the visible spectrum.
    b) A photon of wavelength 700 nm will have higher energy than a photon of infrared radiation.
    c) Electromagnetic radiation of wavelength 700 nm has speed identical to that of radiation of wavelength 400 nm.
    d) Electromagnetic radiation of wavelength 700 nm has a higher frequency than that of X-rays.
    e) Electromagnetic radiation of wavelength 700 nm has a lower frequency than that of X-rays.

Answer: (d)

X-rays have a higher frequency than visible light.

2. What is the wavelength of light that has a frequency of $4.00 \times 10^{14}\ s^{-1}$? (The speed of light is $3.00 \times 10^{8}\ s^{-1}$.)
    a) 7.5 nm
    b) 1333 nm
    c) 750 nm
    d) 1.33 cm^{-1}
    e) 1.2×10^{23} m

Answer: (c)

$c = \lambda\nu$

$3 \times 10^{8} = 4 \times 10^{14}\ \lambda$

$\lambda = \frac{3 \times 18^{8}}{4 \times 10^{14}}$

$\lambda = 7.5 \times 10^{-7} = 750nm$

3. Removing an electron from sodium is an _____ process and removing an electron from fluorine is an _____ process.
    a) endothermic, exothermic
    b) exothermic, endothermic
    c) endothermic, endothermic
    d) exothermic, exothermic
    e) More information is needed.

Answer: (c)

Removing an electron from an atom is always endothermic.

4. Which equation best expresses the energy of a photon?
   a) $E = \frac{1}{2} mv^2$
   b) $E = mc^2$
   c) $E = IR$
   d) $E = hv$
   e) $E = E° - RT\ln K$

Answer: (d)

$E = h\upsilon$

5. Barium salts, when burned, emit a greenish light (often utilized in fireworks). One of the most common barium salts, $BaC1_2$, produces light with the wavelength of 511 nm. What would the corresponding frequency of this wavelength be?
   a) $5.82 \times 10^{10}\ s^{-1}$
   b) $5.87 \times 10^{14}\ s^{-1}$
   c) $8.48 \times 10^{16}\ s^{-1}$
   d) $2.32 \times 10^{18}\ s^{-1}$
   e) $1.73 \times 10^{20}\ s^{-1}$

Answer: (b)

$c = \lambda\nu$

$3 \times 10^8 = 511 \times 10^{-9}\ \nu$

$\nu = \frac{3 \times 18^8}{511 \times 10^{-9}}$

$\nu = 5.87 \times 10^{14}$

III. The Quantum Model of the Atom

The Bohr Model of the Hydrogen Atom

A positively charged nucleus, comprised of protons and neutrons, is surrounded by a negatively charged electron cloud. In the model, electrons orbit the nucleus in atomic shells.

i. Electron Orbits/Energy Levels
   1. Electrons can circle the nucleus only in allowed paths or orbits.
   2. The atom achieves the ground state when atoms occupy the closest possible positions around the nucleus.
   3. The energy to keep an electron in its orbital is greater when the electron is in an orbital farther from the nucleus.
   4. Electromagnetic radiation is emitted when electrons move closer to the nucleus and energy is released.

ii. Energy Transitions
   1. Energies of atoms are fixed with definite quantities.
   2. Energy transitions occur in jumps of discrete amounts of energy.
   3. Electrons only lose energy when they move to a lower energy state.

iii. Shortcomings of the Bohr Model
   1. Bohr model doesn't work for atoms larger than hydrogen.
   2. Bohr model doesn't explain chemical behavior of atoms.

The Quantum Model of the Atom

i. Louis de Broglie (1924) considered the electron as a wave confined to a space, which can only have certain frequencies.
ii. The Heisenberg Uncertainty Principle states that it is impossible to simultaneously determine both the position and velocity of an electron.
iii. The Schrodinger Wave Equation, which provides the basis for quantum theory, proved the quantization of electron energies.
iv. The quantum model of the atom considers electrons as both waves and particles.

Atomic Orbitals and Quantum Numbers

Quantum numbers specify the properties of atomic orbitals and the electrons in an orbital.

i. The principal quantum number (n) indicates the main energy level occupied by the electron. It is the same as the period number in the periodic table. The possible number of orbitals per energy level (or "shell") is equal to n^2.
ii. The angular momentum quantum number (l) indicates the shape of the orbital. The shapes are designated as **s, p, d,** or **f** orbitals.
iii. The magnetic quantum number (m) is the orientation of the orbital around the nucleus.

1. The s orbital (m = 0) has only one possible orientation, the p orbitals (m = −1, 0, 1) have three, the d orbitals (m = −2, −1, 0, 1, 2) have five and the f orbitals (m = −3, −2, −1, 0, 1, 2, 3) have 7 possible orientations as shown below:

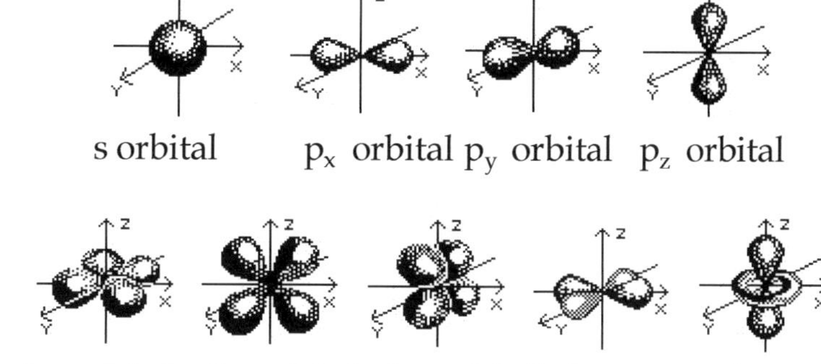

d_{xy} orbital d_{xz} orbital d_{yz} orbital d_x orbital d_z orbital

2. Spin Quantum Number indicates the fundamental spin states of an electron in an orbital. There are two possible values for a spin state, $+\frac{1}{2}$, $-\frac{1}{2}$ and a single orbital can contain only two electrons, which must have opposite spins. The first electron in an orbital will have a spin of $+\frac{1}{2}$.

Summary of Quantum Numbers

Principal Quantum Number (n)	Sublevels in main energy level n	Number of orbitals per sublevel	Number of electrons per sublevel	Number of electrons per main energy level ($2n^2$)
1	s	1	2	2
2	s p	1 3	2 6	8
3	s p d	1 3 5	2 6 10	18
4	s p d f	1 3 5 7	2 6 10 14	32

Section Practice

1. Which of the following principles states that all matter may be considered a wave?
   a) Bohr model
   b) DeBroglie's wave hypothesis
   c) Heisenberg's uncertainty principle
   d) Quantum theory
   e) Atomic theory

Answer: (b)

De Broglie's wave hypothesis states: Consider the electron as a wave confin[ed] to a space that can have only certain frequencies.

2. Which of the following states that one cannot know both position and velocity of an electron at the same time?
   a) Bohr model
   b) deBroglie wave hypothesis
   c) Heisenberg's uncertainty principle
   d) Quantum theory
   e) Atomic theory

Answer: (c)

The Heisenberg Uncertainty Principle states that you can never simultaneous[ly] know the exact position and the exact speed of an object.

3. The lowest principal quantum number that an electron can have is
   a) 0.
   b) 1.
   c) 2.
   d) 3.
   e) 4.

Answer: (b)

Principal quantum number starts wit[h]

4. The sublevel that has only one orbital is identified by the letter
   a) s.
   b) p.
   c) d.
   d) f.
   e) n.

Answer: (a)

s: 1 orbital
p: 3 orbitals
d: 5 orbitals
f: 7 orbitals

5. Which of the following quantum number describes the shape of an orbital?
   a) n
   b) l
   c) m_l
   d) m_s
   e) s

Answer: (b)

The angular momentum quantum number (l) indicates the shape of t[he] orbital.

6. In filling the atom with electrons, the rule(s) that must be considered are

   I. Rydberg equation
   II. Heisenberg's uncertainty principle
   III. Hund's rule
   IV. Pauli exclusion principle
   V. Bohr model

   a) I and III only
   b) II and V only
   c) III and IV only
   d) IV only
   e) III only

Answer: (c)

Three rules in filling the atom with electrons:
Aufbau Principle
Pauli Exclusion Principle
Hund's Rule

7. The best tool to use to calculate the ionization energy of a hydrogen atom is
   a) Rydberg equation
   b) Heisenberg uncertainty principle
   c) Hund's rule
   d) Pauli exclusion principle
   e) Bohr model

Answer: (a)

The Rydberg equation calculates the wavelength of energy emitted or absorbe by a hydrogen atom.

IV. Electron Configurations

Rules that Apply to Electron Configurations

i. The Aufbau principle states an electron occupies the lowest-possible energy orbital.
ii. The Pauli exclusion principle states that no two electrons in the same atom can have the same set of four quantum numbers.
iii. Hund's Rule states that orbitals of equal energy are each occupied by one electron before any orbital is occupied by a second electron, and all electrons in singly occupied orbital must have the same spin.
iv. The following electron configuration sequence shows how orbitals in an atom fill up with electrons.

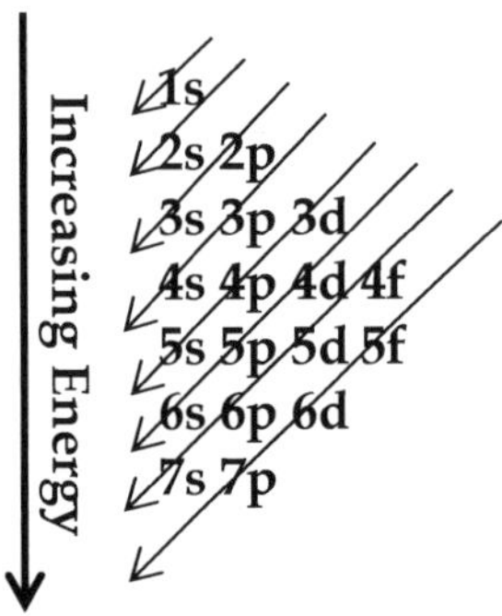

There are two main exceptions to this electron configuration: the chromium and copper groups. In these cases, a completely full or half full **d** sub-level is more stable than a partially filled d sub-level, so an electron from the 4**s** orbital is excited and raised to the 3**d** orbital.

Chromium: Expected: $1s^22s^22p^63s^23p^64s^23d^4$
Actual: $1s^22s^22p^63s^23p^64s^13d^5$

Copper: Expected: $1s^22s^22p^63s^23p^64s^23d^9$
Actual: $1s^22s^22p^63s^23p^64s^13d^{10}$

Section Practice

1. Which of the following has an electron configuration of $1s^22s^22p^63s^23p^1$?
   a) Na^+
   b) Al
   c) F
   d) Ti
   e) B

Answer: (b)

Use electron configuration sequence.

2. Which of the following has the same electron configuration as the neon atom?
   a) Na^+
   b) Al
   c) F
   d) Ti
   e) B

Answer: (a)

Na^+ has 10 electrons.

3. Which of the following elements has an electronic configuration that does NOT follow the Aufbau principle?
   a) Fe
   b) Mg
   c) A1
   d) Ag
   e) Ni

Answer: (d)

Copper group can borrow one electron from s orbital to fill d orbitals.

4. Which of the following is FALSE?
   a) Atoms with electrons in the 4d orbitals are in the fourth period of the periodic table.
   b) The 7s orbitals are in the seventh period of the periodic Table.
   c) The 4f orbitals are in the sixth period of the periodic Table.
   d) The 6s orbitals are spherical in shape.
   e) The 5p orbitals are dumbbell shaped.

Answer: (a)

Atoms in the 4d orbitals are in the fifth period of the periodic table.

5. The f sublevel may contain a maximum of
   a) 2 electrons.
   b) 14 electrons.
   c) 6 electrons.
   d) 10 electrons.
   e) 8 electrons.

Answer: (b)

f: 7 orbitals → 14 electrons

6. For a d orbital,
   a) the value of n must be 2.
   b) the value of m must be $+\frac{1}{2}$.
   c) the value of l must be 3.
   d) the value of m_l must be 3.
   e) the value of l must be 2.

Answer: (e)

l is equal to 2 for d orbitals.

Chapter 2 Atomic Structure and Electron Properties SAT Questions

1. The electron configuration of $1s^22s^22p^63s^23p^64s^23d^7$ represents an atom of the element
   a) Br.
   b) Co.
   c) Cd.
   d) Ga.
   e) Mg.

Answer: (b)

Transition metals have partially filled d orbitals.

2. The total number of electrons that can be accommodated in the fourth principal energy level is _____
   a) 2.
   b) 8.
   c) 18.
   d) 32.
   e) 50.

Answer: (d)

The total number of electrons accommodated in the nth energy level is $2n^2$.

3. If the set of quantum numbers n = 3, l = 1, m_l = 0, m_s = +1/2 represents the last electron to be added to complete the ground state electron configuration of an element, which of the following could be the symbol for that element?
   a) Na
   b) Si
   c) Th
   d) V
   e) Zn

Answer: (b)

The total number of electrons is 2 (for n = 1)+ 8 (for n = 2) + 4 (for $3s^2$ $3p^2$) = 14. Neutral Si atoms have 14 electrons.
Each orbital can only hold two electrons. The first electron in an orbital will have a spin of +1/2.

4. Which of the following elements has the electron configuration of $1s^22s^22p^63s^23p^64s^23d^4$?
   a) Cr
   b) Mn
   c) Mo
   d) S
   e) Se

Answer: (a)

Use electron configuration rules.

5. The sublevel that can be occupied by a maximum of 10 electrons is identified by the letter
   a) d.
   b) f.
   c) p.
   d) s.
   e) n.

Answer: (a)

There are 5 d orbitals that can fill a total of 10 electrons

6. The number of orbitals in the second principal energy level, n = 2, of an atom is
   a) 1.
   b) 9.
   c) 16.
   d) 4.
   e) 8.

Answer: (d)

There are n^2 orbitals in principle energy level n.

7. Which configuration of neutral atom has an outer energy level of $3s^1$?
   a) Li
   b) Na
   c) K
   d) C
   e) F

Answer: (b)

Alkali metal Na has an outer energy level of $3s^1$.

8. Which of the following elements has the greatest affinity for an additional electron?
   a) Li
   b) Na
   c) K
   d) C
   e) F

Answer: (e)

F has the biggest electron affinity.

9. Which of the following elements is the most active metal?
   a) Li
   b) Na
   c) K
   d) C
   e) F

Answer: (c)

The most active metals are alkali metals. The higher the orbitals, the easier it is to lose an electron. K is more active than Na and Li.

10. Which of the following elements has the lowest electronegativity?
   a) Li
   b) Na
   c) K
   d) C
   e) F

Answer: (c)

The easier it is to lose an electron, the lower the electronegativity.

11. Which of the following elements has an outer orbital configuration of $2s^2\ 2p^2$?
   a) Li
   b) Na
   c) K
   d) C
   e) F

Answer: (d)

The electron configuration of C is $1s^2\ 2s^2\ 2p^2$.

12. The maximum number of electrons in a shell with a principal quantum number equal to 4 is
    a) 2.
    b) 10.
    c) 16.
    d) 32.
    e) 64.

Answer: (d)

Maximum number of electrons = $2n^2 = 2 \times 4^2 = 32$

13. If the principal quantum number of a shell is equal to 2, what types of orbitals will be present?
    a) s
    b) s and p
    c) s, p, and d
    d) s, p, d, and f

Answer: (b)

The second shell has s and p orbitals.

14. The total number of electrons that could be held in a sublevel with angular momentum quantum number equal to 2 is
    a) 2.
    b) 6.
    c) 8.
    d) 10.
    e) 12.

Answer: (d)

Angular momentum quantum number equal to 2 is the d orbital, which has 5 sublevel and 10 electrons.

15. With respect to electronic configuration, which of the following is NOT correct?
    a) Se and O have an identical number of valence electrons.
    b) B and Cl both have the same number of unpaired electrons in their ground-state electron configuration.
    c) O^{2-} and F^- have identical electron configurations.
    d) Ne and Ar both have a filled p-orbital in the valence shell.
    e) Se and Br are expected to have similar chemical properties since they are in the same row of the periodic table.

Answer: (e)

Elements in the same family (column) have similar chemical properties.

16. Fill in the missing reactant. $^{1}_{1}H + \_\_ \rightarrow 3\,^{4}_{2}He$
    a) $^{11}_{5}Na$
    b) $^{3}_{1}H$
    c) $^{13}_{7}Al$
    d) $^{11}_{5}B$
    e) $^{3}_{1}Li$

Answer: (d)

Balance the total mass and the number of protons.

Mass = $3 \times 4 - 1 = 13$
Number of Protons = $3 \times 2 - 1 = 5$

The missing reactant is $^{11}_{5}B$.

17. Copper (Cu) can exist as several isotopes, but only two occur naturally: ^{63}Cu and ^{65}Cu. If ^{63}Cu makes up 69.2% of copper atoms and ^{65}Cu makes up 30.8%, what is the atomic mass of copper?
   a) 63.3 amu
   b) 63.4 amu
   c) 63.5 amu
   d) 63.6 amu
   e) 63.7 amu

Answer: (d)

The atomic mass of copper will be 63 × 0.692 + 65 × 0.308 = 63.6 amu.

18. $^{235}_{92}U + ^{1}_{0}n \rightarrow X + ^{92}_{38}Sr + 2\,^{1}_{0}n$
   The reaction above represents the fission of a U-235 nucleus by a slow neutron. The identity of product X is
   a) ^{142}Xe.
   b) ^{144}Xe.
   c) ^{142}Ba.
   d) ^{144}Ba.
   e) ^{142}Cs.

Answer: (a)

Balance the total mass and the number of protons.

Atomic mass of X = 235 + 1 – 92 – 2 = 142
Atomic number of X = 92 – 38 = 54 (Xe)

19. Which of these symbols represent(s) an orbital?
   I. n
   II. s
   III. m_l
   IV. m_s
   V. f
   a) I and II only
   b) II and V only
   c) I, II, and V only
   d) III and IV only
   e) V only

Answer: (b)

Orbitals are s, p, d, and f.

20. Which of these quantum numbers will tell you the shape of the orbital that the electron occupies?
   I. n
   II. s
   III. m_l
   IV. m_s
   V. f
   a) I only
   b) II only
   c) II and V only
   d) IV only
   e) V only

Answer: (c)

*The angular momentum quantum number (l) indicates the shape of the orbital. Shapes are designated **s, p, d,** and f.*

21. The Rydberg equation can be used
    a) to calculate the energy released as an electron drops from a high orbit to a lower one.
    b) to calculate the ionization energy of hydrogen.
    c) to determine the energy needed to promote an electron to a higher energy level.
    d) to understand the spectra of the hydrogen atom.
    e) for all of the above purposes.

Answer: (e)

This is the definition of the Rydberg equation.

22. Which of the following statements regarding electronic configurations is true?
    a) An atom with an electron configuration of $1s^2 2s^2 2p^6 3s^1$ has a higher second ionization energy than an atom with a configuration of $1s^22s^22p^63s^2$.
    b) A neutral atom with the highest electronegativity has two unpaired electrons in its valence shell.
    c) An atom with valence electron configuration $3s^2 3p^5$ has a small electron affinity.
    d) Two ions of different elements with identical ground-state electron configurations are expected to be the same sizes.
    e) An atom with an electron configuration of $1s^2 2s^2 2p^6$ has a lower first ionization energy than an atom with an electron configuration of $1s^2 2s^2 2p^5$.

Answer: (a)

a) The second ionization energy of Alkali metals is much higher than the first, since Alkali metals have only one electron in its third orbital.
b) A neutral atom with the highest electronegativity is a halogen, which has no unpaired electrons.
c) An atom with valence electron configuration $3s^2 3p^5$ has a high electron affinity, since it only needs one more electron to fill its p orbital.
d) Ion sizes also depend on their nuclear charges.
e) Noble gases have the highest first ionization energy.

23. Which model describes electrons circulating in true orbits around the nucleus?
    a) Bohr model
    b) De Broglie's wave hypothesis
    c) Heisenberg's uncertainty principle
    d) Quantum theory
    e) Atomic theory

Answer: (a)

The Bohr hydrogen atom model describes electrons circulating in true orbits around the nucleus.

24. The number of electrons, protons, and neutrons in ^{40}Ar are
    a) 18e, 18p, and 40n, respectively.
    b) 40e, 40p, and 18n, respectively.
    c) 18e, 22p, and 18n, respectively.
    d) 18e, 18p, and 22n, respectively.
    e) 40e, 18p, and 22n, respectively.

Answer: (d)

Argon has 18 protons, 18 electrons, and 40 – 18 = 22 neutrons.

Relationship Analysis Questions

1.	Element Z, with an electronic configuration of $1s^2\ 2s^2\ 2p^5$, can be expected to form the compound MgZ_2.	Each atom of Z needs two electrons to fill its valence shell.	*TF*
2.	Isotopes have different atomic numbers.	Isotopes must have different numbers of electrons.	*FF*
3.	^{40}Ca is a neutral atom.	It has the same number of protons as neutrons.	*TT*
4.	The isotope Cl-37 has 17 protons, 17 neutrons and 17 electrons.	The atomic mass of chlorine is 35.43 amu.	*FT*
5.	Atoms of different elements can have the same mass number.	The atoms of each element have a characteristic number of protons in the nucleus.	*TT*
6.	The element with an electron configuration of $[He]2s^1$ has a larger atomic radius than fluorine.	The element with an electron configuration of $[He]2s^1$ has a greater nuclear charge than fluorine.	*TF*
7.	The maximum number of electrons allowed in the third principal energy level is 18.	The maximum number of electrons allowed in a principal energy level is dictated by the equation $2n^2$.	*TTCE*
8.	^{12}C is an isotope of ^{14}C.	The nuclei of both atoms have the same number of neutrons.	*TF*
9.	Two electrons in the 2s subshell must have opposite spins.	The Pauli exclusion principle states that no two electrons in the same atom can have identical quantum numbers.	*TTCE*
10.	The atomic number of a neutral atom that has a mass of 39 and has 19 electrons is 19.	The number of protons in a neutral atom is equal to the number of electrons.	*TTCE*
11.	An element's nuclear charge equals the number of protons in the nucleus.	The only charged particles in the nucleus are neutrons.	*TF*
12.	Carbon's electron configuration is $1s^22s^22p^2$ rather than $1s^22s^23s^2$.	3s electrons are lower in energy than 2p electrons.	*TF*
13.	Excited tungsten atoms will give off light energy.	As the excited electrons return to their ground state, they emit energy in the form of light.	*TTCE*

Chapter 3 Elements and the Periodic Table

I. Periodic Law

Periods and Blocks

i. Periods are the horizontal rows on the periodic table. The number of the period corresponds to the highest principal quantum number of the elements in that period.

ii. The periodic table can be broken into blocks corresponding to s, p, d, f sublevels.

Electron Configuration and Periodic Trends

i. **Valence electrons** are the electrons available to be lost, gained, or shared in the formation of chemical compounds. They are the electrons in the outermost energy level of s and p orbitals. The number of valence electrons for a neutral atom is equal to its main group number. The main group elements of the periodic table are the elements that belong to the "s" and "p" blocks.

ii. **Atomic radii** tend to decrease across a period due to increasing positive nuclear charge.

iii. **Atomic radii** tend to increase downward within a group due to increasing number energy levels, because outer electrons are farther from the nucleus.

iv. **Ionization energy** of s- and p-block elements tends to increase across each period. Atoms are getting smaller, so the electrons are closer to the nucleus.

v. **Ionization energy** of s- and p-block elements tends to decrease as the atomic number increases in a group because:
   1. The larger the atom, the farther its electrons are from the nucleus.
   2. Outer electrons are shielded from the nucleus by the inner electrons.

vi. **Noble gases** have the highest ionization energy of their periods because they have a completely filled p-sub orbital, which is the most stable configuration of an atom or ion.

vii. **Nonmetals** have higher ionization energy than metals because the electrons of nonmetals are more strongly attracted to each other. Ionization energy increases for each electron removed. The greatest increase in ionization energy comes when trying to remove an electron from a stable, noble gas configuration. As shown in the example below, the biggest increase in ionization energy for sodium is the 2nd ionization energy.

$Na_{(g)} + 496\ kJ/mol \rightarrow Na^{+}_{(g)} + e^{-}$ (1st ionization energy)

$Na^{+}_{(g)} + 4562\ kJ/mol \rightarrow Na^{++}_{(g)} + e^{-}$ (2nd ionization energy)

$Na^{++}_{(g)} + 6912\ kJ/mol \rightarrow Na^{+++}_{(g)} + e^{-}$ (3rd ionization energy)

viii. **Electron affinity** tends to decrease downward within a group because the atoms increase in size. Electron affinity tends to increase across a period because the atoms become smaller and their nuclear charges increase.

ix. **The halogens** have the highest electron affinities since they are only one electron away from having a noble gas configuration. Atoms with filled or half-filled sublevels in their outer energy level tend to have lower electron affinities than other atoms in that period.

x. **Ionic radii** are the radii of atoms forming ionic bonds or becoming ions. Ion size tends to increase going downwards within a group.

1. Cations are positive ions which are smaller than their corresponding neutral atoms and have less shielding of electrons.
2. Anions are negative ions which are larger than their corresponding neutral atoms and have greater electron-electron repulsion.

xi. **Electronegativity** is a measure of the tendency of an atom to attract a bonding pair of electrons. Nonmetals have high electronegativity and metals have low electronegativity. Electronegativity tends to increase across a period and decrease going down a group of elements. Elements like noble gases, which do not form compounds, are not assigned electronegativity.

Section Practice

1. The ionization energy of an element is
   a) a measure of its mass.
   b) the energy required to remove an electron from the element in its gaseous state.
   c) the energy released by the element when forming an ionic bond.
   d) the energy released by the element upon receiving an additional electron.
   e) None of the above

Answer: (b)

This is the definition of ionization energy.

2. The elements within each column of the periodic table
   a) have similar valence electron configurations.
   b) have similar atomic radii.
   c) have the same principal quantum number.
   d) will react to form stable elements.
   e) have no similar chemical properties.

Answer: (a)

Elements of the same family have the same valence electron configurations, which leads to similar chemical properties.

3. Electron affinity is defined as
   a) the change in energy when a gaseous atom in its ground state gains an electron.
   b) the pull of electrons in a chemical bond.
   c) the energy required to remove a valence electron from a neutral gaseous atom in its ground state.
   d) the energy difference between an electron in its ground state and in its excited state.
   e) None of the above

Answer: (a)

This is the definition of electron affinity.

4. The modern periodic table is ordered on the basis of
   a) atomic mass.
   b) atomic radius.
   c) atomic charge.
   d) atomic number.
   e) number of neutrons.

Answer: (d)

Periodic table organization is based on atomic number.

5. Which of the following elements has the greatest electronegativity?
   a) Chlorine
   b) Oxygen
   c) Sulfur
   d) Phosphorus
   e) Fluorine

Answer: (e)

Fluorine has the greatest electronegativity because it is the smallest halogen (needs only one electron to fill its valence shell).

6. Which of the following elements has the greatest electronegativity?
   a) S
   b) Cl
   c) Na
   d) Mg
   e) P

Answer: (b)

Halogens have the highest electronegativity in their period.

7. Which of the following shows Ca^{2+}, Ar, S^{2-}, Cl^-, and K^+ in order of size from smallest to largest?
   a) Ar, S^{-2}, Cl^-, K^+, Ca^{2+}
   b) S^{-2}, Cl^-, Ar, K^+, Ca^{2+}
   c) S^{2-}, Cl^-, Ar, Ca^{2+}, K^+
   d) Ca^{2+}, K^+, Ar, Cl^{-1}, S^{-2}
   e) Ca^{2+}, K^+, Ar, S^{2-}, Cl^-

Answer: (d)

They all have the same number of electrons, so the lesser their nuclear charge, the larger their size.

8. Which of the following is expected to have the largest 3rd ionization energy?
   a) Be
   b) B
   c) C
   d) N
   e) Al

Answer: (a)

The element that has 2 valence electrons will have the largest 3rd ionization energy.

9. Which of the following atoms has the largest radius?
   a) Sodium
   b) Strontium
   c) Uranium
   d) Bromine
   e) Bismuth

Answer: (c)

Uranium has the largest principal quantum number.

II. Blocks and Groups

s-block (groups 1 and 2)

1. Group 1, or **alkali metals**, consists of elements with only one electron in its outer shell. They are soft, silvery metals of low density, low melting points, and high reactivity. The alkali metals are never found in their pure form in nature.

2. Group 2, or **alkaline earth metals**, consists of elements with two **s** electrons in its outer shell. They are denser, harder, stronger, and less reactive than group 1. They are too reactive to be found pure in nature.

The **d-block** (groups 3–12) consists of metals with typical metallic properties. They are referred to as **transition metals**. The group number of a **d**-block element is equal to the sum of its outermost s and d electrons.

The **p-block** (groups 13–18) consists of elements that have valence electrons in the p orbital. It is the only block that has all three types of elements: metals, nonmetals, and metalloids. The **p**-block contains the halogens (group 17), which are the most reactive elements out of the nonmetals, and the noble gases (group 18), which are the most stable elements overall.

The **f-block** elements, the lanthanides and actinides series, are called inner transition metals.

Periodic Trends of the d- and f- Block Elements

i. Atomic radii decrease across a period within the **d**-block due to the added electrons partially shielding the increasing positive nuclear charge. Due to electron-electron repulsion, atomic radii increase slightly at the end of the **d-block**. Atomic radii stay about the same across **f-block** elements.

ii. Ionization energy tends to increase across **d-** and **f-blocks**.

iii. **Ion Formation and Ionic Radii**
   1. Electrons are removed from the outermost energy level, **s**-sublevel first.
   2. Most **d-block** elements form +2 ions (they lose 2 s electrons).
   3. Ions of **d-** and **f-blocks** are called cations, and are smaller than the corresponding atoms.

iv. Electronegativity increases as atomic radii decrease. Metals have characteristically low electronegativity.

Section Practices

1. Which of the following naturally occurs as diatomic elements?
   a) Alkali metals
   b) Alkaline earth metals
   c) Metalloids
   d) Halogens
   e) Rare earth metals

Answer: (d)

*Diatomic elements are H_2, O_2, N_2, and halogens. Remember the acronym HO**F**-BrINCl.*

2. The transition metals are characterized by
   a) completely filled d subshells.
   b) completely filled f subshells.
   c) partially filled d subshells.
   d) partially filled f subshells.
   e) both (a) and (c).

Answer: (c)

Transition metals have partially filled d orbitals.

3. Transition metal compounds generally exhibit bright colors because
   a) electrons in the partially filled d orbitals are easily promoted to excited states.
   b) metals form complex ions with water.
   c) metals conduct electricity and produce colored light.
   d) electrons in the ***d*** orbitals emit energy as they jump back from excited states to ground states.
   e) their valence electrons cause them to bind to other metals.

Answer: (a)

Electrons in partially filled d orbitals are easily promoted to excited states.

4. Which of the following has the highest 1st ionization energy?
   a) Ga
   b) Ba
   c) Ru
   d) F
   e) N

Answer: (d)

Fluorine needs an electron to attain noble gas configuration.

5. Which of the following has the lowest electronegativity?
   a) Ca
   b) Cl
   c) Cs
   d) P
   e) Zn

Answer: (c)

Alkali metals have the lowest electronegativity in their periods.

6. Which element has the greatest electronegativity?
   a) Chlorine
   b) Oxygen
   c) Sulfur
   d) Phosphorus
   e) Fluorine

Answer: (e)

Fluorine has the greatest electronegativity among all elements.

7. Which of the following is used primarily in semiconductors?
   a) Alkali metals
   b) Alkaline earth metals
   c) Metalloids
   d) Halogens
   e) Rare earth metals

Answer: (c)

Metalloids have a combination of metal and nonmetal properties. Therefore, their conductivity are between metals and nonmetral.

8. There are only two liquid elements at room temperature and atmospheric pressure. One of these is
   a) sodium.
   b) strontium.
   c) uranium.
   d) bromine.
   e) bismuth.

Answer: (d)

Bromine and mercury are the only two liquid elements at room temperature and atmospheric pressure.

9. The best way to estimate the boiling point of Pd is to
   a) average the boiling points of Rh and Ag.
   b) average the boiling points of Ni and Pt.
   c) average the boiling points of Ir and Cu.
   d) average the boiling points of Co and Au.
   e) None of the above will work.

Answer: (b)

Elements in the same family have similar properties.

10. A solid element has two valence electrons. This element must be
    a) a halogen.
    b) a noble gas.
    c) a radioactive element.
    d) an alkali metal.
    e) an alkaline earth metal.

Answer: (e)

Alkaline earth metals have two valence electrons.

11. Which of the following elements contains 38 protons?
    a) Sodium
    b) Strontium
    c) Uranium
    d) Bromine
    e) Bismuth

Answer: (b)

The atomic number of strontium is 38.

12. Members of group 1 have similar reactivity because they have
    a) the same number of protons.
    b) the same number of electrons.
    c) similar outer shell configurations.
    d) valence electrons with the same quantum numbers.
    e) the same number of neutrons.

Answer: (c)

Elements with the same number of valence electrons have similar chemical properties.

Chapter 3 Elements and Periodic Table SAT Questions

1. Which of the following has the greatest electronegativity?
   a) Alkali metals
   b) Alkaline earth metals
   c) Metalloids
   d) Halogens
   e) Rare earth metals

Answer: (d)

Halogens have the greatest electronegativity in their periods.

2. Which of the following has the smallest ionization energy?
   a) Alkali metals
   b) Alkaline earth metals
   c) Metalloids
   d) Halogens
   e) Rare earth metals

Answer: (a)

Alkali metals have the smallest ionization energies in their periods.

3. Which of the following forms negative ions in an ionic bond?
   a) Alkali metals
   b) Alkaline earth metals
   c) Noble gases
   d) Halogens
   e) Transition metals

Answer: (d)

Halogens form -1 ions in ionic bonds.

4. Which of the following is a diatomic molecule at room temperature?
   a) Alkali metals
   b) Alkaline earth metals
   c) Noble gases
   d) Halogens
   e) Transition metals

Answer: (d)

Diatomic molecules are H_2, O_2, N_2, and halogens.

5. Which of the following groups possesses the lowest first ionization energy in its respective period?
   a) Alkali metals
   b) Alkaline earth metals
   c) Noble gases
   d) Halogens
   e) Transition metals

Answer: (a)

Alkali metals have the lowest first ionization energies in their periods.

6. The element with the atomic number 32 describes a
   a) metal.
   b) non-metal.
   c) metalloid.
   d) halogen.
   e) noble gas.

Answer: (c)

The atomic number of Ge is 32, and Ge is a metalloid.

7. Which of the following is the biggest in size?
   a) Ca
   b) Ca^{+}
   c) Ca^{2+}
   d) Ca^{-}
   e) Ca^{2-}

Answer: (e)

When atoms lose electrons, they decrease in size due to less shielding and greater nuclear pull. When atoms gain electron, they increase size.

8. Which of the following is a non-metal?
   a) Fr
   b) Pd
   c) I
   d) Sc
   e) Sr

Answer: (c)

Iodine belongs to the halogen family.

9. Which of the following has the greatest affinity for electrons?
   a) F
   b) Cl
   c) Br
   d) K
   e) C

Answer: (a)

F, the smallest halogen, has the greatest affinity for electrons.

10. Which of the following is the most electronegative?
   a) He
   b) I
   c) N
   d) O
   e) C

Answer: (d)

Oxygen is the most electronegative.

11. Which of the following is not a property of Group IA elements?
   a) Low ionization energies
   b) Low electronegativity
   c) High melting points
   d) Metallic bonding
   e) Electrical conductivity

Answer: (c)

Alkali metals have relatively low melting points.

12. Arrange the following elements in order of decreasing nonmetallic character: Ge, Sn, Pb, and Si.
    a) Pb, Sn, Ge, Si
    b) Ge, Sn, Pb, Si
    c) Si, Ge, Sn, Pb
    d) They all have equal nonmetallic character since they are all in the same column of the periodic table.
    e) None of the above

Answer: (a)

Metallic character increases down a group because of the increased ability to lose electrons.

13. Elements in a given period have the same
    a) atomic weight.
    b) maximum angular momentum quantum number.
    c) maximum principal quantum number.
    d) valence electron structure.
    e) atomic number.

Answer: (c)

Elements in the same period have the same principal quantum number.

14. Which of the following elements has the lowest electronegativity?
    a) Cesium
    b) Strontium
    c) Calcium
    d) Barium
    e) Potassium

Answer: (a)

Electronegativity increases across rows and decreases down columns.

15. The order of the elements in the periodic table is based on
    a) the number of neutrons.
    b) the radius of the atom.
    c) the atomic number.
    d) the atomic weight.
    e) the number of oxidation states.

Answer: (c)

The arrangement of the periodic table is based on atomic number.

16. The elements within each column of the periodic table
    a) have similar valence electron configurations.
    b) have similar atomic radii.
    c) have the same principal quantum number.
    d) will react to form stable elements.
    e) have no similar chemical properties.

Answer: (a)

Elements of the same family have the same valence electron configurations, which leads to similar chemical properties.

17. Which of the following is a metalloid?
    a) Fr
    b) Pd
    c) I
    d) B
    e) Sc

Answer: (d)

Boron is a metalloid.

18. Which of the following is/are true regarding Ca and Mg?
    I. Ca has two valence electrons in its outer shell.
    II. The valence electrons of Ca are in the principal energy level n = 4.
    III. All of the electrons belonging to Ca and Mg are paired in the ground state.
    a) I only
    b) II only
    c) I and II only
    d) I and III only
    e) I, II, and III

Answer: (e)

All are true.

19. Which of the following regarding ionization energy is true?
    a) The second ionization energy of Mg should be smaller than the first.
    b) The first ionization energy of Cs is higher than that of Na.
    c) The atom with the highest first ionization energy is H.
    d) The noble gases, as a group, have the highest first ionization energy.
    e) The atom with the lowest ionization energy is He.

Answer: (d)

The second ionization energy is always larger than the first.

The atom with the lowest ionization energy is Cs.

20. Which of the following is NOT true regarding Al?
    a) Al has a higher electronegativity than Mg.
    b) The second ionization energy of Al will have a larger value than the first ionization energy.
    c) Al^{3+} is expected to be smaller than Al^{2+}.
    d) Al is expected to have a more negative electron affinity than sulfur.
    e) The third ionization of Al can be represented by $Al^{2+}(g) \rightarrow Al^{3+}(g) + e^-$.

Answer: (d)

Sulfur has a more negative electron affinity than aluminum.

21. Which of the following has the largest atomic radius?
    a) S
    b) Ar
    c) K
    d) Mg
    e) Rb

Answer: (e)

Atomic radii increase down groups.

22. Which of the following has the highest first ionization energy?
    a) S
    b) Ar
    c) K
    d) Mg
    e) Rb

Answer: (b)

Noble gases have the highest first ionization energy within the same period.

23. The differentiating electrons for transition elements are
    a) d electrons.
    b) s electrons.
    c) p electrons.
    d) f electrons.
    e) valence electrons.

Answer: (a)

Transition metals have partially filled d orbitals.

24. In which of the following pairs of elements is the element with the lower boiling point listed first?
    a) Na, Cs
    b) Te, Se
    c) P, N
    d) Ba, Sr
    e) I, Br

Answer: (d)

Boiling points decrease down groups for metals and increase down groups for nonmetals.

Exceptions are Mg, the lowest in the alkaline earth metals, and Ra, the 2nd highest in its family.

25. Most elements in the periodic table are
    a) nonmetals.
    b) liquids.
    c) gases.
    d) metals.
    e) metalloids.

Answer: (d)

Most elements in the periodic table are metals (the d and f orbitals can fit lots of electrons).

26. The chemical symbol for antimony is
    a) Sn.
    b) Ti.
    c) Sb.
    d) K.
    e) At.

Answer: (c)

27. In which pair of elements is the larger atom listed first?
    a) K, Ca
    b) Na, K
    c) Cl, S
    d) Mg, Na
    e) O, N

Answer: (a)

Atomic sizes decrease down periods and increase down groups (there are some exceptions, of course).

Relationship Analysis Questions

	Statement	Reason	Answer
1.	Bromine has an atomic mass of 79.9.	About 50% of all bromine atoms are ^{79}Br and 50% are ^{81}Br.	TTCE
2.	Nonmetallic atoms have larger ionic radii than atomic radii.	Nonmetallic atoms generally gain electrons when forming ions, increasing the size of their electron cloud.	TTCE
3.	Elements in the upper right corner of the periodic table form acid anhydrides.	Nonmetallic oxides react with water to form acid solutions.	TTCE
4.	The properties of phosphorus should be closer to those of sulfur than those of nitrogen.	Phosphorus and nitrogen are in the same row of the periodic table.	FT
5.	Si, with an atomic number of 14, will probably exhibit an oxidation number of +4 in a compound.	Silicon is an element that has amphoteric compounds.	TT
6.	Sodium has a larger atomic radius than phosphorous.	Sodium is lighter than phosphorous.	TF
7.	Nitrogen has five valence electrons.	The electron configuration for nitrogen is $1s^2 2s^2 2p^6$.	TF
8.	The f subshell contains seven orbitals.	The f subshell is defined by the secondary quantum number 3.	TTCE
9.	Atomic radii increase down a group.	Within a group, the higher the atomic number is, the smaller the atom.	TF
10.	The second ionization energy of B is higher than that of Be.	The second electron to be removed from B and Be comes from the same principal energy level.	TT

Statement I	Statement II	
11. Metalloids have similar characteristics.	Their valence shells have the same configuration.	TF
12. Elements in a group have similar properties.	All the electrons in their valence shells have the same energy.	TF
13. Metals are good conductors of electricity.	Metal atoms are held together by ionic bonds.	TF
14. The halogens, in group 7A, form stable diatomic molecules.	They each need one electron to fill their outer shells.	TTCE
15. The alkali metals are found in their elemental state in nature.	They react vigorously with many other elements.	FT
16. The ion of a nonmetallic atom is larger in radius than its neutral atom.	When a nonmetallic ion is formed, it gains electrons in the outer orbital, thus increasing the size of its electron cloud.	TTCE
17. K is considered a metal.	When K becomes an ion, its atomic radius increases.	TF
18. As you go from left to right across the periodic table, the elements tend to become more metallic in character.	As you go from left to right across the periodic table, the elements tend to lose electrons more easily.	FF
19. Hydrogen has a lower ionization energy than helium.	Hydrogen bonds with halogens to form polar covalent bonds.	TT
20. Elemental iodine has a higher boiling point than elemental bromine.	Iodine forms stronger covalent bonds than bromine.	FF
21. Iron is an element.	It cannot be broken down into other substances by chemical or physical means.	TTCE
22. If an element X has an atomic number of 16, X^{2-} has 14 electrons.	X^{2-} has gained two electrons from its neutral state.	FT
23. Sodium has a smaller atomic radius than chlorine.	A sodium atom does not have as many valence electrons as a chlorine atom.	FT
24. Ne is an inert gas.	Ne has a complete octet valence shell.	TTCE

Chapter 4 Chemical Bonding

I. Introduction to Chemical Bonding

A chemical bond is an attraction between atoms, forming a more stable chemical compound.

Types of Chemical Bonding

i. Ionic Bonding
   1. Chemical bonding results from the electrical attraction between a large number of cations and anions (opposite charges attract each other).
   2. In pure ionic bonding, electrons are transferred between a metal and a non-metal.

ii. Covalent Bonding
   1. Chemical bonding results from the sharing of electron pairs between two non-metal atoms.
   2. A non-polar covalent bond in which the bonding electrons are shared equally results from a balanced distribution of charge.
   3. A polar covalent bond in which electrons are not shared evenly results from an unbalanced distribution of charge.

iii. Multiple Covalent Bonds
   1. A double bond is a covalent bond produced by the sharing of two pairs of electrons between two atoms. It has higher bond energy and shorter bond length than single bonds.

H H
$C = C$
H H

Ethene

   2. A triple bond is a covalent bond produced by the sharing of three pairs of electrons between two atoms. It has higher bond energy and a shorter bond length than single or double bonds.

Ethyne

H — C ≡ C — H

   3. The first bond in the multiple covalent bond is a sigma bond and the rest of them are pi bonds.

Characteristics of Bonds

i. **Ionic Bonds**

1. Metals bond to nonmetals.
2. One atom gains electrons and becomes a positive ion, and the other loses electrons to make a negative ion. Both become stable.
3. Since opposite charges attract each other, the negative ion is attracted to the positive ion.
4. Ionic bonds create crystal structures that can be fractured easily into smaller crystals.
5. Ionic bonds conduct electricity easily in a liquid.

ii. **Covalent Bonds**

1. Non-metals bond to non-metals.
2. Some atoms, especially those with 4 valence electrons, do not give away their electrons. They prefer to share their electrons with other atoms.
3. Each atom gains a full outer shell of electrons by sharing the total number of electrons with others.
4. Covalent bonds are stronger than ionic bonds.
5. Covalent bonds do not conduct electricity easily.

iii. **Metallic Bonds** are the chemical bonds that form from the attraction between metal atoms and the surrounding sea of electrons. Metallic bonds allow outer electrons to move freely throughout the metal. Valence electrons do not belong to any particular atom.

Ag^+ e^- Ag^+ e^- Ag^+ e^- Ag^+ e^- Ag^+ e^- Ag^+ e^-
Ag^+ e^- Ag^+ e^- Ag^+ e^- Ag^+ e^- Ag^+ e^- Ag^+ e^-
Ag^+ e^- Ag^+ e^- Ag^+ e^- Ag^+ e^- Ag^+ e^- Ag^+ e^-
Ag^+ e^- Ag^+ e^- Ag^+ e^- Ag^+ e^- Ag^+ e^- Ag^+ e^-

The Electron Sea Model of Metallic Bonds

1. Metals bond to metals.
2. The metal creates a pool of electrons that can be shared.
3. The more electrons that are shared in the pool, the stronger the bond is.
4. Alkali metals can be cut with a knife.
5. Transition metals are harder metals with more shared electrons.
6. Metals are conductive, with lots of electrons available for electricity to flow.
7. Metals are malleable, which means they can be shaped with a hammer since their electrons are moveable.

Section Practice

1. The type of bond between atoms of potassium and chloride in a potassium chloride crystal is a(n)
   a) hydrogen bond.
   b) ionic bond.
   c) polar covalent bond.
   d) pure covalent bond.
   e) metallic bond.

Answer: (b)

Alkali metals and halogens most commonly form ionic bonds.

2. A triple bond may be best described as
   a) two sigma bonds and one pi bond.
   b) one sigma bond and two pi bonds.
   c) two sigma bonds and two pi bonds.
   d) three sigma bonds.
   e) three pi bonds.

Answer: (b)

The first bond is a sigma bond and the rest of them are pi bonds.

3. Molecules of sodium chloride
   a) display ionic bonding.
   b) display polar covalent bonding.
   c) are polar.
   d) dissociate in water solution.
   e) do not exist.

Answer: (e)

Sodium chloride is an ionic compound so it doesn't have a molecular form.

4. Which of the following is the weakest bond?
   a) Ionic
   b) Covalent
   c) Polar covalent
   d) Metallic
   e) Hydrogen bonding

Answer: (e)

Hydrogen bonding is only an intra-molecular bond.

5. Which of the following oxygen-containing compounds is the most ionic?
   a) SiO_2
   b) NO_2
   c) Al_2O_3
   d) CaO
   e) Cl_2O

Answer: (d)

CaO has the lowest electronegativity.

6. Consider C_2H_4 and C_2H_6. Which of the following is/are true?
   I. The carbon to carbon bond energy in C_2H_4 is greater than in C_2H_6.
   II. The carbon atoms in C_2H_4 are sp^2 hybridized.
   III. Both molecules have a net zero dipole moment.
   a) I only
   b) II only
   c) I and II only
   d) II and III only
   e) I, II, and III

Answer: (e)

C_2H_4 has double bonds; therefore, its bond energy is greater than C_2H_6, which has only single bonds.

C_2H_4 has double bonds, which are sp^2 hybridized.

Both molecules are non-polar molecules.

7. Which of the following has the fewest pi (π) bonds and is non-polar?
   a) HCCH
   b) CO_2
   c) CO_3^{-2}
   d) N_2
   e) SO_2

Answer: (c)

HC≡CH: 2 pi bonds, non-polar
O=C=O: 2 pi bonds, non-polar
CO_3^{-2}: 1 pi bonds, non-polar
N≡N: 2 pi bonds, non-polar
SO_2: 1 pi bonds, polar

8. The oxygen-oxygen bond length in O_3 is greater than the oxygen-oxygen bond length in O_2. Which of the following accounts for this phenomenon?
   a) Electron-electron repulsion is greater in O_3 than in O_2.
   b) The oxygen atoms in O_3 carry a formal charge.
   c) The oxygen–oxygen bonds in O_3 are single bonds.
   d) O_3 has a net dipole moment whereas O_2 does not.
   e) The bond order in O_2 is 2 while the bond order in O_3 is 1.5.

Answer: (e)

O_3 has a resonance structure, meaning it has two double bonds shared amongst the three oxygen atoms.

II. Lewis Structures

Steps to Construct Lewis Structures

i. Calculate the total number of valence electrons from each atom in the molecule.
   1. The number of valence electrons for atoms in groups I through VIII is equal to the group number.
   2. The number of valence electrons for transition metal atoms is equal to the oxidation state of the atom.
   3. Deduct one electron for each positive charge of the positive ion.
   4. Add one electron for each negative charge of the negative ion.

ii. Arrange the atoms appropriately.
   1. The central atom is usually the least electronegative, and the molecule is usually symmetrical.
   2. The molecular formula is usually drawn indicating the order of atoms, i.e. CH_3CNO and CH_3NCO have a different order of the carbon and nitrogen atoms only.

iii. Add lone pairs of electrons to satisfy the octet rule for each atom. Atoms from Period 2 (C, N, O, F) and higher take eight electrons. Hydrogen (H), an atom from Period 1, takes two electrons instead of eight.

iv. The total number of electrons in the structure is equal to two times the sum of the number of bonds and the number of lone pairs.

v. **The Octet Rule:** Chemical compounds tend to form so that each atom, by gaining, losing, or sharing electrons, has an octet of electrons in its highest occupied energy level.

vi. **Formal charge** is equal to
$\text{Number of Valence Electrons} - \text{Number of Lone Pair Electrons} - \text{Number of Bonds}$

   1. The sum of formal charges of the Lewis structure of a molecule or ion must be equal to the net charge of the molecule or ion.
   2. The most electronegative atom usually has a negative formal charge, while the least electronegative atom usually has a positive formal charge.
   3. If there is more than one Lewis structure, a resonance structure can be drawn for a compound. The formal charge closest to zero is the most acceptable structure.

Example: Consider the thiocyanate (CNS^-) ion:

There are three resonance structures as follows:

$$\left[:\overset{..}{\underset{..}{N}}-C\equiv S:\right]^{-}_{I} \leftrightarrow \left[:\overset{..}{\underset{..}{S}}-C\equiv N:\right]^{-}_{II} \leftrightarrow \left[:\ddot{N}=C=\ddot{S}:\right]^{-}_{III}$$

FC: -2 0 +1 -1 0 0 -1 0 0

The structure III is the most stable resonance structure because it has the lowest formal charge and its most electronegative atom, N, has a negative formal charge.

Section Practice

1. The number of bonds predicted for N_2 is
   a) zero.
   b) one.
   c) two.
   d) three.
   e) four.

Answer: (d)

N≡N

2. For which of the following is it possible to draw both polar and non-polar Lewis structures?
   a) $CHCl_3$
   b) NH_3
   c) BF_3
   d) SF_2Cl_4
   e) PCl_5

Answer: (d)

The two F atoms can be arranged with different positions so SF_2Cl_4 can have both polar and non-polar structures.

3. Label formal charges and predict what is the most likely resonance structure is for N_2O.
   a) : N≡N=O::
   b) ::N=O=N::
   c) ::N=N=O::
   d) : N≡N−O:::
   e) : N−N≡O:::

Answer: (d)

: N≡N=O:: violates octet rule
::N=O=N:: −1 +2 −1
::N=N=O:: −1 +1 0
: N≡N−O::: 0 +1 −1
In (d), the most electronegative atom, O, has a negative formal charge.

4. Which of the following sets of molecules contains only non-polar species?
   a) BH_3, NH_3, AlH_3
   b) NO_2, CO_2, ClO_2
   c) HCl, HNO_2, $HClO_3$
   d) BH_3, H_2S, BCl_3
   e) BeH_2, BH_3, CH_4

Answer: (e)

(e) is the only one that have an unshared pair of electrons.

5. How many resonance structures are possible for SO_3?
   a) 1
   b) 2
   c) 3
   d) 4
   e) None

Answer: (c)

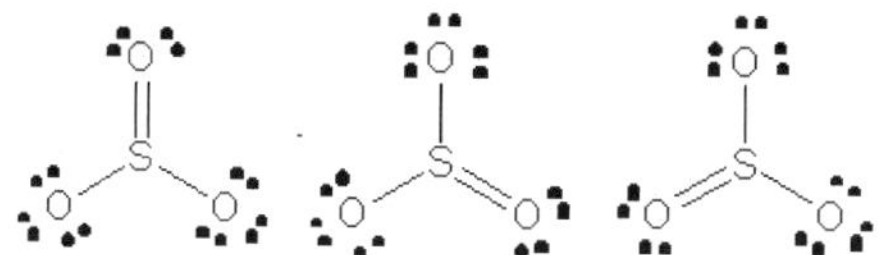

6. How many electrons are available to construct the Lewis structure of the sulfite ion?
   a) 24
   b) 18
   c) 26
   d) 22
   e) 20

Answer: (c)

S: 6 valence electrons
O: 6 valence electrons

SO_3^{-2}: $6 + 3 \times 6 + 2 = 26$

7. The number of bonds predicted for H_2 is:
   a) zero
   b) one
   c) two
   d) three
   e) four

Answer: (b)

$H-H$

H only has one electron.

8. Which molecule contains a triple bond?
   a) C_2H_2
   b) CH_2Cl_2
   c) BF_3
   d) CH_3CH_2OH
   e) HF

Answer: (a)

HC≡CH has one triple bond.

III. Molecular Geometry

VSEPR (Valence Shell Electron Pair Repulsion) Theory

The shape of a molecule can be predicted by assuming that the regions of electron density around an atom will be as far apart as possible. This assumption, when applied to the valence electrons of a molecule, is called VSEPR Theory. Rules are as follows:

i. Draw the Lewis structure.
ii. Count the number of lone pairs and bonded pairs of the central atom.
iii. Obtain the general shape from the table below.
iv. Alter the shape for repulsion between lone pairs.

Summary of VSEPR Rules

Number of Bonds (double or triple bonds count as 1)	Number of Lone Pair Electrons	Angle between Bonds	Molecule Shape	Hybridization
2	0	180°	linear	sp
3	0	120°	trigonal planar	sp^2
3	1	$\theta < 120^\circ$	bent	sp^2
4	0	109.5°	tetrahedral	sp^3
4	1	$\theta < 109.5^\circ$	pyramid	sp^3
4	2	$\theta < 109.5^\circ$	bent	sp^3
5	0	120° & 90°	trigonal bi-pyramid	dsp^3
6	0	90°	octahedral	d^2sp^3

Resonance Structures:

Resonance refers to bonding in molecules or ions that cannot be correctly represented by a single Lewis structure.

- Neither structure is correct.
- Electrons do not move back and forth.
- The two bonds are equal.

Ozone (O_3)

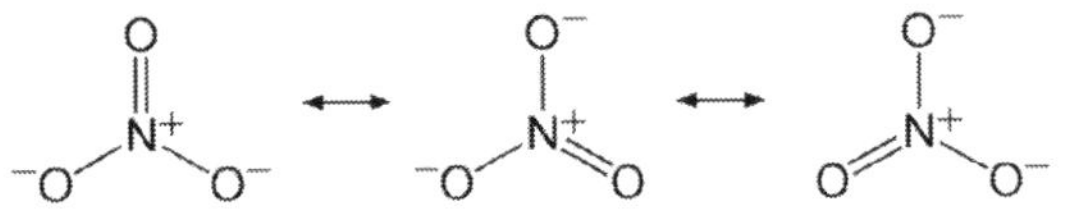

Nitrate Ion (NO_3^-)

- A **covalent network solid** is a compound or an element in which the atoms are bonded by covalent bonds in a continuous network extending throughout the network. Examples are diamonds and quartz. Many covalently bonded compounds do not form individual molecules.

Section Practice

1. Which of these molecules has all of its atoms lying on the same plane?

    I. CBr_4
    II. PF_5
    III. NH_3
    IV. SO_3
    V. HCN

    a) I and III only
    b) II only
    c) III and V only
    d) IV only
    e) IV and V only

Answer: (e)

Sp^2 and Sp have co-planar atoms.

CBr_4: sp^3
PF_5: dsp^3
NH_3: sp^3
SO_3: sp^2
HCN: sp

2. The geometry of ICl_4^-, as predicted by VSEPR, is best described by which of the following?

    a) Pyramidal
    b) Tetrahedral
    c) Square planar
    d) Cuboidal
    e) Trigonal

Answer: (c)

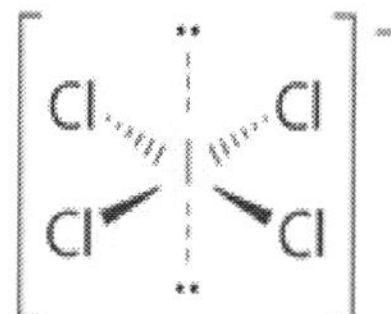

3. The geometry of NH_3 is

    a) linear.
    b) bent.
    c) tetrahedral.
    d) pyramidal.
    e) equilateral triangle.

Answer: (d)

NH_3 is sp^3 hybridized with one unshared paired of electrons.

4. Which of the following species has sp^2 hybridized orbitals?

    a) BeF_2
    b) NH_3
    c) CH_4
    d) CH_2CH_2
    e) CCl_4

Answer: (d)

$CH_2 = CH_2$

Carbon's double bond is sp^2 hybridized.

5. The carbon atoms of acetic acid (CH_3COOH) exhibit what type(s) of hybridization?
   I. sp
   II sp^2
   III. sp^3
   a) I only
   b) II only
   c) I and II only
   d) II and III only
   e) I, II, and III

Answer: (d)

Carbon atoms of acetic acid (CH_3COOH) have single and double bonds.

6. In which of the following pairs are the two items NOT properly related?
   a) sp^3 and 109.5°
   b) Trigonal planar and 120°
   c) Octahedral and sp^3d
   d) sp and 180^0
   e) Square planar and sp^3d^2

Answer: (c)

sp^3d^2 has an octahedral shape.

7. The SF_5^- ion has a square pyramid structure. The hybridization of the s orbitals in sulfur is
   a) sp^3d.
   b) sp.
   c) sp^3d^2.
   d) sp^3.
   e) sp^2.

Answer: (c)

SF_5^- has 5 S – F bonds and one unshared paired of electron. It is sp^3d^2 hybridized.

8. Sulfur forms the following compounds: SO_2, SF_6, SCl_4, and SCl_2. Which form of hybridization is NOT represented by these molecules?
   a) sp
   b) sp^2
   c) sp^3
   d) dsp^3
   e) sp^3d^2

Answer: (a)

SO_2: sp^2
SF_6: sp^3d^2
SCl_4: dsp^3
SCl_2: sp^3

IV. Intermolecular Forces

Intermolecular forces are the forces of attraction between two molecules.

Summary of the Intermolecular Forces

Type of Force	Description	Strength
Network Covalent Bonding	Directional covalent bonds, such as SiO_2, C, diamond, graphite	Strongest
Ionic Bonding	Bonds between ions, such as Na^+Cl^-, $Ba^{+2}SO_4^{-2}$	⇓
Metallic Bonding	Bonds between metal nuclei, such as Cu, Ag	
Hydrogen Bonding	Forces between molecules that occur when an H atom bonds to a highly electronegative atom like N, O, or F, such as H_2O, NH_3, HF	
Dipole-dipole Force	Forces between polar molecules, such as HBr, PH_3	
London Dispersion Force	Forces between non-polar molecules, such as CO_2 , N_2	Weakest

A substance's **boiling point** gives a rough estimate of its intermolecular forces. Stronger intermolecular forces result in higher boiling points.

London dispersion forces are the intermolecular attractions resulting from the constant motion of electrons and the creation of instantaneous dipoles.

i. All molecules experience London forces.
ii. London forces are the only forces of attraction among non-polar molecules, such as noble gas molecules.
iii. London forces increase with the number of electrons in an atom or molecule.
iv. Greater mass = Greater London dispersion forces

Molecular polarity and dipole-dipole forces are the attractions between negative regions of one molecule and positive regions of another.

Hydrogen bonding is the type of intermolecular force that occurs when a hydrogen atom bonds to a highly electronegative atom that holds on to the electrons more tightly. Hydrogen is then attracted to an unshared pair of electrons of an electronegative atom in a nearby molecule. Hydrogen bonds form only when hydrogen binds with oxygen, nitrogen, and fluorine.

Section Practice

1. HCl(g) is a(n)
   a) ionic substance.
   b) polar covalent substance.
   c) non-polar covalent substance.
   d) amorphous substance.
   e) metallic network.

Answer: (b)

HCl has a polar covalent bond.

2. CH_4(g) is a(n)
   a) ionic substance.
   b) polar covalent substance.
   c) non-polar covalent substance.
   d) amorphous substance.
   e) metallic network.

Answer: (c)

CH_4 is a non-polar covalent substance.

3. Which of the following bonds explains water's abnormally high boiling point?
   a) Ionic
   b) Covalent
   c) Polar covalent
   d) Metallic
   e) Hydrogen bonding

Answer: (e)

Hydrogen bonding will increase the boiling point of a molecule.

V. Naming Compounds

Naming Rules

i. Ionic Compounds

Name the cation metal first, followed by the root name of the anion and the suffix "ide". If the anion is a polyatomic ion, use the name of the polyatomic ion. For transition metals, name the metal with the Roman numeral corresponding to its oxidation state.

Examples:

Ionic Compounds	Name
$Al_2(CO_3)_3$	*aluminum carbonate*
Al_2O_3	*aluminum oxide*
NH_4Cl	*ammonium chloride*
Be_3P_2	*beryllium phosphide*
$CaCO_3$	*calcium carbonate*
$CaCl_2$	*calcium chloride*
Li_2SO_4	*lithium sulfate*
Li_2S	*lithium sulfide*
$Mg(C_2H_3O_2)_2$	*magnesium acetate*
$Mg(OH)_2$	*magnesium hydroxide*
KI	*potassium iodide*
NaCN	*sodium cyanide*
Na_3PO_4	*sodium phosphate*
$Co(NO_3)_3$	*cobalt (III) nitrate*

ii. Covalent Compounds

Name the first element with a numerical prefix, unless it is singular. Then name the second element beginning with its prefix and end with "-ide."

Examples:

Compound	Name
CO	*carbon monoxide*
CO_2	*carbon dioxide*
SO_3	*sulfur trioxide*
SF_6	*sulfur hexafluoride*
N_2S_5	*dinitrogen pentasulfide*
P_4O_6	*tetraphosphorus hexoxide*
N_2O	*dinitrogen monoxide*

Multiprotic Acids

i. For binary acids, remove the suffix "**ine**" from the name of the nonmetallic element and add "hydro" as a prefix and "**ic**" as a suffix. For example, the name of HCl is hydrochloric acid.

ii. Oxygen forms a common anion such as in ClO_3^- (chlorate), NO_3^- (nitrate), CO_3^{2-} (carbonate, SO_4^{2-} (sulfate), or PO_4^{3-} (phosphate). Use the suffix "**ate**" in the name of the anion.

iii. If n is the number of oxygens in common anions above, for
- n + 1 oxygens: Add the prefix "per", such as in $HClO_4$ (perchloric acid).
- n – 1 oxygens: Use the suffix "ous", such as in HPO_3 (phosphorous acid).
- n – 2 oxygens: Add the prefix "hypo" and use the suffix "ous", such as HClO (hypochlorous acid).

iv. Oxygen may form less common anions, such as ClO^- (hypochlorite), ClO_2^- (chlorite), ClO_4^- (perchlorate), NO_2^- (nitrite), or SO_3^{2-} (sulfite).

Examples:

Compound	**Name**
H_2CO_3	*carbonic acid*
H_2SO_3	*sulfurous acid*
H_2SO_4	*sulfuric acid*
H_3PO_3	*phosphorous acid*
H_3PO_4	*phosphoric acid*
HBr	*hydrobromic acid*
$HC_2H_3O_2$	*acetic acid*
HCl	*hydrochloric acid*
$HClO_2$	*chlorous acid*
$HClO_3$	*chloric acid*
$HClO_4$	*perchloric acid*
HNO_2	*nitrous acid*
HNO_3	*nitric acid*
H_3PO_4	*phosphoric acid*
$H_2PO_4^-$	*dihydrogen phosphate*
HPO_4^{2-}	*hydrogen phosphate*
PO_4^{3-}	*phosphate*

Section Practice

1. Which of the following is the permanganate ion?
   a) ClO_4^-
   b) PO_4^{-3}
   c) MnO_2
   d) SO_4^{-2}
   e) MnO_4^-

Answer: (e)

'Per' means that there is an extra oxygen.

2. What is the correct name for the compound $Na_2Cr_2O_7$?
   a) Sodium chromium(VII)-ate
   b) Sodium dichromate
   c) Sodium dichromium heptaoxide
   d) Sodium heptaoxochromate
   e) Sodium perchromate

Answer: (b)

$Cr_2O_7^{-2}$ is a dichromate ion.

3. What is the correct formula for hydrochloric acid?
   a) $HClO$
   b) HCl
   c) $HClO_4$
   d) $HClO_2$
   e) $HClO_3$

Answer: (b)

$HClO$: hypochlorous acid
HCl: hydrochloric acid
$HClO_4$: perchloric acid
$HClO_2$: chlorous acid
$HClO_3$: chloric acid

4. What is the name of H_2SO_3?
   a) Sulfuric acid
   b) Sulfurous acid
   c) Hydrosulfuric acid
   d) Hyposulfuric acid
   e) Hyposulfurous acid

Answer: (b)

H_2SO_4: sulfuric acid
H_2SO_3: sulfurous acid
H_2SO_2: hyposulfurous acid

5. Which of the following is a correctly paired formula and name of an acid?
   a) $HClO_2$, chloric acid
   b) HNO_2, hydronitrous acid
   c) H_3PO_4, phosphoric acid
   d) HI, iodic acid
   e) $HClO_4$, chloric acid

Answer: (c)

$HClO_2$: chlorous acid
HNO_2: nitrous acid
H_3PO_4: phosphoric acid
HI: hydroiodic acid
$HClO_4$: perchloric acid

Chapter 4 Chemical Bonding SAT Questions

1. KCl(s) is a(n)
   a) an ionic substance.
   b) a polar covalent substance.
   c) a non-polar covalent substance.
   d) an amorphous substance.
   e) a metallic network.

Answer: (a)

KCl(s) has ionic bonds.

2. Li(s) is a(n)
   a) ionic substance.
   b) polar covalent substance.
   c) non-polar covalent substance.
   d) amorphous substance.
   e) metallic network.

Answer: (e)

Li(s) is a metal.

3. The number of bonds predicted for O_2 is
   a) zero.
   b) one.
   c) two.
   d) three.
   e) four.

Answer: (c)

O=O

4. The geometry of H_2O is
   a) linear.
   b) bent.
   c) tetrahedral.
   d) pyramidal.
   e) equilateral triangle.

Answer: (b)

H_2O is sp^3 hybridized with two unshared pairs of electrons.

5. BeF_2 has a
   a) linear geometry.
   b) bent geometry.
   c) tetrahedral geometry.
   d) pyramidal geometry.
   e) equilateral triangle geometry.

Answer: (a)

BeF_2 has two bonds in total. It is sp hybrid with linear geometry.

6. CH_4 has a
   a) linear geometry.
   b) bent geometry.
   c) tetrahedral geometry.
   d) pyramidal geometry.
   e) equilateral triangle geometry.

Answer: (c)

CH_4 has 4 bonds with sp^3 hybrids.

7. Which of the following species has sp hybridized orbitals?
   a) BeF_2
   b) NH_3
   c) CH_4
   d) CH_2CH_2
   e) CCl_4

Answer: (a)

BeF_2 has two bonds in total. It is sp hybridized with linear geometry.

8. Which of the following bonds attracts atoms of hydrogen to each other in a H_2 molecule?
   a) hydrogen bonding.
   b) ionic bonding.
   c) metallic bonding.
   d) non-polar covalent bonding.
   e) polar covalent bonding.

Answer: (d)

Two hydrogen atoms have the same electronegativity. Hydrogen is also a non-metal. Thus, H_2 forms non-polar covalent bonds.

9. An sp^2 configuration is represented by which orientation?
   a) Tetrahedral
   b) Planar
   c) Linear
   d) Trigonal planar
   e) Square

Answer: (d)

sp^2 has trigonal planar geometric shape.

10. Which of the following elements can form bonds with sp^3 hybridization?
    a) Sodium
    b) Nitrogen
    c) Carbon
    d) Oxygen
    e) Fluorine

Answer: (c)

Carbon has 4 valence electrons that can form sp^3 hybridization.

11. Which of the following molecules has a trigonal pyramidal geometry?
    a) BH_3
    b) H_2O
    c) CH_4
    d) NH_3
    e) $AlCl_3$

Answer: (d)

NH_3 is sp^3 with one unshared pair of electrons. Its geometric shape is pyramidal.

12. The structure of $BeCl_2$ can best be described as
    a) linear.
    b) bent.
    c) trigonal.
    d) tetrahedral.
    e) square.

Answer: (a)

$BeCl_2$ has sp^2 hybridization.

13. If two atoms are bonded in such a way that both members of the pair equally share one electron, what is the bond called?
    a) Ionic
    b) Covalent
    c) Polar covalent
    d) Metallic
    e) Hydrogen

Answer: (b)

This is the definition of a covalent bond.

14. If electron(s) are lost by one atom and completely captured by another, what is this type of bond called?
    a) Ionic
    b) Covalent
    c) Polar covalent
    d) Metallic
    e) Hydrogen bonding

Answer: (a)

This is the definition of ionic bond

15. If one or more valence electrons become detached and migrate in a sea of free electrons among positive ions, what is this type of bond called?
    a) Ionic
    b) Covalent
    c) Polar covalent
    d) Metallic
    e) Hydrogen bonding

Answer: (d)

This is the definition of metallic bond

16. Which of these molecules uses more than an octet of electrons in its Lewis structure?
    I. CBr_4
    II. PF_5
    III. NH_3
    IV. SO_3
    V. HCN
    a) I and III only
    b) II only
    c) III and V only
    d) IV only
    e) V only

Answer: (b)

PF_5 has more than 4 bonds around P.

17. Which of these carries a single negative charge?
    a) Ammonium ion
    b) Calcium ion
    c) Bromide ion
    d) Iron(III)
    e) Phosphate ion

Answer: (c)

Halogen family ions carry a single negative charge.

18. Which of these pairs will form a compound?
    I. Ammonium ion
    II Calcium ion
    III. Bromide ion
    IV. Iron(III)
    V. Phosphate ion
    a) I and II only
    b) II and IV only
    c) III and V only
    d) I and IV only
    e) II and V only

Answer: (e)

$Ca_3(PO_4)_2$ and $Fe(PO_4)$ will be precipitated into a compound.

19. The correct name for $Fe(NO_3)_3$ is
    a) iron nitrite.
    b) Iron(II) nitrate.
    c) ferrous nitroxide.
    d) Iron(III) sulfate.
    e) Iron(III) nitrate.

Answer: (e)

Fe is a transition metal, so use a Roman numeral to indicate its charge.

20. Which of the following pairs of atoms will form isoelectronic ions?
    a) Cl and Na
    b) Cl and F
    c) Na and F
    d) S and Br
    e) Fe and Ca

Answer: (c)

When two elements and/or ions have the same electron configurations, they are said to be "isoelectronic."

21. What is the formula for an ionic compound formed from aluminum and chlorine?
    a) AlCl
    b) Al_3Cl
    c) Al_3Cl_3
    d) $AlCl_3$
    e) Al_2Cl_3

Answer: (d)

Aluminum ions have a charge of +3.

22. The electron configuration $1s^2\ 2s^2\ 2p^6\ 3s^2\ 3p^6$ corresponds to which of the following?
    a) S^{2-}
    b) Ca^{2-}
    c) Cl^-
    d) K^-
    e) All of the above

Answer: (e)

All of the choices have the same number of electrons, and thus the same electron configuration.

23. Which of the following is NOT correctly named?
    a) Cl^- chloride ion
    b) ClO^- hypochlorite ion
    c) ClO_4^- perchlorate ion
    d) ClO_2^- chlorous ion
    e) ClO_3^- chlorate ion

Answer: (d)

ClO_2^- is a chlorite ion.

24. Which of the following is NOT a correct chemical formula?
    a) $SrBr_2$
    b) Ca_2O_3
    c) Mg_3N_2
    d) Na_2S
    e) AlI_3

Answer: (b)

Ca ions have +2 charges.

25. Which of the following is a correct formula?
    a) NH_4SO_3
    b) $CaC_2H_3O_2$
    c) Na_2ClO_4
    d) $Ba(CO_3)_2$
    e) KH_2PO_4

Answer: (e)

Only KH_2PO_4 has the correct formula because their charges are balanced.
$(K^{+1})(H^+)_2(PO_4^{-3})$

26. Which of the following is NOT a linear structure?
    a) I_2
    b) I_3^-
    c) CO_2
    d) H_2S
    e) H−C≡C−H

Answer: (d)

H_2S has a bent geometric shape.

27. Which of the following does the Lewis structure of the cyanide ion most closely resemble?
    a) N_2
    b) O_2
    c) CO_2
    d) NO
    e) C_2H_2

Answer: (a)

CN^- and N_2 have the same electron structure.

28. Which of the following has a nonbonding pair of electrons on the central atom?
    a) BCl_3
    b) NH_3
    c) CCl_2Br_2
    d) PF_5
    e) $SO4^{-2}$

Answer: (b)

NH_3 has one pair of unshared electrons.

29. Which of the following is true when comparing C=C and C≡C bonds?
    a) The triple bond is shorter than the double bond.
    b) The double bond vibrates at a lower frequency than the triple bond.
    c) The double bond energy is lower than the triple bond energy.
    d) Both are composed of sigma and pi bonds.
    e) All of the above are true.

Answer: (e)

All are true.

30. The sulfur hexafluoride molecule is non-polar and contains no lone (unshared) electron pairs on the sulfur atom. Which of the following lists all of the bond angles contained in sulfur hexafluoride?
    a) 120°
    b) 180°
    c) 90° and 180°
    d) 90°, 120°, and 180°
    e) 109.5°

Answer: (c)

Sulfur hexafluoride has an octahedral geometric shape.

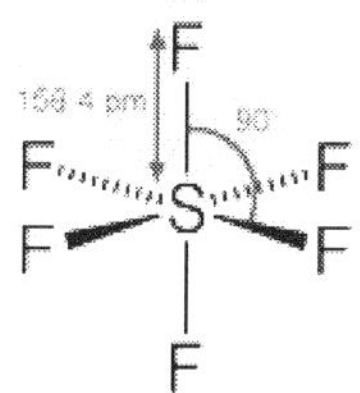

31. Which of the following is octahedral?
    a) $BeCl_2$
    b) SeF_6
    c) BF_3
    d) PF_5
    e) CF_4

Answer: (b)

SeF_6 has 6 bonds.

32. Which angle is NOT expected in any simple molecule?
    a) 60^0
    b) 90^0
    c) 109.5°
    d) 120°
    e) All of these are reasonable angles.

Answer: (a)

Angles less than 90° are uncommon and unstable.

Relationship Analysis Questions

	Statement I	Statement II	Answer
1.	KNO_3 will not dissolve in water.	All chlorides are soluble in water.	FF
2.	Ammonia has a trigonal pyramidal molecular geometry.	Ammonia has tetrahedral electron pair geometry with the three atoms bonded to the central atom.	TTCE
3.	An ionic solid is a good conductor of electricity.	An ionic solid is composed of positive and negative ions joined together by electrostatic forces.	FT
4.	Helium will have fewer atom-to-atom dispersion forces than the other noble gases.	As the mass of non-polar atoms and molecules increases, dispersion forces increase.	TTCE
5.	Atom A with 7 valence electrons forms AB_2 with atom B that has two valence electrons.	B donates its electrons to fill the outer shell of A.	FT
6.	Fluorine's oxidation number is always −1.	Fluorine is the most electronegative element.	TTCE
7.	The boiling point of H_2O is higher than the boiling point of H_2S.	H_2S has a greater molecular mass than H_2O.	TT
8.	He_2 is not known as a common form.	He is lighter than air.	TT
9.	Molecules that contain a polar bond are not necessarily polar compounds.	If polar bonds in a molecule are symmetrically arranged, then their polarities will cancel and they will be non-polar.	TTCE
10.	The molecule SO_2 has a net dipole movement.	Oxygen has higher electronegativity than sulfur.	TT
11.	In a chemical formula, the algebraic sum of the oxidation numbers must be 0.	Oxygen's oxidation number in most compounds is −2.	TT
12.	A non-polar molecule can have polar bonds.	Polar bonds can be symmetrically arranged in a molecule so that there are no net poles.	T,TCE
13.	Water is a polar substance.	The bonding electrons in water are shared equally.	TF

Statement	Reason	Answer
14. Balanced equations have the same number of reactant atoms as the product atoms.	The conservation of matter must apply in all regular chemical equations.	TTCE
15. CCl_4 is a polar molecule.	The dipole arrows for CCl_4 show counterbalance and symmetry.	FT
16. CCl_4 is a non-polar molecule.	The dipole moments in CCl_4 cancel each other out.	TTCE
17. One of the most important factors in determining the chemical properties of an element is the number of electrons in its outermost shell.	The number of electrons in the outer shell determines the bonding characteristics of an element.	TTCE
18. The bond in an O_2 molecule is considered to be non-polar.	The oxygen atoms in an O_2 molecule share the bonding electrons equally.	TTCE
19. The bonds found in a molecule of N_2 are non-polar covalent.	There is an equal sharing of electrons between the nitrogen atoms.	TTCE
20. Nonmetallic atoms of the same element form covalent bonds rather than ionic bonds.	They have the same electronegativity.	TTCE
21. NH_3 is more polarizable than NF_3.	Fluorine atoms are larger than hydrogen atoms.	TT
22. Fluorine has the highest electronegativity.	Fluorine has the greatest attraction for electrons.	TTCE
23. $AlCl_3$ is called aluminum trichloride.	Prefixes are used when naming covalent compounds.	FT
24. The sulfur in SO_2 is sp^2 hybridized.	SO_2 has linear electron pair geometry.	TT
25. The structure of SO_3 can be drawn in more than one way.	SO_3 is very unstable and resonates between these possible structures.	TF

Chapter 5 Chemical Reactions and Stoichiometry

I. The Five Types of Chemical Reactions

Synthesis reactions occur when two or more substances combine to form a more complex substance.

$$A + B \rightarrow AB$$

Types of Synthesis Reactions

i. Metals react with oxygen to form oxides.

$$4Al(s) + 3O_2(g) \rightarrow 2\ Al_2O_3(s)$$

ii. Nonmetals react with oxygen to form oxides.

$$C(s) + O_2(g) \rightarrow CO_2(g)$$

iii. Metals react with halogens to form salts (the word *halogen* means "salt maker").

$$2Na(s) + Cl_2(g) \rightarrow 2NaCl(s)$$

iv. Active metal oxides react with water to form metallic hydroxides.

$$MgO(s) + H_2O(l) \rightarrow Mg(OH)_2(s)$$

v. Nonmetal oxides react with water to form oxyacids (acid rain).

$$SO_2(g) + H_2O \rightarrow H_2SO_3(aq)$$

Decomposition reactions occur when one substance breaks down to form two or more simpler substances.

$$AB \rightarrow A + B$$

Types of Decomposition Reactions

i. Metallic carbonates, when heated, form metallic oxides and carbon dioxide.

$$CaCO_3(s) \rightarrow CaO(s) + CO_2(g)$$

ii. Metallic hydroxides, when heated, decompose into metallic oxides and water.

$$Ca(OH)_2(s) \rightarrow CaO(s) + H_2O(g)$$

iii. Metallic chlorates, when heated, decompose into metallic chlorides and oxygen.

$$2KClO_3(s) \rightarrow 2KCl(s) + 3O_2(g)$$

iv. Some acids, when heated, decompose into nonmetallic oxides and water.

$$H_2SO_4(aq) \rightarrow H_2O(l) + SO_3(g)$$

v. Other peroxides, when heated, decompose into oxides.

$$2PbO_2(s) \rightarrow 2PbO(s) + O_2(g)$$

vi. Some decomposition reactions are caused by an electric current (electrolysis).

$$2NaCl(s) \rightarrow 2Na(s) + Cl_2(g)$$

Single Replacement Reactions occur when one element replaces another element in a compound

$$\mathbf{A + BC \rightarrow B + AC}$$

Types of Single Replacement Reactions

i. A metal in a compound is replaced by a more active metal.

$$Zn(s) + CuSO_4(aq) \rightarrow ZnSO_4(aq) + Cu(s)$$

ii. The hydrogens in water are replaced by an active metal.

$$Ca(s) + 2H_2O(l) \rightarrow Ca(OH)_2(aq) + H_2(g)$$

iii. The hydrogens in an acid are replaced by a metal.

$$Zn(s) + H_2SO_4(aq) \rightarrow ZnSO_4(aq) + H_2(g)$$

iv. Halogens are replaced by more active halogens.

$$Cl_2(g) + 2KBr(aq) \rightarrow 2KCl(aq) + Br_2(g)$$

Examples

1. Solid zinc reacts with sulfuric acid to produce zinc sulfate and hydrogen gas.

$$Zn(s) + H_2SO_4(aq) \rightarrow ZnSO_4(aq) + H_2(g)$$

2. Solid copper reacts with aqueous silver nitrate to produce solid silver and copper (II) nitrate.

$$Cu\ (s) + 2Ag(NO_3)(aq) \rightarrow Cu(NO_3)_2(aq) + 2Ag(s)$$

3. Solid silver reacts with aqueous copper (II) nitrate to produce solid copper and silver nitrate.

$$2Ag_{(s)} + Cu(NO_3)_{2(aq)} \rightarrow 2Ag(NO_3)_{(aq)} + Cu_{(s)}$$

4. Chlorine gas reacts with aqueous sodium bromide to produce liquid bromine and aqueous sodium chloride.

$$Cl_2(g) + 2NaBr(aq) \rightarrow 2NaCl(aq) + Br_2(l)$$

Double Replacement Reactions occur when two compounds interchange elements to form two new compounds.

$$\mathbf{AB + CD \rightarrow AC + BD}$$

Types of Double Replacement Reactions

i. Formation of a Precipitate

$$BaCl_2(aq) + Na2SO_4(aq) \rightarrow 2NaCl(aq) + BaSO4(s)$$

ii. Formation of a Gas

$$FeS(aq) + H2SO_4(aq) \rightarrow FeSO4(aq) + H_2S(g)$$

iii. Formation of Water

$$NaOH(aq) + HCl(aq) \rightarrow NaCl(aq) + H_2O(l)$$

Examples:

1. Aqueous silver nitrate reacts with aqueous sodium chloride to form AgCl, a precipitate.

$$Ag(NO_3)_{(aq)} + NaCl_{(aq)} \rightarrow AgCl_{(s)} + Na(NO_3)_{(aq)}$$

2. Aqueous sodium hydroxide reacts with hydrochloric acid to form water.

$$NaOH_{(aq)} + HCl_{(aq)} \rightarrow NaCl_{(aq)} + H_2O_{(l)}$$

3. Aqueous calcium hydroxide reacts with sulfuric acid to form water. This is called an acid-base reaction.

$$Ca(OH)_{2(aq)} + H_2SO_{4(aq)} \rightarrow Ca(SO_4)_{(aq)} + 2H_2O_{(l)}$$

Combustion Reactions occur when a substance combines with oxygen. Combustion reactions release a large amount of energy in the form of light and heat.

$$2H_2(g) + O_2(g) \rightarrow 2H_2O(g)$$

$$Mg(s) + O_2(g) \rightarrow MgO(s)$$

$$2C_2H_6(g) + 7O_2(g) \rightarrow 4CO_2(g) + 6H_2O(g)$$

Section Practice

$CH_3COONa + HClO_4 \rightarrow CH_3CO_2H + NaClO_4$

1. The above reaction is classified as a
   a) double displacement reaction.
   b) combination reaction.
   c) decomposition reaction.
   d) single displacement and decomposition reaction.
   e) combination and decomposition reaction.

Answer: (a)

AB + CD → AC + BD

2. What are the missing products of the following reaction?

   $NH_4Cl + Ca(OH)_2 \rightarrow$ ______ $+ CaCl_2$

   a) N_2
   b) NH_3
   c) H_2O
   d) $NH_3 + N_2$
   e) $NH_3 + H_2O$

Answer: (e)

This is a double replacement reaction.

$NH_4Cl + Ca(OH)_2 \rightarrow NH_4OH + CaCl_2$

$NH_4OH \rightarrow NH_3 + H_2O$

3. What type of chemical reaction is shown below?

   $2LiH + F_2 \rightarrow 2LiF + H_2$

   a) Single replacement
   b) Decomposition
   c) Double replacement
   d) Combustion
   e) Synthesis

Answer: (a)

AB + C → AC + B

4. What type of chemical reaction is shown below?

   $2Fe(OH)_2 \rightarrow Fe_2O_3 + 3H_2O$

   a) Single replacement
   b) Decomposition
   c) Double replacement
   d) Combustion
   e) Synthesis

Answer: (b)

AB → A + B

5. What type of chemical reaction is shown below?

   $3H_2SO_4 + 2Ga(OH)_3 \rightarrow 6H_2O + 1Ga_2(SO_4)_3$

   a) Single replacement
   b) Decomposition
   c) Double replacement
   d) Combustion
   e) Synthesis

Answer: (c)

AB + CD → AC + BD

6. What type of chemical reaction is shown below?

   $2Ni + 3Pb(NO_3)_2 \rightarrow 2Ni(NO_3)_3 + 3Pb$

   a) Single replacement
   b) Decomposition
   c) Double replacement
   d) Combustion
   e) Synthesis

Answer: (a)

AB + C → AC + B

7. What type of chemical reaction is shown below?

   $2H_2 + O_2 + 2SO_3 \rightarrow 2H_2SO_4$

   a) Single replacement
   b) Decomposition
   c) Double replacement
   d) Combustion
   e) Synthesis

Answer: (e)

A + B → AB

8. What type of chemical reaction is shown below?

   $2NH_3 + 3I_2 \rightarrow N_2I_6 + 3H_2$

   a) Single replacement
   b) Decomposition
   c) Double replacement
   d) Combustion
   e) Synthesis

Answer: (a)

AB + C → AC + B

II. Stoichiometry

Stoichiometry is one of the most important topics in Chemistry. Given a chemical reaction, stoichiometry tells us what quantity of each reactant we need in order to get the right amount of our desired products.

There are four steps to solving any stoichiometry problem:
i. Balance the equation.
ii. Convert the units of each substance to moles.
iii. Find the number of moles of the desired substance using the mole ratio.
iv. Convert the number of moles of the desired substance to the correct units.

The rest of this section will discuss this in more detail and provide examples at each step so that you will be able to handle any stoichiometry problems you see on the actual test.

Balance the equation.
In a chemical reaction, the Law of Conservation of Mass must be obeyed: matter is neither created nor destroyed, so the number of atoms of each type must be the same on the left-hand side as on the right-hand side when the equation is balanced. Proper coefficients are placed in front of the formulas to balance the number of atoms on each side of the equation. The general guidelines of balancing a chemical equation are to:
i. Balance all atoms other than oxygen and hydrogen first.
ii. Then, balance the oxygen atoms using H_2O.
iii. Finally, do the same for hydrogen atoms.

Examples: Identify the type of reaction and balance the equation.

Chemical Reaction	Reaction Type	Equation Balanced
$(NH_4)_2Cr_2O_7 \rightarrow Cr_2O_3 + N_2 + H_2O$	decomposition	$(NH_4)_2Cr_2O_7 \rightarrow Cr_2O_3 + N_2 + 4H_2O$
$AgNO_3 + Cu \rightarrow Cu(NO_3)_2 + Ag$	single replacement	$2AgNO_3 + Cu \rightarrow Cu(NO_3)_2 + 2Ag$
$C_3H_6O + O_2 \rightarrow CO_2 + H_2O$	combustion	$C_3H_6O + 4O_2 \rightarrow 3CO_2 + 3H_2O$
$C_5H_5 + Fe \rightarrow Fe(C_5H_5)_2$	composition	$2C_5H_5 + Fe \rightarrow Fe(C_5H_5)_2$
$C_6H_{12} + O_2 \rightarrow CO_2 + H_2O$	combustion	$2C_6H_{12} + 18O_2 \rightarrow 12CO_2 + 12H_2O$
$Na_3PO_4 + KOH \rightarrow NaOH + K_3PO_4$	double replacement	$Na_3PO_4 + 3KOH \rightarrow 3NaOH + K_3PO_4$
$P_4 + O_2 \rightarrow P_2O_3$	composition	$P_4 + 3O_2 \rightarrow 2P_2O_3$
$RbNO_3 + BeF_2 \rightarrow Be(NO_3)_2 + RbF$	double replacement	$2RbNO_3 + BeF_2 \rightarrow Be(NO_3)_2 + 2RbF$

Keep in mind that the coefficients in front of each compound in a balanced equation represent the mole ratio of that compound in a chemical reaction.

Convert the units of each substance to moles.
i. The mole concept
Because atoms and molecules are too small to easily measure, we use a more convenient unit called the mole to describe a quantity of particles.

Imagine that the mole is a basket holding 6.02×10^{23} particles. The number, 6.02×10^{23}, is called **Avogadro's number**.

ii. Molar mass and mole
The molar mass of a compound is equivalent to the mass of 1 mole of that compound, expressed in grams. To find out a compound's molar mass, add up all the atomic weights of each atom in that compound. For example, to find the molar mass of $CaCO_3$,

$$1\text{Ca}\ (40) + 1\text{C}\ (12) + 3\text{O}\ (16) = 100\ \text{grams/mol}.$$

iii. The relationship between a mole of a compound and its molar mass is

$$\text{Moles} = \frac{\text{Mass (in grams)}}{\text{Molar Mass}}$$

iv. One mole is equivalent to 6.02×10^{23} particles.

$$\text{Moles} = \frac{\text{Number of Molecules}}{6.02 \times 10^{23}}$$

v. Gas volume and the mole
1. Gay-Lussac's Law states that the volume of reacting gases and the volume of gaseous products are in a small whole number ratio.
2. Avogadro's Law states that the same volume of gas under the same temperature and pressure conditions will contain the same number of gas molecules.
3. Under standard temperature and pressure conditions (STP), at 1 atm and 0° C, one mole of gas will occupy 22.4 liters, otherwise known as the molar volume of ideal gas. This is an important number to remember.
4. From Gay-Lussac and Avogadro's Law, we can conclude that the volume ratio of each gaseous compound in a chemical reaction will be equal to their mole ratio.

Find the number of moles of the desired substance using the mole ratio.
Now that we have converted all of our units to moles, it is time to use our balanced equations to find the amount of the desired compounds with the mole ratio. Again, a mole ratio is the ratio of moles of one substance to the moles of another in a balanced equation, and it is equal to the ratio of the coefficients of those compounds.

Convert the number of moles of the desired substance to the correct units.
If a question asks for your answer to be in units other than moles, you must convert the values.

$$\text{mass (in grams)} = \text{\# of moles} \times \text{molar mass}$$
$$\text{\# of molecules} = \text{\# of moles} \times 6.02 \times 10^{23}$$
$$\text{volume of gas (in liters, at STP)} = \text{\# of moles} \times 22.4\ \text{l}$$

Section Practice

1. What volume of H_2O is required to produce 5 L O_2 in the following unbalanced reaction?

$$H_2O(g) \rightarrow H_2(g) + O_2(g)$$

   a) 3 L
   b) 5 L
   c) 10 L
   d) 16 L
   e) 14 L

Answer: (c)

$2H_2O(g) \rightarrow 2H_2(g) + O_2(g)$

Mole ratio of $H_2O : O_2 = 2 : 1$
The volume ratio is the same as the mole ratio.
$5 \times 2 = 10L$

2. What is the empirical formula for a compound containing 63.8% N and 36.2% O?
   a) N_2O_5
   b) N_2O_3
   c) NO_2
   d) NO
   e) N_2O

Answer: (e)

$\frac{63.8}{14} : \frac{36.2}{16} = 2 : 1$

3. What is the empirical formula for a compound containing 36.7% N and 63.3% O?
   a) N_2O_5
   b) N_2O_3
   c) NO_2
   d) NO
   e) N_2O

Answer: (b)

$\frac{36.7}{14} : \frac{63.3}{16} = 2 : 3$

4. How many phosphine molecules are in two moles of phosphine?
   a) 1.807×10^{24}
   b) 3.476×10^{24}
   c) 1.171×10^{24}
   d) 1.204×10^{24}
   e) 2.414×10^{24}

Answer: (d)

Phosphine's chemical formula is PH_3.

$2 \times 6.02 \times 10^{23} = 1.204 \times 10^{24}$ *molecules*

5. How many atoms are in one mole of water?
   a) 1.807×10^{24}
   b) 3.476×10^{24}
   c) 1.171×10^{24}
   d) 1.204×10^{24}
   e) 2.414×10^{24}

Answer: (a)

H_2O has 3 atoms per molecule.
$3 \times 6.02 \times 10^{23}$

$= 1.807 \times 10^{24}$ *atoms*

6. When the following equation is balanced, what is the coefficient of CO_2?

$$C_4H_{10} + O_2 \rightarrow CO_2 + H_2O$$

a) 2
b) 4
c) 8
d) 10
e) 13

Answer: (c)

$2C_4H_{10} + 13O_2 \rightarrow 8CO2 + 10H_2O$

7. In the reaction below, how many moles of aluminum will produce 1 mole of iron?

$$8Al + 3Fe_3O_4 \rightarrow 9Fe + 4Al_2O_3$$

a) 1
b) 3/4
c) 9/8
d) 8/9
e) 4/3

Answer: (d)

Mole ratio of Al : Fe = 8 : 9
$8 : 9 = x : 1$
$x = 8/9$ *moles*

8. When the following equation is balanced, what is the coefficient of H_2O?

$$PH_3 + O_2 \rightarrow P_2O_5 + H_2O$$

a) 1
b) 2
c) 3
d) 4
e) 5

Answer: (c)

$2PH_3 + 4O_2 \rightarrow P_2O_5 + 3H_2O$

9. In the equation, $2NO(g) + 2H_2(g) \rightarrow N_2(g) + 2H_2O(g)$, which of the following is true?
   a) If 1 mole of H_2 is consumed, 0.5 moles of N_2 is produced.
   b) If 1 mole of H_2 is consumed, 0.5 moles of H_2O is produced.
   c) If 0.5 mole of H_2 are consumed, 1 moles of N_2 is produced.
   d) If 0.5 mole of H_2 are consumed, 1 moles of NO is produced.
   e) If 0.5 mole of H_2 are consumed, 1 moles of H_2O is produced.

Answer: (a)

Mole ratios:
$NO : H_2 : N_2 : H_2O$
$= 2 : 2 : 1 : 2$

10. What is the sum of the coefficients when the following reaction is balanced?

$$C_6H_6 + O_2 \rightarrow CO_2 + H_2O$$

a) 7
b) 14
c) 28
d) 35
e) 42

Answer: (d)

$2C_6H_6 + 15O_2 \rightarrow 12CO_2 + 6H_2O$
$2+15 + 12 + 6 = 35$

11. When a solution of phosphoric acid and iron(III) nitrate reacts, which of the following species will be present in the balanced molecular equation?

a) HNO_3(aq)
b) $3HNO_3$(aq)
c) $2FePO_4$(s)
d) $3FePO_4$(s)
e) $2HNO_3$(aq)

Answer: (b)

$H_3PO_4(aq) + Fe(NO_3)_3(aq) \rightarrow 3HNO_3(aq) + Fe(PO_4)(s)$

III. Limiting Reactants and Percent Yield

Limiting Reactants

The limiting reactant is consumed first in a chemical reaction. Therefore, it limits the amounts of other products that can also be formed by the reaction. To identify the limiting reactant in the problems, we need to find the reactant with the smallest:

$$\frac{\text{Number of Moles of the Reactant}}{\text{The Coefficient of the Reactant in the Balanced Equation}}$$

After the limiting reactant has been identified, all the mole ratio calculations should be based on the quantity of the limiting reactant.

Percent Yield

i. The theoretical yield is the amount of a product that should be produced from the given quantity of reactants.
ii. The actual yield is the measured amount of a product obtained from experimental data.
iii. Percent yield is calculated by the following formula:

$$\text{Percent Yield} = \frac{\text{Actual Yield}}{\text{Theoretical Yield}} \times 100\%$$

Section Practice

1. 28 mL of nitrogen react with 15 mL of hydrogen. How many milliliters of which gas are left unreacted?
   a) 5 mL H_2
   b) 5 mL N_2
   c) 7 mL H_2
   d) 11 mL N_2
   e) 23 mL N_2

Answer: (e)

$N_2 + 3H_2 \rightarrow 2NH_3$
Ratio of N_2: 28/1 = 28
Ratio of H_2: 15/3 = 5
H_2 is the limiting reactant.
15 ml of H_2 and 5 ml of N_2 will be used up.
28 – 5 = 23 ml N_2 will be left

2. The balanced net ionic equation for the reaction of aluminum sulfate and sodium hydroxide contains which of the following terms?
   a) $3Al^{3+}(aq)$
   b) $OH^-(aq)$
   c) $3OH^-(aq)$
   d) $2Al^{3+}(aq)$
   e) $2Al(OH)_3(s)$

Answer: (e)

$Al_2(SO_4)_3(aq) + 6NaOH(aq) \rightarrow 2Al(OH)_3(s) + 3Na_2SO_4(aq)$

3. For the following equation, $Fe_2O_3(s) + 3CO(g) \rightarrow 2Fe(s) + 3CO_2(g)$, when 1.0 mole Fe_2O_3 completely reacts with 56 g CO, approximately how many grams of iron, Fe, are produced?
   a) 102
   b) 74.5
   c) 56
   d) 42
   e) 28

Answer: (b)

56 g CO = 2 moles of CO
CO is the limiting reactant.
$CO : Fe = 3 : 2 = 2 : x$
x = 4/3 mole of Fe
$\frac{4}{3} \times 55.85 = 74.5$ *grams of Fe are produced.*

4. If 5.8 g of $Ag(NH3)_2^+$ yields 1.4 g of ammonia, how many moles of silver are produced?
   a) 4.4
   b) 5.8
   c) 0.041
   d) 0.054
   e) 7.2

Answer: (c)

Use conservation of mass.
5.8 − 1.4 = 4.4 grams of Ag = 4.4/108 = 0.041 moles of Ag

5. Aspirin ($C_9H_8O_4$) is prepared by reacting salicylic acid ($C_7H_6O_3$) and acetic anhydride ($C_4H_6O_3$):
   $$C_7H_6O_3 + C_4H_6O_3 \rightarrow C_9H_8O_4 + C_2H_4O_2$$
   How many grams of salicylic acid should be used to prepare six 5-grain aspirin tablets? (1 g = 15.5 grains)
   a) 1.48
   b) 0.74
   c) 2.22
   d) 0.148
   e) 0.222

Answer: (a)

$C_7H_6O_3 : C_9H_8O_4 = 1 : 1 = \frac{x}{7 \times 12+6+3 \times 16} = \frac{6 \times 5/15.5}{9 \times 12+8+4 \times 16}$

$\frac{x}{138} = \frac{1.935}{180}$

x = 1.48 grams

6. Ammonia can be produced by the reaction of nitrogen and hydrogen gas. Suppose the reaction is carried out starting with 14 g of nitrogen and 15 g of hydrogen. How many grams of ammonia can be produced?
   a) 17.04 g
   b) 34.08 g
   c) 51.1 g
   d) 85.2 g
   e) 102 g

Answer: (a)

$N_2 + 3H_2 \rightarrow 2NH_3$
14 g of nitrogen = 0.5 moles of N_2
15 g of hydrogen = 7.5 moles of H_2
N_2 *is the limiting reactant.*
$N2 : NH_3 = 1 : 2 = 0.5 : x$
x = 1 mole of NH_3 *= 17 grams of* NH_3

7. When 7.0 g of ethene (C_2H_4) burns in oxygen to result in carbon dioxide and water, how many grams of CO_2 are formed?

$$C_2H_4 + 3O_2 \rightarrow 2CO_2 + 2H_2O$$

   a) 9.0 g
   b) 22 g
   c) 44 g
   d) 82 g
   e) 180 g

Answer: (b)

$C_2H_4 : CO_2 = 1 : 2 = \frac{7}{2 \times 12+4} : \frac{x}{12+16 \times 2}$

$x = \frac{2 \times 7 \times 44}{28} = 22$ *grams*

8. Consider the reaction below. What mass of CF_4 is formed by the reaction of 8.00 g of methane with an excess of fluorine? $CH_4(g) + 4F_2(g) \rightarrow CF_4(g) + 4HF(g)$
   a) 19 g
   b) 22 g
   c) 38 g
   d) 44 g
   e) 88 g

Answer: (d)

$CH_4 : CF_4 = 1 : 1$

$= \frac{8}{12+4} : \frac{x}{12+4 \times 19}$

$x = \frac{8 \times 88}{16} = 44$ *grams*

9. In the reaction $2AgNO_3 + CaCl_2 \rightarrow 2AgCl + Ca(NO_3)_2$, how many grams of which reactant will remain when 20.0 g $AgNO_3$ (molar mass = 170) is reacted with 15.0 g $CaCl_2$ (molar mass = 111)?
   a) 6.53 g $CaCl_2$
   b) 6.53 g $AgNO_3$
   c) 45.9 g $CaCl_2$
   d) 8.47 g $CaCl_2$
   e) 25.9 g $AgNO_3$

Answer: (d)

20.0 g $AgNO_3 = \frac{20}{170} = 0.1176$ *moles of* $AgNO_3$

15.0 g $CaCl_2 = \frac{15}{111} = 0.1351$ *moles of* $CaCl_2$

$AgNO_3$ *is the limiting reactant.*

$AgNO_3 : CaCl_2$

$= 2 : 1$

$= 0.1176 : x$

$x = 0.0588$ *moles of* $CaCl_2$ *that is used up.*

$(0.1351 - 0.0588) \times 111 = 8.47$ *grams of* $CaCl_2$ *is left.*

Chapter 5 Chemical Reactions and Stoichiometry SAT Questions

1. Which of the following is a single replacement reaction?
   a) Sodium chloride reacting with potassium nitrate
   b) Chlorine gas reacting with sodium metal
   c) Aluminum metal reacting with hydrobromic acid
   d) Ethyl alcohol reacting with oxygen
   e) Magnesium oxide reacting with sulfur trioxide

Answer: (c)

The reactions are:
(a) double replacement
(b) synthesis
(c) single replacement
(d) combustion
(e) synthesis ($MgO + SO_3 = MgSO_4$)

2. The combustion reaction for benzene, C_6H_6, is correctly balanced with the smallest whole number coefficients. What is the sum of the coefficients?
   a) 12
   b) 15
   c) 35
   d) 17.5
   e) 12.5

Answer: (c)

$2C_6H_6 + 15O_2 \rightarrow 12CO_2 + 6H_2O$

3. When the following equation is balanced, what is the sum of the coefficients?
   $Al_2(CO_3)_3 + Mg(OH)_2 \rightarrow Al(OH)_3 + MgCO_3$
   a) 3
   b) 4
   c) 8
   d) 9
   e) 10

Answer: (d)

$Al_2(CO_3)_3 + 3Mg(OH)2 \rightarrow 2Al(OH)_3 + 3MgCO_3$

4. How many moles of NH_3 are needed to produce 2.513 moles of NO in the following reaction?
   $4NH_3(g) + 5O_2(g) \rightarrow 4NO(g) + 6H_2O(g)$
   a) 2.294
   b) 36.51
   c) 1.409
   d) 25.3
   e) 2.513

Answer: (e)

$NH_3 : NO = 4 : 4 = x : 2.513$

$x = 2.513$ *moles of* NH_3

5. How many moles of CO_2 are in 1.53 g of CO_2?
   a) 1.807×10^{-24}
   b) 3.476×10^{-2}
   c) 1.171×10^{-2}
   d) 1.204×10^{24}
   e) 2.414×10^{-1}

Answer: (b)

The molar mass of CO_2 is 44 g/mol.

$\frac{1.53}{44} = 0.0347$

6. What is the mass percentage of silicon in a sample of SiO_2?
   a) 21%
   b) 33%
   c) 47%
   d) 54%
   e) 78%

Answer: (c)

$\frac{28}{28+2 \times 16} = 0.47 = 47\%$

7. What are the product(s) in the following reaction?
   $$H_2SO_4(aq) + Ba(OH)_2(aq) \rightarrow ?$$
   a) O_2
   b) $BaSO_4$
   c) O_2 and $BaSO_4$
   d) O_2 and $BaSO_4$
   e) H_2O and $BaSO_4$

Answer: (e)

$H_2SO_4(aq) + Ba(OH)_2(aq) \rightarrow H_2O + BaSO_4$

8. In the equation,
   $$2Mg(s) + O_2(g) \rightarrow 2MgO(s)$$
   If 48.6 g Mg is placed in a container with 64.0 g O_2 and the reaction is allowed to go to completion, what is the mass of MgO(s) produced?
   a) 15.4 g
   b) 32.0 g
   c) 80.6 g
   d) 96.3 g
   e) 112 g

Answer: (c)

$48.6\ g\ of\ Mg = \frac{48.6}{24.3} = 2\ moles\ of\ Mg$

$64.0\ g\ O_2 = \frac{64}{32} = 2\ moles\ of\ O_2$

Mg is the limiting reactant.

$Mg : MgO = 1 : 1 = 2 : x$

$x = 2\ moles\ of\ MgO = 2 \times 40.3 = 80.6\ g\ of\ MgO$

9. The formula $Cr(NH_3)_5SO_4Br$ consists of
   a) 4 atoms.
   b) 8 atoms.
   c) 12 atoms.
   d) 23 atoms.
   e) 27 atoms.

Answer: (e)

$1 + (1 + 3) \times 5 + 1 + 4 + 1 = 27$

10. What is the molecular formula of a compound made of 25.9% N and 74.1% O?
   a) NO
   b) NO_2
   c) N_2O
   d) N_2O_5
   e) N_2O_4

Answer: (d)

$N : O = \frac{25.9}{14} : \frac{74.1}{16} = 2 : 5$

11. The molar ratio $H_2O_2 : H_2O : O_2$ from the reaction $H_2O_2 \rightarrow H_2O + O_2$ is
    a) 1 : 1 : 1
    b) 2 : 1 : 1
    c) 1 : 2 : 1
    d) 2 : 2 : 1
    e) 2 : 1 : 2

Answer: (d)

$2H_2O_2 \rightarrow 2H_2O + O_2$

12. What is the molecular weight of $HClO_4$?
    a) 52.5
    b) 73.5
    c) 96.5
    d) 100.5
    e) 116.5

Answer: (d)

$1 + 35.5 + 4 \times 16 = 100.5$ *g/mol*

13. Which of the following compounds contains 17 atoms?
    a) $Al_2(SO_4)_3$
    b) $Al(NO_3)_3$
    c) $Ca(HCO_2)_2$
    d) $Mg(IO_3)_2$
    e) None of the above

Answer: (a)

(a) has $2 + (1 + 4) \times 3 = 17$ *atoms*

14. How much reactant remains if 92 g of HNO_3 reacts with 24 g of LiOH, assuming a complete reaction?
    a) 46 g of HNO_3
    b) 29 g of HNO_3
    c) 12 g of HNO_3
    d) 2 g of LiOH
    e) 12 g of LiOH

Answer: (b)

92 g of $HNO_3 = \frac{92}{63} = 1.46$ *moles of* HNO_3

24 g of LiOH $= \frac{24}{24} = 1$ *mole of LiOH*

LiOH is the limiting reactant.

0.46 moles of HNO_3 *are left.*

$0.46 \times 63 = 29$ *g of* HNO_3

15. What is the density, at STP, of a diatomic gas whose gram-formula mass is 80 g/mol?
    a) 1.9 g/L
    b) 2.8 g/L
    c) 3.6 g/L
    d) 4.3 g/L
    e) 5.0 g/L

Answer: (c)

$\frac{80}{22.4} = 3.6$ *g/L*

16. How many mole(s) of CO_2 molecules are found in 1.8×10^{24} atoms?
    a) 1
    b) 2
    c) 3
    d) 4
    e) 5

Answer: (a)

3 moles of atoms = 1 mole of CO_2

$\frac{1.8 \times 10^{24}}{6.02 \times 10^{23}} \times \frac{1}{3} = 1$ *mole of* CO_2

17. How many grams of water will be produced when 8 g of hydrogen react with 8 g of oxygen?
    a) 8 g
    b) 9 g
    c) 18 g
    d) 27 g
    e) 30 g

Answer: (b)

$2H_2 + O_2 \rightarrow 2H_2O$

8 g of H_2 *= 4 moles of* H_2

8 g of $O_2 = \frac{8}{32} = 0.25$ *moles of* O_2

O_2 *is the limiting reactant.*

$O_2 : H_2O = 1 : 2 = 0.25 : x$

$x = 0.5$ *moles of* H_2O *= 9 g of* H_2O.

18. How many atoms are represented in $Na_2CO_3{\cdot}10H_2O$?
    a) 4
    b) 16
    c) 36
    d) 60
    e) 96

Answer: (c)

$2 + 1 + 3 + 10 \times (2 + 1) = 36$

19. What is the density of bromine vapor at STP?
    a) 2.5 g/L
    b) 2.9 g/L
    c) 3.6 g/L
    d) 4.9 g/L
    e) 7.1 g/L

Answer: (e)

The molar mass of Br_2 *is 160 g/mol.*

$\frac{160}{22.4} = 7.1$ *g/L*

20. Fill in the missing reactant: NaOH + _____ → $NaClO_2 + H_2O$
    a) Cl_2
    b) HCl
    c) HClO
    d) $HClO_2$
    e) $HClO_3$

Answer: (d)

This is a double replacement reaction.

$NaOH + HClO_2 \rightarrow NaClO_2 + H_2O$

21. How many grams of Na are present in 30 grams of NaOH?
    a) 10 g
    b) 15 g
    c) 17 g
    d) 20 g
    e) 22 g

Answer: (c)

$Na : NaOH = 23 : 40 = x : 30$
$x = 17\ g\ of\ Na$

22. How many atoms are there in a molecule of $K_3Fe(CN)_6$?
    a) 6
    b) 10
    c) 16
    d) 20
    e) 18

Answer: (c)

$3 + 1 + (1 + 1) \times 6 = 16$

23. What is the formula of a hydrocarbon composed of 86% carbon and 14% hydrogen by weight?
    a) CH_4
    b) C_2H_4
    c) C_2H_6
    d) C_3H_8
    e) C_4H_6

Answer: (b)

$C : H = \frac{86}{12} : \frac{14}{1} : 1 : 2$

The empirical formula for this compound is C_2H_4.

24. Acetylene, used as a fuel in welding torches, is produced in a reaction between calcium carbide and water:
    $CaC_2 + 2H_2O \rightarrow Ca(OH)_2 + C_2H_2$
    How many grams of C_2H_2 are formed from 0.400 moles of CaC_2?
    a) 0.400
    b) 0.800
    c) 4.00
    d) 10.4
    e) 26.0

Answer: (d)

$CaC_2 : C_2H_2 = 1 : 1 = 0.4 : x$
$x = 0.4\ moles\ of\ C_2H_2$

25. The percent composition of an unknown element X in CH_3X is 32%. What is element X?
    a) H
    b) F
    c) Cl
    d) Na
    e) Li

Answer: (e)

$CH3 : x = \frac{68}{17} : \frac{32}{x} = 1 : 1$
$x = 8$
The molar mass of Li, 7, is the closest one.

26. How many moles of $C_6H_{16}N_2$ can be produced when three moles of $C_6H_{10}O_4$ react with four moles of NH_3 and four moles of H_2 in a flask?

$$C_6H_{10}O_4(l) + 2NH_3(g) + 4H_2(g) \rightarrow C_6H_{16}N_2(l) + 4H_2O(l)$$

a) 1
b) 2
c) 3
d) 4
e) 5

Answer: (a)

$C_6H_{10}O_4 : NH_3 : H_2 = 1:2:4$
H_2 is the limiting reactant.
$H_2 : C_6H_{16}N_2 = 4:1 = 4:x$
$x = 1$ *mole of* $C_6H_{16}N_2$

27. Zinc reacts with hydrochloric acid in an aqueous solution according to the reaction above. How many mL of a 0.50 M solution of HCl must be added to Zn to produce 5.6 L of gas at STP?

$$Zn(s) + 2HCl(aq) \rightarrow ZnCl_2(aq) + H_2(g)$$

a) 250 mL
b) 500 mL
c) 750 mL
d) 1000 mL
e) 2000 mL

Answer: (d)

5.6 L of gas at STP $= \frac{5.6}{22.4} = 0.25$ *moles of* H_2
$HCl : H_2 = 2:1 = x : 0.25$
$x = 0.5$ *moles of HCl*
Let y be the number of liters of HCl that is required.
0.5 moles of HCl = 0.5M × y
y = 1 L = 1000 mL of HCl

28. Which of the following may change as temperature changes?

a) Molarity
b) Mass percentage
c) Molar mass
d) Empirical formula
e) Molecular formula

Answer: (a)

Volume can change with temperature. Therefore, anything related to volume will also be affected by temperature.

29. We can determine the _____ if we know the _____ and _____

I. molarity
II. mass percentage
III. molar mass
IV. empirical formula
V. molecular formula

a) I, III, II
b) II, I, V
c) V, III, IV
d) IV, I, II
e) V, III, I

Answer: (c)

If we know the molecular formula of a compound, we can determine its mass percentage, molar mass, and empirical formula.

30. In an experiment, 35.0 mL of 0.345 M HNO_3 is titrated with 0.130 M NaOH. What volume of NaOH will have been used when the indicator changes color?
   a) 35.0 mL
   b) 13.2 mL
   c) 26.4 mL
   d) 50.0 mL
   e) 92.9 mL

Answer: (e)

$35 \times 0.345 = 0.13 \times x$

$x = 92.9\ mL\ of\ NaOH$

31. What is the simplest formula for a compound composed of only carbon and hydrogen and containing 14.3% H?
   a) CH
   b) CH_4
   c) C_4H
   d) CH_2
   e) CH_3

Answer: (d)

$C : H = \frac{85.6}{12} : \frac{14.3}{1} = 1 : 2$

32. In the following reaction , 35.4 mL of 0.125 M KOH is required to titrate 50.0 mL of H_2SO_4. What is the molarity of the H_2SO_4 solution?

$$2KOH + H_2SO_4 \rightarrow K_2SO_4 + 2H_2O$$

   a) 0.0883 M
   b) 0.100 M
   c) 0.0443 M
   d) 0.125 M
   e) 0.177 M

Answer: (c)

$KOH : H_2SO_4 = 2 : 1$

$= 35.4 \times 0.125 : 50x$

$x = 0.0443\ M\ of\ H_2SO_4$

33. A substance has an empirical formula of CH_2. Its molar mass is determined in a separate experiment as 83.5 g/mol. What is the most probable molecular formula for this compound?
   a) C_2H_4
   b) C_6H_2
   c) C_4H_2
   d) CH_{12}
   e) C_6H_{12}

Answer: (e)

$(12+2) \times n = 83.5$

$n \approx 6$

The most probable molecular formula is C_6H_{12}.

34. The mass of one atom of iron is
   a) 1.66×10^{-24} g
   b) 2.11×10^{-22} g
   c) 3.15×10^{-22} g
   d) 9.28×10^{-23} g
   e) 3.36×10^{-25} g

Answer: (d)

$\frac{1}{6.02 \times 10^{23}} \times 55.8 = 9.28 \times 10^{-23}\ g$

35. What is the percentage of potassium in K_3PO_4?
    a) 14.6%
    b) 29.2%
    c) 18.4%
    d) 55.2%
    e) 39.1%

Answer: (d)

$\frac{3 \times 39}{3 \times 39+21+4 \times 16} = 0.552 = 55.2\%$

36. Which of the following is NOT a base metric unit?
    a) Meter
    b) Liter
    c) Mole
    d) Second
    e) Kilogram

Answer: (b)

The seven base units are length (meter), mass (kilogram), time (second), electric current (ampere), temperature (Kelvin), amount of substance (mole), and luminous intensity (candela). Volume is a derived unit and is expressed in terms of length.

37. In the reaction $2AgNO_3+CaCl_2 \rightarrow 2AgCl + Ca(NO_3)_2$, how many grams of AgCl (molar mass = 143.5) will precipitate when 20.0 g of $AgNO_3$ (molar mass = 170) is reacted with 15.0 g of $CaCl_2$ (molar mass= 111)?
    a) 16.9
    b) 38.8
    c) 33.8
    d) 8.45
    e) 67.6

Answer: (a)

20.0 g $AgNO_3 = \frac{20}{170} = 0.118$ moles of $AgNO_3$
15.0 g of $CaCl_2 = \frac{15}{111} = 0.135$ moles of $CaCl_2$
$AgNO_3$ is the limiting reactant.
$AgNO_3 : AgCl$
$= 2 : 2 = 0.118 : x$
$x = 0.118$ moles of $AgCl = 0.118 \times 143.5 = 16.9$ g of AgCl

38. How many liters of air are needed to completely burn 1 mole of methane in air (20% oxygen) at STP according to the reaction $CH_4 + 2O_2 \rightarrow CO_2 + 2H_2O$?
    a) 22.4
    b) 44.8
    c) 11.2
    d) 224
    e) 64.0

Answer: (d)

$CH_4 : O_2 : air = 1 : 2 : 10$
10 moles of air $= 22.4 \times 10$
$= 224$ L of air

39. How many atoms of hydrogen are present in 12.0 g of water?
    a) 1.1×10^{23}
    b) 2.0×10^{23}
    c) 4.0×10^{23}
    d) 8.0×10^{23}
    e) 4.8×10^{24}

Answer: (c)

The molar mass of water is 18 g/mol.

$\frac{12}{18} \times 6.02 \times 10^{23} = 4.0 \times 10^{23}$

40. Which of the following compounds contains the highest percent by mass of hydrogen?
    a) HCl
    b) H_2O
    c) H_3PO_4
    d) H_2SO_4
    e) HF

Answer: (b)

$H_2O: \frac{2}{18} \times 100\% = 11\%$

41. A hydrocarbon (a compound consisting solely of carbon and hydrogen) is found to be 96% carbon by mass. What is the empirical formula for this compound?
    a) C_2H
    b) CH_2
    c) C_3H
    d) CH_3
    e) C_4H

Answer: (a)

$C:H = \frac{96}{12}:\frac{4}{1} = 2:1$

The empirical formula for this compound is C_2H.

Relationship Analysis Questions

	Statement I	Statement II	Answer
1.	When a hydrocarbon is combusted in air, carbon monoxide is the major product.	Air contains much more nitrogen than oxygen.	FT
2.	In a balanced equation, the number of moles of each substance is equal.	Once the limiting reagent has been consumed, the reaction can no longer continue.	FT
3.	The empirical formula of $C_6H_{12}O_6$ is CH_2O.	The empirical formula shows the lowest ratio of the elements present in the molecular formula.	TTCE
4.	When HCl gas and NH_3 gases come into contact, a white smoke forms.	NH3 and HCI react to form a white solid, ammonium chlorate.	TF
5.	Nonmetallic oxides are usually acid anhydrides.	Nonmetallic oxides form acids when placed in water.	TTCE
6.	One mole of CO_2 has a greater mass than 1 mole of H_2O.	The molecular mass of CO_2 is greater than the molecular mass of H_2O.	TTCE
7.	If equal masses of sodium metal and chlorine gas are allowed to react, some sodium will be left over after all the chlorine is used up.	The reaction requires twice as many atoms of chlorine as sodium.	FF
8.	A wooden splint is set on fire and blown out, leaving a hot, glowing end. When the glowing splint is inserted into a sample of purified CO_2 gas, it will reignite.	CO_2 gas contains oxygen gas.	FF

Chapter 6 Gas Phases

I. The Kinetic-Molecular Theory of Gases

An ideal gas is an imaginary, perfect gas that fits all of the assumptions of the kinetic-molecular theory.

Five Assumptions of the Kinetic-Molecular Theory

i. Gases consist of large numbers of tiny particles that are far apart relative to their size.
ii. Gas particles undergo elastic collisions in which no energy is lost.
iii. Gas particles are in constant, rapid motion. Therefore, they possess kinetic energy, the energy of motion.
iv. There are no forces of attraction or repulsion between gas particles.
v. The kinetic energy of the gas particles depends only on the temperature. All gases at the same temperature have the same average kinetic energy. In reality, smaller molecules have higher average speed due to their smaller mass.

Deviations of Real Gases from Ideal Behavior

i. Real gases occupy space and exert attractive forces on one another.
ii. Small non-polar gases at high temperature and low pressure are likely to behave closely to an as ideal gases.

Section Practice

1. Which of the following gases behaves most like an ideal gas at 25 °C and 1 atm?
   a) NO_2
   b) NH_3
   c) CH_4
   d) HF
   e) O_3

Answer: (c)

Non-polar, small gas molecules behave more similarly to an ideal gas.

2. The kinetic molecular theory postulates a direct relationship between what?
   I. Volume
   II. Temperature
   III. Average kinetic energy
   IV. Effusion rate
   V. Pressure
   a) I and III
   b) II and III
   c) III and V
   d) IV and V
   e) I and V

Answer: (b)

The kinetic molecular theory describes the relationship between temperature and average kinetic energy.

3. Ideal gases
   a) have no volume.
   b) have no mass.
   c) have no attractive forces between them.
   d) have a combination of (A) and (C).
   e) have a combination of (A) and (B).

Answer: (d)

The kinetic molecular theory assumptions

4. A gas will behave more like an ideal gas if it has _____ and _____.
   I. large volume
   II. high temperature
   III. high average kinetic energy
   IV. high effusion rate
   V. high pressure
   a) I, II
   b) II, III
   c) III,V
   d) IV,V
   e) V, II

Answer: (a)

The farther apart gas particles are, the more closely they will imitate ideal gas conditions.

5. The kinetic molecular theory predicts that at a given temperature,
   a) all gas molecules have the same kinetic energy.
   b) all gas molecules have the same average velocity.
   c) only ideal gas molecules collide with each other.
   d) on average, heavier molecules move more slowly.
   e) elastic collisions result in the loss of energy.

Answer: (d)

Kinetic molecular theory describes the distribution curve of kinetic energy of gas molecules at different temperature, volume, pressure, etc.

6. Under which conditions will a physical gas behave most like an ideal gas?
   a) High pressure and high temperature
   b) Low pressure and low temperature
   c) Low volume and high temperature
   d) Low pressure and high temperature
   e) High pressure and low temperature

Answer: (d)

Low pressure and high temperature will cause gas molecules to be far apart and therefore closer to ideal standards.

7. With regards to the kinetic molecular theory of gases, which of the following is true?
   a) Particles of gas will have no kinetic energy at 0 K.
   b) The distribution of velocities of particles in a sample of H_2 will be identical at 25 °C and at 75 °C.
   c) The rate of effusion of He will be approximately 5 times faster than that of Ne at 1 atm and 25 °C.
   d) The rate of effusion of H_2 will be approximately 11 times faster than that of I_2 at 1 atm and 25 °C.
   e) The root mean square velocity for oxygen is 500 at 1 atm and 25 °C. This means that the majority of particles in a sample of O_2 will have this velocity at STP.

Answer: (d)

a). 3rd laws of thermodynamic
b). According to the kinetic molecular theory, gas molecules move faster in higher temperatures.
c). $\sqrt{4} : \sqrt{20} \approx 1: 2.24$
d). $\sqrt{2} : \sqrt{254} \approx 1: 11$
e). Only a small portion of O_2 *will have that velocity at STP.*

8. Consider two identical flasks, one filled with $N_2(g)$ and one with $CO_2(g)$ at 1.0 atm and 0 °C. Assuming ideal behavior, which of the following is/are true?
   I. N_2 molecules will have greater average kinetic energy.
   II. N_2 molecules will have greater average velocity.
   III. There are an equal number of N_2 and CO_2 molecules present.
   a) I only
   b) II only
   c) I and II only
   d) II and III only
   e) I, II, and III

Answer: (d)

Ideal gas law: $PV = nRT$

Avaerage gas kinetic energy $\propto T$ *(in Kelvin)*

$$\frac{v_{n2}}{v_{co2}} = \frac{\sqrt{M_{co2}}}{\sqrt{M_{n2}}}$$

9. In the kinetic molecular theory of gases, which of the following statements concerning average speeds is true?
   a) Most molecules are moving at the average speed.
   b) Any given molecule moves at the average speed most of the time.
   c) When temperature increases, more molecules will move at the new average speed.
   d) When temperature increases, fewer molecules will move at the new average speed.
   e) When temperature increases, the average speed decreases.

Answer: (d)

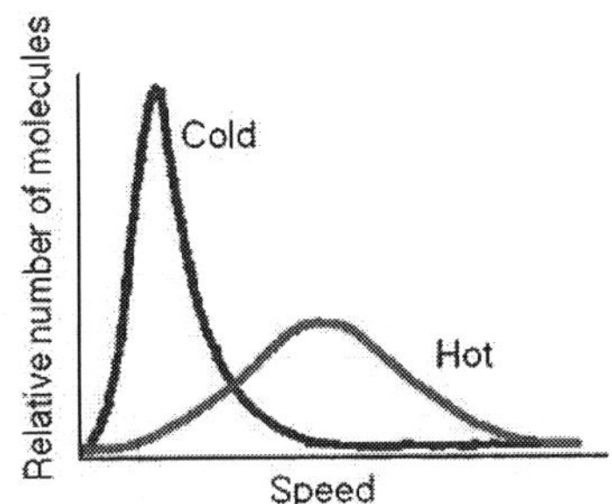

The figure above shows distribution of speeds at two different temperatures. Only (d) is correct.

10. A closed 5.0 L vessel contains a sample of neon. The temperature inside the container is 25 °C and the pressure is 1.5 atm. If the neon gas in the vessel is replaced with an equimolar quantity of helium gas, which of the following will be changed?
   a) Pressure
   b) Temperature
   c) Density
   d) Pressure and temperature
   e) Temperature and density

Answer: (c)

Replacing a sample of gas with the same volume and moles of another gas will not change the temperature or pressure. But the total mass will be reduced, since helium is lighter than neon, so density will also be reduced.

II. Pressure

Pressure and Force

Pressure is defined as the force per unit area on a surface. Gas molecules exert force, which creates pressure on any surface with.

$$\mathbf{P} = \frac{\mathbf{F}}{\mathbf{A}}$$

$$\mathbf{P_{fluid}} = \boldsymbol{\rho}\mathbf{gh}$$

ρ is the density of the fluids, **h** is the height, and **g** is the gravitational constant, $9.8 m/s^2$.

The mercury barometer was invented by Evangelista Torricelli in the 1600s to measure pressure.

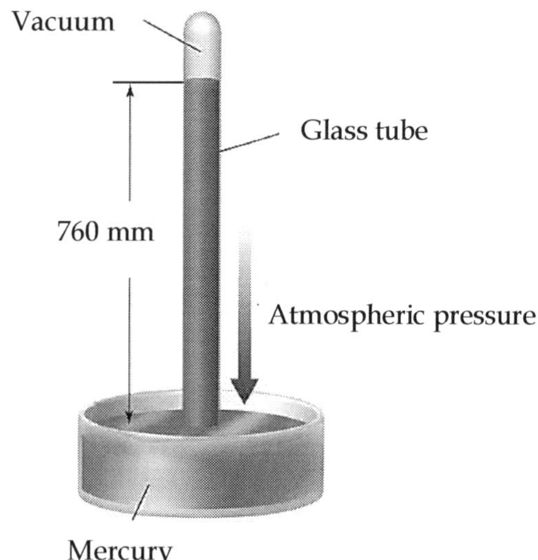

Units of Pressure

Unit	Symbol	Definition/Relationship
Pascal	Pa	SI pressure unit $1\text{ Pa} = \frac{Force(1 Newton)}{Area(1m^2)}$
Millimeter of Mercury (Torr)	mm Hg	The pressure that supports a 1 mm column of mercury in a barometer.
Atmosphere	atm	Average atmospheric pressure at sea level and 0°C 1 atm = 760 mm Hg = 760 torr = 101.3 kPa $= 1.013 \times 10^5$ Pa

Standard temperature and pressure (STP) conditions occur at 0°C and 1 atm.

Manometer

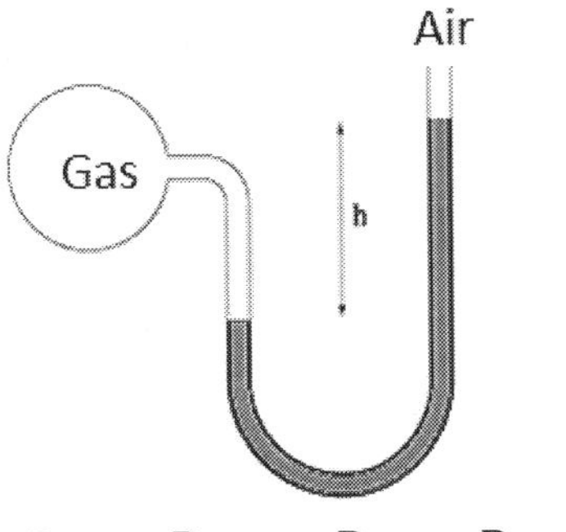

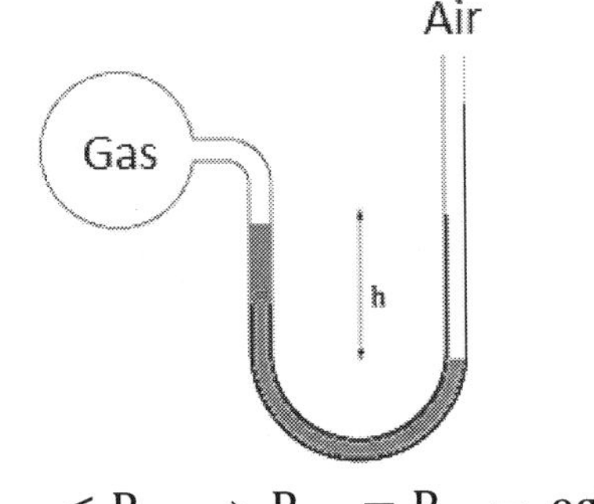

$P_{gas} > P_{air} \rightarrow P_{gas} = P_{air} + \rho gh$ $P_{gas} < P_{air} \rightarrow P_{gas} = P_{air} - \rho gh$

Section Practice

1. Standard conditions are
   a) 0 °C and 14.7 mm Hg.
   b) 32 °F and 76 cm Hg.
   c) 273 °C and 760 mm Hg.
   d) 4 °C and 7.6 m Hg.
   e) 0 K and 1 atm.

Answer: (b)

STP is 1 atm (76 cm Hg) and 0°C (32°F).

2. When the level of mercury inside a gas tube is higher than the level in the reservoir, you can find the correct pressure inside the tube by taking the outside pressure reading and _____ the difference in the height of mercury.
   a) subtracting
   b) adding
   c) dividing
   d) multiplying
   e) doing both (a) and (c)

Answer: (a)

When the level of mercury is higher inside a gas tube than it is outside, the pressure inside is lower than it is outside.

3. What will the total pressure be in a 2.50 L flask at 25 °C if it contains 0.016 moles of CO and 0.035 moles of CH_4?
   a) 31.4 mm Hg
   b) 380 mm Hg
   c) 0.041 mm Hg
   d) 935 mm Hg
   e) 1.23 atm

Answer: (b)

$PV = nRT$

$\frac{P}{760} \times 2.5 = (0.016 + 0.035) \times 0.082 \times (273+25) = 380\ mm\ Hg$

4. Which of the following states the total pressure of a gaseous mixture is equal to the sum of partial pressures?
   a) Boyle's law
   b) Charles' law
   c) Avogadro's law
   d) Ideal gas law
   e) Dalton's law

Answer: (e)

Dalton's law states this.

5. In the laboratory, a sample of hydrogen is collected by water displacement. The sample of hydrogen has a volume of 25 mL at 24.0 °C and a daily barometric pressure of 758 mm Hg. What is the pressure of the dry gas at this temperature? (The vapor pressure of water at 24.0°C is 22.4 mm Hg.)
   a) 455 mm Hg
   b) 470 mm Hg
   c) 736 mm Hg
   d) 758 mm Hg
   e) 780 mm Hg

Answer: (c)

The pressure of the dry gas is equal to the total pressure minus the water vapor pressure.

758 − 22.4 = 735.6 mm Hg

6. Three canisters, A, B, and C, are all at the same temperature, with volumes of 2.0, 4.0, and 6.0 L, respectively. Canister A contains 0.976 g of Ar at 120 torr, canister B contains 1.37 g of N_2 at 120 torr, and canister C is completely empty at the start. Assuming ideal gas conditions, what would be the pressure in canister C if the contents of A and B are completely transferred to C?
   a) 180 torr
   b) 330 torr
   c) 675 torr
   d) 0.25 atm
   e) None of the above

Answer: (e)

At constant temperature, the pressure in C after transferring A and B is $\frac{120\times2}{6} + \frac{120\times4}{6} = 120$ *torr.*

7. At 30 °C, a sample of hydrogen is collected over water ($P_{30^\circ C}$ = 31.82 mm Hg) in a 500 mL flask. The total pressure in the collection flask is 745 mm Hg. What will be the percent error in the amount of hydrogen reported if a correction for the vapor pressure of water is not made?
   a) 0.0%
   b) +4.5%
   c) −4.5%
   d) +4.3%
   e) −4.3%

Answer: (b)

Percent Error = $\frac{\text{Experiment Data} - \text{Actual Data}}{\text{Actual Data}} = \frac{31.82}{745-31.82} \times 100\% = 4.5\%$ *more than actual amount.*

8. A flask contains two moles of hydrogen, three moles of oxygen, and five moles of nitrogen. Which of the following is NOT true?
   a) If the total pressure of the sample is 2 atm, the partial pressure of oxygen is 0.6 atm.
   b) If another flask contains only ten moles of hydrogen (at the same temperature and volume), the total pressure will be the same.
   c) If another flask contains only ten moles of hydrogen (at the same temperature and volume), the density of the gas will be the same.
   d) The mole fraction of nitrogen is 0.5.
   e) Changing the temperature of the flask has no effect on the mole fractions of individual gases.

Answer: (c)

a). Partial pressure of oxygen is $\frac{3}{2+3+5} \times 2 = 0.6$ *atm.*

b). Since the other flask has the same total number of moles, temperature, and volume, it will also have the same pressure.

c). Density is related to the molar mass of the gas, so density will change when you replace the gas with hydrogen.

d). The mole fraction of N_2 *is* $\frac{5}{2+3+5} = 0.5$.

e). Changing the temperature will not change the gas composition.

III. The Gas Laws

Boyle's Law

The volume of a fixed mass of gas varies inversely with the pressure at constant temperature.

$$\mathbf{P_1V_1 = P_2V_2}$$

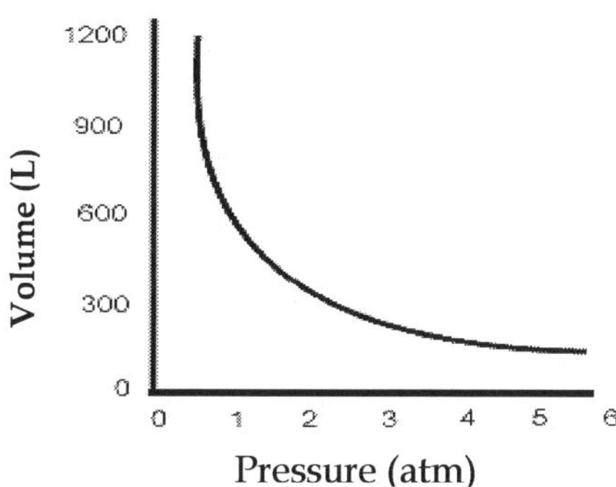

Charles's Law

The volume of a fixed mass of gas at constant pressure varies directly with the temperature (Kelvin).

$$\mathbf{\frac{V_1}{T_1} = \frac{V_2}{T_2}}$$

Gay-Lussac's Law

The pressure of a fixed mass of gas at constant volume varies directly with the Kelvin temperature.

$$\mathbf{\frac{P_1}{T_1} = \frac{P_2}{T_2}}$$

The Combined Gas Law

$$\mathbf{\frac{P_1V_1}{T_1} = \frac{P_2V_2}{T_2}}$$

Ideal Gas Law

$$\mathbf{PV = nRT}$$

P: Pressure (atm)
V: Volume (liters)
n: Number of moles
T: Temperature (Kelvins)
R: Ideal Gas Constant = 0.082 (atm · l/K · mole)

Find a gas' density using the ideal gas law,

$$\mathbf{PM = DRT}$$

M: Gas molar mass (g/mol)
D: Gas density (g/liter)

Dalton's Law of Partial Pressures

i. Dalton's Law states that the total pressure of a mixture of gases is equal to the sum of the partial pressures of the component gases.

$$\mathbf{P_{total} = P_a + P_B + \cdots}$$

$$\mathbf{P_a = P_{total} \cdot x_a}$$

where x_a is the mole fraction of gas a

ii. When gases are collected by water displacement, water vapor will be present in the collected gas, exerting pressure. Therefore,

$$\mathbf{P_{dry\ gas} = P_{total} - P_{water\ vapor}}$$

Stoichiometry of Gases

i. One mole of any gas at STP occupies 22.4 liters of volume.

ii. Volume ratios are the same as mole ratios under the same temperature and pressure.

iii. Under the same conditions of temperature and pressure, an equal volume of gases contains the same number of molecules.

iv. Molecules of active gaseous elements are diatomic, such as H_2, N_2, O_2, F_2, Cl_2, Br_2, and I_2.

v. Molecules of noble gases are monatomic.

Section Practice

1. Boyle's Law can be used for which of the following?
   a) Predicting the expected volumes of two party balloons.
   b) Predicting the relative pressures inside a hot air balloon.
   c) Predicting the change in volume of an inflatable toy from summer to winter.
   d) Predicting the height of a mercury barometer column in a low-pressure system.
   e) Predicting the change in volume of a party balloon subjected to different pressures.

Answer: (e)

Boyle's Law: The volume of a fixed mass of gas varies inversely with the pressure at constant temperature.

2. Considering Boyle's law, a gas will have _____ if the pressure is reduced.

   I. increased volume
   II. increased temperature
   III. increased average kinetic energy
   IV. increased effusion rate
   V. increased pressure

   a) I
   b) II
   c) III
   d) IV
   e) II and III

Answer: (a)

Boyle's Law: The volume of a fixed mass of gas varies inversely with the pressure at constant temperature.

3. The same volume of gas at constant T and P will contain the same number of molecules as stated by
   a) Boyle's law.
   b) Charles' law.
   c) Avogadro's law.
   d) Ideal gas law.
   e) Dalton's law.

Answer: (c)

Avogadro's law states that equal volumes of gas, at the same temperature and pressure, have the same number of molecules.

4. Equimolar quantities of hydrogen gas and oxygen gas are present in a closed container at a constant pressure. Which of the following quantities will be the same for the two gases?
   a) Partial pressure
   b) Partial pressure and average KE
   c) Partial pressure and average molecular velocity
   d) Average KE and average molecular velocity
   e) Partial pressure, average KE, average molecular velocity

Answer: (b)

The same number of moles of ideal gases in the same container (volume), pressure, and temperature will have the same partial pressure and average kinetic energy.

5. What volume does a sample of 1.50×10^{23} atoms of helium at STP take up?
   a) 5.6 L
   b) 11.2 L
   c) 17.8 L
   d) 22.4 L
   e) None of the above

Answer: (a)

At STP, 1 mole of ideal gas takes up 22.4 L.

$\frac{1.5 \times 10^{23}}{6 \times 10^{23}} \times 22.4\ L = 5.6\ L$

6. Which of the following describes the relationship of $P_1V_1 = P_2V_2$?
   a) Boyle's law
   b) Charles's law
   c) Van der Waal's law
   d) The combined gas law
   e) The ideal gas law

Answer: (a)

Boyle's law describes this relationship.

.

7. The relationship between the absolute temperature and volume of a gas at constant pressure is given by
   a) Boyle's law.
   b) Charles's law.
   c) the combined gas law.
   d) the ideal gas law.
   e) None of the above

Answer: (b)

Charles's Law: The volume of a fixed mass of gas at constant pressure varies directly with the temperature (in Kelvin).

8. The relation between the pressure, volume and absolute temperature is given by
   a) Boyle's law.
   b) Charles's law.
   c) the combined gas law.
   d) the ideal gas law.
   e) None of the above

Answer: (c)

The combined gas law deals with temperature, pressure and volume.

9. If ideal gas behavior is assumed, what is the density of neon at STP conditions?
   a) 1.11 gL^{-1}
   b) 448 gL^{-1}
   c) 0.009 gL^{-1}
   d) 0.901 gL^{-1}
   e) 1.25 gL^{-1}

Answer: (d)

Neon gas has a molar mass of 20.18.

Density of neon is $\frac{20.18}{22.4} = 0.901$ *g/L.*

10. If a 360 mL sample of helium contains 0.25 moles of gas, how many molecules of chlorine gas would occupy the same volume at the same temperature and pressure?
   a) 1.2×10^{24}
   b) 6.022×10^{23}
   c) 3.01×10^{23}
   d) 1.51×10^{23}
   e) 7.55×10^{22}

Answer: (d)

The same volume of ideal gas at the same pressure and temperature will have the same number of molecules.

$0.25 \times 6.02 \times 10^{23} = 1.51 \times 10^{23}$ *molecules*

11. The reaction below is used to generate nitrogen gas in an automobile airbag. What mass of NaN_3 is required to inflate a 15 L airbag to a pressure of 1.5 atm at 27 °C?

$$2NaN_3(s) \rightarrow 2Na(s) + 3N_2(g)$$

   a) 5 g
   b) 10.0 g
   c) 20.0 g
   d) 30.0 g
   e) 40.0 g

Answer: (e)

$PV=nRT$
$NaN_3 : N2 = 2 : 3$
Mole of $NaN_3 = \frac{2}{3}$ moles of N_2
$1.5 \times 15 = \frac{x}{23 + 3 \times 14} \times 0.082 \times 300 \times \frac{2}{3}$
$x = 40\ g$

12. A gas mixture contains twice as many moles of O_2 as N_2. Adding 0.200 moles of argon to this mixture increases the pressure from 0.800 atm to 1.10 atm. How many moles of O_2 are in the mixture?
   a) 0.355
   b) 0.178
   c) 0.533
   d) 0.200
   e) 0.075

Answer: (a)

Let x be the total number of moles of the original gas.
$\frac{x}{0.8} = \frac{x+0.2}{1.1}$
$x = 0.533$ *moles in total*
Number of moles of O_2 *in the mixture* $= \frac{2}{3} \times 0.533 = 0.355$ *moles of* O_2

13. A gas in a 1.50 L container is at a pressure of 245 mm Hg. When the gas is transferred completely to a 350 mL container at the same temperature, the pressure will be
   a) 1.05 mm Hg.
   b) 1.05 atm.
   c) 2.14mm Hg.
   d) 1050 mm Hg.
   e) 9.5×10^{-4} atm.

Answer: (d)

$P_1V_1 = P_2V_2$
$1.5 \times 245 = 0.350 \times x$
$x = 1050\ mm\ Hg$

IV. Effusion

Graham's Law of Effusion

$$\frac{\textbf{Effusion Rate of Gas A}}{\textbf{Effusion Rate of Gas B}} = \frac{\sqrt{M_B}}{\sqrt{M_A}}$$

where M_A and M_B are the gas molecular weights

Density can replace molar mass, since density is directly proportional to molar mass.

$$\frac{\textbf{Effusion Rate of Gas A}}{\textbf{Effusion Rate of Gas B}} = \frac{\sqrt{d_B}}{\sqrt{d_A}}$$

Section Practice

1. Graham's Law refers to
   a) the boiling points of gases.
   b) gaseous diffusion.
   c) gas compression.
   d) the volume change of a gas when temperature changes.
   e) the volume change of a gas when pressure changes.

Answer: (b)

Graham's law states that the rate of diffusion of a gas is inversely proportional to the square root of its molecular weight.

2. Which of the following gases will have the slowest rate of effusion?
   a) H_2
   b) He
   c) N_2
   d) Ne
   e) CO_2

Answer: (e)

CO_2 has the highest molar mass and thus the slowest rate of effusion.

3. The ratio of the rate of diffusion of oxygen to that of hydrogen is
   a) 1 : 2
   b) 1 : 4
   c) 1 : 8
   d) 4 : 1
   e) 1 : 32

Answer: (b)

The ratio of the rate of diffusion of oxygen to hydrogen is $\sqrt{2} : \sqrt{32} = 1 : 4$.

4. The rate of diffusion of hydrogen gas is _____ as that of oxygen gas.
   a) ½ as fast
   b) identical
   c) twice as fast
   d) four times as fast
   e) eight times as fast

Answer: (d)

The ratio of the rate of diffusion of oxygen to hydrogen is $\sqrt{2} : \sqrt{32} = 1 : 4$.

5. A rigid metal tank contains helium gas. Which of the following applies to the gas in the tank when some helium is removed at constant temperature?
   a) The volume decreases.
   b) The pressure decreases.
   c) The average speed of the gas molecules decreases.
   d) The total number of gas molecules remains the same.
   e) The average distance between the gas molecules decreases.

Answer: (b)

The pressure and number of molecules will be decreased.

Chapter 6 Gas Phases SAT Questions

1. What is the most abundant element in Earth's crust?
   a) Sodium
   b) Oxygen
   c) Silicon
   d) Aluminum
   e) Nitrogen

Answer: (b)

The most abundant compounds are SiO_2 and Al_2O_3.

2. What is a compound that can be decomposed in the lab to create oxygen gas?
   a) MnO_2
   b) NaOH
   c) CO_2
   d) $KClO_3$
   e) MgO

Answer: (d)

$ClO_3^- \rightarrow ClO + O_2$

3. When oxygen combines with an element to form a compound, the resulting compound is called a(n)
   a) salt.
   b) oxide.
   c) oxidation.
   d) oxalate.
   e) acid.

Answer: (b)

element + oxygen → oxide

4. If you wish to find the correct volume of a gas at 20 °C and 1 atm, and conditions were changed to 0 °C and 0.92 atm, by what fraction would you multiply the original volume?
   a) $\frac{293}{273} \times \frac{1}{0.92}$
   b) $\frac{273}{293} \times \frac{0.92}{1}$
   c) $\frac{273}{293} \times \frac{1}{0.92}$
   d) $\frac{293}{273} \times \frac{0.92}{1}$
   e) $\frac{20}{1} \times \frac{1}{0.92}$

Answer: (c)

Use the combined gas law.

$$\frac{P_1V_1}{T_1} = \frac{P_2V_2}{T_2}$$

$$\frac{1 \times V_1}{273+20} = \frac{0.92 \times V_2}{273}$$

$$V_2 = \frac{273}{293} \times \frac{1}{0.92} V_1$$

5. When a gas is collected over water, the pressure is corrected by
   a) adding the vapor pressure of water.
   b) multiplying by the vapor pressure of water.
   c) subtracting the vapor pressure of water at that temperature.
   d) subtracting the temperature of the water from the vapor pressure.
   e) subtracting the volume of the water from the vapor volume.

Answer: (c)

The total pressure measured includes both the gas and water vapor pressure.

6. At 5 atm and 70 °C, how many moles are present in 1.5 liters of O_2?
   a) 0.036
   b) 0.267
   c) 0.536
   d) 0.10
   e) 0.15

Answer: (b)

$PV = nRT$
$5 \times 1.5 = n \times 0.082 \times (273+70)$
$n = 0.267$ *moles of* O_2

7. What is the density of a gas at 76 torr and 37 °C (molar mass = 25 g/mol)?
   a) 0.1 g/L
   b) 0.8 g/L
   c) 22.4 g/L
   d) 75 g/L
   e) 633 g/L

Answer: (a)

$PM = DRT$
$\frac{76}{760} \times 25 = D \times 0.082 \times (273+37)$
$D = 0.099$ *g/L*

8. What volumes will 2.50 moles of N_2 occupy at 45 °C and 1.50 atm?
   a) 43.5 L
   b) 6.08 L
   c) 0.0233 L
   d) 56.00 L
   e) 14.9 L

Answer: (a)

$PV = nRT$
$1.5 \times V = 2.5 \times 0.082 \times (273 + 45)$
$V = 43.5$ *L*

9. Consider the three gases H_2, Ar, and N_2 at 1 atm and 25 °C. Which of the following is true?
   a) The gas with the highest density is H_2.
   b) The gas with the lowest average molecular speed is Ar.
   c) The gas with the highest average molecular speed is N_2.
   d) The gas with the lowest density is Ar.
   e) All three gases will have the same effusion rates.

Answer: (b)

The less the molar mass of the gases, the lower their densities and the higher their effusion rates are.

10. A sample of N_2 gas in a flask is heated from 27 °C to 150 °C. If the original sample of gas is at a pressure of 1520 torr, what is the pressure in the final sample (in atm)?
    a) 1.4 atm
    b) 2.8 atm
    c) 3.2 atm
    d) 4.3 atm
    e) 5.6 atm

Answer: (b)

$\frac{P_1}{T_1} = \frac{P_2}{T_2}$

$\frac{1520}{27+273} = \frac{x}{150+273}$

$x = 2143.2\ torr = 2.82\ atm$

11. The density of a gas at 2.0 atm and 25 °C is determined to be 3.11 g/L. Which of the following is the identity of the gas?
    a) CH_4
    b) F_2
    c) N_2O_4
    d) O_2
    e) CF_2Cl_2

Answer: (b)

$PM = DRT$

$2 \times M$

$= 3.11 \times 0.082 \times (273+25)$

$M = 38\ g/mol$

The molar mass of F_2 is 38 g/mol.

12. How many moles of helium are needed to fill a balloon that has a volume of 6.45 L and a pressure of 800 mm Hg at a temperature of 24 °C? Assume helium exhibits ideal gas behavior.
    a) 0.288
    b) 2.14
    c) 0.278
    d) 2.65×10^2
    e) 0.255

Answer: (c)

$PV = nRT$

$\frac{800}{760} \times 6.45$

$= n \times 0.082 \times (273 + 24)$

$n = 0.278$ *moles of He*

13. What will be the volume at STP of 10 L of gas currently at 546 K and 2 atm?
    a) 5 L
    b) 10 L
    c) 15 L
    d) 20 L
    e) 25 L

Answer: (b)

$\frac{P_1V_1}{T_1} = \frac{P_2V_2}{T_2}$

$\frac{2 \times 10}{546} = \frac{1 \times V_2}{273}$

$V_2 = 10\ L$

14. A 155 ml sample of CO is at a pressure of 58 mm. When the CO is quantitatively transferred to a 1 .00 L flask, the pressure of the gas will be
    a) 374 mm Hg.
    b) 8990 mm Hg.
    c) 111 mm Hg.
    d) 8.99 mm Hg.
    e) 2.67mm Hg.

Answer: (d)

$P_1V_1 = P_2V_2$

$58 \times 155 = P_2 \times 100$

$P2 = 8.99\ mm\ Hg$

15. Carbon dioxide from the combustion of 1.50 g of C_2H_6 is collected over water at 25 °C. The pressure of CO_2 in the collection flask is 746 mm Hg, and the volume is 2.00 L. How much of the CO_2 is dissolved in the water of the pneumatic trough?
    a) 0.0814 moles
    b) 0.88 g
    c) 1.79 g
    d) 0.100 moles
    e) 2.55 g

Answer: (b)

$2C_2H_6 + 7O_2 \rightarrow 4CO_2 + 6H_2O$

$1.50\ g\ of\ C_2H_6 = \frac{1.5}{30} = 0.05$ *moles*

$C_2H_6 : CO2 = 2 : 4 = 0.05 : x$

$x = 0.1$ *moles of* CO_2

$PV = nRT$

$\frac{746}{760} \times 2 = n \times 0.082 \times (273 + 25)$

$n = 0.08$ *moles of gas* CO_2.

$0.1 - 0.08 = 0.02$ *moles of* CO_2 *was dissolved in water.*

$0.02 \times 44 = 0.88\ g\ of\ CO_2$

16. Which of the following can we do to a sample of gas so that it will be impossible to predict whether the pressure of the gas will increase, decrease, or stay the same?
    a) Heating it.
    b) Heating it and increasing the volume.
    c) Cooling it and withdrawing some gas.
    d) Adding additional gas to the sample.
    e) Cooling it and increasing the volume.

Answer: (b)

Use the combined gas law.

$$\frac{P_1V_1}{T_1} = \frac{P_2V_2}{T_2}$$

Considering that all other conditions are kept constant, increasing the temperature will increase the pressure and increasing the volume will decrease the pressure. So the pressure will be changed based on which factors changes more.

17. Under identical conditions, gaseous CO_2 and CCl_4 are allowed to effuse through a pinhole. If the rate of effusion of the CO_2 is 6.3×10^{-2} mole^{-1}, what is the rate of effusion of the CCl_4?
    a) 6.3×10^{-2} mole/s
    b) 2.2×10^{-1} mole/s
    c) 1.8×10^{-2} mole/s
    d) 3.4×10^{-2} mole/s
    e) 1.2×10^{-1} mole/s

Answer: (d)

$$\frac{r_1}{r_2} = \frac{\sqrt{M_2}}{\sqrt{M_1}}$$

$$\frac{6.3 \times 10^{-2}}{x} = \frac{\sqrt{12+4 \times 35.5}}{\sqrt{44}}$$

$x = 3.4 \times 10^{-2}$ *mole* s^{-1}

18. The number of moles of an ideal gas in a 2.50L container at 300 K and a pressure of 0.450 atm is (R = 0.0821 L atm mol^{-1} K^{-1}) is
    a) 0.0457
    b) 21.9
    c) 4.93×10^{-5}
    d) 2.03×10^{4}
    e) 6.02

Answer: (a)

$PV = nRT$

$0.45 \times 2.5 = n \times 0.0821 \times 300$

$n = 0.0457$

19. What volume of hydrogen gas at STP condition will a 0.100 g sample of magnesium (molar mass = 24.31) produce when reacted with an excess of HCl?

$$Mg + 2HCl \rightarrow MgCl_2 + H_2$$

   a) 92.1 mL
   b) 46.1 mL
   c) 184 mL
   d) 9.2 mL
   e) 4.6 L

Answer: (a)

0.100 g of Mg $= \frac{0.1}{24.31} = 0.0041$ *moles of Mg*

$Mg : H_2 = 1 : 1 = 0.0041 : x$
$x = 0.0041$ *moles of* H_2 $=$
$0.0041 \times 22.4 = 0.00921$ L $=$
92.1 mL

20. Which law states that the volume of a gas is directly proportional to its temperature?
   a) Boyle's law
   b) Charles' law
   c) Avogadro's law
   d) Ideal gas law
   e) Dalton's law

Answer: (b)

Charles's law: $\frac{V_1}{T_1} = \frac{V_2}{T_2}$

21. A closed 5.0 L vessel contains a sample of neon. The temperature inside the container is 25 °C and the pressure is 1.5 atm. Which of the following expressions is equal to the number of moles of gas in the sample?
   a) (1.5 × 5.0) / (0.082 × 25)
   b) (0.08 × 250 / (1.5 × 5.0)
   c) (1.5 × 25) / (0.082 × 5.0)
   d) (0.08 × 298) / (1.5 × 5.0)
   e) (1.5 × 5.0) / (0.082 × 298)

Answer: (e)

$PV = nRT$

$$n = \frac{PV}{RT} = \frac{1.5 \times 5}{0.082 \times (25 + 273)}$$

$$= \frac{1.5 \times 5}{0.082 \times 298}$$

22. A closed 5.0 L vessel contains a sample of neon. The temperature inside the container is 25 °C and the pressure is 1.5 atm. The volume was changed while the temperature was held constant until the pressure became 1.6 atm. Which of the following expressions is equal to the new volume?
   a) 5.0 × 1.5 / 1.6 L
   b) 5.0 × 1.6 / 1.5 L
   c) 25 × 1.5 / 1.6 L
   d) 0.08 × 1.6 / 1.5 L
   e) 0.08 × 1.5 / 1.6 L

Answer: (a)

$P_1V_1 = P_2V_2$
$1.5 \times 5 = 1.6 \times V_2$

$$V_2 = \frac{1.5 \times 5}{1.6}$$

23. A flask contains three times as many moles of H_2 as it does O_2. If hydrogen and oxygen were the only gases present, what is the total pressure in the flask if the partial pressure of oxygen is P?
    a) 4P
    b) 3P
    c) $\frac{4}{3}$P
    d) $\frac{3}{4}$P
    e) 7P

Answer: (a)

$H_2 : O_2 = 3 : 1 = x : P$

$x = 3P$

Total Pressure $= P + 3P = 4P$

24. An ideal gas in a large cylinder is at a pressure of 3040 torr. Without changing the temperature, what volume of this gas can you compress into a 100 L box at 8 atm?
    a) 20 L
    b) 200 L
    c) 5,000 L
    d) 50,000 L
    e) 500,000 L

Answer: (b)

$P_1V_1 = P_2V_2$

$\frac{3040}{760} \times V = 8 \times 100$

$V = 200\ L$

25. Which of the following will always decrease the volume of a gas?
    I. Decreasing the pressure while holding temperature constant.
    II. Increasing the pressure while decreasing temperature.
    III. Increasing the temperature while increasing pressure.
    a) I only
    b) II only
    c) I and III only
    d) II and III only
    e) I, II, and III

Answer: (b)

$\frac{P_1V_1}{T_1} = \frac{P_2V_2}{T_2}$

Increasing pressure and decreasing temperature will decrease the volume of gas.

26. A gas has a volume of 10 L at 50 °C and 200 mm Hg. What conversion factor is needed to give a volume at STP?
    a) 10 × (0/50) × (200/760)
    b) 10 × (0/50) × 760/200)
    c) 10 × (273/323) × (200/760)
    d) 10 × (273/323) × (760/200)
    e) 10 × (323/273) × (760/200)

Answer: (c)

$\frac{P_1V_1}{T_1} = \frac{P_2V_2}{T_2}$

$\frac{200 \times 10}{50 + 273} = \frac{760 \times V}{273}$

$V = \frac{273}{323} \times \frac{200}{760} \times 10\ L$

27. Which of the following are the standard conditions using a Kelvin temperature scale?
    a) 760 torr and 273 K
    b) 760 torr, 273 K, and 1 L
    c) 760 torr and 0 K
    d) 0 torr and 0 K
    e) 0 torr, 273 K, and 1 L

Answer: (a)

1 atm; 0°C = 760 torr, 273 k

28. The relationship between the pressure and volume of a gas at constant temperature is given by
    a) Boyle's law.
    b) Charles's law.
    c) the combined gas law.
    d) the ideal gas law.
    e) None of the above

Answer: (a)

Boyle's law: $P_1V_1 = P_2V_2$

29. How many atoms are present in 22.4 L of O_2 at STP?
    a) 3×10^{23}
    b) 6×10^{23}
    c) 9×10^{23}
    d) 12×10^{23}
    e) 15×10^{23}

Answer: (d)

22.4 L = 1 mole of O_2 *= 2 moles of O* $= 2 \times 6.02 \times 10^{23}$

30. A gas at STP that contains 6.02×10^{23} atoms and forms diatomic molecules will occupy
    a) 11.2 L.
    b) 22.4 L.
    c) 33.6 L.
    d) 67.2 L.
    e) 1.06 quarts.

Answer: (a)

6.02 x 10^{23} *atoms of diatomic molecules = 0.5 moles of gas =* $\frac{22.4}{2} = 11.2$ *L*

Relationship Analysis Questions

	Statement	Relationship	Answer
1.	As pressure on a gas increases, the volume of the gas decreases.	Pressure and volume have a direct relationship.	TF
2.	At constant pressure, a certain amount of gas will double in volume as the temperature is halved.	Temperature and volume are inversely proportional.	FF
3.	When an ideal gas is cooled, its volume will increase.	Temperature and volume are proportional.	FT
4.	An increase in temperature will cause a gas to expand.	Temperature and volume have a direct relationship.	TTCE
5.	Under the conditions of low pressure and high temperature, the ideal gas law is inaccurate.	Any deviation from the ideal gas law is due to the non-negligible volume of the molecules and the interactions between molecules.	FT
6.	At isothermal and isobaric condition, helium effuses faster than neon.	Neon has a higher molar mass than helium.	TTCE
7.	At STP, 22.4 liters of He will have the same volume as one mole of H_2. (Assume ideal gases.)	One mole or 22.4 liters of any gas at STP will have the same mass.	TF
8.	Decreasing the volume of a system decreases pressure.	Pressure and volume are inversely related.	FT

Chapter 7 Liquids and Solids

I. Properties of Liquids

Fluids are substances that can flow and therefore take the shape of their container. They have the following properties:

i. High density
ii. Incompressibility: the volume of liquids changes little when pressure is applied.
iii. Surface tension: a force that pulls adjacent parts of a liquid's surface together. The higher the surface tension, the more the fluid attempts to minimize its surface area.
iv. Capillary action is the attraction of the surface of a liquid to the surface of a solid. Hydrogen bonding in water creates stronger than normal surface tension and capillary action.

Evaporation and Boiling

i. Vaporization is the process by which a liquid or solid changes to a gas.
ii. Evaporation is the process by which particles escape from the surface of a non-boiling liquid. Evaporation is a form of vaporization, but at any temperature.
iii. Boiling is the rapid vaporization of a liquid when the liquid is heated to its boiling point, or the temperature at which the vapor pressure of the liquid is equal to the pressure of the surrounding.

Section Practice

1. Which of the following factors determines whether two liquids are miscible?
   a) Molecular size
   b) Molecular polarity
   c) Density
   d) Both B and C
   e) None of the above

Answer: (b)

"Like dissolves like": a polar solute will dissolve in a polar solvent, while a non-polar solute will dissolve in a non-polar solvent.

2. Foam is an example of
   a) a gas dispersed in a liquid.
   b) a liquid dispersed in a gas.
   c) a solid dispersed in a liquid.
   d) a liquid dispersed in a liquid.
   e) None of the above

Answer: (a)

Foam is gas dispersed in a liquid or solid.

3. Which of the following sections shows increasing kinetic energy of a liquid?

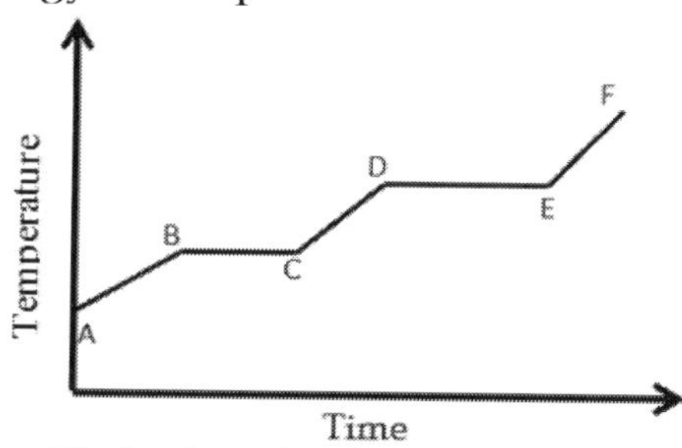

The heating curve of a pure substance

a) AB
b) BC
c) CD
d) DE
e) EF

Answer: (c)

Increasing temperature is equivalent to increasing kinetic energy. The substance is a liquid in section CD and a gas in section EF.

4. A small amount of acetone sprayed on the back of the hand will feel cooler than water would. This is because
   a) acetone is an organic compound.
   b) acetone has a lower viscosity and transfers heat quanta better.
   c) water has a higher heat capacity than acetone, therefore retains more heat.
   d) the higher vapor pressure of acetone results in more rapid evaporation and heat loss.
   e) the observed effect is not always true.

Answer: (d)

Acetone is more easily vaporized than water, meaning that acetone has a higher vapor pressure than water.

5. Which of the following compounds can NOT form hydrogen bonds with itself?
   a) CF_4
   b) CH_3OH
   c) $H_2NCH_2CH_2CH_3$
   d) $HOCH_2CH_2OH$
   e) HClO

Answer: (a)

Hydrogen bonds occur between an H atom and an O atom, an N atom, or an F atom.

6. When water is boiling, small bubbles form at the bottom of the pan and rise to the surface. What is inside these bubbles?
   a) Steam
   b) Hydrogen gas
   c) Oxygen gas
   d) A vacuum
   e) Air

Answer: (a)

Liquid water is vaporized into steam.

7. A liquid substance that exhibits low intermolecular attractions is expected to have
   a) low viscosity, low boiling point and low heat of vaporization.
   b) high viscosity, low boiling point, and low heat of vaporization.
   c) low viscosity, high boiling point, and low heat of vaporization.
   d) low viscosity, low boiling point, and high heat of vaporization.
   e) high viscosity, high boiling point, and high heat of vaporization.

Answer: (a)

Lowering intermolecular attractions results in a lower boiling point, viscosity and heat of vaporization.

8. When the following compounds are kept at the same temperature, which of the following is expected to evaporate most quickly?
   a) C_8H_{18}
   b) C_8H_7OH
   c) $C_8H_{17}NH_2$
   d) C_6H_{14}
   e) $C_7H_{15}COOH$

Answer: (d)

C_6H_{14} is non-polar and has the lowest molar mass, therefore we would expect it to have the lower boiling point and heat of vaporization.

9. In which of the following are the intermolecular forces listed from the weakest to the strongest?
   a) Dipole-dipole > London > Hydrogen bonds
   b) London < Dipole-dipole < Hydrogen bonds
   c) Hydrogen bonds < Dipole-dipole < London
   d) London> Hydrogen bonds > Dipole-dipole
   e) London < Hydrogen bonds < Dipole-dipole

Answer: (b)

London force: attractive force between non-polar molecules
Dipole-dipole force: attractive force between polar molecules
Dipole-dipole forces are stronger than London Dispersion forces.

II. Properties of Solids

Solids are substances with definite shape and volume.

i. Solids have a relatively high density, incompressibility, and relatively low rate of diffusion.
ii. Different types of solids categorized by their binding forces are listed below:
    1. Ionic crystals: such as NaCl and CaO_2
    2. Covalent network crystals: such as diamond and quartz
    3. Metallic crystals: such as copper and other metals
    4. Covalent molecular crystals: such as solid methane and water molecules in ice

Crystalline solids are substances that are arranged in a repeating pattern which is called a unit cell. Crystalline solids have definite melting points.

Amorphous solids are substances that are arranged randomly. Amorphous solids do not have definite melting points.

Section Practice

1. Which of the following indicates the relative randomness of molecules in the three states of matter?
   a) Solid > Liquid > Gas
   b) Liquid < Solid < Gas
   c) Liquid > Gas > Solid
   d) Gas > Liquid > Solid
   e) None of the above

Answer: (d)

Molecules in gas form have more randomness than in liquid form, and similarly they have more randomness in liquid form than in solid form.

2. Which of the following is a solid at 25 °C and 1 atm?
   a) H_2
   b) CH_3OH
   c) CH_2Cl_2
   d) KCl
   e) CO

Answer: (d)

KCl is an ionic compound, which have the highest melting points.

3. Diamond is classified as a(n)
   a) covalent crystal.
   b) ionic crystal.
   c) amorphous solid.
   d) metallic crystal.
   e) molecular crystal.

Answer: (a)

Diamond: sp^3, 3D network covalent bonds.

4. The extremely high melting point of diamond (carbon) may be explained by its
   a) network covalent bonds.
   b) ionic bonds.
   c) hydrogen bonds.
   d) van der Waals forces.
   e) None of the above

Answer: (a)

Diamond: sp^3, 3D network covalent bonds

5. Which of the following statements is NOT consistent with the crystal properties of the substance?
   a) SiC is used to grind metal parts to shape.
   b) Tungsten is drawn into thin wires.
   c) Aluminum is used to cut glass.
   d) Graphite is used to lubricate locks.
   e) MgF_2 shatters when dropped.

Answer: (c)

Aluminum is a relatively soft metal.
Diamond is used to cut glass.

6. An aqueous solution of KCl is heated from 15 °C to 85 °C. Which of the following properties of the solution remains the same?

   I. Molality
   II. Molarity
   III. Density

   a) I only
   b) III only
   c) I and II only
   d) II and III only
   e) I, II, and III

Answer: (a)

Changing the temperature will change the volume of the solution, therefore it will change the density and molarity of the solution.

III. Changes of State

Phase changes are the transitions between solid, liquid, and gaseous phases; typically involved with the transfer of large amounts of energy compared to the specific heat.

Heating Curve of Phase Changes

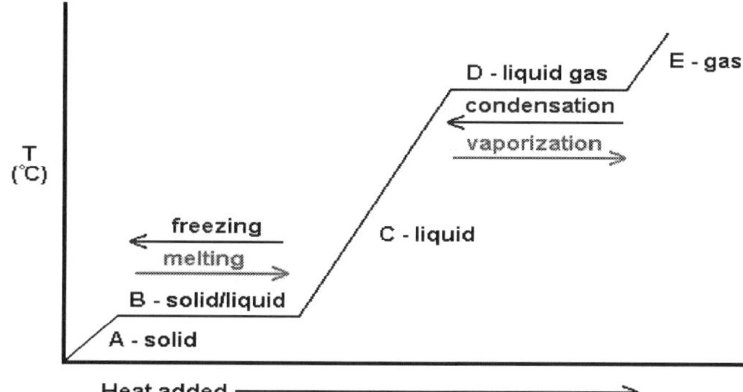

i. During phase changes, for a pure element, the temperature remains constant in the heating curve.
ii. This constant temperature property is sometimes used to determine if the sample is pure or mixed.

Phase Diagrams:

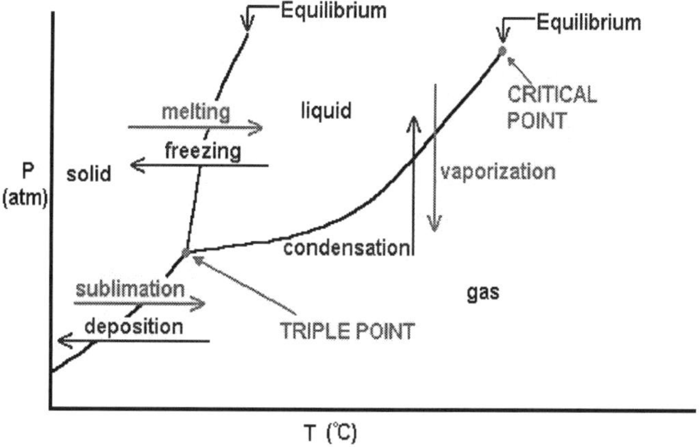

i. The triple point is the temperature and pressure condition at which the solid, liquid, and vapor states of the substance can coexist at equilibrium.
ii. The critical temperature is the temperature at which the substance cannot exist in the liquid state, regardless of pressure.
iii. The critical pressure is the lowest pressure at which the substance can exist as a liquid at the critical temperature.
iv. The critical point is the point on the graph that simultaneously describes the critical temperature and the critical pressure.

Equilibrium between Vaporization and Condensation

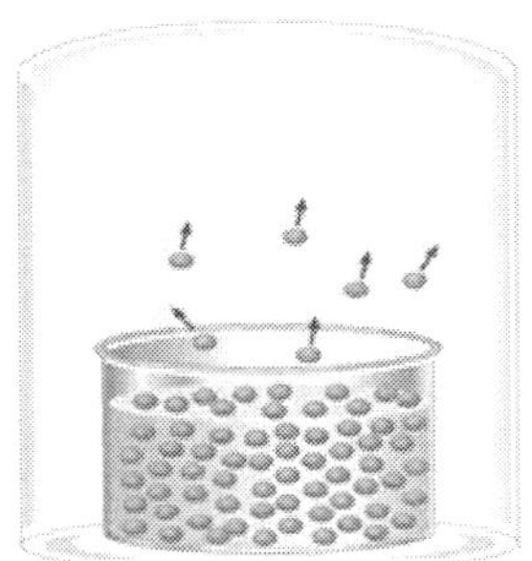

Vaporization Only

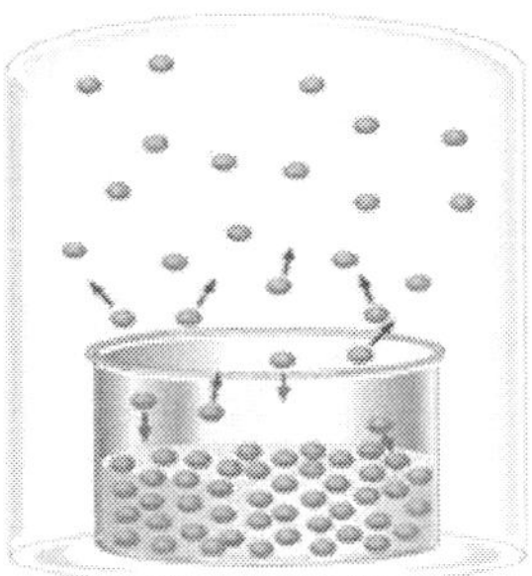

Vaporization Rate > Condensation Rate

At Equilibrium: Vaporization Rate = Condensation Rate

i. Equilibrium vapor pressure is the pressure that is exerted by a vapor in equilibrium with its corresponding liquid at a given temperature.
ii. Volatile liquids have weak forces of attraction and evaporate easily.
iii. Nonvolatile liquids have strong forces of attraction and do not evaporate easily.
iv. Boiling occurs when the equilibrium vapor pressure of the liquid equals the atmospheric pressure.
v. The boiling point is the temperature at which the equilibrium vapor pressure of the liquid equals the atmospheric pressure. Water boils at 100 °C at 1 atm pressure (normal boiling point).

Molar Heat of Vaporization is the amount of heat energy required to vaporize one mole of a liquid at its boiling point. Strong attractive forces between particles result in a high molar heat of vaporization.

Freezing and Melting points are the equilibrium temperatures between solid and liquid at 1 atm. For pure crystalline solids, the melting point and freezing point are the same. Temperature remains constant during a phase change.

Molar Heat of Fusion is the amount of heat energy required to melt one mole of solid at its melting point.

Sublimation is the direct change of state of a solid to a gas. For example, dry ice sublimes to gaseous CO_2.

Deposition is the change of state from a gas directly to a solid.

Section Practice

1. The process of turning a solid into gas is called
   a) sublimation.
   b) condensation.
   c) evaporation.
   d) deposition.
   e) melting.

Answer: (a)

This is the definition of sublimation.

2. In the figure below, which section represents boiling?

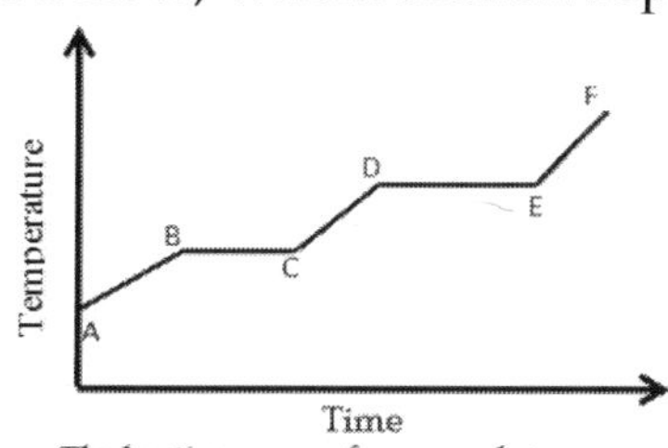

The heating curve of a pure substance

   a) AB
   b) BC
   c) CD
   d) DE
   e) EF

Answer: (d)

Temperature is constant during a phase change. Section BC shows melting and DE shows boiling.

3. The normal boiling point of the substance shown below is approximately

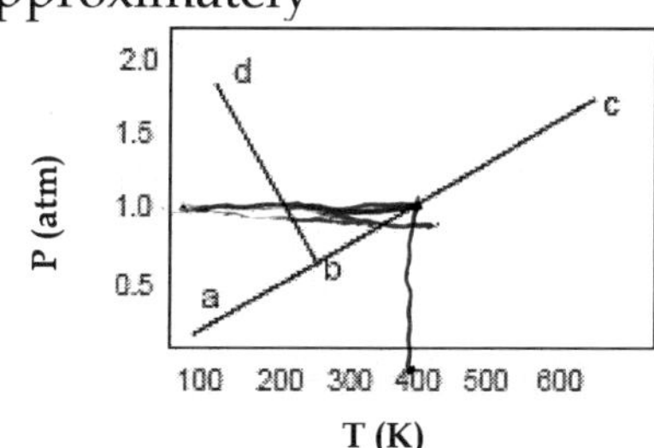

   a) 100 K.
   b) 200 K.
   c) 300 K.
   d) 400 K.
   e) 500 K.

Answer: (d)

At 1 atm pressure, a liquid boils at its normal boiling point.

On the line bc, the temperature is 400K when the pressure is 1 atm.

4. The process of turning a gas into solid is called
   a) sublimation.
   b) condensation.
   c) evaporation.
   d) deposition.
   e) melting.

Answer: (d)

This is the definition of deposition process.

5. The process of turning a gas into liquid is called
   a) sublimation.
   b) condensation.
   c) evaporation.
   d) deposition.
   e) melting.

Answer: (b)

This is the definition of condensation.

6. Put the following from least to greatest in terms of increasing melting point: SiH_4, SiO_2, CH_4, NH_3, and PH_3.
   a) NH_3, PH_3, CH_4, SiH_4, SiO_2
   b) SiO_2, PH_3, NH_3, CH_4, SiH_4
   c) SiH_4, CH_4, NH_3, PH_3, SiO_2
   d) CH_4, SiH_4, PH_3, NH_3, SiO_2
   e) CH_4, SiH_4, SiO_2, NH_3, PH_3

Answer: (d)

SiO_2 is a crystalline solid with the highest melting point.
NH_3 is a polar molecule. Its melting point should be higher than other non-polar compounds.
For non-polar molecule, the higher the molar mass, the higher melting point is.

7. At a certain temperature and pressure, ice, water, and steam are found to coexist at equilibrium. This pressure and temperature corresponds to
   a) the critical temperature.
   b) the critical pressure.
   c) the sublimation point.
   d) the triple point.
   e) None of the above

Answer: (d)

Solid, liquid, and gas coexist at the triple point.

8. Which pair of temperatures and pressures will produce a supercritical fluid?

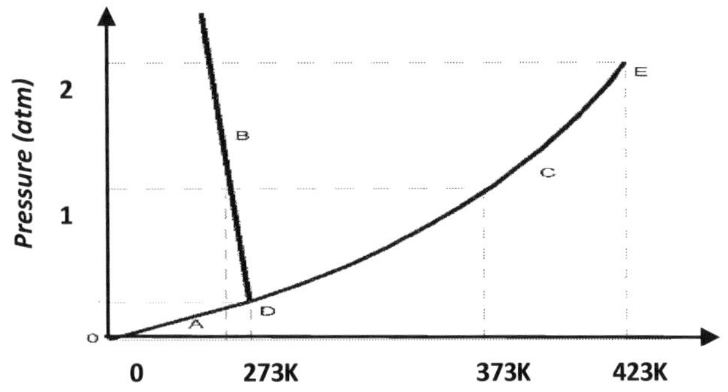

   a) 151 °C and 2.00 atm
   b) 95 °C and 100 atm
   c) 105 °C and 230 atm
   d) 10 °C and 0.15 atm
   e) 100 °C and 2.00 atm

Answer: (a)

Temperature needs to be above the critical point temperature.

9. At 125 °C and 1.50 atm of pressure this substance will be?

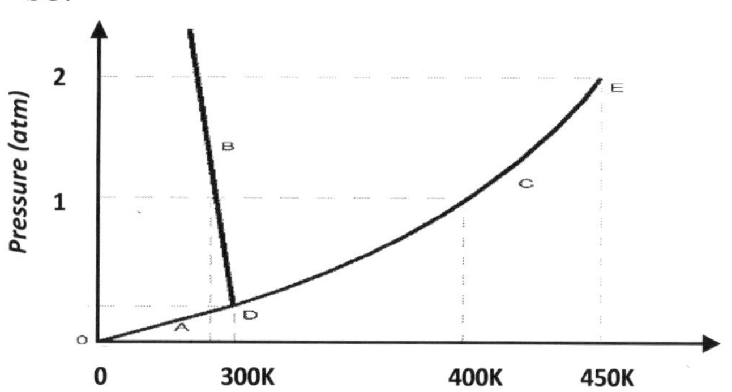

a) A liquid
b) A solid
c) A gas
d) A solid and liquid at equilibrium
e) A gas and liquid at equilibrium

Answer: (a)

K = 125°C+273 = 398K
Between the DB line and the line DC is the liquid phase region.

10. Which of the following will be true on top of a high mountain?
    a) The boiling point of water will be higher than water at sea level.
    b) The vapor pressure of water at 60 °C will be the same as water at sea level at an identical temperature.
    c) An egg placed in boiling water at the summit will cook faster than one placed in boiling water at sea level.
    d) Atmospheric pressure will be approximately the same as that at sea level.
    e) The water will be vaporized slower than water placed at sea level at the same temperature.

Answer: (b)

The boiling point of water will be lower at higher altitude.
Vapor pressure of pure water only depends on temperature.

IV. Water Properties

Basic Information about Water

Bond type	Polar
Bond angle	104.5°
Boiling point	100 °C
Melting point	0 °C
Density of ice (0 °C)	0.917 g/cm3
Density of water (0 °C)	0.999 g/cm3
Point of maximum density	3.98 °C
Molar heat of fusion	6.009 kJ/mol
Molar heat of vaporization	40.79 kJ/mol

i. **Lower Solid Density**
Ice has a lower density than liquid water because the orientation of hydrogen bonds causes molecules to spread out further in the crystal structure.

ii. **High Surface Tension**
Because of the high attraction of water molecules to itself, water has a high surface tension compared to other liquids.

iii. **High Boiling Point**
Large amounts of hydrogen bonding in water results in high cohesion. This prevents water molecules from easily escaping the water's surface. Therefore water has a low vapor pressure and high boiling point.

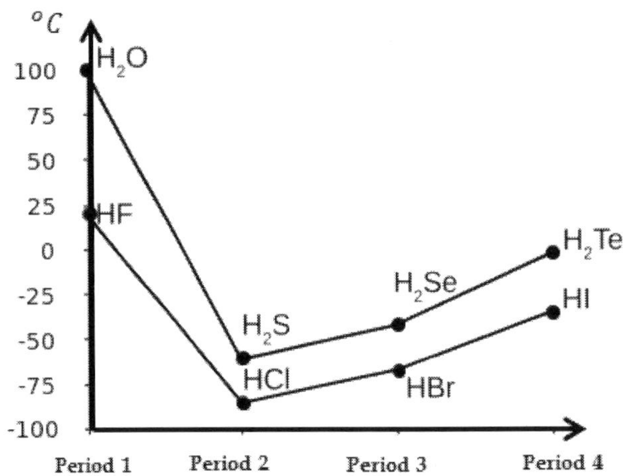

Because of the hydrogen bonds, the boiling points of HF and H_2O do not follow the trend lines.

iv. **High Heat of Vaporization**
Water has a higher heat of vaporization than any other liquid. This is because of large amounts of hydrogen bonding holding the molecules close together. A great deal of energy is required to separate the water molecules to convert the water to gas.

Section Practice

1. Decomposing water by an electric current will give what volumetric ratio of hydrogen to oxygen?
   a) 1 : 9
   b) 2 : 1
   c) 1 : 2
   d) 1 : 8
   e) None of the above

Answer: (b)

$2H_2O \rightarrow 2H_2 + O_2$
2 moles of H_2 are produced for every mole of O_2, so the ratio would be $H_2 : O_2 = 2 : 1$

2. If 10 grams of ice melts at 0 °C, the total quantity of heat absorbed is
   a) 10 cal.
   b) 80 cal.
   c) 800 cal.
   d) 800 kcal.
   e) None of the above

Answer: (c)

The heat of fusion of water is approximately 80 cal/gram.

3. $C_{30}H_{62}$ is a non-polar compound that is a solid at room temperature. Water has hydrogen bonds but it is a liquid because
   a) water molecules are very light.
   b) water molecules ionize easily.
   c) London dispersion forces build up a large dipole moment across the 62 hydrogen atoms in $C_{30}H_{62}$ and lead to attractive forces that exceed that of water's hydrogen bonds.
   d) $C_{30}H_{62}$ is so large that it cannot melt easily.
   e) $C_{30}H_{62}$ has a lower melting point if dissolved in non-polar hexane.

Answer: (c)

Bigger molecules tend to be more difficult to melt because of a bigger effect from London dispersion forces.

4. The ratio in water of hydrogen to oxygen by mass is
   a) 1 : 9.
   b) 2 : 1.
   c) 1 : 2.
   d) 1 : 8.
   e) None of the above

Answer: (d)

There are two H for every O, so we get the H : O mass ratio to be 2 : 16 = 1 : 8

5. Which of the following is responsible for the abnormally high boiling point of water?
   a) Covalent bonding
   b) Hydrogen bonding
   c) High polarity
   d) Large dielectric constant
   e) Low molecular weight

Answer: (b)

Hydrogen bonding contributes to the abnormally high boiling point of water.

6. The phase diagram of water is shown below. Which point on the diagram corresponds to the boiling point of water?

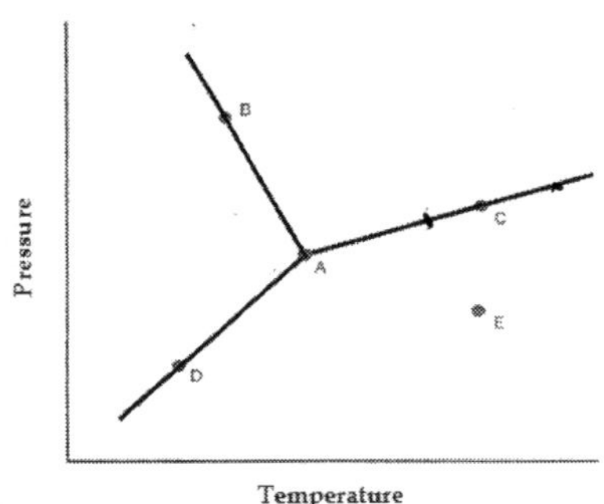

a) A
b) B
c) C
d) D
e) E

Answer: (c)

The water is boiling at point C.

Chapter 7 Liquids and Solids SAT Questions

1. What state is the substance in state B?

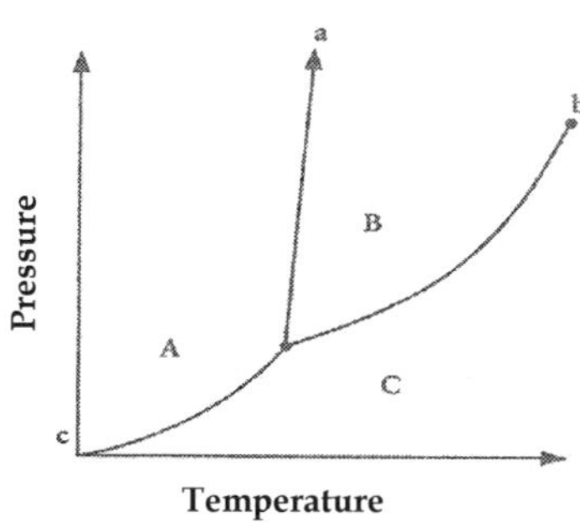

a) Pure crystalline solid
b) Amorphous solid
c) Gas
d) Liquid
e) None of the above

Answer: (d)

The substance is a solid in state A, liquid in state B, and gas in state C

2. What state is the substance in state C?

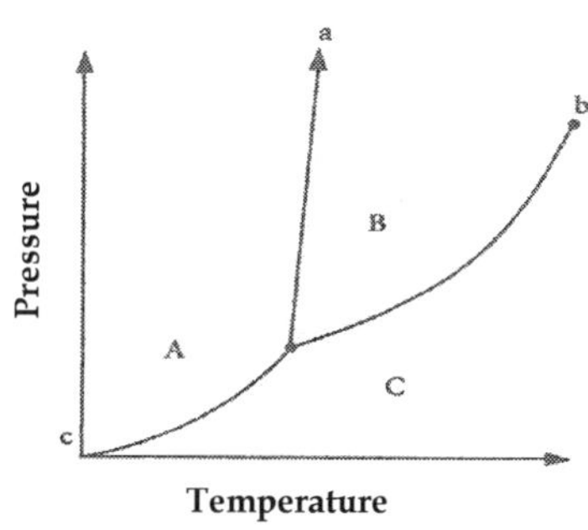

a) Pure crystalline solid
b) Amorphous solid
c) Gas
d) Liquid
e) None of the above

Answer: (c)

The substance is a solid in state A, liquid in state B, and gas in state C

3. Which of the following is capable of hydrogen bonding?
   a) H_2
   b) CH_3OH
   c) CH_2Cl_2
   d) KCI
   e) CO

Answer: (b)

Hydrogen bonds can form because of the -OH group.

4. A 75 gram sample of an unknown solid is dissolved in 1 kg of water. The resulting solution is found to have a freezing point of −0.93 °C. If the freezing point depression constant for water (K_f) is 1.86 °C/m, which of the following is most likely to be solid?
   a) Citric acid (MW = 60 g/mo1)
   b) Ribose (MW = 150 g/mol)
   c) Ascorbic acid (MW = 176 g/mol)
   d) Dextrose (MW = 180 g/mol)
   e) Maltose (MW = 360 g/mol)

Answer: (b)

$0.93 = 1.86 \times m$

$m = 0.5 = \frac{\frac{75}{M}}{1}$

$M = 150\ g/mol$

5. Which of the following aqueous solutions will have the highest boiling point?
   a) 0.5m NaBr
   b) 0.75 m $C_2H_6O_2$ (ethylene glycol)
   c) 1.25 m $C_6H_{12}O_6$ (glucose)
   d) 1.0 m $KMnO_4$ (potassium permanganate)
   e) 0.75 m LiCl

Answer: (d)

a). $m = 0.5 \times 2 = 1$
b). $m = 0.75 \times 1 = 0.75$
c). $m = 1.25 \times 1 = 1.25$
d). $1 \times 2 = 2$
e). $0.75 \times 2 = 1.5$

6. 50.0 grams of vitamin A (molar mass = 286.5 g/mol) are dissolved in 100.0 mL of ethanol (molar mass = 46.07). The density of ethanol is 0.787 g/ml. If the vapor pressure of pure ethanol at 20 °C is 44.4 torr, what is the observed vapor pressure of the retinol solution at this temperature?
   a) 35.4 torr
   b) 36.9 torr
   c) 38.2 torr
   d) 40.4 torr
   e) 46.3 torr

Answer: (d)

$P_A = P^0_A\ X_A$

$= 44.4 \times \frac{\frac{100 \times 0.787}{46.06}}{\frac{50}{286.5} + \frac{100 \times 0.787}{46.06}} =$

40.4torr

7. What mass of $FeSO_4{\cdot}6H_2O$ (260 g/mol) is required to produce 500 mL of a 0.10 M iron(II) sulfate solution?
   a) 9 g
   b) 13 g
   c) 36 g
   d) 72 g
   e) 144 g

Answer: (b)

$\frac{500}{1000} \times 0.1 \times 260 = 13\ g$

8. Sodium carbonate (Na_2CO_3) is the least soluble in which of the following liquids?
   a) CH_3OH
   b) CF_3COOH
   c) H_2O
   d) $CH_3(CH_2)_4CH_3$
   e) $CHCl_3$

Answer: (d)

Polar dissolves in polar, and $CH_3(CH_2)_4CH_3$ is non-polar.

9. Which of the following will have the greatest change in its boiling point if the pressure at which it is boiled is changed from 1.00 atm to 0.900 atm? (The numbers in the parentheses are the heats of vaporization in kilojoules per mole.)
   a) Water (43.9)
   b) Ammonia (21.7)
   c) Methane (8.2)
   d) Bromine (15.0)
   e) Fluorine (5.9)

Answer: (a)

The higher the heat of vaporization, the greater the change in boiling point.

10. On the basis of this heating curve, which of the following statements is true?

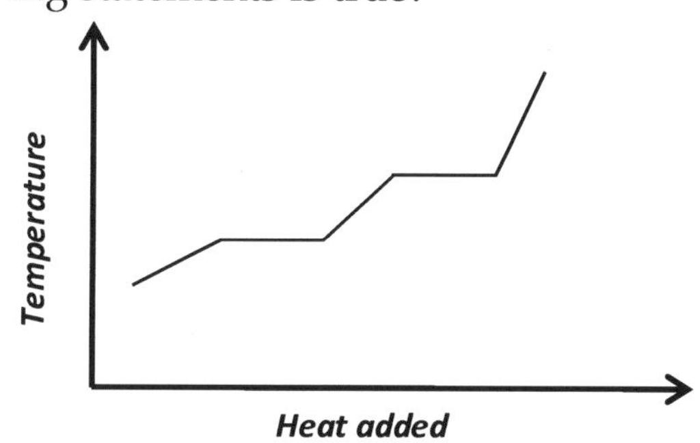

   a) The heat of fusion and heat of vaporization are about equal.
   b) The heat capacities of the solid, liquid and gas are approximately equal.
   c) The heat capacity of the gas is greater than that of the liquid.
   d) The heat capacity of the gas is greater than the heat of fusion.
   e) The heat of vaporization is less than the heat of fusion.

Answer: (a)

The slope of the heating curve for gas is higher than that for liquid and solid. Therefore the heat capacity of the gas is greater than that of the liquid.

11. On the basis of this heating curve, which of the following statements is correct about the substance?

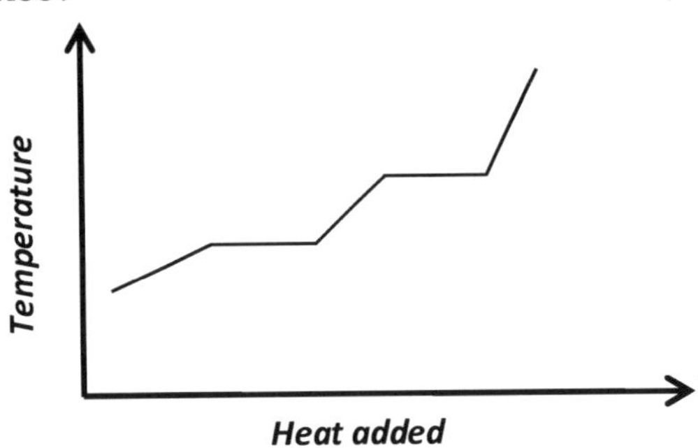

a) The substances supercool easily.
b) The gas is a metastable state.
c) The substance must be a salt that dissociates on heating.
d) The density of the liquid is greater than that of the solid.
e) The specific heat can be determined if the mass is known.

Answer: (e)

The specific heat of the substance can be determined by the slope and amount of mass.

12. A substance is initially at 0.5 atm and 200 K. The pressure on this substance is steadily increased while its temperature is kept constant. What phase change will eventually occur?

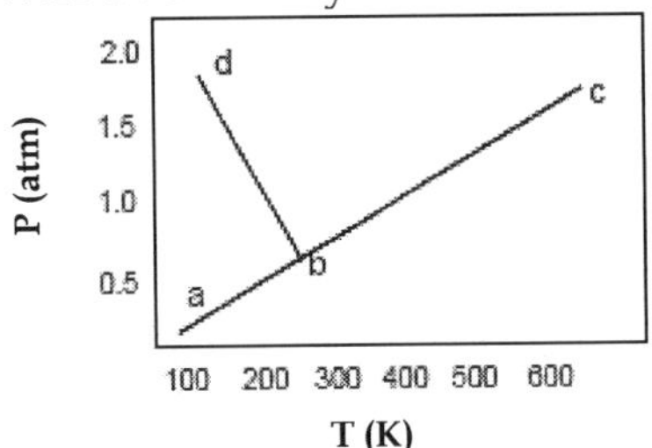

a) Condensation
b) Freezing
c) Melting
d) Sublimation
e) Vaporization

Answer: (c)

The transition from solid to liquid is called melting.

Relationship Analysis Questions

	Statement	Reason	Answer
1.	Bromine has a higher boiling point than chlorine.	Bromine has stronger dispersion forces than chlorine.	TTCE
2.	Decreasing the atmospheric pressure on a pot of boiling water causes the water to stop boiling.	Changes in pressure are directly related to the boiling point of water.	FT
3.	As ice absorbs heat and begins to melt, its temperature remains constant.	Changes of state bring about changes in a substance's potential energy, not in its kinetic energy.	TTCE
4.	Water boils at a lower temperature at higher altitudes.	The vapor pressure of water is lower at higher altitudes.	TF
5.	At 1 atm, pure water can boil at a temperature less than 273 K.	Water boils when its vapor pressure is equal to the atmospheric pressure.	FT
6.	The heat of fusion plus the heat of vaporization for a particular substance is not equal to the heat of sublimation.	ΔH_{fus}, ΔH_{vap}, and ΔH_{sub} are state functions.	FT
7.	A liquid can boil at different temperatures.	The atmospheric (or surrounding) pressure can vary.	TTCE
8.	Water boils at a higher temperature on the moon.	The atmospheric pressure of the moon is less than that on earth.	FT

Chapter 8 Mixtures

I. Solution

A solution is a homogeneous mixture of two or more substances in a single phase. The dissolving medium is the solvent and the dissolved substance is the solute in a solution.

Types of Solutions

i. Gaseous mixtures (i.e. air)
ii. Solid solutions (i.e. metal alloys)
iii. Liquid solutions
   1. Liquid dissolved in a liquid (i.e. alcohol in water).
   2. Solid dissolved in a liquid (i.e. salt water).
   3. An aqueous solution is a solution where water is the solvent.

Electrolyte vs. Non-electrolyte Solutes

i. An electrolyte is a substance that dissolves in water to produce a solution that conducts electric current (ions are produced).
ii. A non-electrolyte is a substance that dissolves in water to produce a solution that does not conduct an electric current (no ions are produced).

Suspensions are mixtures where the solute particles are so large that they will settle out of the solution if it is not constantly stirred or agitated. Particles in a suspension are on the order of 1000 nm in diameter and can be filtered out.

Colloids are mixtures where the solute particles are between 2 nm to 1000 nm in diameter. The solutes in colloids are larger than those in solutions, but smaller than those in suspensions. Colloid particles can't be filtered out easily.

The scattering that occurs when light is shined through a colloid or suspension mixture is called the **Tyndall effect.**

Section Practice

1. The ionization of salt in water is useful in explaining
   I. its unusually high solubility in water.
   II. its electrical conductivity in solution.
   III. the lowered freezing points and increased boiling points of salt solutions.
   a) I, II, and III
   b) I and II only
   c) II and III only
   d) I only
   e) III only

Answer: (a)

The ionization of salt causes its high solubility in water, increases electrical conductivity, lowers freezing points, and increases boiling points of its solution.

2. Which of the following sequences lists the relative sizes of particles in water, from smallest to largest?
   a) Solutions, suspensions, colloids
   b) Solutions, colloids, suspensions
   c) Colloids, solutions, suspensions
   d) Colloids, suspensions, solutions
   e) Suspensions, colloids, solutions

Answer: (b)

Solutions have the smallest particle size, followed by colloids and then suspensions.

3. Which of the following words describes the interaction between solutes and solvents?
   a) Solute
   b) Solvent
   c) Solubility
   d) Aqueous solution
   e) Solvation

Answer: (e)

This is the definition of solvation.

4. What condition must exist when a water solution that has been at equilibrium is heated to a higher temperature, thus increasing its solubility, but no additional solute is added?
   a) Dilute
   b) Concentrated
   c) Unsaturated
   d) Saturated
   e) Supersaturated

Answer: (c)

The solution goes from being a saturated solution to an unsaturated solution.

II. Solvation

Factors Affecting the Rate of Dissolution

i. Solutes can be dissolved more quickly when their surface area is increased.
ii. Solutes can be dissolved more quickly by stirring or shaking. This brings the solvent into contact with more particles.
iii. Increasing the temperature of a solvent always increases the rate of dissolution of solids in liquids.

The **solubility** of a substance is the amount of that substance required to form a saturated solution with a specific amount of solvent and a specified temperature. The rate at which a substance dissolves does not alter the solubility of the substance.

Levels of Saturation

i. A saturated solution is a solution that contains the maximum amount of dissolved solute.
ii. An unsaturated solution is a solution that contains less solute than a saturated solution under the existing conditions.
iii. A supersaturated solution is a solution that contains more dissolved solute than a saturated solution under the same conditions.

An Important Solubility Rule

The "**like dissolves like**" rule states that polar substances dissolve in polar solvents and non-polar substances dissolve in non-polar solvents.

Dissolving Ionic Compounds in Aqueous Solutions

i. The electropositive hydrogen of water is attracted to negatively charged ions.
ii. The electronegative oxygen of water is attracted to positively charged ions.
iii. Hydration is the solvation process with water as the solvent.
iv. Hydrates are the ionic substances that incorporate water molecules into their structure during the re-crystallization process, such as $CuSO_4 \cdot 5H_2O$.

Effects of Pressure on Solubility

i. Pressure has no real effect on the solubility of liquids and solids in liquid solvents.
ii. Increasing pressure will increase the solubility of gases in liquids.
iii. **Henry's law** states that the solubility of a gas in a liquid is directly proportional to the partial pressure of that gas on the surface of the liquid.

Effects of Temperature on Solubility

i. The solubility of solids increases when temperature increases, with some exceptions. Such as Cerium(III) sulphate $Ce_2(SO_4)_3$, due to its exothermic heat of solution.
ii. The solubility of gases decreases when temperature increases. Increased temperature causes an increase in kinetic energy. The higher kinetic energy

causes more motion in the gas molecules which break intermolecular bonds and escape from solution.

The **heat of solution** is the amount of heat energy absorbed or released when a specific amount of solute dissolves in a solvent.

It will be incredibly useful to memorize the solubility rules in the table below.

Solubility Rules in Water

Rules	Important Exceptions
All nitrate (NO_3^-), nitrite (NO_2^-), chlorate (ClO_3^-), and perchlorate (ClO_4^-) salts are soluble.	Silver nitrite ($AgNO_3$) and potassium perchlorate ($KClO_4$) are slightly soluble.
All alkali metal (Li+, Na+, K+, Rb+, Cs+) and ammonium (NH_4^+) salts are soluble.	No exceptions!
Most halogen (Cl^-, Br^-, I^-) salts are soluble.	Halogen salts with Ag^+, Hg_2^{2+}, Cu^+, and Tl^+ are not soluble. $HgBr_2$ is slightly soluble. Pb^{2+} halogen salts are soluble in hot water.
Most acetate ($C_2H_3O_2^-$) salts are soluble.	Ag^+, Hg_2^{2+}
Most sulfate (SO_4^{2-}) salts are soluble.	Ca^{2+}, Sr^{2+}, Ba^{2+}, Ra^{2+}, Pb^{2+}, Ag^+, Hg^{2+}
Many sulfides (S^{2-}) are insoluble.	All alkali metal and alkaline earth (Be^{2+}, Mg^{2+}, Ca^{2+}, Sr^{2+}, Ba^{2+}, Ra^{2+}) sulfides are soluble. Ammonium sulfide, $(NH_4)_2S$, is soluble.
Most hydroxide (OH^-) salts are insoluble.	Alkali metal hydroxides are soluble. Ba^{2+}, Sr^{2+}, Ca^{2+} and Tl^+ are considered slightly soluble.

Section Practice

1. Which of the following indicates that the rate of dissolution is equal to the rate of precipitation in a solution?
   a) Dilute
   b) Concentrated
   c) Unsaturated
   d) Saturated
   e) Supersaturated

Answer: (d)

A saturated solution is at equilibrium, so the amount of solute that precipitates out is equal to the amount that dissolves.

2. A tiny crystal of NaCl is added to a sodium chloride solution, resulting in additional sodium chloride precipitating out. This solution had been
   a) unsaturated.
   b) saturated.
   c) supersaturated.
   d) diluted.
   e) concentrated.

Answer: (c)

Supersaturated conditions can be disturbed by adding a tiny crystal as a seed to the solution.

3. Sodium chloride would be most soluble in
   a) ether.
   b) benzene.
   c) water.
   d) carbon tetrachloride.
   e) gasoline.

Answer: (c)

Ionic compounds dissolve easily in water and other polar solvents.

4. A compound which, when dissolved in water, barely conducts electrical current is probably a(n)
   a) strong electrolyte.
   b) ionic salt.
   c) strong acid.
   d) strong base.
   e) nonelectrolyte.

Answer: (e)

The solution is a nonelectrolyte solution.

5. Which of the following choices correctly describes the solubility of potassium chloride (KCl)?
   a) Solubility in CCl_4 > Solubility in CH_3CH_2OH > Solubility in H_2O
   b) Solubility in H_2O > Solubility in CH_3CH_2OH > Solubility in CCl_4
   c) Solubility in CH_3CH_2OH > Solubility in CCl_4 > Solubility in H_2O
   d) Solubility in H_2O > Solubility in CCl_4 > Solubility in CH_3CH_2OH
   e) None of the above

Answer: (b)

Ionic compounds dissolve easily in water and other polar solvents.

6. Which of the following is the most electrically conductive?
   a) Sugar dissolved in water
   b) Salt water
   c) Salt dissolved in an organic solvent
   d) An oil and water mixture
   e) None of the above

Answer: (b)

Salt water is the most electrically conductive.

7. Ethyl alcohol, C_2H_5OH, and water become warmer when mixed. This is due to
   a) the decrease in volume when they are mixed.
   b) smaller attractive forces in the mixture than in the pure liquids themselves.
   c) the hydrogen bonding of the two liquids.
   d) the change in vapor pressure above the mixture.
   e) stronger attractive forces in the mixture than in the pure liquids themselves.

Answer: (e)

Mixing alcohol and water is an exothermal process due to the large attractive forces between the water and alcohol molecules.

III. Concentration of Solutions

Molarity (M) is defined as the number of moles of solute per liter of solution.
Molality (m) is defined as the number of moles of solute per kilogram of solvent.
The **mass percent of** a solution is the mass of solute per mass of solution.
The **volume percent** of a solution is the volume of solute per volume of solution.

Example: What is the molality of a solution if it contains 10% by mass of NaCl in water?

Answer: Molality (m) = $\frac{Moles\ of\ Solute}{Kg\ of\ Solvent}$

If there are 100 g of solution, then it contains 10 g of NaCl and 90 g of water.

$$m = \frac{\frac{10}{58.5l}}{\frac{90}{1000}} = 1.9 \text{ mole/kg}$$

Concentrations of Mixing Solutions

The molarity of the mixture of two or more solutions, including when solutions are diluted (one of the solutions has a concentration of 0), can be found with the following equation:

$$M_1V_1 + M_2V_2 \ldots = (V_1 + V_2 \ldots) \times M_{mixture}$$

Section Practice

1. A 10% solution of NaCl means that in 100 g of solution, there are
   a) 5.85 g of NaCl.
   b) 58.5 g of NaCl.
   c) 10 g of NaCl.
   d) 90 g of NaCl.
   e) 94 g of NaCl.

Answer: (c)

$10\% = \frac{x}{100} \times 100\%$

$x = 10g$

2. The molarity of a solution made by placing 98 g H_2SO_4 in water to make 500 mL of solution is
   a) 0.5.
   b) 1.
   c) 2.
   d) 2.5.
   e) 3.

Answer: (c)

Molar Mass of $H_2SO_4 = 98\,g$

$\frac{\frac{98}{98} moles}{0.5\ kg} = 2\ Moles$

3. When 74 grams of $Ca(OH)_2$ are completely dissolved in a container holding 2 liters of water, what is the concentration of the solution?
   a) 1 molar
   b) 1 molal
   c) 0.5 molar
   d) 0.5 molal
   e) 2.5 molar

Answer: (d)

Molar Mass of $Ca(OH)_2 = 74$ *g/mol*
Mass of 2 Liters of Water = 2 kg

$$\frac{\frac{74}{74} moles}{2\ kg} = 0.5\ m$$

4. When 684 grams of sucrose, $C_{12}H_{22}O_{11}$, are completely dissolved in 2,000 grams of water, what is the concentration of the solution?
   a) 1 molar
   b) 1 molal
   c) 0.5 molar
   d) 0.5 molal
   e) 2.5 molar

Answer: (b)

Molar mass of $C_{12}H_{22}O_{11} =$ *342g*

$$\frac{\frac{684}{342} moles}{2\ kg} = 1\ m$$

5. How much NaOH must be added to make 200 mL of a 1M NaOH solution?
   a) 8 g
   b) 16 g
   c) 40 g
   d) 80 g
   e) None of the above

Answer: (a)

Molar mass of NaOH = 40 g

$$1\ M = \frac{\frac{x}{40}}{0.2}$$

$$x = 8\ g$$

6. To what volume, in mL, must 50.0 mL of 3.50 M H_2SO_4 be diluted in order to make a 2 M H_2SO_4 solution?
   a) 25
   b) 60.1
   c) 87.5
   d) 93.2
   e) 101

Answer: (c)

$$50 \times 3.5 = x \times 2$$

$$x = 87.5\ mL$$

IV. Colligative Properties

Colligative properties are properties that depend on the concentration of solute particles, but do not depend on their identity.

Vapor Pressure Lowering

Any nonvolatile solute will lower the vapor pressure of a solution, resulting in two noticeable effects:

i. The boiling point of the solution will increase.

ii. The freezing point of the solution will decrease.

Lowering the Freezing Point

The difference between the freezing points of the pure solvent and the solution will be:

$$\Delta T_f = i \times K_f \times m$$

Where **m** is the molality of solution and **i** is the total number of ions dissociated in the solution. The value **i** is equal to the number of particles produced per unit of solute. It is 1 in a non-electrolyte solution. The K_f of water is equal to 1.86.

Raising the Boiling Point:

The difference between the boiling points of the pure solvent and a solution of a non-electrolyte in the solvent is:

$$\Delta T_b = i \times K_b \times m$$

where the K_b of water is equal to 0.52.

Section Practice

1. If 684 g of sucrose (MW = 342 g) is dissolved in 2000 g of H_2O, what will be the freezing point of this solution?
   a) −0.51 °C
   b) −1.86 °C
   c) −3.72 °C
   d) −6.58 °C
   e) −7.09 °C

Answer: (b)

$\frac{\frac{684}{342}}{2} = 1\ m$ *of sucrose*
$\Delta T_f = 1.86 \times 1 = 1.86$
$T_f = -1.86\ ^\circ C$

2. What is the melting point of 0.2 L of water containing 6.20 g of dissolved $C_2H_6O_2$?
   a) −1.86 °C
   b) −0.93 °C
   c) 0 °C
   d) 0.93 °C
   e) 1.86 °C

Answer: (b)

Molar Mass of $C_2H_6O_2 = 62g$
$\Delta T_f = 1.86 \times \frac{\frac{6.2}{62}}{0.2} = 0.93\ ^\circ C$

3. One mole of NaCl in 1000 g of H_2O will change the boiling point of water to
   a) 100.51 °C.
   b) 101.04 °C.
   c) 101.53 °C.
   d) 101.86 °C.
   e) 103.62 °C.

Answer: (b)

One mole of NaCl produces two moles of ions.
$\Delta T_b = 2 \times 0.52 \times \frac{1}{1} = 1.04\ ^\circ C$

4. What is the molar mass of a non-ionizing solid if 10 g of this solid is dissolved in 100 g of water with its freezing point at −1.21 °C?
   a) 0.65 g
   b) 6.5 g
   c) 130 g
   d) 154 g
   e) 265 g

Answer: (d)

$\Delta T_f = 1.86 \times \frac{\frac{10}{M}}{0.1} = 1.21$

$M = 154\ g/mol$

5. Which of the following solutes, when added to 1.00 kg H_2O, is expected to give the greatest increase to the boiling point of water?
   a) 1.25 mole sucrose
   b) 0.25 mole iron(III) nitrate
   c) 0.50 mole ammonium chloride
   d) 0.6 mole calcium sulfate
   e) 1.0 mole acetic acid

Answer: (a)

a) $\Delta T_b = i \times m = 1.25 \times 0.52$
b) $\Delta T_b = i \times m = 0.25 \times 4 \times 0.52$
c) $\Delta T_b = i \times m = 0.5 \times 2 \times 0.52$
d) $\Delta T_b = i \times m = 0.6 \times 2 \times 0.52$
e) $\Delta T_b = i \times m = 1 \times 1 \times 0.52$

6. At 85 °C, liquid A has a vapor pressure of 437 mm Hg and liquid B has a vapor pressure of 0.880 atm. Which of the following represents a possible solution of the two liquids?
   a) A mixture with a vapor pressure of 345 mm Hg at 85 °C
   b) A mixture with a vapor pressure of 0.750 atm at 85 °C
   c) A mixture with a boiling point of 165 °C
   d) A mixture with a vapor pressure of 1106 mm Hg
   e) A mixture with a boiling point of 85 °C

Answer: (b)

437 mm Hg = 0.575 atm
The vapor pressure of the solution is between 0.575 atm and .88 atm.

7. The freezing point depression constant for water is 1.86 °C/m. When 100 g of a compound is dissolved in 500 g of H_2O, the freezing point is −10.0 °C. Which of the following is the identity of this compound?
   a) $Mg(NO_3)_2$
   b) KCl
   c) Na_2SO_4
   d) HCOOH
   e) HF

Answer: (b)

$$\Delta T_f = i \times 1.86 \times \frac{\frac{100}{M}}{0.5} = 10$$

$$\frac{M}{i} = 37.2$$
KCl gives an i = 2 and a molar mass of 74.5.

8. If 684 grams of sucrose (molecular mass = 342 g) is dissolved in 2,000 grams of water, what will be the freezing point of this solution?
   a) −.51 °C
   b) −1.86 °C
   c) −3.72 °C
   d) −6.58 °C
   e) None of the above

Answer: (b)

$$\Delta T_f = 1.86 \times \frac{\frac{684}{342}}{2} = 1.86\ °C$$

9. All of the following physical properties change as solute is added to the solution. Which one is NOT a colligative property?
   a) Boiling point
   b) Surface tension
   c) Vapor pressure
   d) Melting point
   e) Osmotic pressure

Answer: (b)

The surface tension of a solution depends on the identity of the solute particles.

Chapter 8 Mixtures SAT Questions

1. Which of the following is defined as moles of solute per kilogram of solvent?
   a) Molarity
   b) Formality
   c) Density
   d) Molality
   e) Normality

Answer: (d)

This is the definition of molality.

2. Which of the following is defined as moles of solute per liter of solution?
   a) Molarity
   b) Formality
   c) Density
   d) Molality
   e) Normality

Answer: (a)

This is the definition of molarity

3. Which of the following is the lesser component present in all solutions?
   a) Solute
   b) Solvent
   c) Ions
   d) Solution
   e) Water

Answer: (a)

There is a lesser amount of solute than solvent in a solution.

4. Which of the following is the descriptive term that indicates that there is a larger quantity of solute in one solution compared another?
   a) Diluted
   b) Concentrated
   c) Unsaturated
   d) Saturated
   e) Supersaturated

Answer: (b)

Solutions that have a large quantity of solute compared to another are more concentrated. Diluted and concentrated are relative terms. Supersaturated solutions are a specific type of solution where there are more solutes dissolved in the solution than would naturally be dissolved at the current temperature and pressure conditions. Unsaturated, saturated, and supersaturated are not relative terms.

5. What is the molarity of a 500 mL solution containing 20 g of $CaBr_2$?
   a) 0.1 M
   b) 0.2 M
   c) 0.5 M
   d) 1 M
   e) 5 M

Answer: (b)

Molar Mass of $CaBr_2$ = 200 g/mol

$\frac{\frac{20}{200}}{0.5} = 0.2\ M$

6. How many moles of sulfate ions are in 200 mL of a 2 M sodium sulfate solution?
   a) 0.2 moles
   b) 0.4 moles
   c) 0.6 moles
   d) 0.8 moles
   e) 1.0 moles

Answer: (b)

$NaSO_4$ dissociates into two ions.

$2 \times \frac{200}{1000} = 0.4$ *moles of ions*

7. A 0.5 M solution could be prepared by dissolving 20 g NaOH in how much water?
   a) 0.5 L
   b) 0.5 kg water
   c) 1 L water
   d) 1 kg water
   e) 2 L water

Answer: (d)

Molar Mass of NaOH = 40

$0.5 = \frac{\frac{20}{40}}{x}$

$x = 1\ L$

8. What volume of water would be needed to dilute 50 mL of a 3 M HCl solution to 1 M?
   a) 25 mL
   b) 50 mL
   c) 75 mL
   d) 100 mL
   e) 150 mL

Answer: (d)

$50 \times 3 = (x + 50) \times 1$

$x = 100\ mL$

9. About how many grams of sodium chloride would be dissolved in water to form a 0.5 M 500 mL solution?
   a) 7
   b) 29
   c) 14.6
   d) 58
   e) 112

Answer: (c)

Molar Mass of NaCl = 58.5

$.5\ M = \frac{\frac{x}{58.5}}{0.5}$

$x = 14.6\ g$

10. A one liter solution of 2 M NaOH can be prepared with
    a) 20 g NaOH
    b) 40 g NaOH
    c) 60 g NaOH
    d) 80 g NaOH
    e) 100 g NaOH

Answer: (d)

Molar Mass of NaOH = 40

$2\ M = \frac{\frac{x}{40}}{1}$

$x = 80\ g$

11. What is the molarity of a 10 mL solution in which 3.7 g of KCl are dissolved?
    a) 0.05 M
    b) 0.1 M
    c) 1 M
    d) 5 M
    e) 10 M

Answer: (d)

The molar Mass of KCl = 74.5

$M = \frac{\frac{3.7}{74.5}}{0.01} = 5\ M$

12. A solution of 10 M NaOH is used to prepare 2 L of 0.5 M NaOH. How many mL of the original NaOH solution are needed?
    a) 10 mL
    b) 100 mL
    c) 1000 mL
    d) 200 mL
    e) 2000 mL

Answer: (b)

$10 \times x = 2 \times 0.5$

$x = 0.1\ L = 100\ mL$

13. A 1 molal solution of NaCl results when 58.5 g of sodium chloride is dissolved in
    a) 1 liter of water.
    b) 100 mL of water.
    c) 1 kilogram of water.
    d) 100 g of water.
    e) one cubic meter of water.

Answer: (c)

Molality is the number of moles of a solvent dissolved in 1 kg of water.

14. Which of the following would produce a highly conductive aqueous solution?
    a) Cyclohexane
    b) Hydrochloric acid
    c) Benzene
    d) Sucrose
    e) Acetic acid

Answer: (b)

Strong acids, strong bases, and ionic salts are great conductors of electricity in water solution.

15. A 10% solution of HNO_3 would be produced by dissolving 63 g HNO_3 in how many mL of water?
    a) 100
    b) 300
    c) 567
    d) 630
    e) 1000

Answer: (c)

$10\% = 0.1 = \frac{63}{63+x}$

$x = 567\ g$

16. What is the boiling point of an aqueous solution containing 117 g of NaCl in 1000 g of H_2O? (K_b = 0.52 °C kg/mol)
    a) 98.96 °C
    b) 99.48 °C
    c) 100.52 °C
    d) 101. 04 °C
    e) 102.08 °C

Answer: (e)

Molar mass of NaCl = 58.5

Molality of NaCl $= \frac{\frac{117}{58.5}}{1} = 2\ m$

$i = 2$

$\Delta T = 0.52 \times 2 \times 2 = 2.08\ °C$

Boiling Point = 100 + 2.08 = 102.8 °C

17. How much water, in liters, must be added to 0.5 L of 6 M HCl to make it 2 M?
    a) 0.33
    b) 0.5
    c) 1
    d) 1.5
    e) 2

Answer: (c)

$0.5 \times 6M = (x + 0.5) \times 2M$

$x = 1\ L$

18. A 10% solution of NaCl means that in 100 grams of solution, there is
    a) 5.85 g of NaCl.
    b) 58.5 g of NaCl.
    c) 10 g of NaCl.
    d) 94 g of H_2O.
    e) None of the above

Answer: (c)

$10\% = 0.1 = \frac{x}{100}$

$x = 10\ g\ of\ NaCl$

19. The molarity of a solution made by placing 98 grams of H_2SO_4 in sufficient water to make 500 milliliters of solution is
    a) 0.5.
    b) 1.
    c) 2.
    d) 2.5.
    e) 3.

Answer: (c)

Molar Mass of $H_2SO_4 = 98$

$M = \frac{\frac{98}{98}}{0.5} = 2\ M$

20. The osmotic pressure at STP of a solution made from 1 L of solution containing 117 g of NaCl (aq) is
   a) 44.77 atm.
   b) 48.87 atm.
   c) 89.54 atm.
   d) 117 atm.
   e) None of the above

Answer: (c)

Molar Mass of NaCl = 58.5

$M = \frac{\frac{117}{58.5}}{1} = 2\ M$

$\pi = iMRT$

$= 2 \times 2 \times 0.082 \times 273 = 85.54\ atm$

21. The solubility of cadmium chloride, $CdCl_2$, is 140 g per 100 mL of solution. What is the molar molarity of a saturated solution of $CdCl_2$?
   a) 0.763 M
   b) 1.31 M
   c) 7.63 M
   d) 12.61 M
   e) 0.131 M

Answer: (c)

Molar Mass of $CdCl_2$ = 183.4

$M = \frac{\frac{140}{183.4}}{0.1} = 7.63\ M$

22. The vapor pressure of an ideal solution is 456 mm Hg. If the vapor pressure of the pure solvent is 832 mm Hg, what is the mole fraction of the nonvolatile solute?
   a) 0.548
   b) 0.354
   c) 0.645
   d) 1.825
   e) 0.452

Answer: (e)

Raoult's law

$P_a = P^o \times X_a$

$X_a = \frac{456}{832} = 0.452$

23. K_f and K_b values for water are 1.86 and 0.52 °C/m , respectively. An aqueous solution boils at 107.5 °C. At what temperature does this solution freeze?
   a) 7.5 °C
   b) −7.5 °C
   c) 0.0 °C
   d) −26.8 °C
   e) −284.5 °C

Answer: (d)

$1.86 : 0.52 = x : 7.5$

$x = 26.8\ °C$

Freezing Point = – 26.8 °C

24. When KCl dissolves in water, the solution cools noticeably to the touch. It may be concluded that
   a) the solvation energy is greater than the lattice energy.
   b) KCl is relatively insoluble in water.
   c) entropy decreases when KCl dissolves.
   d) the boiling point of the solution will be less than 100 °C.
   e) the entropy increase overcomes the unfavorable heat of dissolution.

Answer: (e)

When KCl dissolves in water, entropy increases. The solution is exothermic.

25. The solubility of acetylene, CHCH, in water at 30 °C is 0.975 g/L when the pressure of acetylene is 1.00 atm. What is the solubility, at the same temperature, when the pressure of acetylene above the water is reduced to 0.212 atm?
   a) $4.60gL^{-1}$
   b) $0.207gL^{-1}$
   c) $0.975\ gL^{-1}$
   d) $0.212\ gL^{-1}$
   e) The answer cannot be determined from the data given.

Answer: (b)

Henry's law states that at a constant temperature, the amount of a given gas that dissolves in a liquid is directly proportional to the partial pressure of that gas.

$0.975 : x = 1 : 0.212$
$x = 0.207\ g/L$

26. If 20.0 g of ethanol (molar mass = 46) and 30.0 g of water (molar mass = 18) are mixed together, the mole fraction of ethanol in the mixture is
   a) 0.207
   b) 0.261
   c) 0.739
   d) 0.793
   e) 4.83

Answer: (a)

$$X_{Ethanol} = \frac{\frac{20}{46}}{\frac{20}{46}+\frac{30}{18}} = 0.207$$

27. Which of the following must be measured in order to calculate the molality of a solution?
   I. Mass of the solute
   II. Mass of the solvent
   III. Total volume of the solution
   a) I only
   b) I and III only
   c) II and III only
   d) I and II only
   e) I, II, and III

Answer: (d)

Molality is equal to the number of moles of solute dissolved in the mass of the solvent.

Relationship Analysis Questions

	Statement I	Statement II	
1.	A 0.2 M solution of carbonic acid is a weaker conductor of electricity than a 0.2 M solution of HBr.	In a solution with the same concentration of solute molecules, HCO_3 is less dissociated than HBr.	TTCE
2.	NaCl (aq) is an electrolyte.	It forms ions in solution.	TTCE
3.	A solution of NaCl will conduct electricity.	NaCl will not form ions in solution.	TF

	Statement	Explanation	
4.	A salt dissolved in an organic solvent will be a good electrical conductor.	Salts will not dissolve appreciably in an organic solvent.	FT
5.	Hydrocarbons will dissolve in water.	Substances that have the same polarity are miscible and can dissolve each other.	FT
6.	Salt dissolved in water lowers the freezing point.	The change in freezing point is given by $\Delta T_f = i \times K_f \times m$.	TTCE
7.	Combining equal volumes of 0.2 M AgNO3 and 0.2 M HC1 does not produce a precipitate of AgCl.	The silver ion is rapidly reduced to silver metal, producing chlorine gas.	FF
8.	Sodium chloride forms an aqueous solution of ions.	The sodium in NaCl has a +1 charge while the chlorine has a −1 charge. The compound is then hydrated by the water molecules.	TTCE
9.	Crystals of sodium chloride go into solution in water as ions.	The sodium in NaCl has a +1 charge while the chlorine has a −1 charge. The compound is then hydrated by the water molecules.	TTCE
10.	A saturated solution is not necessarily concentrated.	Dilute and concentrated are terms that relate only to the relative amount of solute dissolved in the solvent.	TTCE
11.	A super saturated solution of glucose in boiling water crystallizes as it cools.	The solubility increases as the temperature decreases.	TF
12.	AgCl is insoluble in water.	All chlorides are soluble in water except for those of silver, lead and mercury.	TTCE
13.	When a solute is added to pure water, the vapor pressure of the water will decrease.	All solutes dissociate into positive and negative ions.	TF
14.	A 1 M NaCl(aq) solution will freeze at a temperature below 273 K.	As a solute is added to a solvent, the boiling point increases while the freezing point decreases.	TTCE

Chapter 9 Energy and Thermodynamics

I. Energy and Work

The **SI unit of energy** is the joule. 4.184 joules are equal to one calorie.

Work (w) and Heat (q)

i. **Work** is the amount of force applied to an object over a distance, given by the equation:

$$w = F \cdot d$$

ii. **PV (pressure/volume) work** is the work done by the expansion or compression of a gas.

$$w = -P\Delta V$$

iii. **Heat** is the energy transferred from a hotter object to a colder one.

$$Q = m \times C \times \Delta T$$

Q: transferred heat; m: mass; C: specific heat; ΔT: changing temperature

iv. **Internal Energy**

1. The total energy of a system is called the internal energy.
2. The absolute internal energy of a system cannot be measured, so only the changes in internal energy (known as ΔE) can be measured.

Example: A mixture of $H_{2(g)}$ and $O_2(g)$ has a higher internal energy than $H_2O(g)$. Going from $H_2(g)$ and $O_2(g)$ to $H_2O(g)$ results in a negative change in internal energy.
$H_2(g) + O_2(g) \rightarrow 2\,H_2O(g)$ **$\Delta E < 0$**

Going from $H_2O(g)$ to $H_2(g)$ and $O_2(g)$ results in a positive change in internal energy.
$2\,H_2O(g) \rightarrow H_2(g) + O_2(g)$ **$\Delta E > 0$**

The First Law of Thermodynamics

$$\Delta E = Q + w$$

i. When heat is flowing from the surroundings to the system, **$Q > 0$.** (Think of it as heat being added to the system.)
ii. Heat flowing from the system into the surroundings is negative (heat is leaving the system, or the system is losing heat): **$Q < 0$**
iii. Similarly, work done by the surroundings on the system is positive: **$w > 0$**

iv. Work done by the system is negative: $\mathbf{w < 0}$

Example: Calculate the change in energy for a system that loses 15 kJ of heat and does 25 kJ of work.

$\Delta E = Q + w$

$Q = -15$ kJ (Heat is lost from the system.)

$w = -25$ kJ (Work is done by the system.)

Thus, $\Delta E = -15 \text{ kJ} + -25 \text{ kJ} = -40 \text{ kJ}$

Endothermic and Exothermic Processes

i. An **endothermic** process is a process that absorbs heat from the surroundings.
ii. An **exothermic** process is a process that transfers heat to the surroundings.

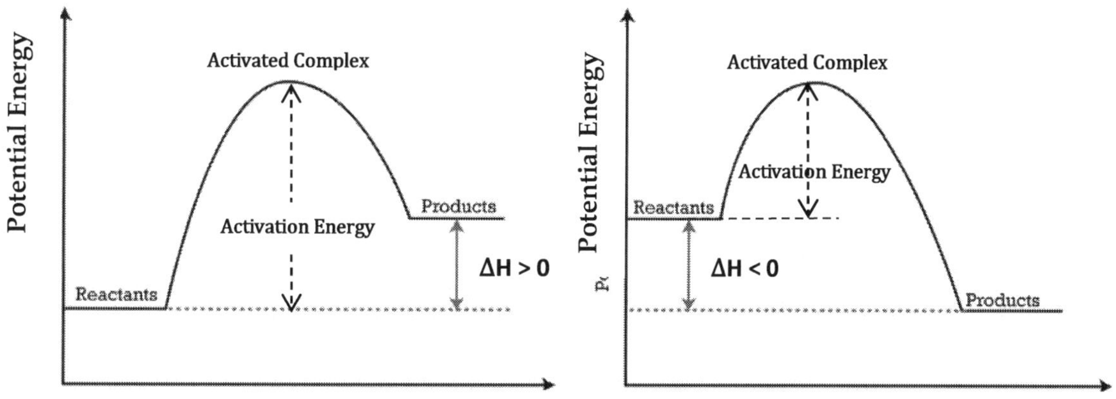

Section Practice

1. A reaction that absorbs heat is
   a) endothermic.
   b) an equilibrium process.
   c) spontaneous.
   d) non-spontaneous.
   e) exothermic.

Answer: (a)

An endothermic process absorbs heat from the surroundings. An exothermic process transfers heat to the surroundings.

2. What is the heat capacity of a 10 g sample that absorbs 100 calories over a temperature change of 30 °C?
   a) 0.333 cal/g °C
   b) 0.666 ca1/g °C
   c) 3 cal/g °C
   d) 30 cal/g °C
   e) 300 cal/g °C

Answer: (a)

$Q = mc\Delta T$

$100 = 10 \times C \times 30$

$C = 0.33$ cal/g °C

3. Calculate the amount of heat needed to bring 10 g of ice from -45 °C to steam at 110 °C. (The heat of fusion of ice is 80 cal/g, the heat of vaporization of water is 540 cal/g, and the heat capacities of both ice and steam are 0.5 cal/g°C)
   a) 7.325 cal
   b) 7.450 cal
   c) 7.325 kcal
   d) 7.475 kcal
   e) 74.75 kcal

Answer: (d)

Ice at – 45 °C→ Ice at 0 °C → Water at 0 °C → Water at 100 °C→ Steam at 100 °C→ Steam at 110 °C

$Q = 10 \times 0.5 \times 45 + 80 \times 10 + 10 \times 1 \times 100 + 10 \times 540 + 10 \times 0.5 \times 10 = 7475$ cal = 7.475 Kcal.

4. A 50 g sample of metal was heated to 100 °C and then dropped into a beaker containing 50 g of water at 25 °C. If the specific heat capacity of the metal is 0.25 cal/g· °C, what is the final temperature of the water?
   a) 27 °C
   b) 40 °C
   c) 60 °C
   d) 66 °C
   e) 86 °C

Answer: (b)

Assume that there is no heat loss during this process.

Let the final temperature be T.

$Q = 0 = 50 \times 0.25 \times (T - 100) + 50 \times 1 \times (T - 25)$

$T = 40$ °C

5. A gas is allowed to expand from an initial volume of 5.00 L and pressure of 3.00 atm to a volume of 15.0 L and pressure of 1.00 atm. What is the value of work?
   a) +15.0 L atm
   b) +10.0 L atm
   c) -16.5 L atm
   d) -15.0 L atm
   e) −10.0 L atm

Answer: (c)

This is isothermal expansion.

$W = -\ nRT\, ln\frac{V_2}{V_1} = P_1 V_1$

$ln(\frac{V2}{V1}) = 3 \times 5 \times ln(\frac{15}{5}) =$
$-16.5\ L\ atm$

6. The energy of a system can be
   a) easily changed into mass.
   b) transformed into a different form.
   c) measured only in terms of potential energy.
   d) measured only in terms of kinetic energy.
   e) None of the above

Answer: (b)

Energy can be easily transferred between forms.

7. Two solutions are mixed separately, and both solutions are found to be the same temperature. The two solutions are mixed, and a thermometer shows that the final mixture's temperature has decreased in temperature. Which of the following statements is true?
   a) The chemical reaction is exothermic.
   b) The chemical reaction is absorbing energy.
   c) The chemical reaction is releasing energy.
   d) The energy released could be found by multiplying the temperatures together.
   e) The energy absorbed by the solution is equal to the difference in temperature of the solutions.

Answer: (b)

The process is endothermic as heat has been absorbed.

II. Enthalpy (H)

Properties of Enthalpy

i. Enthalpy is the heat transferred between the system and the surroundings during a chemical reaction that occurs under constant pressure.

ii. We can measure the change in enthalpy using the following equation:

$$\Delta H = H\,final - H\,initial = Q$$

where Q = heat at constant pressure

iii. Enthalpy is a state function, which means that ΔH depends *solely* on the initial and final states.

iv. When heat is transferred from the surroundings to the system, **ΔH > 0**. (The reaction is endothermic).

v. When heat is transferred from the system to the surroundings, **ΔH < 0.** (The reaction is exothermic).

Heat Capacity and Specific Heat

$$Q = m \times C \times \Delta T$$

$$m: mass, C: specific\ heat, \Delta T: changing\ temperature$$

The **enthalpy of reaction** is the enthalpy change that accompanies a reaction.

$$\Delta H = H(products) - H(reactants)$$

We can visualize this change in energy (as heat) from reactants to products on a reaction coordinate diagram.

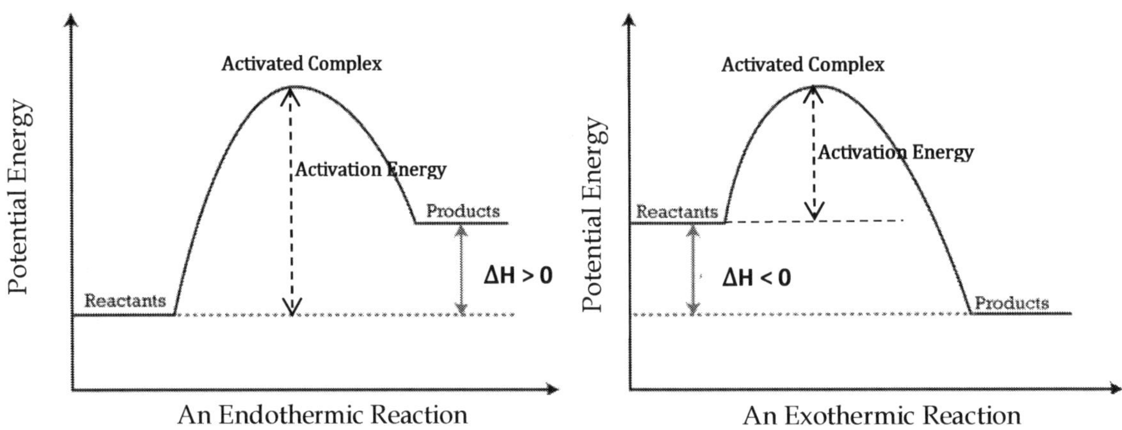

Example:

$CH_4(g) + 2O_2(g) \rightarrow CO_2(g) + 2H_2O(l)$ ΔH = −890 kJ

$CO_2(g) + 2H_2O(l) \rightarrow CH_4(g) + 2O_2(g)$ ΔH = +890 kJ

The **heat of formation** is the amount off heat released or absorbed when one mole of a compound is formed from its elements.

$$\Delta H_{reaction} = \sum H_{f_{products}} - \sum H_{f_{reactants}}$$

i. If a compound is formed from its constituent elements, then the enthalpy change for the reaction is called the enthalpy of formation, ΔH_f.
ii. Standard conditions (or standard state) are 1 atm and 25 °C.
iii. Standard enthalpy, ΔH^o, is the enthalpy measured when everything is at standard conditions.
iv. The standard enthalpy of formation of the most stable form of an element is zero.

Bond energy is the energy required to break a bond. Energy is released when chemical bonds are formed.

$$\Delta H_{reaction} = \sum BE_{reactants} - \sum BE_{products}$$

Hess's Law states if a reaction is carried out in a series of steps, ΔH for the reaction is the sum of the ΔHs for each step. The total change in enthalpy for any final reaction is independent of the number of steps taken in between. Total ΔH is also independent of the nature of the path.

Example:

$CH_4(g) + 2O_2(g) \rightarrow CO_2(g) + \cancel{2H_2O(g)}$	$\Delta H = -802$ kJ
$\cancel{2H_2O(g)} \rightarrow 2H_2O(l)$	$\Delta H = -88$ kJ
$CH_4(g) + 2O_2(g) \rightarrow CO_2(g) + 2H_2O(l)$	$\Delta H = -890$ kJ

Section Practice

1. If the ΔH of a reaction is negative, the reaction is
   a) endothermic.
   b) unstable.
   c) exothermic.
   d) reversible.

Answer: (c)

A negative ΔH implies that the reaction is an exothermic reaction.

2. Which of the following has a standard enthalpy of formation equal to zero?
   a) $S_8(g)$
   b) $CO_2(g)$
   c) $HCl(g)$
   d) $Cl_{2(g)}$
   e) $O_3(g)$

Answer: (d)

The standard enthalpy of formation of the most stable form of an element is zero.

The most stable form of sulfur is S_8 in its solid state.

3. Calculate the bond energy of a Br—F bond given the information below.

$$Br(g) + 5\ F(g) \rightarrow BrF_5(g)$$
$$\Delta H_f \text{ of } BrF_5(g) = -429 \text{ kJ/mol}$$
$$\Delta H_f \text{ of } Br(g) = 112 \text{ kJ/mol}$$
$$\Delta H_f \text{ of } F(g) = 79 \text{ kJ/mol}$$

a) 936 kJ/mol
b) 187 kJ/mol
c) 125 kJ/mol
d) 86 kJ/mol
e) 47 kJ/mol

Answer: (b)

Let x be the bond energy of a BrF bond.
The total energy in the system before the reaction must be equal to the total energy of the system afterwards.
This total energy is equal to the energy of formation plus the total bond energy.
$112 + 79 \times 5 = -429 + 5x$
$x = 187.2$ kJ/ mol

4.

Bond	Average Bond Energy
C ≡ O	1075 kJ/mol
C = O	728 kJ/mol
C - Cl	326 kJ/mol
Cl - Cl	243 kJ/mol

Calculate the heat of reaction for the following equation using the information given above.

$$CO + Cl_2 \rightarrow COCl_2$$

a) 62 kJ
b) − 62 kJ
c) − 409 kJ
d) 706 kJ
e) – 706 kJ

Answer: (b)

ΔH = Bond Energy of Reactants – Bond Energy of Products

The Lewis structure of CO: C≡ O

$(1075 + 243) - (728 + 2\times326) = -62$ kJ

5. At which of the following temperatures will the process, shown below, spontaneously occur at 1 atm?

$$CHCl_{3\,(l)} \rightarrow CHCl_3(g)$$

$\Delta H = 31.4$ kJ/mol and $\Delta S = 94.0$ J/mol·K

a) 61°C
b) 58 °C
c) 43 °C
d) 25 °C
e) 14 °C

Answer: (a)

$\Delta G = \Delta H - T \times \Delta S$
$= 31.4 \times 1000 - T \times 94$
When $T > 334$ K, $\Delta G < 0$

$T > 61$ °C

6. Enthalpy is an expression for the _____ of a reaction.
a) heat content
b) energy state
c) reaction rate
d) activation energy
e) equilibrium state

Answer: (a)

Enthalpy refers to the heat content.

7. The ΔH_f^o of a reaction is recorded at
   a) 0 °C.
   b) 25 °C.
   c) 100 °C.
   d) 200 °C.
   e) 0 K.

Answer: (b)

Standard state is 1 atm and 25°C.

8. What is the ΔH of the reaction that forms CO_2 from C + O_2?

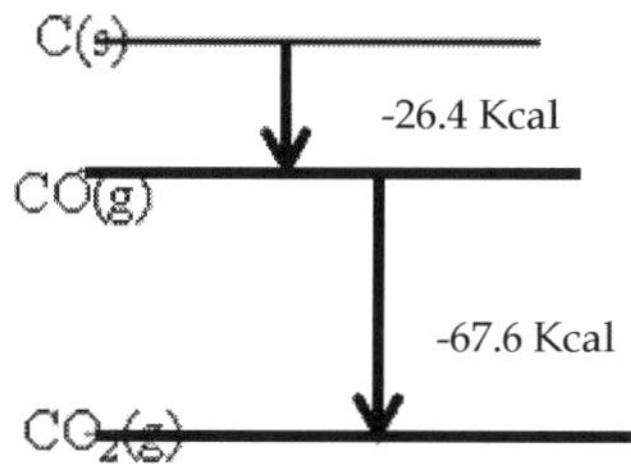

   a) −94.0 kcal
   b) −26.4 kcal
   c) −67.6 kcal
   d) −41.2 kcal
   e) 26.4 kcal

Answer: (a)

ΔH of the Total Reaction = ΔH of Reaction 1 + ΔH of Reaction 2 = – 26.4 – 67.6 = – 94 Kcal.

9. When 1 mole of sulfur burns to form SO_2, 1300 calories are released. When 1 mole of sulfur burns to form SO_3, 3600 calories are released. What is ΔH when 1 mole of SO_2 burns to form SO_3?
   a) 3900 cal
   b) −1950 cal
   c) 1000 cal
   d) −500 cal
   e) −2300 cal

Answer: (e)

Use Hess's law.

$S + O_2 \rightarrow SO_2 \; \Delta H = -1300 \; cal$

$S + \frac{3}{2}O_2 \rightarrow SO_3 \; \Delta H = -3600 \; cal$

$SO_2 + \frac{1}{2}O_2 \rightarrow SO_3$

$\Delta H = -3600 - (-1300) = -2300 \; cal$

10. The graphical representation of the energy levels of the reactants and products in a chemical reaction is shown below. Which of the following statements is/are true?

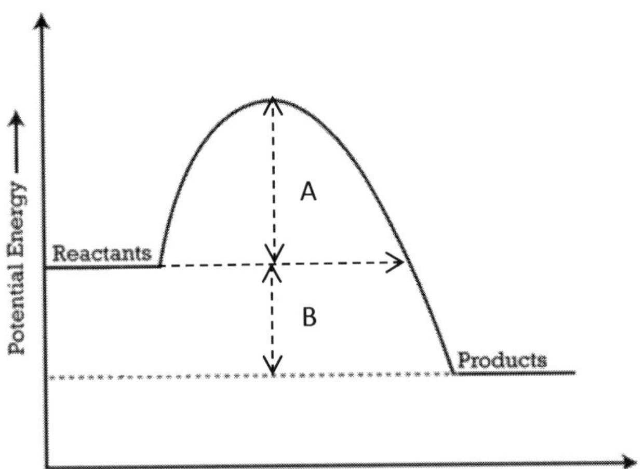

I. The forward reaction is an exothermic reaction.
II. The activation energy for the forward reaction is represented by B.
III. The energy shown in A is released from the system in the forward reaction.

a) I only
b) II only
c) I, III only
d) II, III only
e) I, II, and III

Answer: (a)

ΔH = Product Energy – Reactant Energy.
An exothermic reaction has negative ΔH.

The activation energy for the forward reaction is represented by A.

B is the energy given off in the forward reaction.

III. Entropy (S)

Entropy is a measure of the degree of randomness in a system.

What Increases Entropy?

i. Adding more particles increases the frequency of collisions and the randomness of motion.
ii. Adding energy or increasing temperature increases the velocity and randomness of the particles.
iii. Increasing volume allows particles to roam in a greater amount of space and leads to more random motion.

Entropy increases with the freedom of motion of the particles. Gases tend to have more randomness, followed by liquids and then solids.

Increasing entropy →

$H_2O(s)$ $H_2O(l)$ $H_2O(g)$

iv. The entropy of a system tends to increase over time.

Examples: Predict the sign of ΔS for the following reactions (+ for increasing entropy, − for decreasing entropy, 0 for no entropy change).

$ClF(g) + F_2(g) \rightarrow ClF_3(g)$	−
$NH_3(g) \rightarrow NH_3(aq)$	−
$CH_3OH(l) \rightarrow CH_3OH(aq)$	+
$C_{10}H_8(l) \rightarrow C_{10}H_8(s)$	−

Free Energy(G) is the energy available to do work (useful energy). G depends on both enthalpy and entropy.

$$\Delta G^\circ = \Delta H^\circ - T\Delta S^\circ$$

i. A reaction proceeds spontaneously in the way that lowers its free energy ($\Delta G < 0$).
ii. The more negative the ΔH°, the more negative the ΔG.
iii. The higher the temperature and the more positive the ΔS, the more negative the ΔG.

Section Practice

1. All of the following are correct statements concerning entropy EXCEPT
   a) all spontaneous processes tend towards an increase in entropy.
   b) the more highly ordered the system, the higher the entropy.
   c) the entropy of a pure crystalline solid at 0 K is 0.
   d) the change in entropy of an equilibrium process is 0.
   e) All of the above are correct

Answer: (b)

The less ordered the system, the higher the entropy is.

2. The evaporation of any liquid is expected to have
   a) a positive ΔH and a negative ΔS.
   b) a negative ΔH and a negative ΔS.
   c) a positive ΔH and a positive ΔS.
   d) a positive ΔH and a negative ΔS.
   e) unpredictable ΔH and ΔS.

Answer: (c)

Evaporation increases randomness and absorbs energy.

3. Which of the following is most likely to be true?
   a) No products are formed in a nonspontaneous reaction.
   b) A positive $\Delta G°$ indicates a spontaneous reaction.
   c) A positive $\Delta S°$ always means that the reaction is spontaneous.
   d) A spontaneous reaction always goes to completion.
   e) Combustion of organic compounds has a negative $\Delta H°$.

Answer: (e)

Combustion of organic compounds will always release heat.

4. Which of the following explains the fact that, when KCl is dissolved, water condenses on the outside of a beaker?
   a) $\Delta H°$ is positive and $\Delta S°$ is negative.
   b) $\Delta H°$ is positive and $\Delta S°$ is positive.
   c) $\Delta H°$ is negative and $\Delta S°$ is negative.
   d) $\Delta H°$ is negative and $\Delta S°$ is positive.
   e) $\Delta H°$ is 0.00 and $\Delta S°$ is negative.

Answer: (b)

KCl dissolving in water increases randomness and absorbs energy.

5. Which of the following describes a system that CANNOT be spontaneous?
   a) $\Delta H°$ is positive and $\Delta S°$ is negative.
   b) $\Delta H°$ is positive and $\Delta S°$ is positive.
   c) $\Delta H°$ is negative and $\Delta S°$ is negative.
   d) $\Delta H°$ is negative and $\Delta S°$ is positive.
   e) $\Delta H°$ is 0.00 and $\Delta S°$ is positive.

Answer: (a)

A positive ΔH and negative ΔS will result in a positive ΔG.

6. Which of the following are extensive values?
   I. $\Delta G°$
   II. $\Delta S°$
   III. $\Delta H°$
   IV. G
   V. H
   a) I, III only
   b) II, V only
   c) I, II, and IV only
   d) IV, V only
   e) I, III, and V only

Answer: (d)

An intensive property does not depend on the number of molecules in a system.

An extensive property is proportional to the number of molecules in the system.

G and H describe the amount of energy that a system has and do depend on the number of molecules in the system.

7. If _____ is negative and _____ is positive, a reaction will never be spontaneous.
   I. ΔG
   II. ΔS
   III. ΔH
   IV. G
   V. H
   a) II, III
   b) III, IV
   c) I, II
   d) IV, III
   e) I,V

Answer: (a)

$\Delta G = \Delta H - T\Delta S$

Nonspontaneous processes have positive ΔG.

A positive ΔH and negative ΔS will result in a positive ΔG.

8. Which of the following thermodynamic quantities is decreased by the addition of a catalyst?
   a) ΔG
   b) ΔH
   c) ΔS
   d) E_A
   e) K_{EQ}

Answer: (d)

Adding a catalyst will change the activation energy of the reactions.

9. Which reaction has the greatest expected entropy decrease?
   a) $CH_4(g) + 2O_2(g) \rightarrow CO_2(g) + 2H_2O(g)$
   b) $CH_4(l) + 2O_2(g) \rightarrow CO_2(g) + 2H_2O(g)$
   c) $CH_4(g) + 2O_2(g) \rightarrow CO_2(s) + 2H_2O(l)$
   d) $CH_4(g) + 2O_2(g) \rightarrow CO_2(s) + 2H_2O(g)$
   e) $CH_4(l) + 2O_2(g) \rightarrow CO_2(g) + 2H_2O(l)$

Answer: (c)

Randomness increases from solid to liquid to gas.

10. Which of the following thermodynamic quantities is always negative for a spontaneous process?
    a) ΔG
    b) ΔH
    c) ΔS
    d) E_A
    e) K_{EQ}

Answer: (a)

Spontaneous processes have negative ΔG.

11. Which of the following thermodynamic quantities has the units J/mol·K?
    a) ΔG
    b) ΔH
    c) ΔS
    d) E_A
    e) K_{EQ}

Answer: (c)

Entropy has a unit of J/mol·K.

12. Which of the following processes may result in a decrease in entropy?
    I. Water freezing
    II. Water vaporizing
    III. Dry ice subliming (vaporizing)
    IV. Extracting Mg^{2+} and pure water from seawater
    a) I and II only
    b) II and IV only
    c) I and IV only
    d) III only
    e) II and III only

Answer: (c)

Entropy increases from solid to liquid to gas.

Chapter 9 Energy and Thermodynamics SAT Questions

1. The reaction of aluminum with dilute H_2SO_4 can be classified as a
   a) synthesis reaction.
   b) decomposition reaction.
   c) single replacement reaction.
   d) double replacement reaction.
   e) combustion reaction.

Answer: (c)

$Al + H_2SO_4 \rightarrow Al_2(SO_4)_3 + H_2$

2. Using the information given in the reaction equations below, calculate the heat of formation for 1 mole of carbon monoxide.

   $2\,C(s) + 2O_2 \rightarrow 2CO_2 \quad \Delta H = -787\ kJ$

   $2CO + O_2 \rightarrow 2CO_2 \quad \Delta H = -566 kJ$

   a) – 221 kJ/mol
   b) −410 kJ/mol
   c) −110 kJ/mol
   d) 410 kJ/mol
   e) 221 kJ/mol

Answer: (c)

$2C + O_2 \rightarrow 2CO$

$\Delta H = -787 - (-566) = -221$ kJ

1 mole of CO will need $\frac{-221}{2}$ *kJ* $= -110.5$ *kJ.*

3. When a solid sample of $NaNO_3$ is added to a cup of water, the temperature of the solution decreases. Which of the following MUST be true?

   I. The entropy of solution must be positive.
   II. The entropy of solution must be negative.
   III. The enthalpy of solution must be negative.

   a) I only
   b) II only
   c) I and III only
   d) II and III only
   e) I, II, and III

Answer: (a)

The process is endothermic. Both entropy and enthalpy increase.

$\Delta S > 0$

$\Delta H > 0$

4. The combustion of propane is shown below. What would be the value of ΔH° if the reaction produced $H_2O(g)$ instead of liquid water?

   $C_3H_8(g) + 5O_2(g) \rightarrow 3CO_2(g) + 4H_2O(1) \quad \Delta H° = -2220\ kJ$

   a) – 2044 kJ
   b) – 2176 kJ
   c) – 2264 kJ
   d) – 2396 kJ
   e) – 2440 kJ

Answer: (a)

$-2220 + 44 \times 4 = -2044$ kJ

5. Which of the following must be negative for a reaction to be spontaneous?
   I. ΔG
   II. ΔS
   III. ΔH
   IV. G
   V. H
   a) I only
   b) III only
   c) I, II, and IV only
   d) IV only
   e) I, III, and V only

Answer: (a)

A reaction is a spontaneous reaction when ΔG is a negative.

6. Which of the following cannot be determined in any reaction?
   I. ΔG
   II. ΔS
   III. ΔH
   IV. G
   V. H
   a) I and III only
   b) II only
   c) I, II, and IV only
   d) I, III, and IV only
   e) IV and V only

Answer: (e)

No absolute value of enthalpy and Gibbs free energy can be determined in any reaction.

7. 0.400 g of CH_4 is burned in excess oxygen in a bomb calorimeter that has a heat capacity of 3245 J °C. A temperature increase of 6.795 °C is observed. Determine ΔH for the combustion of methane.
   a) 22.05 kJmole $^{-1}$
   b) −882 kJ
   c) +22.05 kJ
   d) 8.820 kJ g^{-1}
   e) ΔH cannot be determined because the amount of work done is unknown.

Answer: (b)

$Q = Cp \times \Delta T = 6.795 \times 3245 = 22.05$ kJ

0.400 g of $CH_4 = \frac{0.4}{14} = 0.025$ moles of CH_4

There is a temperature increase, so the process must be exothermic ($Q_v < 0$).

$\Delta H = -\frac{22.05}{0.025} = -882$ kJ/mol

8. Which of the following is the LEAST likely to occur for a combustion reaction?
   a) ΔG° is a large negative number.
   b) ΔS° is a large negative number.
   c) ΔH° is a large negative number.
   d) K_{eq} is a large positive number.
   e) Q, the reaction quotient, is a small number.

Answer: (a)

Normally, combustion reactions are not spontaneous reactions at room temperature and normal pressure. ΔG° cannot be a large negative number.

9. Water boils at 100 °C with a molar heat of vaporization of +43.9 kJ. At 100 °C, what is the entropy change?

$$H_2O(g) \rightarrow H_2O(l)$$

a) −439 J K^{-1}
b) +0.439 J K^{-1}
c) −118 J K^{-1}
d) ΔG° must also be known to determine the entropy change.
e) We cannot determine the entropy change as this is not a chemical reaction.

Answer: (c)

At equilibrium, ΔG = 0.

$\Delta G = \Delta H - T\Delta S$

$\Delta S = \frac{\Delta H}{T} = \frac{-43900}{373} = -118\ J\ K^{-1}$

10. The heat of formation of a few different substances is given below.

$CH_3OH(l) = -238.6$ kJ mol^{-1}
$CO_2(g) = -393.5$ kJ mol^{-1}
$H_2O(g) = -241.8$ kJ mol^{-1}

What is ΔH° for the heat of combustion of methanol?

a) −396.7 kJ
b) −1277 kJ
c) −638.5 kJ
d) +396.7 kJ
e) The heat of combustion cannot be calculated without the heat of formation for $O_2(g)$.

Answer: (b)

$2CH_3OH + 3O_2 \rightarrow 2CO_2 + 4H_2O$

$\Delta H = 4(-241.8) + 2(-393.5) - 2(-238.6) = -1277\ kJ =$

11. The standard heat of formation of $SO_3(g)$ is −396 kJ $mole^{-1}$. The standard entropies of S(s), $O_2(g)$ and $SO_3(g)$ are 31.8, 205.0, and 256 J $mole^{-1}$ K^{-1}, respectively. Calculate the free energy for the decomposition of SO_3 in the following reaction:

$$2SO_3(g) \rightarrow 2S(s) + 3O_2(g) \text{ at } 25\ °C$$

a) +396 kJ
b) −446 kJ
c) +346 kJ
d) −346kJ
e) +742 kJ

Answer: (e)

$\Delta G = \Delta H - T\Delta S$

$\Delta H = 396kJ \times 2 = 792\ kJ$

$\Delta S = 2(31.8) + 3(205) - 2(256) = 166.6\ J/K$

$\Delta G = 792000 - 298(166.6) = 742353\ J \approx 742\ kJ$

12. What is the ΔH of the reaction that forms CO_2 from $C + O_2$?

a) −94.0 kcal
b) −26.4 kcal
c) −67.6 kcal
d) − 41.2 kcal
e) 26.4 kcal

Answer: (a)

Combine step 1 and step 2.

$-26.4 + (-67.6) = -94\ Kcal$

13. What is the ΔH of the reaction that forms CO_2 from $CO + O_2$?

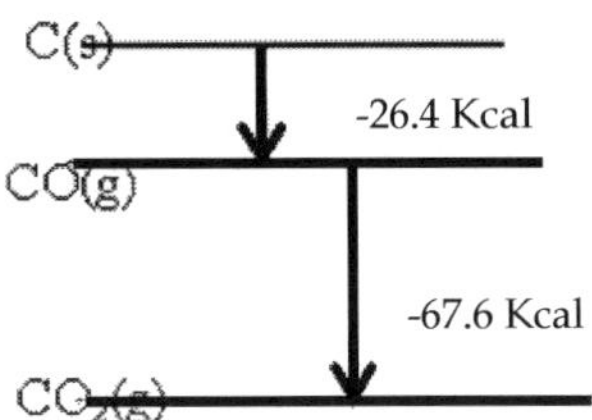

a) −94.0 kcal
b) −26.4 kcal
c) −67.6 kcal
d) -41.2 kcal
e) 26.4 kcal

Answer: (c)

The reaction that forms CO_2 from $CO + O_2$ is the second step in the step diagram.

14. Which step in the state change curve below will all molecules be in the solid state?

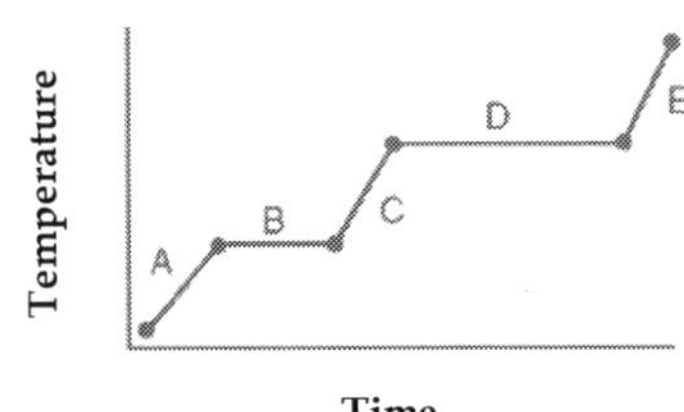

Answer: (a)

Segment A represents the solid-only phase.

15. According to the state change curve below, where would the greatest amount of heat be required for a phase change?

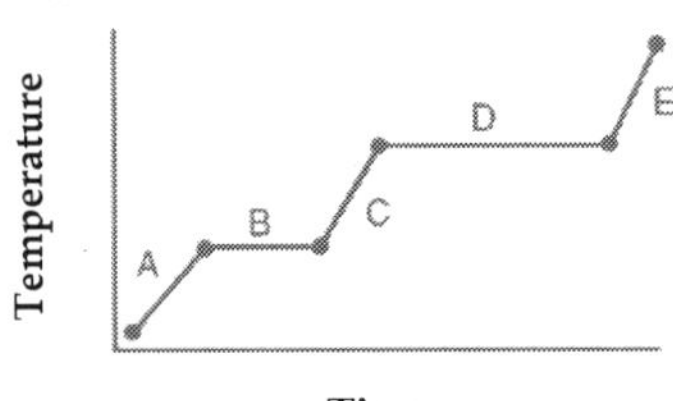

Answer: (d)

The phase change from liquid to gas, which is segment D, requires the greatest amount of energy.

16. According to the graph below, which interval shows the potential energy of the products?

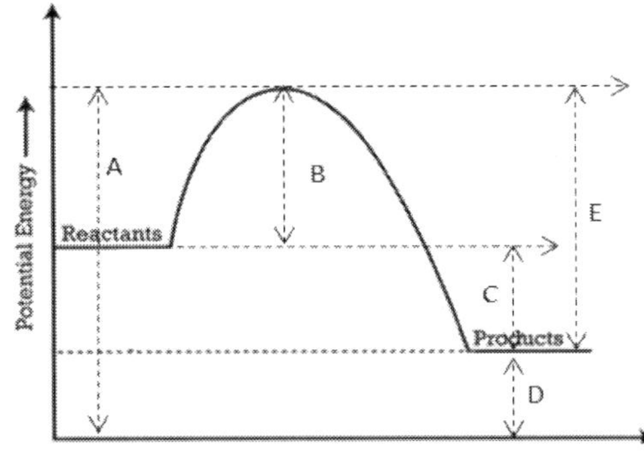

Answer: (d)

The reactants are on the left and the products are on the right. D indicates the potential energy of the products.

17. According to the state change curve below, at which segment will the temperature of one gram of H_2O change at 1 °C per cal of energy?

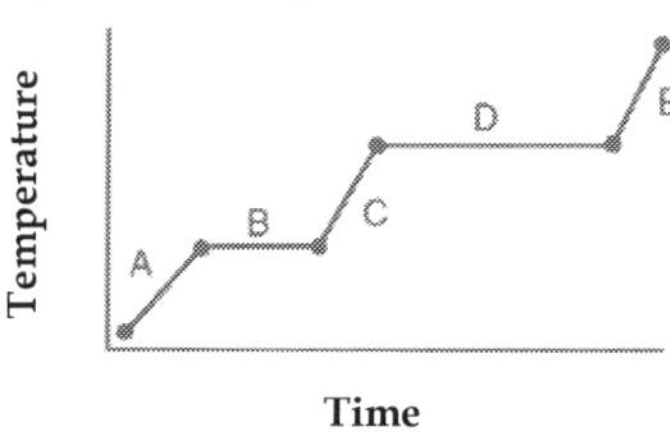

Answer: (c)

Liquid water has a specific heat of 1 °C/g·cal. C is the region where water is fully liquid.

18. Which step in the state change curve below will all molecules be in the liquid state?

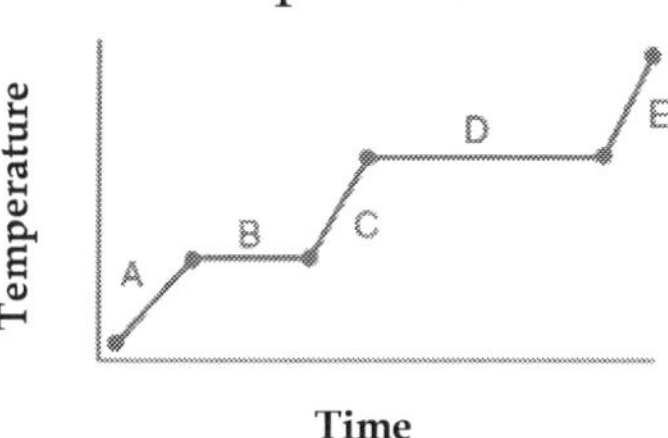

Answer: (c)

Segment C represents the liquid-only phase.

19. Which step in the state change curve below will all molecules be in the gaseous state?

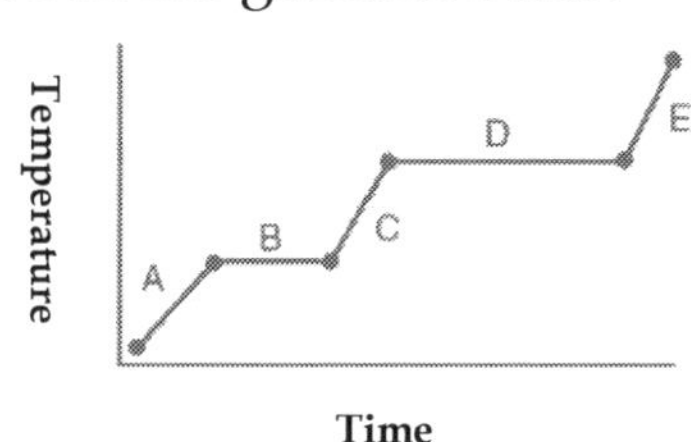

Answer: (e)

Segment E represents the gas-only phase.

20. Which step in the state change curve below could molecules be in both the liquid and gaseous state?

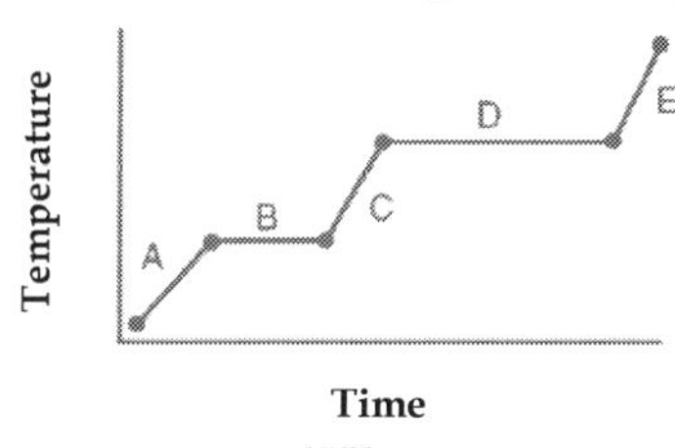

Answer: (d)

Segment D represents a phase where liquid and gas may coexist.

21. The reaction $2C_6H_6(l) + 15O_2(g) \rightarrow 12CO_2(g) + 6H_2O(l)$ is expected to have a(n)
    a) positive ΔH and a negative ΔS.
    b) negative ΔH and a negative ΔS.
    c) positive ΔH and a positive ΔS.
    d) negative ΔH and a negative ΔS.
    e) unknown ΔH and ΔS.

Answer: (b)

This reaction reduces the total number of gas molecules and is also exothermic.

$\Delta H < 0$

$\Delta S < 0$

22. How much heat is given off when 8 g of hydrogen reacts in the following process?
$2H_2 + O_2 \rightarrow 2H_2O$ $\Delta H° = -115.60$ kcal
a) −57.8 kcal
b) −115.6 kcal
c) −173.4 kcal
d) −231.2 kcal
e) −462.4 kcal

Answer: (d)

$8\ g\ of\ H_2 = \frac{8}{2} = 4\ moles\ of\ H_2$

$2 : -115.6 = 4 : x$

$x = -231.2\ Kcal$

23. The change in heat energy for a reaction is best expressed as a change in
a) enthalpy (H).
b) absolute temperature (T).
c) specific heat (C).
d) entropy (S).
e) kinetic energy (K_E).

Answer: (a)

This is the definition of enthalpy.

24. When the temperature of a 20 gram sample of water is increased from 10 °C to 30 °C, the amount heat absorbed by the water is
a) 600 cal.
b) 30 cal.
c) 400 cal.
d) 20 cal.
e) 200 cal.

Answer: (c)

$c_{water} = 1\ cal/g°C$

$Q = mc\Delta T = 20 \times 1 \times (30 - 10) = 400\ cal$

25. How many grams of CH_4 will produce 425.6 kcal in the reaction below?
$CH_4 + 2O_2 \rightarrow CO_2 + 2H_2O + 212.8$ kcal
a) 8 g
b) 16 g
c) 24 g
d) 32 g
e) 64 g

Answer: (d)

$1\ mole\ of\ CH_4 : 212.8 = x : 425.6$

$x = 2\ moles\ of\ CH_4 = 32\ g\ of\ CH_4$

26. What is ΔH_{rxn} for the decomposition of 1 mole of sodium chlorate? (ΔH_f values are as follows: $NaClO_3(s) = -85.7$ kcal/mol; $NaCl(s) = -98.2$ kcal/mol; $O_2(g) = 0$ kcal/mol)
a) −183.9 kcal
b) −91.9 kcal
c) +45.3 kcal
d) +22.5 kcal
e) −12.5 kcal

Answer: (e)

$2NaClO_3(s) \rightarrow 2NaCl + 3O_2$

$\Delta H_{rxn} = \frac{2\times(-98.2)+0-2(-85.7)}{2} = -12.5\ Kcal$

27. When enthalpy is negative and entropy is positive,
    a) free energy is always negative.
    b) free energy is negative at low temperatures.
    c) free energy is negative at high temperatures.
    d) free energy is never negative.
    e) the system is at equilibrium.

Answer: (a)

$\Delta G = \Delta H - T\Delta S$

A negative ΔH minus a positive $T\Delta S$ always results in a negative ΔG.

28. When enthalpy is positive and entropy is positive,
    a) free energy is always negative.
    b) free energy is negative at lower temperatures.
    c) free energy is negative at high temperatures.
    d) free energy is never negative.
    e) the system is at equilibrium and there is no net reaction.

Answer: (c)

$\Delta G = \Delta H - T\Delta S$

A positive ΔH minus a positive $T\Delta S$ can result in either a negative or positive ΔG. ΔG could be negative at a high temperature, for example.

29. When enthalpy is negative and entropy is negative,
    a) free energy is always negative.
    b) free energy is negative at low temperatures.
    c) free energy is negative at high temperatures
    d) free energy is never negative.
    e) the system is at equilibrium.

Answer: (b)

$\Delta G = \Delta H - T\Delta S$

ΔG is negative at lower temperatures.

Relationship Analysis Questions

1.	A catalyst will change the heat of reaction.	A catalyst will lower the potential energy of the activated complex in a reaction.	FT
2.	A reaction with a positive ΔH is considered to be exothermic.	An exothermic reaction releases more heat than it absorbs.	FT
3.	An exothermic reaction has a positive ΔH value.	Heat must be added to the reaction for the reaction to occur.	FF
4.	An increase in entropy leads to a decrease in randomness.	The low energy state of ordered crystals has high entropy.	FF
5.	A calorimeter can be used to measure the amount of heat lost or absorbed in a process.	Calorimeters are used to measure heat lost or gained by a system and its surroundings.	TF

	Statement I	Statement II	
6.	The heat of formation of a compound can be calculated by algebraically adding two or more thermal reaction equations.	Hess's Law states that a heat of reaction can be derived by the algebraic summation of two or more other thermal reactions.	TTCE
7.	The reaction in which HgO is heated to release O_2 is called decomposition.	In a decomposition reaction, the original compound is broken apart into equal numbers of atoms.	TF
8.	An exothermic reaction has a negative ΔH.	In an exothermic reaction, the products have less potential energy than the reactants.	TTCE
9.	The entropy of a solid decreases when it is dissolved.	The dissolved solid becomes less ordered.	FT
10.	The temperature of a substance always increases as heat is added to the system.	The average kinetic energy of the particles in a system increases with an increase in temperature.	FT
11.	If the heat of formation of a compound is a large negative number, the reaction is exothermic.	The First Law of Thermodynamics states that a negative heat of formation is associated with an exothermic reaction.	TF
12.	The burning of carbon with excess O_2, forming CO_2, will go to completion.	When a reaction results in the release of a gas that is allowed to escape, the reaction will go to completion.	TTCE
13.	Entropy can be described as the state of disorder of a system.	When high amounts of energy are released from a reaction, the reaction is said to be exothermic.	TT
14.	When the ΔG of a reaction at a given temperature is negative, the reaction occurs spontaneously.	When ΔG is negative, ΔH is also negative.	TF
15.	If ΔH is positive and ΔS is positive, ΔG must be positive.	$\Delta G = \Delta H - T\Delta S$	FT
16.	A reaction will be spontaneous if ΔH is negative and ΔS is positive.	ΔG will be negative when there is a decrease in enthalpy and an increase in entropy.	TTCE
17.	The freezing of water is an exothermic process.	Energy is released when covalent bonds are formed.	TF

Statement	Reason	
18. An exothermic reaction has a positive ΔH.	Heat is released in an exothermic reaction.	FT
19. Covalent bonds must be broken for a liquid to boil.	Heat must be released for a liquid to change into a gas.	FF
20. A reaction with a positive enthalpy and negative entropy will be spontaneous.	The Gibbs free energy for a spontaneous reaction is negative.	FT
21. Candles can be safely stored at room temperature, even though their reaction with air is spontaneous at room temperature.	The reaction that takes place when a candle is burned involves a decrease in entropy.	FF

Chapter 10 Chemical Kinetics

I. Chemical Reaction Rate

Properties of a substance such as mass, concentration, color, or pH can be observed to determine the chemical reaction rate.

$$\text{Chemical Reaction Rate} = \frac{\textit{Change in Substance}}{\textit{Change in Time}}$$

Theories of Reaction Rate

i. Collision Theory
   1. Chemical reactions occur when molecules collide, so the more collisions there are, the faster the reaction proceeds.
   2. A chemical reaction also needs a minimum amount of energy, or activation energy, to occur, as well as molecules colliding in the correct orientation.

ii. Transition State Theory
   1. Rates of reactions can be studied by examining activated complexes which lie near the saddle point of a potential energy surface. The saddle point itself is called the transition state.
   2. The activated complexes are in a special equilibrium (quasi-equilibrium) with the reactant molecules.
   3. The activated complexes can be converted into products, and kinetic theory may be used to calculate the rate of this conversion.

Factors Effecting Reaction Rate

i. The types of bonds in the reactants influence the reaction rate. Weaker bonds require less activation energy and react faster.

ii. Greater concentrations of reactants will increase the number of collisions and hence increase the reaction rate.

iii. Increasing the surface area of a reactant will increase the amount of reactant that is able to react.

iv. Increasing the temperature of the reaction will increase the number of collisions and the number of reactant molecules which will have enough kinetic energy to exceed the activation energy. As a rule of thumb, for many common chemical reactions at room temperature, the reaction rate doubles with every 10 °C increase of temperature.

v. Adding a catalyst will lower the activation energy, therefore increase the reaction rate.

Section Practice

1. All of the following are true statements concerning reaction orders EXCEPT?
   a) Zeroth order reactions are common.
   b) After three half-lives, a radioactive sample will be one-eighth of its original concentration.
   c) The units for the rate constant of first order reactions are sec^{-1}.
   d) If the concentration of a reactant is doubled, the rate of the reaction will double. The reaction is first order in that reactant.
   e) The units for the rate constant for zero order reactions are $M{\cdot}sec^{-1}$.

Answer: (a)

Zeroth order reactions, like radioactive reactions, are uncommon

2. All of the following are true statements concerning catalysts EXCEPT
   a) A catalyst will speed up the rate-determining step.
   b) A catalyst will be used up in a reaction.
   c) A catalyst may induce steric strain in a molecule to make it react more readily.
   d) A catalyst will lower the activation energy of a reaction.
   e) None of the above

Answer: (b)

A catalyst is not part of the reactants in a chemical reaction.

3. An increase in concentration of the reactants in a reaction
   a) is directly related to the number of collisions in that reaction.
   b) is inversely related to the number of collisions in that reaction.
   c) has no effect on the number of collisions in that reaction.
   d) must increase the reaction rate.
   e) has no effect on the reaction rate.

Answer: (a)

An increase in concentration of the reactants will increase the number of collisions, but not necessarily the reaction rate

4. Normally, at the beginning of a reaction, the reaction rate for the reactants is
   a) greatest, then decreases.
   b) greatest, and remains constant.
   c) smallest, then increases.
   d) smallest, and remains constant.
   e) constant at all times.

Answer: (a)

Because the beginning of a reaction has the highest concentration of reactants, the reaction rate is greatest then.

5. According to chemical kinetic theory, a reaction can occur under which conditions?
   a) If the reactants collide with the proper orientation.
   b) If the reactants possess sufficient energy of collision.
   c) If the reactants are able to form a correct transition state.
   d) All of the above are correct.
   e) Only (a) and (b) are correct.

Answer: (d)

All of the choices are true.

6. Which of the following is true?
   a) The rate of a reaction is always proportional to the concentration of the reactants.
   b) The activation energy of a reaction is constant with respect to temperature.
   c) The rate constant is constant with respect to temperature.
   d) A reaction with a large negative ΔG° will occur at a faster rate.
   e) For the second-order reaction 2A → B + C, we can calculate the rate constant using a plot of ln([A]) versus time.

Answer: (b)

The activation energy required for a chemical reaction is temperature independent. ΔG° is only associated with equilibrium conditions, not with kinetics conditions.

For the second-order reaction:

$R = -kA^2$

$\frac{dA}{dt} = -kA^2$

$\frac{dA}{A^2} = -kdt$

$\frac{1}{A} - \frac{1}{A_0} = kt$

7. A fast reaction should have a(n)
   a) high activation energy.
   b) catalyst present.
   c) large equilibrium constant.
   d) low activation energy.
   e) exothermic heat of reaction.

Answer: (d)

The lower the activation energy, the easier it is to break chemical bonds and the faster the chemical reactions are.

II. Rate Laws

$$A + B \rightarrow C + D$$
$$Rate = k[A]^n[B]^m$$
$$where\ k = Rate\ law\ constant;\ \ n, m = Reaction\ order$$

Examples: Given the following reactions and sample rates, find the rate law for the reaction.

1. $2N_2O_5 \rightarrow 4NO_2 + O_2$

$[N_2O_5]$(M)	Rate (mole/L·s)
90 M	5.4×10^{-4}
45 M	2.7×10^{-4}

Since rate doubles when concentration doubles, the order of reaction with respect to $[N_2O_5]$ is one.

Rate = k × $[N_2O_5]$

2. $NH_4^+ + NO_2^- \rightarrow N_2 + 2H_2O$

$[NH_4^+]$(M)	$[NO_2^-]$(M)	Rate(mole/L·s)
0.100 M	.0050 M	1.35×10^{-7}
0.100 M	.0100 M	2.70×10^{-7}
0.200 M	.0100 M	5.40×10^{-7}

When $[NO_2^-]$ is doubled, rate is also doubled. When $[NH_4^+]$ is doubled, rate is doubled as well. Therefore, both orders of reaction are 1.

Rate = k × $[NH_4^+]$ × $[NO_2^-]$

3. $BrO_3^- + 5Br^- + 6H^+ \rightarrow 3Br_2 + 3H_2O$

10	10	.10	8.0×10^{-4}
20	10	.10	1.6×10^{-3}
20	20	.10	3.2×10^{-3}
10	10	.20	3.2×10^{-3}

When either $[BrO_3^-]$ or $[Br^-]$ is doubled, the rate is doubled.

When $[H^+]$ is doubled, the rate is quadrupled.

Rate = k × $[BrO_3^-]$ × $[Br^-]$ × $[H^+]^2$

Section Practice

1. Which of the following rate laws has a rate constant with units of L^2 $mole^{-2}$ s^{-1}?
   a) Rate = k [A]
   b) Rate = k $[A]^2$
   c) Rate = k [A] [B]
   d) Rate = k $[A][B]^2$
   e) Rate = k $[A]^0$

Answer: (d)

$$\frac{Rate}{K} = \frac{Mole\ L^{-1}\ s^{-1}}{L^2\ Mole^{-2}\ s^{-1}} = \frac{Mole^3}{L^3}$$

The reaction must be a 3rd order reaction.

2. CO_2 is produced at rate of 2.2×10^{-2} mole L^{-1} s^{-1} in the following reaction:
   $$2C_6H_6(g) + 15O_{2(g)} \rightarrow 12CO_2(g) + 6H_2O(l)$$
   What is the rate at which O_2 is consumed?
   a) 2.2×10^{-2} mole L^{-1} s^{-1}
   b) 1.3×10^{-1} mole L^{-1} s^{-1}
   c) 2.8×10^{-2} mole L^{-1} s^{-1}
   d) 1.8×10^{-3} mole L^{-1} s^{-1}
   e) -2.2×10^{-2} mole L^{-1} s^{-1}

Answer: (c)

$O_2 : CO_2 = 15 : 12$
$= x : 2.2 \times 10^{-2}$

$x = 2.8 \times 10^{-2}$ mole L^{-1} s^{-1}

3. If a reactant's concentration is doubled and the reaction rate increases by a factor of 8, the exponent for that reactant in the rate law should be
   a) 0
   b) 1
   c) 2
   d) 3
   e) ½

Answer: (d)

$2^3 = 8$

4. Based on the following reaction and rate data:
   $$A(g) + B(g) \rightarrow \text{products}$$

Experiment	[A] (mol/L)	[B] (mol/L)	Initial rate (M/s)
1	0.06	0.01	0.04
2	0.03	0.01	0.04
3	0.03	0.02	0.08

What is the order of reaction with respect to A?
   a) 0
   b) 1
   c) 2
   d) 3
   e) 4

Answer: (a)

The reaction rate does not change when [A] is reduced is halved.
Rate $\propto [A]^0$

5. For the reaction A + B → C, determine the order of reaction with respect to B from the information given below:

$[A]_o$(M)	$[B]_o$(M)	Initial Rate (M/s)
1	1	2
1	2	8.1
2	2	15.9

a) Zeroth order
b) First order
c) Second order
d) Third order
e) Fourth order

Answer: (C)

Doubling [B], the rate in the reaction quadruples.

Rate $\propto [B]_o^2$

6. A sample of the unstable isotope ^{20}Na is generated in the laboratory. Initially, 2.40 moles of the isotope are detected. After 0.30 seconds, 0.30 moles of ^{20}Na are detected. Which of the following is the half-life for this reaction?
a) 0.10 seconds
b) 0.15 seconds
c) 0.20 seconds
d) 0.25 seconds
e) 0.30 seconds

Answer: (a)

$\frac{2.4}{0.3} = 8 = 2^3$

3 half-lives have passed in 0.3 seconds. One half-life is 0.1 seconds.

III. Reaction Mechanisms

A reaction mechanism is the series of steps which produce a chemical reaction. The steps must add up to the overall balanced equation of the reaction; no matter can be created or destroyed.

In the equation below:

$$\begin{array}{ll} NO_2 + NO_2 \rightarrow NO_3 + NO & \text{(slow)} \\ \underline{NO_3 + CO \rightarrow NO_2 + CO_2} & \underline{\text{(fast)}} \\ NO_2 + CO \rightarrow NO + CO_2 & \end{array}$$

The rate law for this equation is Rate = $k[NO_2]^2$ because the coefficient of NO_2 is 2. Thus, if $[NO_2]$ is doubled, the rate is quadrupled.

Rate Law Determined by the Reaction Mechanism

i. The rate law is based on the reaction mechanism.
ii. The sum of the steps must equal the overall balanced equation.
iii. The mechanisms must agree with the experimentally proven rate law.
iv. The rate determining step is the slowest step in the reaction. The slowest step bottlenecks the rate of the reaction.

Example: For the chemical reaction $2NO + Br_2 \rightarrow 2NOBr$, the following mechanism was proposed:

$$\begin{array}{ll} Br_2 + NO \rightarrow NOBr_2 & \text{(slow)} \\ NOBr_2 + NO \rightarrow 2NOBr & \text{(fast)} \end{array}$$

Find the rate law for this reaction.

Answer: Based on the slowest step in the reaction, the rate is:
Rate = $k \times [Br_2] \times [NO]$

Example: The proposed mechanism for the depletion of O_3 in the upper atmosphere is shown below:

Step 1: $O_3 + Cl \rightarrow O_2 + ClO$
Step 2: $ClO + O \rightarrow Cl + O_2$

a. Write a balanced equation for the overall reaction represented by steps 1 and 2.
Answer: $O_3 + O \rightarrow 2O_2$

b. Clearly identify the intermediate in the mechanism above.
Answer: The intermediate is ClO and Cl is a catalyst.

c. If the rate law for the overall reaction is found to be Rate = $k[O_3][Cl]$, what is the rate determining step of the reaction and what is the overall order of the reaction?

Answer: The rate determining step determines the rate equation, so1st step is the rate determining step. The overall order of the reaction is 1 since [Cl] stays almost constant.

Section Practice

1. In a multistep chemical process, the rate-limiting step is the step with the
   a) highest activation energy and fastest reaction rate.
   b) highest activation energy and slowest reaction rate.
   c) lowest activation energy and fastest reaction rate.
   d) lowest activation energy and slowest reaction rate.
   e) greatest concentration of the reactants and products.

Answer: (b)

The rate limiting step has the slowest rate and highest activation energy.

2. The reaction between nitrogen monoxide and oxygen is shown below:

$$2NO(g) + O_2(g) \rightarrow 2NO_2(g)$$

One proposed mechanism is the following:

Step 1: $NO(g) + O_2(g) \rightarrow NO_2(g) + O(g)$ (slow)

Step 2: $NO(g) + O(g) \rightarrow NO_2(g)$ (fast)

Which of the following rate expressions best agrees with this possible mechanism?
   a) Rate = k [NO] [O]
   b) Rate = k [NO] $[O_2]$
   c) Rate = k $[NO]^2$ $[O_2]$
   d) Rate = k [NO] / $[O_2]$
   e) Rate = k [NO]/ [O]

Answer: (b)

The 1st step is the rate determining step.

R = k[NO]$[O_2]$

3. A catalyst increases the rate of a reaction by
   a) increasing the concentration of reactant(s).
   b) decreasing the concentration of the reactant(s).
   c) increasing the activation energy needed for the reaction.
   d) decreasing the activation energy needed for the reaction.
   e) increasing the collision rate among reactants.

Answer: (d)

A catalyst decreases the activation energy needed for a reaction to occur, and thus increases the rate of the reaction.

4. $CF_2Cl_2(g)$ undergoes the following decomposition when it absorbs a high-energy photon of light:

$$CF_2Cl_2(g) \rightarrow CF_2C1 + Cl$$

The following represents a proposed mechanism for ozone destruction:

Step 1: $O_3 + Cl \rightarrow O_2 + ClO$ (slow)
Step 2: $ClO + O \rightarrow Cl + O_2$ (fast)

Which of the following is NOT true with respect to this mechanism?

a) Cl is a catalyst for the destruction of ozone.
b) The rate equation is Rate = $k[O_3][Cl]$
c) Step 1 is the rate-limiting step for this reaction.
d) Increasing ClO will increase the reaction rate.
e) The balanced chemical reaction for the destruction of ozone by this mechanism is given by $O_3 + O \rightarrow 2O_2$.

Answer: (d)

ClO is an intermediate compound in this reaction and is not included in the rate equation.

5. Consider the following reaction mechanism:

Step 1: $M + X \rightarrow MX$
Step 2: $MX + A \rightarrow D + X$

The chemical species MX is a(n)

a) catalyst.
b) inhibitor.
c) final product.
d) reaction intermediate.
e) reactant.

Answer: (d)

MX is a reaction intermediate because it disappears from the final equation (cancels out when you add the two steps together).

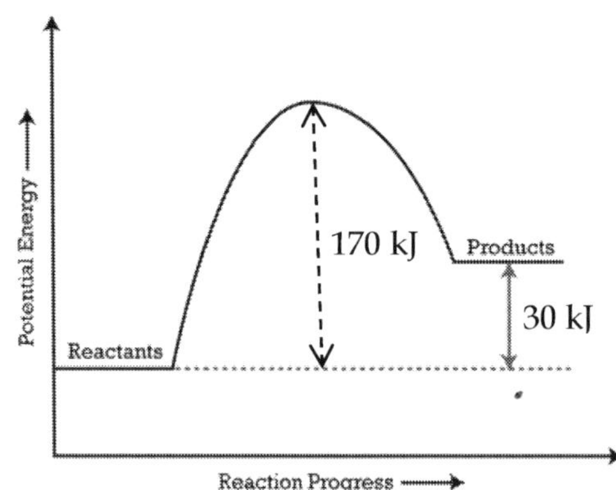

6. Consider the potential energy diagram above. The activation energy for the reverse reaction is

a) 30 kJ
b) 140 kJ
c) 170 kJ
d) 200 kJ
e) 205 kJ

Answer: (b)

170 – 30 = 140 kJ

7. The activated complex may be described as
   a) The compound at the maximum energy point along the reaction curve
   b) The shape of the molecules at the moment of collision
   c) The shape of the reaction product
   d) The phase (liquid, solid, or gas) in which the reaction takes place
   e) A coordination state

Answer: (a)

The activated complex is an intermediary compound that has the highest potential energy of any compound in the reaction.

8. The activated complex is a compound that is
   a) stable and has low potential energy.
   b) stable and has high potential energy.
   c) unstable and has low potential energy.
   d) unstable and has high potential energy.
   e) one of the reactants.

Answer: (d)

Activated complexes are unstable (hence why they are usually intermediate compounds) and have high potential energy.

9. Which combination of factors will affect the rate of the following reaction?
   $MgCO_3(s)+2HCl(aq) \rightarrow CO_2(g)+H_2O(l)+MgCl_2(aq)$
   a) Temperature and surface area only
   b) Temperature and concentration only
   c) Concentration and surface area only
   d) Temperature, concentration, and surface area only
   e) Concentration, surface area, and pressure only

Answer: (d)

Anything that changes the rate of collision and the activation energy needed, (i.e. temperature, concentration, and surface area), will affect the reaction rate.

Chapter 10 Chemical Kinetics SAT Questions

1. The half-life of radioactive sodium is 15.0 hours. How many hours would it take for a 64 g sample to decay to one-eighth of its original concentration?
   a) 3
   b) 15
   c) 30
   d) 45
   e) 60

Answer: (d)
$\frac{1}{8} = (\frac{1}{2})^3$
3 half-lives = 45 hours

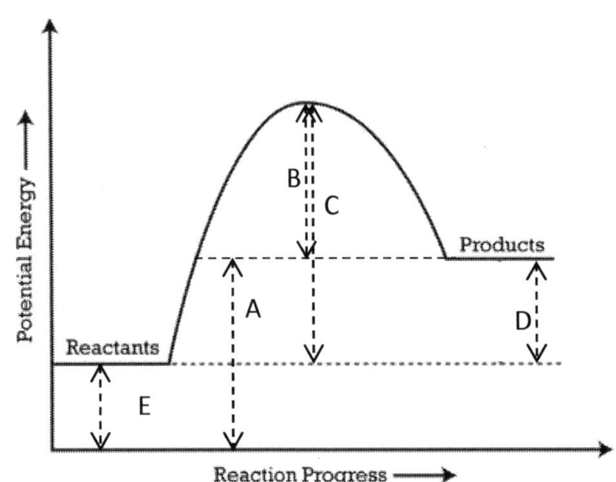

2. In the diagram above, which arrow represents the activation energy for the reverse reaction?
   a) A
   b) B
   c) C
   d) D
   e) None of the above

Answer: (b)
The activation energy for a reaction is the difference in potential energy of the highest-energy state and the energy state of the reactants. Thus, in the reverse reaction, the products will be the reactants, and B represents the difference.

3. The number of un-decayed nuclei in a sample of Bromine-87 is decreased by a factor of 4 over a period of 112 sec. What is the rate constant for the decay of bromine-87?
   a) 56 sec
   b) 6.93×10^{-1} sec^{-1}
   c) 1.24×10^{-2} sec^{-1}
   d) 6.19×10^{-3} sec^{-1}
   e) 3.1×10^{-3} sec^{-1}

Answer: (c)

A radioactive decay is a 1st order reaction.

$R = -k[A] = \frac{d[A]}{dt}$

$ln(\frac{A}{A_o}) = (-kt)$

$k = -\frac{ln(\frac{1}{4})}{112} = 0.0124\ s^{-1}$

4. At equilibrium,
    a) the forward reaction will continue.
    b) a change in conditions may shift the equilibrium.
    c) the reverse reaction will not continue.
    d) Both a) and b) are true.
    e) Both a) and c) are true.

Answer: (d)

At equilibrium, both the forward and the reserve reactions occur. A change in pressure, temperature, or concentration may shift the equilibrium. Thus, both (a) and (b) are true

5. The addition of a catalyst to a reaction
    a) changes the enthalpy.
    b) changes the entropy.
    c) changes the nature of the products.
    d) changes the activation energy needed.
    e) None of the above

Answer: (d)

A catalyst changes the intermediate paths of the reactions, which changes the activation energy of the reaction.

6. The reaction rate law applied to the limiting reaction aA + bB → AB gives the expression
    a) r $\propto [A]^b[B]^a$
    b) r $\propto [A]^a[AB]^b$
    c) r $\propto [A]^b[B]^a$
    d) r $\propto [A]^a[B]^b$
    e) r $\propto [AB]$

Answer: (d)

This is the rate law expression.

7. The heat of a reaction is best deduced from the
    a) activation energy
    b) orientation
    c) potential energy curve
    d) frequency
    e) activated complex

Answer: (c)

We can calculate the heat of reaction from the potential energy curve of the reaction.

8. A reaction in which the rate and the rate constant have the same units is
    a) radioactive decay.
    b) Second-order reaction.
    c) reaction with a one-step mechanism.
    d) first-order reaction.
    e) zeroth-order reaction.

Answer: (e)

Rate = K × $[A]^0$
For zeroth-order reactions, the rate is a constant.

9. Which of the following statements(s) is/are correct? Assume that in each case $\Delta H°$ closely approximates the overall energy change.
   I. For an endothermic reaction, E_a is always greater than $\Delta H°$.
   II. For an exothermic reaction, the magnitude of E_a is always greater than that of $\Delta H°$.
   III. For an exothermic reaction, adding a catalyst will decrease the magnitude of $\Delta H°$.
   a) I only
   b) II only
   c) I and II only
   d) II and III only
   e) I, II, and III

Answer: (a)

The activation energy is always higher than the $\Delta H°$ in an endothermic reaction (shown below).

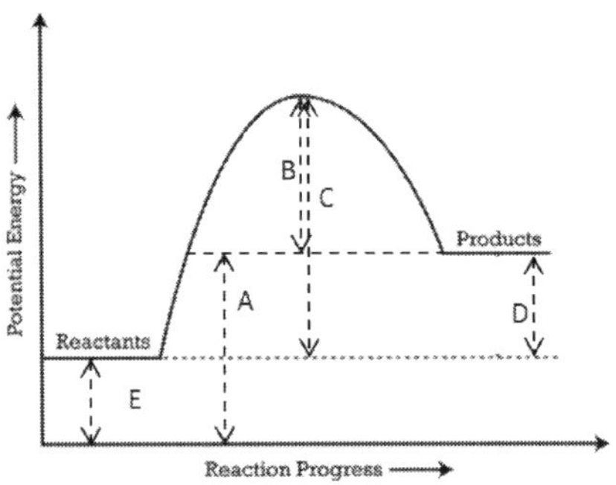

10. The collision theory explains the reaction rates of chemical reactions using which of the following?
   I. Activation energy q
   II. Molecule orientation
   III. Potential energy curve
   IV. Frequency of collisions
   V. Activated complex
   a) I and III only
   b) II only
   c) II and IV only
   d) IV only
   e) I, III, and V only

Answer: (c)

The collision theory describes the relationship between reaction rates and the frequency of molecular collisions and the orientation at which compounds collide.

11. The transition state theory explains the reaction rates of chemical reactions using which of the following?
   I. Activation energy
   II. Molecule orientation
   III. Potential energy curve
   IV. Frequency of collisions
   V. Activated complex
   a) I and III only
   b) III only
   c) III and V only
   d) IV only
   e) I, III, and V only

Answer: (e)

The transition state theory states that chemical reactions are always progressing in both the forward and reverse direction and in and out of various transition states.

12. A reaction in which the rate and the rate constant have the same units is
    a) radioactive decay.
    b) second-order reaction.
    c) reaction with a one-step mechanism.
    d) first-order reaction.
    e) zeroth-order reaction.

Answer: (e)

Rate = K × $[A]^0$
For zeroth-order reactions, the rate is a constant.

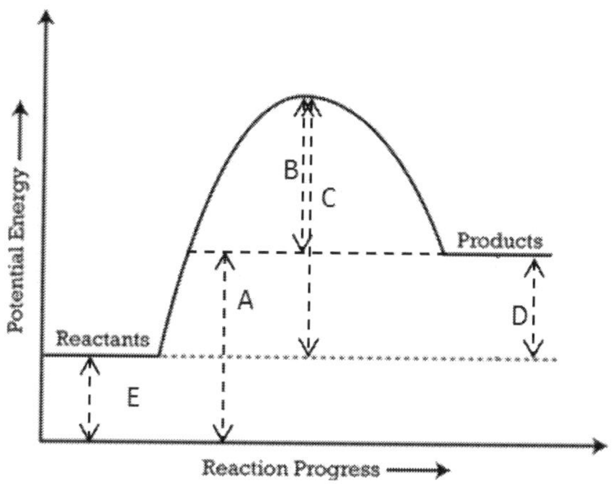

13. In the reaction described by the reaction profile above:
    a) Forward Ea > Reverse Ea and ΔH is exothermic
    b) Reverse Ea > Forward Ea and ΔH is endothermic
    c) Forward Ea < Reverse Ea and ΔH is exothermic
    d) Reverse Ea < Forward Ea and ΔH is endothermic
    e) Reverse Ea = Forward Ea and ΔH is zero

Answer: (d)

This is an endothermic reaction. The forward activation energy is C and reverse activation energy is C – D.

14. If the temperature of a reaction is raised from 300 K to 320 K, the reaction rate will increase by a factor of approximately
    a) 320/300
    b) 22/2
    c) 4
    d) 2
    e) 20

Answer: (c)

The reaction rate is approximately doubled for every 10 °C increase of temperature.

15. Addition of a catalyst to a reaction mixture will affect which part of the graph below?

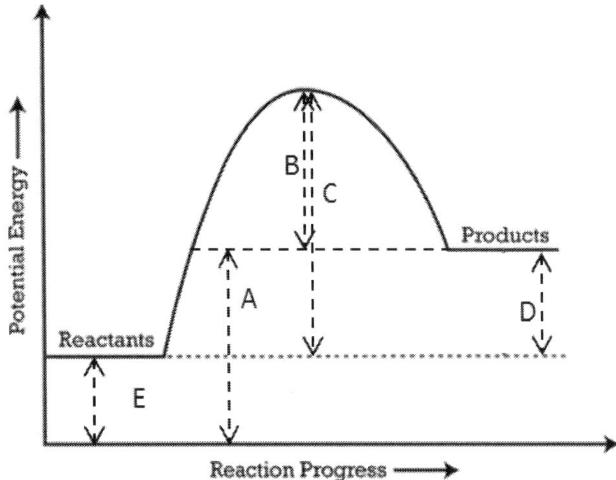

a) B
b) C
c) D
d) E
e) A

Answer: (c)

The addition of a catalyst to the reaction changes only the activation energy.

16. Which of the following is the LEAST effective in increasing the rate of a reaction?
    a) Increasing the pressure by adding an inert gas
    b) Grinding a solid reactant into small particles
    c) Increasing the temperature
    d) Eliminating reverse reactions
    e) Adding a catalyst

Answer: (a)

Adding an inert gas into a reaction chamber will not affect the collision frequency of the reactants.

17. When graphing the reciprocal of reactant concentration versus time, the graph will be a straight line for which of the following?
    a) zeroth-order reaction
    b) a first-order reaction
    c) a second-order reaction
    d) Both a) and c)
    e) a), b), and c)

Answer: (c)

0th order: $A = -kt + Ao$
1st order: $A = Ao\, e^{(-kt)}$
2nd order: $\frac{1}{A} = kt + \frac{1}{A_0}$

18. An Arrhenius plot is a graph of
    a) the rate constant versus concentration.
    b) the natural logarithm (ln) of the rate constant versus concentration.
    c) the reciprocal of the rate constant versus in temperature.
    d) the rate constant versus ln(1/T), where T is the temperature in K.
    e) the natural logarithm (ln) of the rate constant versus 1/T, where T is the temperature in K.

Answer: (e)

An Arrhenius plot displays the log of kinetic constants plotted against inverse temperature. Arrhenius plots are often used to analyze the effect of temperature on the rates of chemical reactions.

19. A rate law is found to be Rate = $k[A]^2[B]$. Which of the following actions will NOT change the initial reaction rate?
    a) Doubling the concentrations of both A and B
    b) Doubling the concentration of A and halving the concentration of B
    c) Halving the concentration of A and doubling the concentration of B
    d) Halving the concentration of A and quadrupling the concentration of B
    e) Doubling the concentration of A and quadrupling the concentration of B

Answer: (d)

$k[\frac{1}{2}A]^2\,[4B] = k[A]^2\,[B]$

20. Which of the following describes an endothermic reaction?
    a) Positive ΔH
    b) Negative ΔH
    c) Positive ΔG
    d) Negative ΔG
    e) Positive ΔS

Answer: (a)

The ΔH of an endothermic reaction is positive.

21. Which describes a spontaneous reaction?
    a) Positive ΔH
    b) Negative ΔH
    c) Positive ΔG
    d) Negative ΔG
    e) Positive ΔS

Answer: (d)

The ΔG of a spontaneous reaction is negative.

22. Which describes a nonspontaneous reaction?
    a) Positive ΔH
    b) Negative ΔH
    c) Positive ΔG
    d) Negative ΔG
    e) Positive ΔS

Answer: (c)

Positive ΔG indicates that the reaction is not spontaneous.

23. Which of the following is multiplied by temperature in K in the equation used to calculate free energy?
    a) Positive ΔH
    b) Negative ΔH
    c) Positive ΔG
    d) Negative ΔG
    e) Positive ΔS

Answer: (e)

$\Delta G = \Delta H - T\Delta S$

24. Which of the following increases the number of molecular effective collisions without increasing the average kinetic energy?
    a) An increase in the reaction concentration
    b) An increase in temperature
    c) A decrease in pressure
    d) Catalysis
    e) pH value

Answer: (a)

The higher the concentration of reactants, the higher of their collision frequency.

25. Which of the following decreases the activation energy?
    a) An increase in the reaction concentration
    b) An increase in temperature
    c) A decrease in pressure
    d) A catalysis
    e) A change in pH value

Answer: (d)

A catalyst can reduce the activation energy of the reaction.

26. Which of the following is the amount of energy that must be added to raise the temperature of 1 gram of a substance by 1 ^{o}C?
    a) Enthalpy change
    b) Entropy change
    c) Gibbs free energy change
    d) Activation energy
    e) Specific heat capacity

Answer: (e)

This is the definition of specific heat capacity.

27. Which of the following indicates a spontaneous reaction?
    a) Enthalpy change
    b) Entropy change
    c) Gibbs free energy change
    d) Activation energy
    e) Specific heat capacity

Answer: (c)

A negative Gibbs free energy change indicates a spontaneous reaction.

28. Which of the following values determines whether a reaction is endothermic or exothermic?
    a) Enthalpy change
    b) Entropy change
    c) Gibbs free energy change
    d) Activation energy
    e) Specific heat capacity

Answer: (a)

The enthalpy change (ΔH) indicates whether the reaction is an endothermic or an exothermic reaction.

Relationship Analysis Questions

	Statement	Reason	Answer
1.	When salt dissolves in water, ΔS is positive.	Aqueous ions have greater entropy than ions in solid form.	TTCE
2.	Reactions happen faster at higher temperatures.	As temperature increases, the number of collisions with the required activation energy also increases.	TTCE
3.	Increasing the temperature of a reaction increases the reaction rate.	At higher temperatures, molecules or atoms tend to be further apart.	TT
4.	Catalysts may speed up or slow down a reaction.	Catalysts change the energy released from a reaction.	TF
5.	Catalysts decrease the rate of a chemical reaction.	Catalysts decrease the activation energy needed for a reaction.	FT
6.	In the kinetic theory of gas, collisions between gas particles and the walls of container are considered elastic.	Gas molecules are considered volume-less particles that are in constant motion with no intermolecular forces.	TT
7.	The entropy of a solid increases when it is dissolved in a solvent.	The solid becomes less ordered.	TTCE
8.	The reaction of $BaCl_2$ and Na_2SO_4 does not go to completion.	The compound barium sulfate is formed in the reaction.	FT

	Statement I	Statement II	
9.	In a second-order reaction with one reactant, doubling the concentration of the reactant quadruples the rate.	The rate equation is Rate = $k[A]^2$ for such a reaction.	TTCE
10.	Adding more reactants will usually speed up a reaction.	The reactants will collide less frequently.	TF
11.	A catalyst changes the equilibrium of a reaction.	Catalysts can only lower the activation energy of the forward reaction.	FF
12.	The addition of a catalyst will decrease the ΔH for a reaction.	Catalysts provide alternate reaction paths with lower activation energy.	FT
13.	The activation energy of a reaction is decreased by a catalyst.	Catalysts are not used up in the reaction process.	TT

Chapter 11 Chemical Equilibrium

I. Equilibrium Conditions

Equilibrium is established when the rate of the forward reaction equals the rate of the reverse reaction.

$2H_2(g) + O_2(g) \leftrightarrow 2H_2O(g)$
Forward: $2H_2(g) + O_2(g) \rightarrow 2H_2O(g)$
Reverse: $2H_2O(g) \rightarrow 2H_2(g) + O_2(g)$

An equilibrium expression is shown below for the reaction aA + bB ↔ cC + dD, where K_{eq} is the equilibrium constant.

$$K_{eq} = \frac{[C]^c[D]^d}{[A]^a[B]^b}$$

Example: The reaction $2H_2O(g) \leftrightarrow 2H_2(g) + O_2(g)$ can be split into a forward reaction, $2H_2O(g) \rightarrow 2H_2(g) + O_2(g)$, and a reverse reaction, $2H_2(g) + O_2(g) \rightarrow 2H_2O(g)$. Write the equilibrium expression of this reaction.

Answer: $K_{eq} = \frac{[H_2]^2[O_2]}{[H_2O]^2}$

Pure solids and pure liquids are not included in equilibrium expressions. If you know K_{eq} you can use it to find out if a reaction is at equilibrium. For example, let's say that you start a reaction by mixing H_2 and I_2 gases. Say you know that K_{eq} is 125. You periodically measure the concentrations of H_2, I_2, and HI that are present. After 1 minute, the concentrations are as follows:

$H_2 + I_2 \rightarrow 2HI$

Compound	Concentration (M)
$[H_2]$	1 M
$[I_2]$	4 M
[HI]	8 M
$K_{eq} = 125$	$Q = (8^2)/4 = 16$

The reaction is not yet at equilibrium because the reaction quotient, Q, is not 125. Since 16 < 125, the reaction will proceed in a direction that causes an increase in the amount of product (the forward direction).

Section Practice

1. A change in which of the following conditions will cause a change in the equilibrium constant of the reaction?
   a) Temperature
   b) Pressure
   c) Volume
   d) Concentration of reactants
   e) Concentration of products

Answer: (a)

The equilibrium constant is associated only with the nature of the reaction and the temperature of the system.

2. For the reaction A + B ↔ C + D, the equilibrium constant can be expressed as:
   a) $K_{eq} = \frac{[A][B]}{[C][D]}$
   b) $K_{eq} = \frac{[C][B]}{[A][D]}$
   c) $K_{eq} = \frac{[C][D]}{[A][B]}$
   d) $K_{eq} = \frac{[A][B]}{[C][D]}$
   e) $K_{eq} = \frac{C \times D}{A \times B}$

Answer: (c)

This is the definition of the equilibrium constant.

3. The equilibrium expression for the reaction $BaSO_4(s) \leftrightarrow Ba^{+2}(aq) + SO_4^{-2}(aq)$ is equal to
   a) $[Ba^{+2}][SO_4^{-2}]$
   b) $\frac{[Ba^{+2}][SO_4^{-2}]}{BaSO_4}$
   c) $\frac{[Ba^{+2}]+[SO_4^{-2}]}{[BaSO_4]}$
   d) $\frac{[Ba^{+2}][SO_4^{-2}]^2}{BaSO_4}$
   e) $\frac{[BaSO_4]}{[Ba^{+2}][SO_4^{-2}]}$

Answer: (a)

Pure solids are not part of the equilibrium expression.

4. If $K_{eq} \gg 1$, the reaction
   a) the equilibrium mixture will favor products over reactants.
   b) the equilibrium mixture will favor reactants over products.
   c) will favor reactants and products equally.
   d) the reaction is irreversible.
   e) the reaction is spontaneous.

Answer: (a)

If $K_{eq} > 1$, the reaction will favor the reactants. If $K_{eq} < 1$, the reaction will favor the products. If $K_{eq} = 1$, the reaction will favor reactants and products equally.

5. Which of the following is an appropriate equilibrium expression for the following reaction?
$MgCO_3(s)+2HCl(g) \leftrightarrow MgCl_2(s)+CO_2(g)+H_2O(l)$
   a) $\frac{[CO_2]}{[HCl]}$
   b) $\frac{[MgCl_2][CO_2][H_2O]}{[HCl]^2[MgCO_3]}$
   c) $\frac{[HCl]^2[MgCO_3]}{[MgCl_2][CO_2][H_2O]}$
   d) $\frac{[CO_2]}{[HCl]^2}$
   e) $\frac{[CO_2][H_2O]}{[HCl]^2}$

Answer: (a)

Pure solids and liquids are not part of the equilibrium expression.

6. For which of the following reactions will $K_p = K_c$?
   a) $MgCO_3(s) + 2HCl(g) \leftrightarrow MgCl_2(s) + CO_2(g) + H_2O(l)$
   b) $C(s) + O_2(g) \leftrightarrow CO_2(g)$
   c) $CH_4(g) + 3O_2(g) \leftrightarrow CO_2(g) + 2H_2O(g)$
   d) $Zn(s) + 2HCl(aq) \leftrightarrow H_2(g) + ZnCl_2(aq)$
   e) $2NO_2(g) + O_2(g) \leftrightarrow N_2O_5(g)$

Answer: (b)

When the sum of the coefficients of the gaseous compounds on the reactant side is equal to the sum of the coefficients of the gaseous compounds on the product side, $K_p = K_c$.

7. After the equilibrium represented below is established, some pure H_2O vapor is injected into the reaction vessel at constant temperature and equilibrium is allowed to be reestablished. Which of the following values has decreased?

$$2H_2O_2(g) \leftrightarrow 2H_2O(g) + O_2(g)$$

   a) K_{eq}
   b) $[H_2O_2]$
   c) $[H_2O]$
   d) $[O_2]$
   e) The total pressure in the reaction vessel

Answer: (d)

The reaction shifts to the left.

II. Le Chatelier's Principle

If the conditions of a system are changed, a reaction at equilibrium will proceed in a direction that relieves the stress that was added.
The equilibrium concentrations may changes, but the equilibrium constant does not change unless the temperature changes.

Possible Stresses

i. **Temperature**

1. In an exothermic reaction, a temperature increase will cause the reaction to proceed to the left (increase the concentration of the reactants). In an endothermic reaction, a temperature increase will cause the reaction to proceed to the right (increasing the concentration of the products).
2. Increasing the temperature will increase the reaction rate.

ii. **Volume**

1. Decreasing the volume will increase the pressure and cause the reaction to proceed towards the side with fewer moles of gas.
2. Changing the volume does not change K_{eq}.

iii. **Pressure**

Pressure can be changed in two ways:

1. Changing the volume: Decreasing the volume will increase the pressure and cause the reaction to proceed towards the side with fewer moles of gas.
2. Adding an inert gas: Adding gas increases the pressure but does NOT change equilibrium concentrations.

iv. **Concentration**

If the concentration of a reactant is increased, the reaction shifts towards the products. If the concentration of a product is increased, the reaction shifts towards the reactants.

Example: What happens to the following reaction at equilibrium if…

$$2H_2(g) + O_2(g) + \text{Energy} \leftrightarrow 2H_2O(g)$$

1. $[H_2]$ increases?
   Answer: The reaction will proceed to the right to produce more products and use up the excess H_2.

2. $[H_2]$ decreases?
   Answer: The reaction will proceed to left to produce some of the H_2 that was lost.

3. Temperature increases?
   Answer: Because energy is a reactant, the reaction will proceed to the right to use up the energy.

4. Temperature decreases?
   Answer: Because energy is a reactant, the reaction will proceed to the left to produce some of the energy that was lost.

5. Pressure increases (or volume decreases)?
   Answer: The reaction will proceed to the side that produces fewer moles of gas, and equilibrium will shift to the right.

6. Pressure decreases (or volume increases)?
   Answer: The reaction will proceed to the side that produces more moles of gas, and equilibrium will shift to the left.

Section Practice

1. For the following reaction, which of the following will be true if the temperature of the system is decreased and pressure is held constant?
   $2NOBr(g) \leftrightarrow 2NO(g) + Br_2(g) \quad \Delta H^\circ = 16.1\ kJ/mol$
   a) K_{eq} will increase.
   b) The concentration of NO will increase.
   c) The concentration of Br_2 will decrease.
   d) The concentration of NOBr will decrease.
   e) The reaction $2NO(g) + Br_2(g) \leftrightarrow 2NOBr(g)$ will become endothermic.

Answer: (c)

When the temperature of the system is decreased, the equilibrium will shift to the left because the reaction is endothermic. The concentration of Br_2 will decrease.

2. Assume that the reaction below is initially at equilibrium. The pressure of the reaction vessel is increased by compression to a smaller volume at constant temperature. What will happen to the concentrations below and to K_{eq} once equilibrium is reached again.
   $2SO_3(g) \leftrightarrow 2SO_2(g) + O_2(g) \quad \Delta H = 197\ kJ$

	$[SO_3]$	$[SO_2]$	$[O_2]$	K_{eq}
(a)	Increase	Increase	Decrease	Same
(b)	Decrease	Increase	Increase	Increase
(c)	Increase	Decrease	Decrease	Decrease
(d)	Increase	Decrease	Increase	Same
(e)	Increase	Increase	Increase	Same

Answer: (e)

When pressure is increased, the equilibrium will shift to the side with fewer gas molecules, which is the left. But the concentration of each component is increased because of the smaller volume.

3. For the following reaction, which change will NOT be effective in increasing the amount of N_2O_4 (g)?

$$Heat + 2NO_2(g) \leftrightarrow N_2O_4(g)$$

   a) Decreasing the volume of the reaction vessel
   b) Increasing the temperature
   c) Adding N_2 to increase the pressure
   d) Absorbing the N_2O_4(g) with a solid absorbent
   e) Adding more NO_2(g) to the reaction vessel

Answer: (c)

Adding an inert gas will not shift the equilibrium.

4. Which of the following cases describes a reaction that is expected to be exothermic?
   a) Increasing the pressure increases the amount of product formed.
   b) Increasing the amount of reactant increases the amount of product formed.
   c) Increasing the temperature increases the amount of product formed.
   d) Increasing the volume decreases the amount of product formed.
   e) Increasing the temperature decreases the amount of product formed.

Answer: (e)

The equilibrium will shift to the left when increasing the temperature in an exothermic reaction.

5. Which of the following CANNOT affect the extent of a reaction?
   a) Changing the temperature
   b) Adding a catalyst
   c) Increasing the amount of reactant
   d) Removing some products
   e) Changing the volume

Answer: (b)

Adding a catalyst will not change the equilibrium conditions of a chemical reaction.

6. The Haber process is used to produce ammonia from nitrogen and hydrogen. This reaction could be forced to produce more ammonia by
   a) increasing the reaction pressure.
   b) decreasing the reaction pressure.
   c) adding a catalyst.
   d) Both b) and c).
   e) None of the above

Answer: (a)

$H_2 + N_2 \rightarrow NH_3$

Increasing the reaction pressure will shift the equilibrium of the (unbalanced) reaction above to the right.

7. An increase in pressure will change the equilibrium by
   a) shifting the reaction to the side resulting in a smaller volume results.
   b) shifting the reaction to the side resulting in a larger volume results.
   c) favoring the endothermic reaction.
   d) favoring the exothermic reaction.
   e) None of the above

Answer: (e)

Depends on how the pressure has been changed. For example, if the pressure is changed by adding an inert gas, no change will result.

8. Consider the system below at equilibrium. Which of the following changes will shift the equilibrium to the right?

$$H_2 + N_2 \rightarrow NH_3 + 92.94 \text{ kJ}$$

   I. Increasing the temperature
   II. Decreasing the temperature
   III. Increasing the pressure on the system
   a) I only
   b) II only
   c) III only
   d) I and III only
   e) II and III only

Answer: (e)

Decreasing the temperature and increasing the pressure will shift the equilibrium to the right.

9. A reaction at equilibrium may be forced to completion by
   a) adding a catalyst.
   b) increasing the pressure.
   c) increasing the temperature.
   d) removing the products from the reaction mixture as they are formed.
   e) decreasing the reactant concentration.

Answer: (d)

Removing the products from the reaction will shift the equilibrium to the right.

III. Solving Equilibrium Reaction Problems

i. Write a balanced equation for the chemical reaction and list the initial concentrations of reactants and products.

ii. Calculate the reaction quotient, Q, by using the initial concentrations. If the equilibrium constant, K_{eq}, is greater than the reaction quotient, Q, the reaction will proceed forward. If K_{eq} is less than Q, the reaction will proceed in the reverse direction. If Q is equal to K_{eq}, then the system is already at equilibrium.

iii. Set x as the change in concentration of one specie and find the changes in concentration of all other species in terms of x. Remember, mass cannot be created nor destroyed!

iv. Substitute the equilibrium concentration values (in terms of x) into the equilibrium constant expression and solve for x.

Example: $H_2O(g) + Cl_2O(g) \leftrightarrow 2HOCl(g)$

The equilibrium constant for the reaction above is 0.0900 at 25 °C.

For the following conditions, will the system be at equilibrium? If not, in which direction will the reaction shift?

1) $P_{H_2O} = 200\ torr, P_{Cl_2O} = 49.9\ torr,$ and $P_{HOCl} = 21.0\ torr$

$$Q = \frac{[HOCl]^2}{[H_2O][Cl_2O]} = \frac{21^2}{200 \times 49.8} = 0.0443 < 0.09$$

The reaction is not yet at equilibrium, so the reaction will shift to the right.

2) $P_{H_2O} = 1\ atm,\ P_{Cl_2O} = 1\ atm,$ and $P_{HOCl} = 1atm$

$$Q = \frac{[HOCl]^2}{[H_2O][Cl_2O]} = \frac{1^2}{1 \times 1} > 0.09$$

Q is greater than the equilibrium constant, so the reaction will shift to the left.

3) $P_{H_2O} = 296\ torr,\ P_{Cl_2O} = 15.0\ torr,$ and $P_{HOCl} = 20.0\ torr$

$$Q = \frac{[HOCl]^2}{[H_2O][Cl_2O]} = \frac{20^2}{296 \times 15} = 0.09 = K_p$$

The reaction is at equilibrium.

Example: The value of the equilibrium constant for the following reaction is 1.5×10^{-5} at 298K.

$$2HF(g) \leftrightarrow H_2(g) + F_2(g)$$

If the [HF] = 2.0M, what are the final concentrations of all species once equilibrium is established?

$2HF(g) \leftrightarrow H_2(g) + F_2(g)$
2.0 0 0 (initial)
$2-2x$ x x (at equilibrium)

$$K_p = 1.5 \times 10^{-5} = \frac{x^2}{(2-2x)^2}$$

$$\frac{x}{2-2x} = 0.00387$$
$x = 0.0077$
$[HF] = 2 - 2 \times 0.0077 = 1.9846$ M
$[H_2] = [F_2] = 0.0077$ M

Example: $PCl_5(g) \leftrightarrow PCl_3(g) + Cl_2(g)$

Phosphorus pentachloride at initial partial pressure of 189.2 torr was placed into an empty flask and allowed to decompose into PCl_3 and Cl_2 by the reaction above at 557K.

At equilibrium, the total pressure inside the flask was observed to be 358.7 torr. Calculate the partial pressure of each gas at equilibrium and the value of K_p at 557 K.

$PCl_5(g) \leftrightarrow PCl_3(g) + Cl_2(g)$
189.2 0 0
$189.2 - x$ x x

189.2 $-x + x + x =$ *358.7*

$x = 169.5$ torr

$$K_p = \frac{169.5 \times 169.5}{189.2 - 169.5} = 1458 \text{ torr}$$

Section Practice

1. The reaction $2NO_2(g) \leftrightarrow N_2O_4(g)$ has an equilibrium constant of 4.5×10^3 at a certain temperature. What is the equilibrium constant of $2N_2O_4(g) \leftrightarrow 4NO_2(g)$ at the same temperature?
   a) 5×10^{-8}
   b) 4500
   c) 2.2×10^{-4}
   d) 2.0×10^{7}
   e) 5×10^{8}

Answer: (a)

$$K = \frac{[NO_2]^4}{[N_2O_4]^2} = \left(\frac{1}{4.5 \times 10^3}\right)^2$$
$= 5 \times 10^{-8}$

2. The solubility of $AuCl_3$ is 1.0×10^{-4} g L^{-1}. What is the solubility product constant of $AuCl_3$, which has a molar mass of 303 g/mol?
   a) 1.00×10^{-16}
   b) 2.7×10^{-15}
   c) 1.2×10^{-26}
   d) 3.2×10^{-25}
   e) 9.6×10^{-25}

Answer: (d)

$AuCl_3 \rightarrow Au^{3+} + 3Cl^-$

$x \quad 3x$

Let x be the concentration of Au^{3+} at equilibrium (and 3x the concentration of Cl^-).

$x = \frac{1.0 \times 10^{-4}/303}{1} = 3.3 \times 10^{-7}$

$K_{sp} = [x][3x]^3 = 3.2 \times 10^{-25}$

3. One liter of solution contains 2.4×10^{-3} moles of sulfate ions. What is the molar solubility of $BaSO_4$ in this solution? ($K_{sp} = 1.1 \times 10^{-10}$ for $BaSO_4$)
   a) 1.05×10^{-5}
   b) 1.1×10^{-9}
   c) 2.6×10^{-13}
   d) 2.2×10^{7}
   e) 4.6×10^{-8}

Answer: (e)

$BaSO_4 \rightarrow Ba^{2+} + SO_4^{2-}$

$x \quad x + 2.4 \times 10^{-3}$

Let x be the concentration of Ba^{2+} at equilibrium (and $x + 2.4 \times 10^{-3}$ the concentration of SO_4^{2-}).

$K_{sp} = 1.1 \times 10^{-10} = [x][x+0.0024]$

$x + 0.0024 \approx 0.0024$ *for small x.*

$x = \frac{1.1 \times 10^{-10}}{0.0024} = 4.58 \times 10^{-8}$ M

4. For the reaction $2NO_2(g) \leftrightarrow N_2O_4(g)$ ($K_p = 8.8$), under which of the following conditions will the reaction proceed in the forward direction?

	$NO_2(g)$	$N_2O_4(g)$
(a)	0.2 atm	0.352 atm
(b)	250 mm Hg	400 mm Hg
(c)	0.00255 atm	0.000134 atm
(d)	46.5 mm Hg	82.3 mm Hg
(e)	0.138 atm	0.764 atm

Answer: (b)

$Q = \frac{N_2O_4}{NO_2^2}$

Convert all pressures to atm.

(a) $\frac{0.352}{0.2^2} = 8.8 = K_p$

The reaction is at equilibrium.

(b) $\frac{\frac{400}{760}}{\left(\frac{250}{760}\right)^2} = 4.86 < K_p$

The reaction will move forward.

(c) $\frac{0.000134}{0.00255^2} = 20.6 > K_p$

The reaction will shift to the left.

(d) $\frac{82.3/760}{\left(\frac{46.5}{760}\right)^2} = 29 > K_p$

The reaction will shift to the left.

(e) $\frac{0.764}{0.138^2} = 40.1 > K_p$

The reaction will shift to the left.

5. The weak acid H_2A ionizes in two steps with these equilibrium constants:

$$H_2A \leftrightarrow H^+ + HA^- \quad K_{a1} = 2.3 \times 10^{-4}$$
$$HA^- \leftrightarrow H+ + A^{-2} \quad K_{a2} = 4.5 \times 10^{-7}$$

What is the equilibrium constant for the following reactions?

$$H_2A \leftrightarrow 2H^+ + A^{2-}$$

a) 6.8×10^{-11}
b) 1.0×10^{-10}
c) 2.3045×10^{-4}
d) 2.0×10^{-3}
e) 5.1×10^{2}

Answer: (b)

$H_2A \rightarrow H^+ + HA^-$
$+ HA^- \rightarrow H+ + A^{-2}$
$H_2A \rightarrow 2H^+ + A^{2-}$

$K = K_{a1} \times K_{a2} = 2.3 \times 10^{-4} \times 4.5 \times 10^{-7} = 1.0 \times 10^{-10}$

6. In an experiment, 0.0300 moles each of $SO_3(g)$, $SO_2(g)$, and $O_2(g)$ were placed in a 10.0 L flask at a certain temperature. When the reaction reached equilibrium, the concentration of $SO_2(g)$ in the flask was 3.5×10^{-5} M. What is K_c for the following reaction?

$$2SO_2(g) + O_2(g) \leftrightarrow 2SO_3(g)$$

a) 3.5×10^{-5}
b) 1.9×10^{7}
c) 5.2×10^{5}
d) 1.2×10^{9}
e) 8.2×10^{8}

Answer: (b)

$2SO_2(g) + O_2(g) \rightarrow 2SO_3(g)$
0.003 0.003 0.003
0.003−2x 0.003−x
0.003+2x

$$K_c = \frac{[0.003+2x]^2}{[0.003-2x]^2[0.003-x]}$$

$0.003 - 2x = 3.5 \times 10^{-5}$
$x = 0.00148$
$K_c = 1.9 \times 10^{7}$

7. What is the concentration of the Ag^+ ion in a saturated solution of AgCl? (K_{sp} for AgCl is 1.7×10^{-10}.)

a) 1.7×10^{-10} M
b) 3.4×10^{-10} M
c) 1.3×10^{-5} M
d) 2.6×10^{-5} M
e) 5.2×10^{-5} M

Answer: (c)

$AgCl \rightarrow Ag^+ + Cl^-$
x x
$x^2 = 1.7 \times 10^{-10}$
$x = 1.3 \times 10^{-5}$

8. The K_{sp} of AgCl is 1.0×10^{-10} and the K_{sp} of AgI is 8.3×10^{-17}. A solution has ~~0.1 M of I-~~ and 0.1 M of Cl^-. What is the molarity of the iodide ions when AgCl just starts to precipitate?

a) 1.0×10^{-5}
b) 9.1×10^{-9}
c) 8.3×10^{-13}
d) 8.3×10^{-8}
e) 1.2×10^{4}

Answer: (d)

Since K_{sp} of AgI is smaller, AgI will be precipitated first until $[Ag^+][Cl^-] = K_{sp}$ of AgCl.
$[Ag^+][0.1] = 1.0 \times 10^{-10}$
$[Ag^+] = 1.0 \times 10^{-9}$
$[Ag^+][I^-] = 8.3 \times 10^{-17}$
$1.0 \times 10^{-9} \times [I^-] = 8.3 \times 10^{-17}$
$[I^-] = 8.3 \times 10^{-8}$

Chapter 11 Chemical Equilibrium SAT Questions

1. The concentrations in an equilibrium expression have units of
   a) mole/mL.
   b) g/L.
   c) gram.
   d) mole/L.
   e) g/mL.

Answer: (d)

The concentrations in an equilibrium expression are measured using molarity, or mole/L.

2. In the Haber process for making ammonia, an increase in pressure favors
   a) the forward reaction.
   b) the reverse reaction.
   c) neither direction.
   d) either a forward or reverse reaction depending on the temperature of the system.
   e) either a forward or reverse reaction depending on the volume.

Answer: (a)

$3H_2 + N_2 \leftrightarrow 2NH_3$

An increase in pressure will move the equilibrium to the right to reduce the total pressure.

3. If $Ca(OH)_2$ is dissolved in a solution of NaOH, its solubility compared to that of $Ca(OH)_2$ in pure water is
   a) higher.
   b) lower.
   c) unaffected.
   d) uncertain.
   e) higher, then lower.

Answer: (b)

The solubility of $Ca(OH)_2$ in water will be greater than its solubility in a solution with a high concentration OH^-.

4. The following reaction is at equilibrium in a 1 L flask at 25 °C:

$$P_4(g) + 5O_2(g) \leftrightarrow P_4O_{10}(g)$$

If 0.25 moles of oxygen are added to the flask, which of the following is/are true?

I. $[P_4]$ will increase.
II. $[P_4O_{10}]$ will increase.
III. $[O_2]$ will decrease.

   a) I only
   b) II only
   c) I and II only
   d) II and III only
   e) I, II, and III

Answer: (d)

When 0.25 moles of O_2 are added to the flask, the equilibrium shifts to the right. Therefore, $[P_4O_{10}]$ increases and $[P_4]$ decreases.
$[O_2]$ increases even though the equilibrium shifts to the right because a large quantity of oxygen was added to the flask.

5. Which of the following is NOT true?
   a) The molar solubility of CaF_2 ($K_{sp} = 4.0 \times 10^{-11}$) is less than that of BaF_2 ($K_{sp} = 2.4 \times 10^{-5}$).
   b) The solubility of $MnCO_3$ will be higher in an acidic solution than in a basic solution.
   c) The solubility of AgCl will be higher in an acidic solution than in a basic solution.
   d) The solubility of Ag_3PO_4 will be lower in a basic solution than in an acidic solution.
   e) The solubility of $Ca(OH)_2$ will be lower in a basic solution than in an acidic solution.

Answer: (c)

Normally, an acidic compound will increase its solubility in a basic solution, but decrease its solubility in an acidic solution. On the contrary, a basic compound will increase its solubility in an acidic solution, but decrease its solubility in a basic solution.

6. Assume that the reaction below is initially at equilibrium. The temperature is increased from 25 °C to 75 °C. How would these changes affect the concentrations below once a new equilibrium is established?

$2SO_3(g) \leftrightarrow 2SO_2(g) + O_2(g) \quad \Delta H = 197\ kJ$

	$[SO_3]$	$[SO_2]$	$[O_2]$	K_{eq}
a)	Increase	Increase	Decrease	
b)	Decrease	Increase	Increase	Increase
c)	Increase	Decrease	Decrease	Decrease
d)	Increase	Decrease	Increase	
e)	Increase	Increase	Increase	

Answer: (b)

A positive ΔH indicates that this is an endothermic reaction. The increase in temperature will shift the equilibrium to the right, therefore increasing the equilibrium constant.

7. The effect of temperature on a system at equilibrium is best described by
   I. K_a
   II. K_{sp}
   III. Q
   IV. K_c
   V. Le Chatelier's principle
   a) I and III only
   b) II only
   c) III and V only
   d) IV only
   e) V only

Answer: (e)

Le Chatelier's principle can be used to determine the effect of a change in conditions on an equilibrium system.

8. Which of the following may be described as being in a state of chemical equilibrium?
   a) Chemical reactions
   b) Acids and bases
   c) Solubility
   d) Both a) and c)
   e) a), b), and c)

Answer: (e)

a), b), and c) are all correct.

9. Which of the following is/are most useful in determining the solubility of a substance?
   I. K_a
   II. K_{sp}
   III. Q
   IV. K_c
   V. Le Chatelier's principle
   a) I and III only
   b) II only
   c) III and V only
   d) IV only
   e) V only

Answer: (b)

K_{sp} is the solubility equilibrium constant.

10. A chemical system at equilibrium will
    a) have the same concentrations of all products and reactants.
    b) form more products if the temperature is increased and the system is allowed to reestablish equilibrium.
    c) maintain a constant ratio of product concentration(s) to reactant concentration(s).
    d) not have any precipitates.
    e) represent a spontaneous chemical process.

Answer: (c)

A chemical system at equilibrium will follow the equilibrium constant calculations.

11. What are the units of the equilibrium constant, K_c, for the following reaction ?

$$CH_4(g) + 3O_2(g) \rightarrow CO_2(g) + 2H_2O(g)$$

    a) M^{-2}
    b) M^2
    c) M
    d) M^{-1}
    e) M^3

Answer: (d)

$$Kc = \frac{[H_2O]^2[CO_2]}{[CH_4][O_2]^3} = \frac{1}{M}$$

12. A reaction has a very large equilibrium constant of 3.3×10^{13}. Which of the following statement is NOT true about this reaction?
    a) The reaction will be very fast.
    b) The reaction will essentially run to completion.
    c) The reaction is spontaneous.
    d) The equilibrium constant will change if the temperature is changed.
    e) The products will react to yield very little reactant.

Answer: (a)

Reaction rates and equilibrium constants are not directly related.

13. $BaCl_2$ dissociates in water to release one Ba^{2+} ion and two Cl^- ions. If an HCl solution is added to this solution, then
   a) $[Ba^{2+}]$ increases.
   b) $[OH^-]$ increases.
   c) $[Ba^{2+}]$ remains constant.
   d) $[H^+]$ decreases.
   e) the number of moles of un-dissociated $BaCl_2$ increases.

Answer: (e)

By adding extra Cl^- to the solution, the solubility of $BaCl_2$ will be reduced.

14. Consider the following reaction:

$$H_2(g) + Br_2(g) \leftrightarrow 2HBr(g)$$

The concentrations of H_2, Br_2, and HBr are 0.05 M, 0.03 M, and 500.0 M, respectively. The equilibrium constant for this reaction at the current temperature is 2.5×10^3. Is this system at equilibrium?
   a) Yes, the system is at equilibrium.
   b) No, the reaction must shift to the right in order to reach equilibrium.
   c) No, the reaction must shift to the left in order to reach equilibrium.
   d) It cannot be determined.
   e) The reaction will never be at equilibrium.

Answer: (c)

$K_c = \frac{[HBr]^2}{[H_2][Br_2]} = \frac{500^2}{0.05 \times 0.03} = 1.67 \times 10^8 > 2.5 \times 10^3$

The system is not at equilibrium yet, so the reaction must shift to the left.

15. An increase in pressure in the reaction $2HI(g) \leftrightarrow H_2(g) + I_2(g)$ will
   a) produce more $I^-(aq)$.
   b) produce more H_2.
   c) not affect the system.
   d) drive it to the right.
   e) drive it to the left.

Answer: (c)

An increase in pressure will not change the equilibrium conditions because the concentration of gas molecules on the reactants side is the same as that of the products side.

16. Which of the following is true for a liquid/gas mixture at equilibrium?
   a) The equilibrium constant is dependent on temperature.
   b) The amount of gas present at equilibrium is independent of pressure.
   c) All interchanging of elements between liquid and gas phases has ceased.
   d) All of the above
   e) None of the above

Answer: (a)

Only (a) is true.

17. In the following equilibrium reaction taking place in a closed container, how could the forward reaction rate be increased?

$$A + B \leftrightarrow AB + Heat$$

I. Increasing [AB]
II. Increasing [A]
III. Reducing [AB]

a) I only
b) III only
c) I and III only
d) II and III only
e) I, II, and III

Answer: (d)

By increasing [A] and [B] or removing [AB]], the reaction will shift to the right.

18. Which of the following statements best describes the condition(s) needed for a successful formation of a product in a chemical reaction?
    a) The collision of reactants must involve a sufficient amount of energy to overcome the activation energy.
    b) The relative orientation of the particles has little or no effect on the formation of the product.
    c) The relative orientation of the particles has an effect only if the kinetic energy of the particles is below some minimum value.
    d) The relative orientation of the particles must allow for formation of new bonds in the product.
    e) The energy of the incoming particles must be above a certain minimum value and the relative orientation of the particles must allow for formation of new bonds in the product.

Answer: (a)

This is the collision theory that qualitatively explains how chemical reactions occur and why reaction rates differ for different reactions.

19. A catalyzed pathway in a reaction mechanism has a _____ activation energy and thus causes a _____ reaction rate than its non-catalyzed counterpart.
    a) higher, lower
    b) higher, higher
    c) lower, higher
    d) lower, steady
    e) higher, steady

Answer: (c)

A catalyst can change the pathway of a chemical reaction so that the activation energy of the reaction is lowered and the reaction rate is increased.

20. Write the equilibrium expression for the following reaction:

Answer: (b)

$$2A + B \rightarrow 3C + D$$

This is the expression of the equilibrium constant.

a) $[A]^2[B][D]$

b) $\frac{[C]^3[D]}{[A]^2[B]}$

c) $\frac{[2C][D]}{[2A][B]}$

d) $\frac{[D]}{[A]^2[B]}$

e) $\frac{[A]^2[B]}{[C]^3[D]}$

21. At a given temperature, if the equilibrium constant for the reaction, $H_2 + Cl_2 \leftrightarrow 2HCl$, is K_p, the equilibrium constant for the reaction, $HCl \leftrightarrow \frac{1}{2}H_2 + \frac{1}{2}Cl_2$ can be represented as

    a) $\frac{1}{K_{p2}}$.

    b) K_p^2.

    c) $\frac{1}{\sqrt{K_p}}$.

    d) $\sqrt{K_p}$.

    e) K_p^3.

Answer: (c)

$HCl \leftrightarrow \frac{1}{2}H_2 + \frac{1}{2}Cl_2$

$K_{eq} = (\frac{1}{K_p})^{1/2} = \frac{1}{\sqrt{K_p}}$

Relationship Analysis Questions

1.	At equilibrium, the concentrations of reactants and products remain constant.	At equilibrium, the rates of the forward and reverse reactions are equal.	TTCE
2.	A system is at equilibrium when the rate of the forward reaction is equal to the rate of the reverse reaction.	At equilibrium, the concentration of the products is equal to that of the reactants.	TF
3.	The reaction of barium chloride with sodium sulfate will not go to completion.	The compound barium sulfate is formed as an insoluble precipitate.	FT
4.	In a reaction that has both a forward and a reverse reaction ($A + B \leftrightarrow AB$),	The reverse reaction does not begin until equilibrium is reached.	TF

	when A and B (and no other species) are introduced into a vessel, the forward reaction rate is the highest at the beginning and begins to decrease from that point until equilibrium is reached.		
5.	In the system where $N_2(g) + O_2(g) \leftrightarrow NO(g)$ is at equilibrium, decreasing the pressure will not cause a shift in position of the equilibrium.	There is no net change in the number of moles of gas from one side of the reaction to another.	TTCE
6.	At equilibrium, the forward reaction and reverse reaction stop.	At equilibrium, the reactants and products have reached the equilibrium concentrations.	FT
7.	When the temperature of a reaction at equilibrium is increased, the equilibrium will shift to favor the endothermic direction.	Endothermic reactions involve heat acting as a reactant and Le Chatelier's principle states that an equilibrium shift will occur to offset temperature changes.	TTCE
8.	In an equilibrium reaction, if the concentration of the reactants is increased, the forward reaction rate will increase.	When a stress is applied to a reaction at equilibrium, the equilibrium shifts in the direction that alleviates the stress.	TTCE
9.	The reaction of HCl(aq) and KOH(aq) goes to completion.	This is a neutralization reaction between a strong acid and a strong base.	TTCE

Chapter 12 Acid - Base Titration and pH

I. Properties of Acids and Bases

Properties of Acids

i. Aqueous acid solutions taste sour.

ii. Some acids react with active metals to release hydrogen.

$$Zn(s) + H_2SO_4(aq) \rightarrow ZnSO_4(aq) + H_2(g)$$

iii. Acids react with bases to produce salts and water.

$$HCl(aq) + NaOH(aq) \rightarrow NaCl(aq) + H_2O(l)$$

Properties of Bases

i. Aqueous solutions of bases have a bitter taste.

ii. Dilute aqueous solutions of bases feel slippery.

iii. Bases react with acids to produce salts and water.

Properties of Both Acids and Bases

i. Both acids and bases conduct electricity.

ii. Both cause acid-base indicators to change color.

Naming Acid Compounds

i. Binary acids are acids that contain hydrogen atoms and a very electronegative element.

1. prefix "hydro-"
2. Root of element name
3. "-ic" ending

Such as HBr = hydrobromic acid

ii. Oxyacids are acids that contain hydrogen, oxygen, and a third element, usually a nonmetal.

Rules for Naming Oxyacids

Description	Rule	Example
The oxyacid containing the ion with one more oxygen than the ion with the "ate" prefix	Prefix: "per" Suffix: "ic"	Ion: ClO_4^- Formula: $HClO_4$ Name: perchloric acid
The oxyacid containing the ion with the "ate" prefix	Suffix: "ic"	Ion: ClO_3^- Formula: $HClO_3$ Name: chloric acid
The oxyacid containing the ion with the "ite" prefix	Suffix: "ous"	Ion: ClO_2^- Formula: $HClO_2$ Name: chlorous acid

The oxyacid containing the ion with one less oxygen than the "ite" ion.	Prefix: "hypo" Suffix: "ous"	Ion: ClO Formula: HClO Name: hypochlorous acid

Some Common Industrial Acids

i. H_2SO_4 - Sulfuric Acid

1. Used in making fertilizer, paper, petroleum products, and car batteries
2. Most commonly produced chemical in the U. S.

ii. HNO_3 - Nitric Acid

1. Unstable, volatile liquid in pure state
2. Can be yellow due to the formation of nitrogen dioxide gas
3. Used in making fertilizers, explosives, rubber, plastics, and pharmaceuticals
4. Stains skin and other proteins yellow

iii. H_3PO_4 - Phosphoric Acid

Used in making fertilizers and detergents

iv. HCl - Hydrochloric Acid

1. Aids the digestion of proteins in the stomach
2. Used in pickling steel, recovering magnesium from sea water, cleaning masonry, and correcting pool pH

v. Acetic Acid

1. Acid component of vinegar
2. Concentrated "glacial" acetic acid used in making chemicals for plastic manufacturing

Acid Strength

i. Strong acids ionize completely in solution.

ii. Weak acids ionize incompletely and are weak electrolytes.

Strong Acids	Weak Acids
H_2SO_4	HSO_4^-
$HClO_4$	H_3PO_4
HCl	HF
HNO_3	CH_3COOH
HBr	H_2CO_3
HI	H_2S
	HCN
	HCO_3^-

Monoprotic and Polyprotic Acids

i. Monoprotic acids, such as HCl, HNO_3, $HClO_4$, donate only one proton per molecule.

ii. Polyprotic acids can donate more than one proton per molecule.

1. Diprotic, such as H_2SO_4, H_2CO_3, can give out two protons.
2. Triprotic, such as H_3PO_4, can donate three protons.

$$H_3PO_4(aq) + H_2O(l) \rightarrow H_3O^+(aq) + H_2PO_4^-(aq)$$
$$H_2PO_4^-(aq) + H_2O(l) \rightarrow H_3O^+(aq) + HPO_4^{2-}(aq)$$
$$HPO_4^{2-}(aq) + H_2O(l) \rightarrow H_3O^+(aq) + PO_4^{3-}(aq)$$

Section Practice

1. The hydronium ion is represented as
   a) H_2O^+.
   b) H_3O^+.
   c) HOH^+.
   d) H^-.
   e) H^+.

Answer: (b)

The hydronium ion is represented as H_3O^+.

2. Which of the following has the highest pH?
   a) 0.1 M HCl
   b) 0.200 M $HC_2H_3O_2$
   c) 0.1 M Na_2CO_3
   d) 0.200 M NaCl
   e) 0.500 M $NaC_2H_3O_2$

Answer: (c)

The strongest base has the highest pH value. Na_2CO_3 is the strongest base here.

3. Which of the following is the acid anhydride of a monoprotic acid?
   a) CaO
   b) SO_3
   c) FeO
   d) CO_2
   e) N_2O_5

Answer: (e)

CaO and FeO are bases in solutions.
$SO_3 + H_2O = H_2SO_4$
$CO_2 + H_2O \rightarrow H_2CO_3$
$N_2O_5 + H_2O \rightarrow 2HNO_3$

4. A strip of litmus paper will appear blue in a
   a) HBr(aq) solution.
   b) NH_3(aq) solution.
   c) H_2O(l) solution.
   d) HF(aq) solution.
   e) H_2CO_3(aq) solution.

Answer: (b)

Litmus paper will appear blue in a base solution. Only NH_3 is a base in water.

5. Which of the following is essentially a non-electrolyte solution?
   a) HBr(aq)
   b) NH_3(aq)
   c) H_2O(l)
   d) HF(aq)
   e) H_2CO_3(aq)

Answer: (c)

Water is a non-electrolyte compound. It does not conduct electricity.

6. Which of the following ionizations goes virtually to completion?
   a) HBr(aq)
   b) NH_3(aq)
   c) H_2O(l)
   d) HF(aq)
   e) H_2CO_3(aq)

Answer: (a)

Strong acids or bases ionize completely in an aqueous solution.

7. NH_3 is a
   a) strong acid.
   b) strong base.
   c) weak acid.
   d) weak base.
   e) salt.

Answer: (d)

NH_3 is a weak base.

8. Cl^- is a
   a) strong acid.
   b) strong base.
   c) weak acid.
   d) weak base.
   e) salt.

Answer: (d)

HCl is a strong acid, so its conjugate base, Cl^-, is a weak base.

9. The product of a group IA element and water is an example of a(n)
   a) acid.
   b) base.
   c) acidic salt.
   d) basic salt.
   e) amphoteric substance.

Answer: (b)

Alkali metals react with water to form strong basic solutions.

10. Bicarbonate ions are an example of a(n)
    a) acid.
    b) base.
    c) acidic salt.
    d) basic salt.
    e) amphoteric substance.

Answer: (e)

Bicarbonate ions can accept a proton, thus acting as a base, or they can donate a proton, thus acting as an acid.

$HCO_3^- + H_2O \rightarrow H_2CO_3 + OH^-$

$HCO_3^- + H_2O \rightarrow CO_3^{2-} + H_3O^+$

11. A compound that dissolves in water and barely conducts electrical current is probably
    a) a strong electrolyte.
    b) an ionic salt.
    c) a strong acid.
    d) a strong base.
    e) None of the above

Answer: (e)

All of them can conduct an electrical current in aqueous solutions.

II. Acid-Base Theory

Arrhenius Acids and Bases

i. An Arrhenius acid is an acid that provides hydrogen ions, H^+, in an aqueous solution.
ii. An Arrhenius base is a base that provides hydroxide ions, OH^-, in an aqueous solution.

Brønsted-Lowry Acids and Bases

i. A Brønsted–Lowry acid is an acid that donates protons.
ii. A Brønsted-Lowry base is a base that is a proton acceptor.
iii. The hydroxide ion is a base by accepting an H^+. The concept of acids and bases only exist with regard to how they react with each other.

Lewis Acids and Bases

i. A Lewis acid is a compound that **accepts an electron** pair to form a bond.
ii. A Lewis base is a compound that **donates an electron** pair to form a bond.
iii. The hydroxide ion donates a pair of electrons to form a covalent bond in the following reaction, so OH^{-1} is a Lewis base in this reaction. The hydrogen ion accepts the pair of electrons, so it is acting as a Lewis acid.

$$H^{1+} + [:\ddot{O}-H]^{1-} \longrightarrow H-\ddot{O}-H$$

Section Practice

1. According to the Brønsted-Lowry Theory, an acid is a(n)
   a) proton donor.
   b) proton acceptor.
   c) electron donor.
   d) electron acceptor.
   e) H^+ donor.

Answer: (a)

A Brønsted-Lowry acid donates protons.

2. Which of the following can be the product of a Lewis acid reacting with a Lewis base?
   I. $Cu(NH_3)_4^{+2}$
   II. KOH
   III. HCO_3^-
   IV. CO_3^{-2}
   V. SO_3^{-2}
   a) I and II only
   b) II only
   c) I and III only
   d) IV only
   e) IV and V only

Answer: (c)

Cu^{2+} and NH_3 can act as a Lewis acid and base respectively.

3. Which of the following always dissociates completely in an aqueous solution?
   a) A Brønsted acid
   b) A Brønsted base
   c) A strong acid
   d) A weak base
   e) A buffer solution

Answer: (c)

Strong acids or bases ionize completely in an aqueous solution.

4. Which of the following characteristics is associated with Lewis bases?
   a) They react with metal to produce hydrogen gas.
   b) They donate an unshared electron pair.
   c) They always contain the hydroxide ion in their structures.
   d) They taste sour.
   e) They are formed by the reaction of a nonmetal oxide and water.

Answer: (b)

This is the definition of a Lewis base.

5. A molecule or ion is classified as a Lewis base if it
   a) accepts a proton from water.
   b) donates a proton to water.
   c) accepts a pair of electrons.
   d) donates a pair of electrons.
   e) results in a basic solution when dissolved in water.

Answer: (d)

This is the definition of a Lewis base.

III. Acid-Base Reactions

Conjugate Acids and Bases

i. A **conjugate base** remains after an acid has given up a proton. The stronger the acid, the weaker its conjugate base.

$$H_3PO_4(aq) + H_2O(l) \rightarrow H_3O^+(aq) + H_2PO_4^-(aq)$$

Acid Conjugate Base

ii. A **conjugate acid** is formed when a base gains a proton. The stronger the base, the weaker its conjugate acid.

$$H_3PO_4(aq) + H_2O(l) \rightarrow H_3O^+(aq) + H_2PO_4^-(aq)$$

Base Conjugate Acid

Examples: Using your knowledge of the Brønsted-Lowry theory of acids and bases, write equations for the following acid-base reactions and indicate each conjugate acid-base pair:

a. $\underset{\text{Acid}}{HNO_3} + \underset{\text{Base}}{OH^-} \rightarrow \underset{\text{Conjugate Acid}}{H_2O} + \underset{\text{Conjugate Base}}{NO_3^{-1}}$

b. $\underset{\text{Base}}{CH_3NH_2} + \underset{\text{Acid}}{H_2O} \rightarrow \underset{\text{Conjugate Acid}}{CH_3NH_3^+} + \underset{\text{Conjugate Base}}{OH^-}$

c. $\underset{\text{Acid}}{HPO_4^{-2}} + \underset{\text{Base}}{OH^-} \rightarrow \underset{\text{Conjugate Acid}}{H_2O} + \underset{\text{Conjugate Base}}{PO_4^{-3}}$

Amphoteric Compounds can react as either an acid or a base.

i. Water as a base:

$$H_3PO_4(aq) + H_2O(l) \rightarrow H_3O^+(aq) + H_2PO_4^-(aq)$$

ii. Water as an acid:

$$NH_3(g) + H_2O(l) \rightarrow NH_4^+(aq) + OH^-(aq)$$

A **neutralization reaction** is when an acid and a base react to produce water and a salt.

$$KOH(aq) + HNO_3(aq) \rightarrow KNO_3(aq) + H_2O(l)$$

Section Practice

1. The reaction of zinc metal and HCl produces which of the following?
   I. $H_2(g)$
   II. $Cl_2(g)$
   III. $ZnCl_2(aq)$
   a) II only
   b) III only
   c) I and II only
   d) I and III only
   e) I, II, and III

Answer: (d)

$2HCl + Zn \rightarrow H_2 + ZnCl_2$

2. In $NH_3(aq) + H_2CO_3(aq) \leftrightarrow NH_4^+(aq) + HCO_3^-(aq)$, $NH_4^+(aq)$ acts as a(n)
   a) indicator.
   b) hydrate.
   c) acid.
   d) base.
   e) salt.

Answer: (c)

$NH_4^+(aq)$ is a conjugate acid of the base NH_3.

3. You wish to construct a buffer of pH = 7.0. Which of the following weak acids would you select?
   a) $HClO_2$ (chlorous acid), $K_a = 1.2 \times 10^{-2}$
   b) HF (hydrofluoric acid), $K_a = 7.2 \times 10^{-4}$
   c) HOCl (hypochlorous acid), $K_a = 3.5 \times 10^{-8}$
   d) HCN (hydrocyanic acid), $K_a = 4.0 \times 10^{-10}$
   e) C_2H_3OH (ethanol), $K_a = 1.0 \times 10^{-25}$

Answer: (c)

You would select a weak acid or base with a K_a or K_b around 10^{-7}.

4. pH is equal to pKa
   a) when [conjugate acid] = [conjugate base].
   b) at the end point of a titration.
   c) in the buffer region.
   d) in the Henderson–Hasselbalch equation.
   e) at equilibrium.

Answer: (a)

$pKa = \frac{[H^+][conjugate\ base]}{[conjugate\ acid]}$

The Henderson–Hasselbalch equation states that $pH = pKa + log\frac{[A^-]}{[HA]}$.

5. In $HNO_3(aq) + OH^-(aq) \leftrightarrow H_2O(l) + NO_3^-(aq)$, which of the following species is the conjugate acid?
   a) $HNO_3(aq)$
   b) $OH^-(aq)$
   c) $H_2O(l)$
   d) $NO_3^-(aq)$
   e) There is no conjugate acid.

Answer: (c)

The conjugate acid, H_2O, forms from the base, OH^-.

6. When 0.250 moles of NaOH is added to 1.00 L of 0.1 M H_3PO_4, the solution will contain
   a) HPO_4^{-2}.
   b) $H_2PO_4^-$.
   c) PO_4^{-3}.
   d) a) and b).
   e) a) and c).

Answer: (e)

0.25 moles of NaOH will react with 0.1 moles of H_3PO_4 past the 2nd equivalence point. Therefore, the solution will contain $H_2PO_4^{-1}$, HPO_4^{-2}, and PO_4^{-3} at equilibrium conditions.

7. Aqueous solutions contain 1:1 mole ratios of the following pairs of substances. Assuming all concentrations are 1 M, which of the following is the solution with the lowest pH?
   a) NaCl and NaOH solution.
   b) NaOAc and HOAc solution.
   c) HNO_3 and $NaNO_3$ solution.
   d) NH_3 and NH_4Cl solution.
   e) NaC1 and K_2SO_4 solution.

Answer: (c)

Strong acids and weak bases in a solution would result in the lowest pH values.

8. Aqueous solutions contain 1:1 mole ratios of the following pairs of substances. Assuming all concentrations are 1 M, which of the following is a buffer solution with a pH > 8?
   a) NaCl and NaOH solution
   b) NaOAc and HOAC solution
   c) HNO_3 and $NaNO_3$ solution
   d) NH_3 and NH_4Cl solution
   e) NaCl and K_2SO_4 solution

Answer: (d)

A weak base plus the salt of its conjugate base becomes a buffer solution.

9. $NaHCO_3$ is a
   a) strong acid.
   b) strong base.
   c) weak acid.
   d) weak base.
   e) salt.

Answer: (e)

$NaHCO_3$ is a salt that forms from NaOH reacting with H_2CO_3.

10. A solution made by the combination of a weak acid and the salt of its conjugate base is a
    a) Brønsted acid.
    b) Brønsted base.
    c) strong acid.
    d) weak base.
    e) buffer solution.

Answer: (e)

A buffer solution is made by a weak acid and the salt of its conjugate base or by a weak base and the salt of its conjugate acid.

IV. Aqueous Solutions and pH

The dissociation of water at 25 °C is shown below:

$$2H_2O(l) \rightarrow H_3O^+(aq) + OH^-(aq)$$

$$K_w = [H_3O^+] \times [OH^-] = 1.0 \times 10^{-14}\ M^2$$

The pH Scale

$$pH = -\log[H^+]$$
$$pOH = -\log[OH^-]$$
$$pH + pOH = 14$$

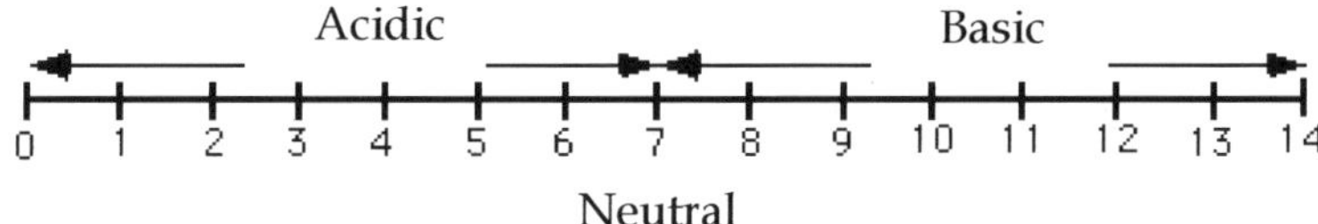

Strong acids and bases are assumed to dissociate completely in a dilute solution.

Example: One gram of concentrated sulfuric acid (H_2SO_4) is diluted to 1.0 L of water. What is the molar concentration of the hydrogen ion in this solution? What is the pH?

Answer: First determine the number of moles of H_2SO_4.

1 g of $H_2SO_4 = \frac{1}{98}$ moles = 0.010 moles of H_2SO_4

$H_2SO_4 \rightarrow 2H^+ + SO_4^{2-}$

0.01 M 0.02 M

(In dilute solutions, this reaction goes to 100% completion.)

pH = $-\log[H^+] = -\log[0.02\ M] = 1.69$

Example: A volume of 5.71 cm³ of pure acetic acid, $HC_2H_3O_2$, is diluted with water at 25 °C to form a solution with a volume of 1.0 L. What is the molar concentration of the hydrogen ion, H^+, in this solution? (The density of pure acetic acid is 1.05 g/cm³. The K_a of acetic acid is 1.8×10^{-5})

Answer: Mass of Acid = Acid Density × Acid Volume = 1.05 × 5.71= 6.00 g of acetic acid

6.00 g = $\frac{6}{60}$ moles = 0.10 moles acetic acid (in 1 L)

$[HC_2H_3O_2]$ = 0.10 mole / 1 L

Find $[H^+]$ by using $K_a = \frac{[H+][C_2H_3O_2^{-1}]}{[HC_2H_3O_2]}$.

$1.8 \times 10^{-5} = \frac{x^2}{0.1-x} \approx \frac{x^2}{0.1}\ (assume\ x \ll 0.1)$

$x = 1.3 \times 10^{-3}$ M

(Our assumption is acceptable since x is much smaller than 0.1.)

Section Practice

1. The pH of a solution with a hydrogen ion concentration of 1×10^{-3} is
   a) +3.
   b) −3.
   c) −11.
   d) 11.
   e) 10^{-3}.

Answer: (a)

$pH = -\log[H^+] = -\log(10^{-3}) = 3$

2. At 25 °C, a 0.25 M solution of hydrocyanic acid (HCN) is prepared. Which of the following is/are true at equilibrium?
   I. $[H^+] > 1 \times 10^{-7}$ M
   II. $[OH^-] < 1 \times 10^{-7}$ M
   III. $[H+][OH^{-1}] = 1 \times 10^{-14}$
   a) I only
   b) II only
   c) I and II only
   d) II and III only
   e) I, II, and III

Answer: (e)

HCN is a weak acid.

$[H^+] > 10^{-7}$

3. The dissociation of sulfurous acid (H_2SO_3) in an aqueous solution occurs as follows:
   $H_2SO_3(aq) \rightarrow H^+(aq) + HSO_3^-(aq)$
   $K_{a1} = \frac{[H^+][HSO_3^-]}{[H_2SO_3]} = 1.5 \times 10^{-2}$
   $HSO_3^{-1}(aq) \rightarrow H^+(aq) + SO_3^{-2}(aq)$
   $K_{a2} = \frac{[H^+][SO_3^{-2}]}{[HSO_3^{-1}]} = 1.0 \times 10^{-7}$
   If 0.50 moles of sulfurous acid are dissolved to form a 1 L solution, which of the following species will be the LEAST concentrated at equilibrium?
   a) H_2SO_3
   b) H^+
   c) H_3O^+
   d) HSO_3^{-1}
   e) SO_3^{-2}

Answer: (e)

Normally, the second acid dissociation constant is much lower than the first.

4. At 25 °C, an aqueous solution has a proton concentration, $[H^+]$, of 1.0×10^{-10} M. The hydroxide ion concentration, $[OH^-]$, is equal to
   a) 0.
   b) 1.0×10^{-2}.
   c) 1.0×10^{-4}.
   d) 5.0×10^{-6}.
   e) 1.0×10^{-10}.

Answer: (c)

$[H^+][OH^-] = 10^{-14}$

5. The pH of a 1.23×10^{-3} M aqueous solution of $Al(OH)_3$ is
   a) 2.91.
   b) 2.43.
   c) 11.09.
   d) 13.52.
   e) 11.57.

Answer: (e)

$Al(OH)_3 \rightarrow Al^{+3} + 3OH^-$
Assume $Al(OH)_3$ ionizes completely in the above reaction.
$OH^- = 3 \times 1.23 \times 10^{-3} = 3.69 \times 10^{-3}$
$pH = 14 + \log(3.69 \times 10^{-3})$
$= 11.57$

6. A buffer has a pH of 4.87. If the buffer is made from a weak acid ($K_a = 3.30 \times 10^{-5}$) and its conjugate base, what is $\frac{\text{Conjugate Base}}{\text{Weak Acid}}$?
   a) 4.87
   b) 4.48
   c) 1.00
   d) 2.45
   e) 0.41

Answer: (d)

$[H^+] = 10^{-4.87} = 1.35 \times 10^{-5}$

$K_a = 3.30 \times 10^{-5} = \frac{[H^+][Conjugate\ Base]}{Conjugate\ Acid}$

$\frac{Conjugate\ Base}{Weak\ Acid} = 2.45$

7. The pH of a 0.125 M solution of a weak base is 10.45. What is the K_b of this base?
   a) 3.5×10^{-11}
   b) 6.4×10^{-7}
   c) 2.8×10^{-4}
   d) 2.3×10^{-3}
   e) 1.2×10^{-2}

Answer: (b)

$[OH^-] = 10^{-(14-10.45)} = 2.8 \times 10^{-4}$

$Kb = \frac{[2.8 \times 10^{-4}]^2}{0.125} = 6.4 \times 10^{-7}$

8. What is the H_3O^+ concentration of a 0.100 M acetic acid solution ($K_a = 1.8 \times 10^{-5}$)?
   a) 1.8×10^{-5}
   b) 1.8×10^{-4}
   c) 1.3×10^{-2}
   d) 1.3×10^{-3}
   e) 0.9×10^{-3}

Answer: (d)

$HA \rightarrow H^+ + A^-$
$0.1 - x \quad x \quad x$
$1.8 \times 10^{-5} = \frac{x^2}{0.1 - x}$
$x = 1.31 \times 10^{-3}$

V. Determining pH and Titrations

A ***pH indicator*** is a substance that changes color depending on the pH of a solution. Indicators are useful when they display a range of colors corresponding to a continuous change in pH values, including the start and end points of a reaction.

Acid-Base Indicators

Solution	Endpoint	Best Indicator(s)
Strong Acid + Strong Base	The endpoint pH is 7.	Litmus Bromthymol blue
Strong Acid + Weak Base	The endpoint pH is less than 7.	Methyl orange Bromphenol blue
Weak Acid + Strong Base	The endpoint pH is greater than 7.	Phenolphthalein Phenol red
Weak Acid + Weak Base	The endpoint pH can fall within a wide range.	No single indicator is suitable.

Acid-Base Titration

Titrations are common quantitative methods of chemical analysis where a solution of a known concentration is used to determine the concentration of an unknown solution.

The **equivalence point** of an acid-base reaction is the point at which **chemically equivalent** quantities of acids and bases have been mixed.

Two common **titration curves** are shown below:

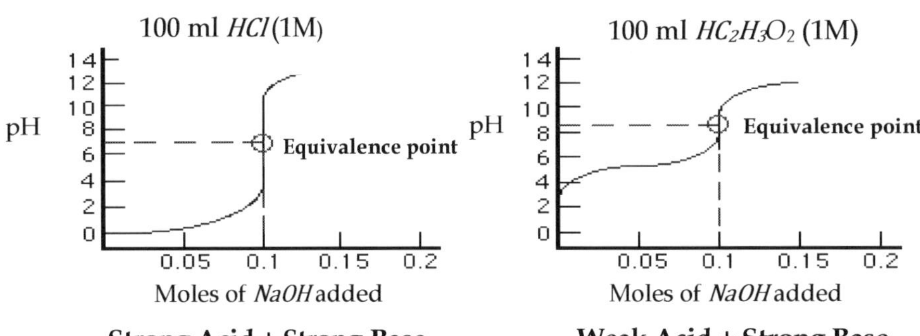

Strong Acid + Strong Base **Weak Acid + Strong Base**

Normality (N) is the equivalent concentration of a solution and is defined as:

$$\text{Normality (N)} = \text{Molarity (M)} \times i$$

where i is the number of moles of H^+ each acid will donate or each base will accept.

In a titration,

$$N_1V_1 = N_2V_2$$

where N_1, N_2 are the normalities of the acid and base and V_1, V_2 are the volumes.

A **buffer solution** is a solution that resists changes in pH when a strong acid or strong base is added. A buffer solution should contain either a weak acid and its conjugate base or a weak base and its conjugate acid.

Blood buffering is a buffer system for maintaining the acid-base balance in our bloodstream. It consists of a carbonic acid and bicarbonate buffer.

Section Practice

1. A solution of 10 M NaOH was used to prepare 2 L of 0.5 M NaOH. How many milliliters of 10 M NaOH solution were used?
   a) 10 mL
   b) 100 mL
   c) 1000 mL
   d) 200 mL
   e) 2000 mL

Answer: (b)

$M_1V_1 = M_2V_2$
$10 \times x = 0.5 \times 2$
$x = 0.1\ L = 100\ mL$

2. If 10.0 mL of 1 M HCl was required to titrate a 20 mL NaOH solution of unknown concentration to its endpoint, what was the concentration of the NaOH?
   a) 0.5 M
   b) 1.5 M
   c) 2.0 M
   d) 2.5 M
   e) 3.5 M

Answer: (a)

$N_1V_1 = N_2V_2$
$1 \times 10 = x \times 20$
$x = 0.5\ M$

3. Which of the following is the correct method for preparing a buffer solution?
   a) Mix the correct amounts of a weak acid and its conjugate base.
   b) Partially neutralize a weak base with a strong acid.
   c) Partially neutralize a weak acid with a strong base.
   d) Add the appropriate amount of strong acid to an acid salt.
   e) All of the above methods may be used to prepare buffers.

Answer: (e)

A buffer solution should contain either a weak acid and its conjugate base or a weak base and its conjugate acid.

4. If 50.0 g of formic acid ($HCHO_2$, $K_a = 1.8 \times 10^{-4}$) and 30.0 g of sodium formate ($NaCHO_2$) are dissolved to make 500 mL of solution, the pH of this solution is
   a) 4.76.
   b) 3.76.
   c) 3.35.
   d) 4.12.
   e) 3.02.

Answer: (c)

M *of* $HCHO_2 = \frac{\frac{50}{46}}{0.5} = 2.17\,M$

of $NaCHO_2 = \frac{\frac{30}{68}}{0.5} = 0.88$

$HCHO_2 \rightarrow H^+ + CHO_2^-$

$2.17 - x \quad x \quad 0.88 + x$

$K_a = \frac{x \times (0.88+x)}{2.17-x} = 1.4 \times 10^{-4}$

$x = 4.4 \times 10^{-4}$

$pH = -\log(4.4 \times 10^{-4}) = 3.35$

5. A solution containing HF is titrated with KOH. At the endpoint of the titration, the solution contains
   a) equal amounts of HF and KOH.
   b) H_2O, H^+, OH^-, K^+, F^-, and HF.
   c) K^+ and F^-.
   d) KF and H_2O.
   e) K^+, F^-, and H_2O.

Answer: (b)

HF is a weak acid so F^- *can hydrolyze into HF and* OH^-.

6. A buffer solution with a pH of 10.0 is needed. Which of the following should be used?
   a) Acetic acid with a K_a of 1.8×10^{-5}
   b) Ammonia with a K_b of 1.8×10^{-5}
   c) Nitrous acid with a K_a of 7.1×10^{-4}
   d) $H_2PO_4^-$ and PO_4^{-3} with a Ka of 4.5×10^{-13}
   e) Dimethyl amine with a K_b of 1.05×10^{-3}

Answer: (b)

The solution needs a weak base with a K_b *close to* 10^{-4}.

7. A buffer is generated using NH_3 and NH_4Cl. Which of the following is/are true?
   I. Any buffers generated with the same $\frac{[NH_3]}{[NH_4Cl]}$ will have an identical pH.
   II. If $[NH_3] = [NH_4C1]$, the pH will equal the pKa of NH_4^+.
   III. Any buffers generated with the same $\frac{[NH_3]}{[NH_4Cl]}$ will have an identical buffering capacity.
   a) I only
   b) II only
   c) I and II only
   d) I and III only
   e) I, II, and III

Answer: (c)

$NH_4^- \rightarrow NH_3 + H^+$

$pH = pKa - \log\frac{NH_3}{NH_4^+}$

8. Which of the following would make the best buffer solution?
   a) H_2O, 1 M NaOH, 1 M H_2SO_4
   b) H_2O, 1 M CH_3COOH, 1 M $NaCH_3COO^-$
   c) H_2O, 1 M CH_3COOH, 6 M $Na^+CH_3COO^-$
   d) H_2O, 1 M CH_3COOH, 1 M NaOH
   e) H_2O, 1 M HCl, 1 M NaOH

Answer: (b)

A good buffer solution needs the same concentration of weak acid or base and its conjugate salt.

9. An indicator has a K_a of 6.4×10^{-6}. The conjugate acid shows up red and the conjugate base shows up yellow. At what pH will the solution be red?
   a) 5.2
   b) 5.5
   c) 4.0
   d) 4.7
   e) 6.4

Answer: (c)

$pH > pka + 1 =$ color of the conjugate base
$pH < pKa - 1 =$ color of the conjugate acid
$pKa = log[6.4 \times 10^{-6}] = 5.1$
A $pH < 4.1$ will be red.

10. A buffer with pH 5.32 is prepared from a weak acid with a pKa of 5.15. If 100 mL of this buffer is diluted to 200 mL with distilled water, the pH of the dilute solution is
    a) 5.62.
    b) 5.02.
    c) 5.32.
    d) unknown. The identity of the acid is needed to answer this question.
    e) unknown. The concentrations of the acid and salt are needed to answer this question.

Answer: (c)

The pH will not change very much since the solution is a buffer.

Chapter 12 Acid - Base Titration and pH SAT Questions

1. The difference between HCl and $HC_2H_3O_2$ is that
   a) the first dissociates fewer hydrogen ions in solution.
   b) the second dissociates more ionized hydrogens.
   c) the first is highly ionized in water.
   d) the second is highly ionized in water.
   e) one is an acid and the other is a base in solution.

Answer: (c)

HCl is a strong acid and $HC_2H_3O_2$ is a weak acid.

2. In solution, which of the following produces the greatest $[H_3O^+]$?
   a) HCN
   b) HNO_3
   c) H_2O
   d) OH^-
   e) CH_3OH

Answer: (b)

HNO_3 is the strongest acid among the answer choices.

3. At 25 °C, which of the following is not true for a solution that has a hydroxide concentration of 1.0×10^{-6} M?
   a) $K_w = 1 \times 10^{-14}$
   b) The solution is acidic.
   c) The solution is basic.
   d) The $[H^+]$ is 1×10^{-8} M.
   e) The pOH equals 6.0.

Answer: (b)

$[OH^-][H^+] = 10^{-14}$

$[H^+] = \frac{10^{-14}}{10^{-6}} = 10^{-8}$

$pH = -\log[10^{-8}] = 8 > 7$

This is a basic solution.

$pOH = 14 - 8 = 6$

4. Which of the following would produce a basic aqueous solution?
   a) SO_2
   b) KCl
   c) CO_2
   d) NH_4Cl
   e) Na_2O

Answer: (e)

Alkali oxides are basic ionic compounds.

5. Which of the following equimolar solutions would produce the most acidic solution?
   a) H_3PO_4
   b) HClO
   c) $HClO_2$
   d) $HClO_3$
   e) $HClO_4$

Answer: (e)

$HClO_4$ is the strongest acid among the answer choices.

6. The point at which a titration is complete is called the
   a) endpoint.
   b) equilibrium point.
   c) calibrated point.
   d) chemical point.
   e) half equivalent point.

Answer: (a)

The point at which a titration is complete is called the endpoint or the equivalent point.

7. HI is a strong acid whereas HF is a weak acid. Which of the following is NOT true?
   a) If a 1 M solution of HI is prepared, $[I^-]$ is approximately 1 M.
   b) For an HF solution at equilibrium, $[HF] \gg [H^+]$.
   c) For an HF solution at equilibrium, $[H]^+ > [OH]^-$.
   d) A solution of NaF is expected to be basic.
   e) A solution of NaI is expected to be basic.

Answer: (e)

Strong acids dissociate almost completely in solution.
Strong Acid + Strong Base = Neutral Solution
Weak Acid + Strong Base = Weak Basic Solution

8. In a 0.20 M aqueous solution, lactic acid is 2.6% dissociated. What is the value of K_a for lactic acid?
   a) 4×10^{-6}
   b) 8.3×10^{-5}
   c) 1.4×10^{-4}
   d) 5.2×10^{-3}
   e) 9.8×10^{-3}

Answer: (c)

$HC_3H_5O_3 \rightarrow C_3H_5O_3^- + H^+$

$0.2 - x \quad x \quad x$

$x = 0.026 \times 0.2 = 0.0052$

$$K_a = \frac{0.0052^2}{0.2 - 0.0052} = 1.4 \times 10^{-4}$$

9. Aqueous solutions contain 1:1 mole ratios of the following pairs of substances. Which of the following solutions has a pH of 7?
   a) NaCl and NaOH
   b) NaOAc and HOAc
   c) HNO_3 and $NaNO_3$
   d) NH_3 and NH_4Cl
   e) NaCl and K_2SO_4

Answer: (e)

Both NaC1 and K_2SO_4 solutions are pH = 7. Neither is an acid nor base (they are salts).

10. The only acid that can be both a strong and a weak acid after dissociation is
   a) hydrochloric acid.
   b) perchloric acid.
   c) nitric acid.
   d) sulfuric acid.
   e) phosphoric acid.

Answer: (d)

The first dissociation of H^+ in sulfuric acid occurs as a strong acid but the 2nd dissociation of H^+ in sulfuric acid occurs as a weak acid.

11. At 25 °C, which of the following has a pH > 7?
    a) HBr(aq)
    b) NH_3(aq)
    c) H_2O(l)
    d) HF(aq)
    e) H_2CO_3(aq)

Answer: (b)

Among the choices, only NH_3 in an aqueous solution is a basic solution.

12. Which of the following has a very high K_a?
    a) A Brønsted acid
    b) A Brønsted base
    c) A strong acid
    d) A weak base
    e) A buffer

Answer: (c)

A strong acid has a very high K_a because of its almost 100% dissociation rate in water.

13. NaOH is a
    a) strong acid.
    b) strong base.
    c) weak acid.
    d) weak base.
    e) salt.

Answer: (b)

NaOH is a strong base.

14. Amino acids are an example of a(n)
    a) acid only.
    b) base only.
    c) acidic salt.
    d) basic salt.
    e) amphoteric substance.

Answer: (e)

Amino acids, of the form $HCOO - R - NH_2$, can act as an acid or a base.

15. Ammonia is an example of a(n)
    a) acid.
    b) base.
    c) acidic salt.
    d) basic salt.
    e) amphoteric substance.

Answer: (b)

Ammonia, NH_3, is a base.

16. Ammonium sulfate is an example of a(n)
    a) acid.
    b) base.
    c) acidic salt.
    d) basic salt.
    e) amphoteric substance.

Answer: (c)

Ammonium sulfate, $(NH_4)_2SO_4$, is an acidic salt.

17. Aluminum chloride is an example of a(n)
    a) acid.
    b) base.
    c) acidic salt.
    d) basic salt.
    e) amphoteric substance.

Answer: (c)

Aluminum chloride, $Al(Cl)_3$, is an acidic salt.

18. Which of the following is a poor electrolyte?
    a) A hydrochloric acid solution
    b) A sodium hydroxide solution
    c) Vinegar
    d) A sodium chloride solution
    e) Molten sodium chloride

Answer: (c)

Vinegar, or an acetic acid solution, is a weakly acidic solution.

19. The pH of a solution that has a hydroxide ion concentration of 1×10^{-4} M is
    a) 4.
    b) −4.
    c) 10.
    d) −10.
    e) 1×10^{-4}.

Answer: (c)

$[OH^-] = 10^{-4}$

$pOH = 4$

$pH = 14 - 4 = 10$

20. What is the hydroxide ion concentration in a solution with a pH of 5?
    a) 10^{-3}
    b) 10^{-5}
    c) 10^{-7}
    d) 10^{-9}
    e) 10^{-11}

Answer: (d)

$[H^+] = 10^{-5}$

$[OH^-] = \frac{10^{-14}}{10^{-5}} = 10^{-9}$

21. An aqueous solution with pH = 5 at 25 °C has a hydroxide ion concentration of
    a) 1×10^{-11} M.
    b) 1×10^{-9} M.
    c) 1×10^{-7} M.
    d) 1×10^{-5} M.
    e) 1×10^{-3} M.

Answer: (b)

$pOH = 14 - 5 = 9$

$pOH = -\log[OH^-] = 9$

$OH^- = 10^{-9}$

22. What is the pH of a solution with a hydroxide ion concentration of 0.00001 M?
    a) −5
    b) −1
    c) 5
    d) 9
    e) 14

Answer: (d)

$[OH^-] = 10^{-5}$

$[H^+] = \frac{10^{-14}}{10^{-5}} = 10^{-9}$

$pH = -\log(10^{-9}) = 9$

23. A titration experiment is conducted in which 15 mL of a 0.015 M $Ba(OH)_2$ solution is added to 30 mL of an HCl solution of unknown concentration. When the titration is complete, what is the approximate concentration of the HCl solution?
    a) 0.015 M
    b) 0.03 M
    c) 1.5 M
    d) 2.5 M
    e) 3.0 M

Answer: (a)

$N_1V_1 = N_2V_2$

$0.015 \times 2 \times 15 = N_2 \times 30$

$N_2 = 0.015\ N = 0.015\ M$

24. Hydrolysis will give an acidic solution reaction when which of the following is placed in solution with water?
    a) Na_2SO_4
    b) K_2SO_4
    c) $NaNO_3$
    d) $Cu(NO_3)_2$
    e) KCl

Answer: (d)

Only weak acid or weak bases can be hydrolyzed.

Among the answer choices, only Cu^{2+} is a weakly acidic ion.

25. Which of the following is true regarding an aqueous solution of H_3PO_4 at 25 °C?
    a) It has a very large acid ionization constant.
    b) It has a bitter taste.
    c) The concentration of [OH-] is greater than 1.0×10^{-7} M.
    d) It is a weak electrolyte.
    e) It can be formed by the reaction of a metal oxide and water.

Answer: (d)

H_3PO_4 in solution is weakly acidic.

Relationship Analysis Questions

	Statement I	Statement II	
1.	Cl^- is the conjugate base of HCl.	A conjugate base is formed when an acid gains a proton.	TF
2.	Water makes a good buffer.	A good buffer will resist changes in pH.	FT
3.	A solution with a pH of 5 is less acidic than a solution with a pH of 8.	A solution with a pH of 5 has 1000 times more hydronium ions than a solution with a pH of 8.	FT
4.	Acetic acid is a strong acid.	Acetic acid ionizes completely in solution.	FF

	Statement	Reason	Answer
5.	NH_3 is a Lewis base.	Ammonia can accept a proton.	TT
6.	A solution with a pH of 12 has a higher concentration of hydroxide ions than a solution with a pH of 10.	At 25 °C, pH + pOH = 14	TT
7.	The pH of 0.01 M HCl(aq) is 2.	HCl is essentially an ionic species, completely dissociating so that $[H^+]$ = [HCl].	TTCE
8.	HCl is an Arrhenius acid.	HCl will yield hydronium ions as the only positive ions in solution.	TTCE
9.	An aqueous solution of HI is considered to be a Brønsted-Lowry base.	HI(aq) can accept H+ ions from another species.	FF
10.	The reaction of zinc with hydrochloric acid goes to completion in an open container.	Hydrogen gas bubbles out from the reaction of zinc and hydrochloric acid.	TTCE
11.	NaCl is a basic salt.	Hydrolysis of NaCl reveals the formation of NaOH and HCl.	FT
12.	Hydrofluoric acid etches glass.	Hydrofluoric acid is a strong acid.	TF
13.	A 1 N ("normal") solution of H_2SO_4 is the same as a 1 M ("molar") solution of H_2SO_4.	Molarity refers to the moles of solute per liter of solution, whereas normality refers to the molarity of hydrogen ions.	FT
14.	$Cl^-$is the conjugate base of HCl.	A conjugate base is formed once a Brønsted-Lowry acid accepts a proton.	TF
15.	If an acid is added to pure water, it increases the water's pH.	Adding an acid to water raises the hydrogen ion concentration in the water.	FT
16.	Pure water has a pH of 7.	The number of H^+ ions is equal to the number of OH^- ions.	TTCE

Chapter 13 Oxidation-Reduction Reactions

I. Oxidation States

Rules for Assigning Oxidation Numbers

i. The oxidation number of a free element is 0.
ii. The oxidation number of a monatomic ion is equal to the charge on the ion.
iii. The oxidation number of hydrogen is +1.
iv. The oxidation number of oxygen is −2 except in peroxides, where the oxidation number of oxygen is −1.
v. The oxidation number of fluorine is always −1.
vi. The sum of the oxidation numbers in a polyatomic ion is equal to the charge on the ion.
vii. The oxidation number of elements in groups 1, 2, and aluminum are always equal to their group number.

Example: Use the oxidation number rules to determine the oxidation number of the element in **bold** for each formula.

$\mathbf{Sb}_2O_5$	+5	$Mg\mathbf{Si}F_6$	+4
$Al(\mathbf{N}O_3)_3$	+5	$\mathbf{I}O_3^-$	+5
$Mg_3(\mathbf{P}O_4)_2$	+5	$(\mathbf{N}H_4)_2S$	+3
$(NH_4)_2\mathbf{S}O_4$	+6	$\mathbf{Mn}O_4^-$	+7
$\mathbf{Cr}O_4^{-2}$	+6	$\mathbf{Br}O_3^-$	+5
$\mathbf{Cl}O_4^-$	+7	$\mathbf{Cl}O^-$	+1

Oxidation and Reduction Processes

i. A molecule, atom, or ion is **oxidized** when it loses electrons or when its *oxidation* number is increased.

Example: $Na \rightarrow Na^{+1} + e^-$
Na has an oxidation number of 0 and Na^{+1} has an oxidation number of 1.

ii. A molecule, atom, or ion is **reduced** when it gains electrons or when its *oxidation* number is decreased.

Example: $Cl + e^- \rightarrow Cl^{-1}$
Cl has an oxidation number of 0 and Cl^{-1} has an oxidation number of −1.

iii. A **redox reaction** is the chemical process in which elements undergo changes in oxidation number.
   1. Oxidation cannot occur without reduction. Oxidation and reduction occur simultaneously.

2. The number of electrons lost is equal to the number of electrons gained in a redox reaction.

iv. A **half-reaction** is the part of the redox reaction that is either oxidized or reduced, and can be written separately. For example,

$$\begin{array}{llll} 2Na & \rightarrow & 2Na^{+1} + 2e^{-} & \text{Oxidation} \\ Cl_2 + 2e^{-} & \rightarrow & 2Cl^{-1} & \text{Reduction} \\ \hline 2Na + Cl_2 & \rightarrow & 2NaCl & \text{Combined} \end{array}$$

In any redox equation, at least one particle will gain electrons and one particle will lose electrons.

The next example shown below occurs in an acidic solution. Permanganate(VII) is reduced to the colorless manganese(II), or Mn^{2+}, ion. The top arrow indicates the element that gains electrons from reduction and the bottom arrow shows the element that loses electrons from oxidation.

gains $5e^-$ (reduction)

$$\overset{+7\ -2}{MnO_4^-} + \overset{+4}{H_2SO_3} \rightarrow \overset{+2}{Mn^{+2}} + \overset{+6}{HSO_4^-}$$

loses $2e^-$ (oxidation)

Section Practice

1. What is the charge of calcium in $CaCl_2$?
   a) 0
   b) −1
   c) +1
   d) −2
   e) +2

Answer: (e)

Ca^{+2}

2. What is the oxidation number of Cl in Cl_2?
   a) 0
   b) −1
   c) +1
   d) −2
   e) +2

Answer: (a)

If there is no charge, there is no oxidation number.

3. What is the oxidation number of sulfur in $NaHSO_4$?
   a) 0
   b) +2
   c) −2
   d) +4
   e) +6

Answer: (e)

+6

4. Which of the following is TRUE?
   a) The number of positive ions in a solution equals the number of negative ions.
   b) The positive ions are called anions.
   c) The positive ions are called cathodes.
   d) The total positive charge equals the total negative charge in a solution.
   e) None of the above

Answer: (d)

An anion has a negative charge and a cation has a positive charge.
The total negative charge is equal to the total positive charge in a solution.

5. A positive reaction potential indicates that
   a) the reaction will not occur.
   b) the reaction will occur and give off energy.
   c) the reaction will occur if heat or energy is added.
   d) the reaction will power an outside alternating electric current.
   e) None of the above

Answer: (b)

A positive reaction potential indicates a spontaneous reaction.

6. Which of the following metals reacted with hydrochloric acid does NOT produce hydrogen gas?

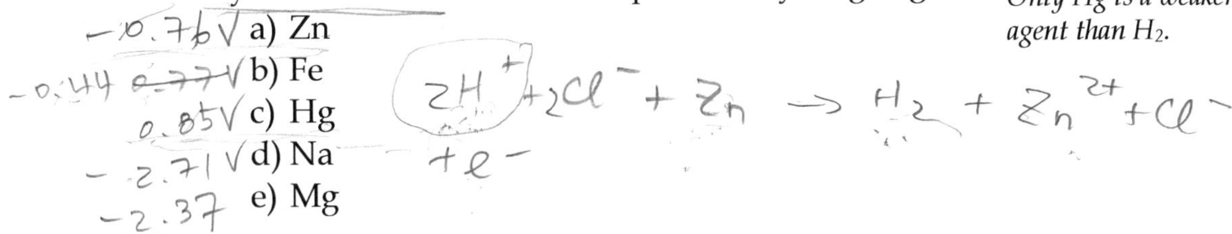

   a) Zn
   b) Fe
   c) Hg
   d) Na
   e) Mg

Answer: (c)

Only Hg is a weaker reduction agent than H_2.

7. The loss of electrons is a(n)_____ process.
   a) Nernst equation
   b) spontaneous
   c) reduction
   d) oxidation
   e) electrolysis

Answer: (d)

An oxidation process is a loss of an electron.

8. For the reaction below, indicate which element is reduced and which element is oxidized.

$$2Cu(NO_3)_2 \rightarrow 2CuO + 4NO_2 + O_2$$

	Oxidized	Reduced
a)	Nitrogen	Oxygen
b)	Copper	Oxygen
c)	Copper	Nitrogen
d)	Nitrogen	Copper
e)	Oxygen	Nitrogen

Answer: (e)

Cu^{2+} keeps the same oxidation number.
The oxidation number of N changes from +5 to +4 (reduced).
The oxidation number of O changes from – 2 to 0 (oxidized).

9. _____ cannot occur without _____ also occurring within the same system.

I. Nernst equation
II. spontaneous
III. reduction
IV. oxidation
V. electrolysis

a) I, III
b) II, V
c) III, IV
d) IV, V
e) V, II

Answer: (c)

Reduction and oxidation processes have to occur at the same time.

10. Which of the following pairs of constants are NOT mathematically related to each other?

a) Equilibrium constant and Gibbs free energy
b) Rate constant and activation energy
c) Standard cell voltage and equilibrium constant
d) Standard cell voltage and rate constant
e) Gibbs free energy and standard cell voltage

Answer: (d)

Rate equations are not related to equilibrium conditions.

II. Balancing Redox Equations

The Electron Transfer Method

$$NH_3 + CuO \rightarrow Cu + H_2O + N_2$$

i. Assign oxidation numbers to all elements and determine what will be oxidized and what will be reduced.

loses $3e^-$ × 2 (oxidation)

-3 +1 +2 -2 0 +1 -2 0

$$\mathbf{2NH_3 + CuO \rightarrow Cu + H_2O + N_2}$$

gains $2e^-$ × 3 (reduction)

ii. Balance the total number of electrons gained and lost the same way you would balance a chemical reaction.

$$2NH_3 + 3CuO \rightarrow 3Cu + H_2O + N_2$$

iii. Balance the rest of the non-redoxed elements (in this case, hydrogen and oxygen).

$$2NH_3 + 3\,CuO \rightarrow 3Cu + 3H_2O + N_2$$

Examples: Balance each reaction below.

Reaction	*Solution*
$Cl_2 + I^- \rightarrow Cl^- + I_2$	$Cl_2 + 2I^- \rightarrow 2Cl^- + I_2$
$BrO_3^- + MnO_2 \rightarrow Br^- + MnO_4^-$	$2OH^- + BrO_3^- + 2MnO_2 \rightarrow Br^- + 2MnO_4^- + H_2O$
$Cr + NO_2^- \rightarrow CrO_2^- + N_2O_2^{-2}$	$2H_2O + 4Cr + 6NO_2^- \rightarrow 4CrO_2^- + 3N_2O_2^{-2} + 4H^+$
$Cr + Sn^{+4} \rightarrow Cr^{+3} + Sn^{+2}$	$2Cr + 3Sn^{+4} \rightarrow 2Cr^{+3} + 3\,Sn^{+2}$
$Fe^{+2} + MnO_4^- \rightarrow Mn^{+2} + Fe^{+3}$	$8\,H^+ + 5Fe^{+2} + MnO_4^- \rightarrow Mn^{+2} + 5Fe^{+3} + 4H_2O$
$IO_4^- + I^- \rightarrow I_2$	$8\,H^+ + IO_4^- + 7\,I^- \rightarrow 4I_2 + 4H_2O$
$Mg + O_2 \rightarrow MgO$	$2Mg + O_2 \rightarrow 2MgO$
$MnO_4^- + C_2O_4^{-2} \rightarrow Mn^{+2} + CO_2$	$16H^+ + 2MnO_4^- + 5C_2O_4^{-2} \rightarrow 2Mn^{+2} + 10CO_2 + 8H_2O$
$NO_2 + ClO^- \rightarrow NO_3^- + Cl_2$	$2NO_2 + 2ClO^- \rightarrow 2NO_3^- + Cl_2$
$NO_3^- + S \rightarrow NO_2 + H_2SO_4$	$6H^+ + 6NO_3^- + S \rightarrow 6NO_2 + H_2SO_4 + 2H_2O$

Half-Reaction Method

i. Write down the reduction and the oxidation half-reactions.

ii. To balance oxygen, add an appropriate amount of H_2O to the side with the least amount of oxygen, and then add H^+ to the other side to balance hydrogen.

iii. The number of electrons gained must equal the number of electrons lost.

1. Find the least common multiple of the electrons gained and lost.
2. In each half-reaction, multiply the electron coefficient by a number to reach the common multiple.
3. Multiply all of the coefficients in the half-reaction by this same number.

iv. Add the two half-reactions.

v. Check the equation.

1. There should be no electrons in the equation at this time.
2. The number of each element should be the same on both sides.
3. It doesn't matter what the charge of an element is.
4. If any of these are not balanced, the equation is incorrect. The only thing to do is go back to step 1 and begin looking for your mistake.

gains $5e^-$ (reduction)

+7 -2 +4 +2 +6

$$MnO_4^- + H_2SO_3 \rightarrow Mn^{+2} + HSO_4^-$$

loses $2e^-$ (oxidation)

MnO_4^- reaction: $(8H^{+1} + 5e^- + MnO_4^- \rightarrow Mn^{+2} + 4H_2O) \times 2$
H_2SO_3 reaction: $(H_2O + H_2SO_3 \rightarrow HSO_4^{-1} + 2e^- + 3H^+) \times 5$

$$16H^+ + 10e^- + 2MnO_4^- \rightarrow 2Mn^{+2} + 8H_2O$$
$$+ 5H_2O + 5H_2SO_3 \rightarrow 5HSO_4^- + 10e^- + 15H^+$$

$$\cancel{16H^+} + \cancel{10e^{-1}} + 2MnO_4^- + \cancel{5H_2O} + 5H_2SO_3 \rightarrow$$
$$2Mn^{+2} + \cancel{8H_2O} + 5HSO_4^- + \cancel{10e^-} + \cancel{15H^+}$$

Final balanced equation: $H^+ + 2MnO_4^- + 5H_2SO_3 \rightarrow 2Mn^{+2} + 3H_2O + 5HSO_4^-$

Examples: Balance these redox equations using the half-reaction method.

1. $HNO_3 + H_3PO_3 \rightarrow NO + H_3PO_4 + H_2O$

   $2HNO_3 + 6e^- + 6H^+ \rightarrow 2NO + 4H_2O$
   $3H_3PO_3 + 3H_2O \rightarrow 3H_3PO_4 + 6e^- + 6H^+$

   $2HNO_3 + 3H_3PO_3 \rightarrow 2NO + 3H_3PO_4 + H_2O$

2. $Cr_2O_7^{-2} + H^+ + I^- \rightarrow Cr^{+3} + I_2 + H_2O$
   $Cr_2O_7^{-2} + 6e^- + 14H^+ \rightarrow 2Cr^{+3} + 7H_2O$
   $6I^- \rightarrow 3I_2 + 6e^-$

   $Cr_2O_7^{-2} + 14H^+ + 6I^- \rightarrow 2Cr^{+3} + 3I_2 + 7H_2O$

3. $MnO_4^- + H_2O_2 \rightarrow Mn^{+2} + O_2$
   $16H^+ + 2MnO_4^- + 10e^- \rightarrow 2Mn^{+2} + 8H_2O$
   $5H_2O_2 \rightarrow 5O_2 + 10e^- + 10H^+$

   $2MnO_4^- + 5H_2O_2 + 6H^+ \rightarrow 2Mn^{+2} + 5O_2 + 8H_2O$

Section Practice

1. What is the oxidation number of Na in NaCl?
   a) 0
   b) −1
   c) +1
   d) −2
   e) +2

Answer: (c)

Na: +1
Cl: − 1

2. When the equation $Cu(s) + NO_3^-(aq) + H^+(aq) \rightarrow Cu^{2+}(aq) + NO_2(g) + H_2O(l)$ is balanced, what is the coefficient of H^+?
   a) 1
   b) 2
   c) 3
   d) 4
   e) 5

Answer: (d)

$Cu(s) + 2NO_3^-(aq) + 4H^+(aq) \rightarrow Cu^{2+}(aq) + 2NO_2(g) + 2H_2O(l)$

3. When the equation $HMnO_4 + H_2SO_3 \rightarrow MnSO_4 + H_2O + H_2SO_4$ is balanced, what is the smallest possible whole number coefficient of H_2SO_3?
   a) 1
   b) 2
   c) 3
   d) 4
   e) 5

Answer: (e)

$2HMnO_4 + 5H_2SO_3 \rightarrow 2MnSO_4 + 3H_2O + 3H_2SO_4$

4. What is the sum of the coefficients of the products for the following reaction?
   $K_2Cr_2O_7 + HCl \rightarrow KCl + CrCl_3 + H_2O + Cl_2$
   a) 10
   b) 12
   c) 13
   d) 14
   e) 15

Answer: (d)

$K_2Cr_2O_7 + 14HCl \rightarrow 2KCl + 2CrCl_3 + 7H_2O + 3Cl_2$
The sum of the coefficients of the products is 2 + 2 + 7 + 3 = 14.

5. When the following redox equation is balanced and all coefficients are reduced to lowest whole number terms, what is the coefficient of H^+?
   $$H^+(aq) + MnO_4^{-1}(aq) + Fe^{+2}(aq) \rightarrow Fe^{+3}(aq) + Mn^{+2}(aq) + H_2O(l)$$
   a) 2
   b) 4
   c) 7
   d) 8
   e) 9

Answer: (d)

$8H^+(aq) + MnO_4^{-1}(aq) + 5Fe^{+2}(aq) \rightarrow 5Fe^{+3}(aq) + Mn^{+2}(aq) + 4H_2O(l)$

6. What is the minimum number of electrons needed to balance the following half-reaction with whole number coefficients?

$$IO_3^- \rightarrow I_2$$

a) 1
b) 2
c) 5
d) 10
e) 12

Answer: (d)

$12H^+ + 2IO_3^- + 10e^- \rightarrow I_2 + 6H_2O$

7. An electrochemical cell is constructed using Cd and Ag. Which of the following is true?
   a) Ag must be the anode.
   b) Cd must be the cathode.
   c) The $E°_{cell}$ is 1.20V.
   d) The $E°_{cell}$ is 0.40 V.
   e) Cd is reduced in the cell according to the following half-reaction: $Cd^{+2} + 2e^- \rightarrow Cd(s)$.

Answer: (c)

Metal Cd is more active than Ag. In the electrochemical cell, Cd should be the anode and Ag should be the cathode.
Cd Reduction Potential = – 0.4V
Ag Reduction Potential = 0.8
$E°_{cell} = 0.8 - (-0.4) = 1.2$

8. The diagram shown below represents an electroplating arrangement. The object to be plated with metal would be the

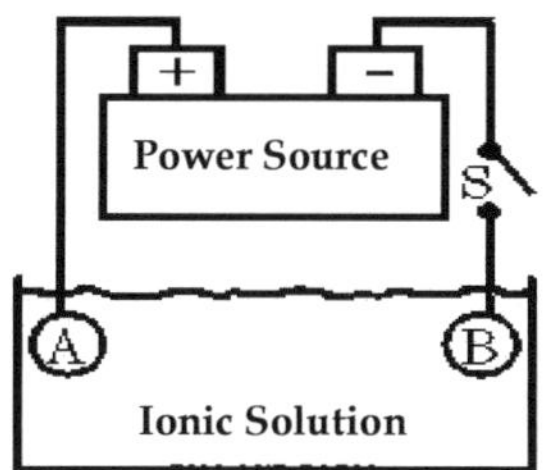

a) anode at A.
b) anode at B.
c) cathode at A.
d) cathode at B.
e) None of the above

Answer: (d)

The cathode is where the reduction occurs.

III. Oxidizing and Reducing Agents

Oxidizing Agents

1. A substance that has the potential to cause another substance to be oxidized
2. The substance that is reduced in a redox reaction
3. Halogens and oxygen are active oxidizing agents.

Reducing Agents

1. A substance that has the potential to cause another substance to be reduced
2. The substance that is oxidized in a redox reaction
3. Group 1 and 2 metals are active reducing agents.

Strong Oxidizing Agents

1. Substances that readily gain electrons are strong oxidizing agents.
2. Halogens and oxygen are among the strongest oxidation agents.

Strong Reducing Agents

1. Substances that readily lose electrons are strong reducing agents, such as Group I and Group II metals.
2. Once oxidized, the strong reducing agent becomes a poor oxidizing agent. It does not want to gain back the electrons it lost.

Redox reactions take place in electrochemical cells. There are two types of electrochemical cells. Spontaneous reactions occur in galvanic (voltaic) cells, while nonspontaneous reactions occur in electrolytic cells. Both types of cells contain electrodes where the oxidation and reduction reactions occur. Oxidation occurs at the electrode, which is called the anode, and reduction occurs at the electrode, which is called the cathode.

Relative Strengths of Oxidizing and Reducing Agents

Reducing Agents		Oxidizing Agents	
Increasing Strength →	Li	Li	Increasing Strength→
	K	K	
	Ca	Ca^{+2}	
	Na	Na^{+}	
	Mg	Mg^{+2}	
	Al	Al^{+3}	
	Zn	Zn^{+2}	
	Cr	Cr^{+3}	
	Fe	Fe^{+2}	
	Ni	Ni^{+2}	
	Sn	Sn^{+2}	
	Pb	Pb^{+2}	
	H_2	H_3O^{+}	
	H_2S	S	
	Cu	Cu^{+2}	
	I^{-}	I_2	
	Hg	Hg_2^{+2}	
	Ag	Ag	
	Br	$Br2$	
	Cr^{+3}	$Cr_2O_7^{-2}$	
	Cl^{-}	Cl_2	
	Mn^{+2}	MnO_4^{-}	
	F^{-}	F_2	

Section Practice

1. Which of the following is a good reducing agent?
   a) Group IA
   b) Group IIA
   c) Group IIIA
   d) Group VIA
   e) Group VIIA

Answer: (a)

The best reducing agent, which loses electrons during redox reactions, has the lowest electronegativity.

2. Which of the following is the best reducing agent?
   a) Ca
   b) Au
   c) H
   d) Fe
   e) Cu

Answer: (a)

The best reducing agent, which loses electrons during redox reactions, has the lowest electronegativity.

3. In $Cu(s) + NO_3^-(aq) + H^+(aq) \rightarrow Cu^{2+}(aq) + NO_2(g) + H_2O(l)$, which of the following takes place?
   a) Cu(s) is oxidized.
   b) $H^+(aq)$ is oxidized.
   c) Cu(s) is reduced.
   d) $H^+(aq)$ is reduced.
   e) NO_3^- is oxidized.

Answer: (a)

Cu(s) is oxidized and NO_3^- is reduced.

4. How many moles of electrons are required to reduce 103.6 g of lead from Pb^{2+} to the metal?
   a) 0.5 moles
   b) 1 mole
   c) 2 moles
   d) 4 moles
   e) 8 moles

Answer: (b)

$Pb^{2+} + 2e^- \rightarrow Pb$
One mole of lead needs two moles of electrons.
$\frac{103.6}{207.2} \times 2 = 1$ *mole of electrons*

5. Which of the following shows reducing agents correctly ordered by decreasing strength?
   a) Na, Mg, Fe, Ag, Cu
   b) Mg, Na, Fe, Cu, Ag
   c) Ag, Cu, Fe, Mg, Na
   d) Na, Fe, Mg, Cu, Ag
   e) Na, Mg, Fe, Cu, Ag

Answer: (e)

More active metals, which lose electrons more easily, are better reducing agents.

Na > Mg > Fe > Cu > Ag

6. Which of the following elements will be produced in the cathode when we electrolyze a dilute solution of sodium chloride?
   a) Sodium
   b) Chlorine
   c) Hydrogen
   d) Oxygen
   e) None of the above

Answer: (c)

Since Na has a higher reduction potential than H_2 in the cathode, H^+ will be reduced to H_2 instead of Na^+.

7. In which of the following compounds does manganese have the same oxidation number as it does in $KMnO_4$?
   a) $MnCl_2$
   b) MnO_2
   c) Mn_2O_3
   d) Mn_2O_7
   e) Mn

Answer: (d)

The oxidation number of Mn in $KMnO_4$ is +7, the same as the oxidation number of Mn in Mn_2O_7.

8. In the electroplating of tin, 0.500 Faradays of electrical charge are passed through a solution of $SnSO_4$ at 25 °C. What is the mass of tin deposited?
   a) 14.8 g
   b) 29.7 g
   c) 59.4 g
   d) 119 g
   e) 237 g

Answer: (b)

0.500 Faradays of electrical charge are equal to 0.5 moles of electrons.
$Sn^{2+} + 2e^- \rightarrow Sn$
0.5 moles of electrons will deposit 0.25 moles of Sn.
0.25 × 118.7 = 29.7 g of tin.

9. Consider the following reaction:

   $$Cl_2(g) + 2OH^-(aq) \rightarrow Cl^-(aq) + OCl^-(aq) + H_2O$$

   Which of the following is/are true regarding this reaction?
   I. Cl_2 undergoes both oxidation and reduction.
   II. The oxidation state of O in OCl^- is −1.
   III. OH^- is the reducing agent.
   a) I only
   b) II only
   c) II and III only
   d) I and III only
   e) I, II, and III

Answer: (a)

Cl_2 undergoes two different reactions here.

$Cl_2 \rightarrow OCl^-$ and its oxidation number changes from 0 to +1.

$Cl_2 \rightarrow Cl^-$ and its oxidation number changes from 0 to −1.

Cl_2 undergoes both oxidation and reduction.

IV. Electrochemistry

Electrochemistry is the branch of chemistry that deals with electricity-related applications of oxidation–reduction reactions.

Electrochemical Cells

i. **The electrode** is a conductor used to establish contact with a nonmetallic part of a circuit, such as an electrolyte.
ii. **A half-cell** is a single electrode immersed in a solution of its ions.
iii. **The anode** is the electrode where oxidation occurs.
iv. **The cathode** is the electrode where reduction occurs.
v. **A voltaic cell** is an electrochemical cell in which the redox reaction takes place spontaneously and produces electrical energy.

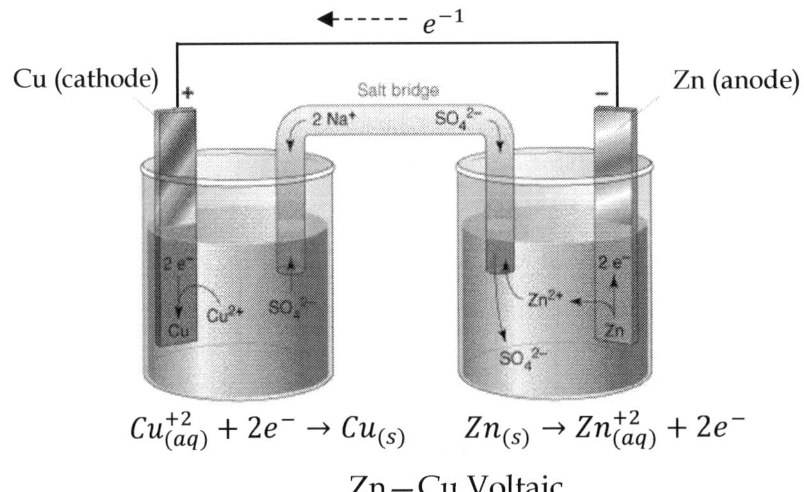

Zn—Cu Voltaic

Battery

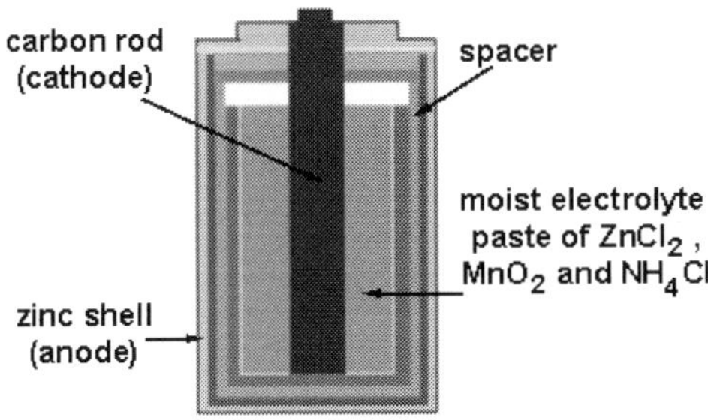

In the most common type of dry cell battery, graphite serves as the cathode and a zinc shell serves as the anode.

Cathode: $2\,NH_4 + 2\,MnO_2 + 2e^- \rightarrow Mn_2O_3 + 2NH_3 + H_2O$
Anode: $Zn_{(s)} \rightarrow Zn^{+2} + 2e^{-1}$

Electrolytic Cells

i. **Electrolysis** is a process by which an electric current is used to drive non-spontaneous redox reactions.

ii. **Electroplating** is an electrolytic process in which a metal ion is reduced and a solid metal is deposited on a surface.

1. The solution contains the salt of the plating metal.
2. The cathode is the object to be plated.
3. The anode is the plating metal.

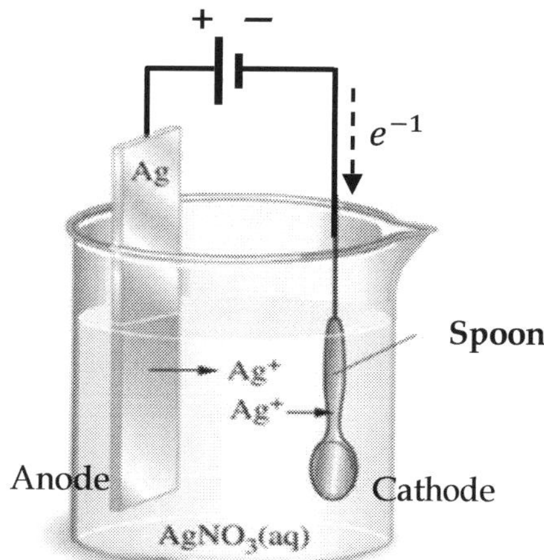

Silver ions are reduced (and plated) at the cathode: $Ag^{+1} + e^- \rightarrow Ag$

Electrode Potentials

$$\mathbf{E°_{cell} = E°_{reduction} + E°_{oxidation}}$$

Example: For a Zn-Cu cell,

$$Cu^{+2} + 2e^- \rightarrow Cu \quad E° = +0.24 \text{ volts}$$

$$Zn^{+2} + 2e^- \rightarrow Zn \quad E° = -0.76 \text{ volts}$$

The copper reduction will occur at the cathode and proceed as written. Zinc will be oxidized at the anode, and the reaction will be written as:

$$Zn \rightarrow Zn^{2+} + e^- \quad E° = +0.76 \text{ volts}$$

The sign on the potential changes (E°) will change when the direction of the reaction is reversed.

$$\begin{array}{lll} Cu^{+2} + 2e^- & \rightarrow Cu & E^o = +0.24\,V \\ \underline{Zn} & \underline{\rightarrow Zn^{+2} + 2e^-} & \underline{E^o = +0.76\,V} \\ Zn + Cu^{+2} & \rightarrow Zn^{+2} + Cu & E^o = 1.0\,V \end{array}$$

Electrodes and Charge

The anode of an electrolytic cell is positive (while the cathode is negative), since the anode attracts anions from the solution. However, the anode of a galvanic cell is negatively charged, since the spontaneous oxidation at the anode is the source of the cell's electrons or negative charge. The cathode of a galvanic cell is its positive terminal. In both galvanic and electrolytic cells, oxidation takes place at the anode and electrons flow from the anode to the cathode.

Cell potentials are measured in volts or energy per unit charge. This energy can be related to the theoretical maximum free energy or Gibbs free energy of the total redox reaction.

$$\Delta G^o = -nFE^o_{cell}$$

Where: $\Delta G°$ is the free energy of the reaction.
n is the number of moles of electrons exchanged in the reaction.
F is Faraday's constant (9.648456×10^4 C/mole).
$E°_{cell}$ is the cell potential.

Section Practice

1. The standard reduction potential of $Cu^{+2}(aq)$ is +0.34 V. What is the oxidation potential of Cu(s)?
   a) +0.68 V
   b) +0.34 V
   c) – 0.34 V
   d) – 0.68 V
   e) None of the above

Answer: (c)

The oxidation potential is the opposite of the standard reduction potential of Cu^{+2}.

2. What is the standard EMF if the following half-reactions are combined in a galvanic cell?

   $$Co^{+3}(aq) + e^- \rightarrow Co^{+2}(aq) \quad E° = 1.82\ V$$
   $$Na^+(aq) + e^- \rightarrow Na(s) \quad E° = -2.71V$$

   a) 4.53 V
   b) 0.89 V
   c) −0.89 V
   d) −4.53V
   e) None of the above

Answer: (a)

$1.82 - (-2.71) = 4.53\ V$

3. What is $E°_{cell}$ for a reaction where $\Delta G° = -553.91$ kJ and 2 electrons are transferred?
   a) −2.87 V
   b) −0.00287 V
   c) 0.00287 V
   d) 2.87 V
   e) None of the above

Answer: (d)

$\Delta G° = -nFE°_{cell}$
$-553910 = -2 \times 96485 \times E$
$E = 2.87\ V$

4. When the following half-reactions are combined in a galvanic cell, which species will be reduced and which will be oxidized?

$$F_2 + 2e^- \rightarrow 2F^-(aq)\ E° = +1.87\ V$$
$$Ca^{+2} + 2e^- \rightarrow Ca(s)\quad E° = -2.76\ V$$

a) F^- will be oxidized and Ca^{+2} will be reduced.
b) Ca^{+2} will be oxidized and F_2 will be reduced.
c) Ca(s) will be oxidized and F_2 will be reduced.
d) F_2 will be oxidized and Ca(s) will be reduced.
e) None of the above

Answer: (c)

In order to make the overall potential change positive, Ca(s) must be oxidized and F_2 must be reduced.

5. The gold-plating process involves the following reaction:

$$Au^{+3}(aq) + 3e^- \rightarrow Au(s)$$

If 0.600 g of Au is plated onto a metal, how many coulombs are used?

a) 440 C
b) 882 C
c) 1,760 C
d) 8,800 C
e) None of the above

Answer: (b)

0.600 g of Au is equal to $\frac{0.6}{197}$ moles of Au.
$\frac{0.6}{197} \times 3 \times 96485 = 882$ C

6. Electrode potentials are:

$$Zn \rightarrow Zn^{+2} + 2e^-\quad E^o = 0.76\ V$$
$$Au \rightarrow Au^{+3} + 3e^-\quad E° = -1.42\ V$$

If gold foil were placed in a solution containing Zn^{+2} ions, what would the reaction potential be?

a) −1.84 V
b) −2.18 V
c) −0.66 V
d) +2.18 V
e) +1.34 V

Answer: (b)

$-1.42 - 0.76 = -2.18$ V

7. Which of the following acts as the cathode?

a) Zn(s)
b) $Cu^{2+}(aq)$
c) $Zn^{2+}(aq)$
d) Cu(s)
e) H_2O

Answer: (d)

Oxidation occurs at the anode and reduction occurs at the cathode.
Cu is less active than Zn. Cu^{2+} ions will be reduced in the cathode.

8. In the electrochemical cell shown below, which of the following half-reaction occurs at the anode?

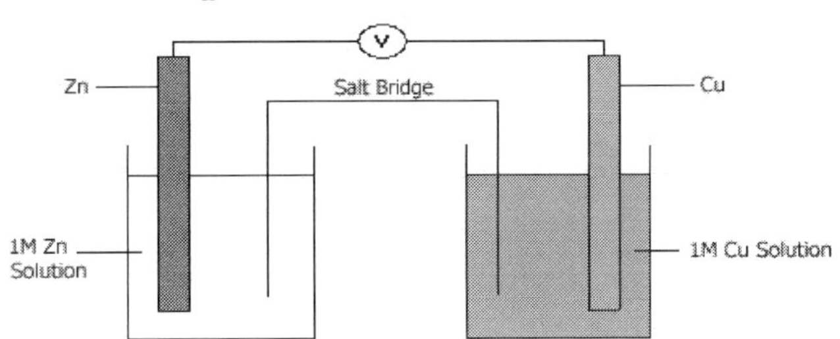

a) $Cu^{+2} + e^- \rightarrow Cu^+$
b) $Zn(s) \rightarrow Zn^{+2} + 2e^-$
c) $Zn^{+2} + 2e^- \rightarrow Zn(s)$
d) $Cu(s) \rightarrow Cu^{+2} + 2e^-$
e) $Cu^{+2} + 2e^- \rightarrow Cu(s)$

Answer: (b)

The anode is the electrode where oxidation occurs. Zn is more active than Cu, so Zn will be oxidized at the anode.

9. The Nernst equation is given by the following:

$$E_{cell} = E°_{cell} - \ln(Q)$$

Which of the following is/are true?

I. E_{cell} is always greater than $E °C_{ell}$.
II. When $Q = K_{eq}$, $E_{cell} = 0$.
III. When all concentrations are equal to 1 M (standard state), $E_{cell} = 0$.

a) I only
b) II only
c) I and II only
d) II and III only
e) I, II, and III

Answer: (b)

At equilibrium, $Q = K_{eq}$ and $E_{cell} = 0$
At the standard state, $E_{cell} = E°_{cell}$

10. In the reduction of MnO_4^{-1} to Mn^{+2}, the correct form of the Nernst equation is

a) $E = E° + \frac{0.0591}{3} log \frac{[Mn^{+2}]}{[MnO_4^-][H^+]^8}$
b) $E = E° - \frac{0.0591}{5} log \frac{[Mn^{+2}]}{[MnO_4^-][H^+]^8}$
c) $E^o = E - \frac{0.0591}{5} log \frac{[Mn^{+2}]}{[MnO_4^-][H^+]^8}$
d) $E = E° + \frac{0.0591}{5} log \frac{[MnO_4^-][H^+]^8}{[Mn^{+2}]}$
e) $E = E° + \frac{0.0591}{5} log \frac{[Mn^{+2}]}{[MnO_4^-][H^+]^8}$

Answer: (b)

$8H^+ + MnO_4^{-1} + 5e^- \rightarrow Mn^{+2} + 4H_2O$

$Q = \frac{[Mn^{+2}]}{[MnO_4^-][H^+]^8}$

$n = 5e^-$ *transferred*

$E_{cell} = E°_{cell} - \frac{0.052}{n} log(Q)$

$= E° - \frac{0.0591}{5} log \frac{[Mn^{+2}]}{[MnO_4^-][H^+]^8}$

11. When the temperature of the galvanic cell is increased from 20 °C to 30 °C, the cell voltage changes by a factor of 1.034. Which of the following conclusions may be drawn from this observation?
    a) $\Delta G°$ must be positive since the reaction is not spontaneous.
    b) The increase is due solely to the temperature in the equation $\Delta G° = -RT\ln K$.
    c) $\Delta S°$ for this reaction must be negative.
    d) The reaction is spontaneous because $\Delta G°$ is negative.
    e) The voltage change must be due to the change in the equilibrium constant with the change in temperature.

Answer: (b)

Changing the temperature will change the equilibrium constant and $\Delta G°$.

12. Which of the following half-cell reactions describes what is happening at the anode in the following diagram?

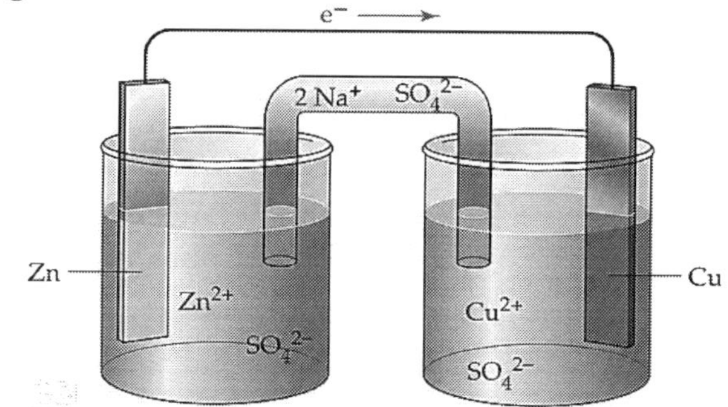

a) $Zn \rightarrow Zn^{2+} + 2e^-$
b) $H_2 \rightarrow 2H^+ + 2e^-$
c) $2Cl^- \rightarrow Cl_2 + 2e^-$
d) $SO_4^- \rightarrow S + 2O_2 + 6e^-$
e) $2H^+ + 2e^- \rightarrow H_2$

Answer: (a)

The anode is the electrode where oxidation occurs.

Chapter 13 Oxidation-Reduction Reactions SAT Questions

1. In which of the following compounds would nitrogen have the highest oxidation number?
   a) NO
   b) N_2O
   c) NO_2
   d) N_2O_3
   e) HNO_3

Answer: (e)

a) +2
b) +1
c) +4
d) +3
e) +5

2. Given the following chemical reaction for the formation of lithium oxide, which of the following statements is true?

$$4Li(s) + O_2(g) \rightarrow 2Li_2O(s)$$

   a) Lithium metal is the oxidizing agent.
   b) Oxygen gas is the reducing agent.
   c) Lithium is oxidized.
   d) Oxygen is oxidized.
   e) Oxygen loses two electrons to become a −2 ion.

Answer: (c)

$Li \rightarrow Li^+$: Li loses one e^-, which makes it oxidized and a reducing agent.

$O_2 \rightarrow O^{-2}$: Each O gains one e^-, which means it was reduced and an oxidizing agent.

3. What is the charge of chlorine in KCl?
   a) 0
   b) −1
   c) +1
   d) −2
   e) +2

Answer: (b)

The charge of Cl^- is −1.

4. Which type of element is missing?

   _____$_3(PO_4)_2$

   a) Group IA
   b) Group IIA
   c) Group IIIA
   d) Group VIA
   e) Group VIIA

Answer: (b)

$(X^{2+})_3(PO_4{}^{-3})_2$

The X ion should bear +2 charges. Alkaline earth metals are ionized to form 2+ charges.

5. Which type of element is missing?

   _____$_2O_2$ (oxidation state of oxygen is −1.)

   a) Group IA
   b) Group IIA
   c) Group IIIA
   d) Group VIA
   e) Group VIIA

Answer: (a)

X_2O_2

The X ion should have a +1 charge, so it must be a group IA ion.

6. Which type of element is missing?

   Cu_____2

   a) Group IA
   b) Group IIA
   c) Group IIIA
   d) Group VIA
   e) Group VIIA

Answer: (e)

$Cu^{2+} (X)_2$

The X ion should have a -1 charge, so it must be a group VIIA ion.

7. Which of the following is true of an electrolytic cell?
   a) An electric current causes an otherwise non-spontaneous chemical reaction to occur.
   b) Reduction occurs at the anode.
   c) A spontaneous electrochemical reaction produces an electric current.
   d) The electrode to which the electrons flow is where oxidation occurs.
   e) None of the above

Answer: (a)

Electrolysis is a process by which an electric current is used to drive non-spontaneous redox reactions.

8. In the electrolysis of molten copper chloride, what is the substance liberated at the anode?
   a) Copper
   b) Chlorine
   c) Hydrogen
   d) Copper chloride
   e) None of the above

Answer: (b)

Oxidation occurs at the anode.
$2Cl^- \rightarrow Cl_2 + 2e^-$

9. When salt is dissolved in water and placed in a conductivity apparatus, it will cause the light bulb to glow. The reason that a current can flow is because
   a) ions combine to form molecules.
   b) molecules migrate to the charge plates.
   c) ions migrate to the charge plates.
   d) sparks cross the gap.
   e) None of the above

Answer: (c)

Electric current, which consists of moving electrons, can be transported by ions in the solution.

10. The degree of ionization depends on the
    a) nature of the solvent.
    b) nature of the solute.
    c) concentration of the solution.
    d) temperature of the solution.
    e) All the above

Answer: (e)

All of the choices are true.

11. Which of the following is the hydronium ion?
    a) H_2O^+
    b) H_3O^+
    c) HOH^+
    d) H^+
    e) OH^-

Answer: (b)

Hydronium ion is produced in the following reaction:
$H^+ + H_2O \rightarrow H_3O^+$

12. In which state will ionic compounds conduct an electric current?
    a) Solidified
    b) Melted
    c) Frozen
    d) Dehydrated
    e) None of the above

Answer: (b)

Ionic compounds will conduct an electric current in an aqueous solution or a melted state.

13. If one Faraday is equivalent to 96,487 C/mole of e^-, what is the charge of an individual electron?
    a) 5.76×10^{28} C/e^-
    b) 6.02×10^{23} C/e^-
    c) 1.6×10^{19} C/e^-
    d) 1.6×10^{-19} C/e^-
    e) None of the above

Answer: (d)

Charge of an Electron =
$\frac{96487}{6.02 \times 10^{23}} = 1.6 \times 10^{-19}$ C/e^-

14. How many Faradays are required for the reduction of 1 mole of Ni^{+2} to Ni(s)?
    a) 1 F
    b) 2 F
    c) 96,487 F
    d) 6.022×10^{23} F
    e) None of the above

Answer: (b)

$Ni^{+2} + 2e^- \rightarrow Ni$

1 mole of Ni needs 2 moles of e^- = 2 F of C.

15. If the following reactions are used to make a galvanic cell, which species will be reduced and which species will be oxidized?

$$F_2 + 2e^- \rightarrow 2F^-(aq) \quad E = +2.87 \text{ V}$$
$$Ca^{+2} + 2e^- \rightarrow Ca(s) \quad E = -2.76 \text{ V}$$

    a) F^- will be oxidized and Ca^{2+} will be reduced.
    b) Ca^{2+} will be oxidized and F_2 will be reduced.
    c) Ca(s) will be oxidized and F_2 will be reduced.
    d) F_2 will be oxidized and Ca(s) will be reduced.
    e) None of the above

Answer: (c)

In order to make the overall potential change positive, Ca should be oxidized and F_2 should be reduced.

16. What is the $\Delta G°$ for the following reaction?

$Ti^{2+}(aq) + Mg(s) \rightarrow Ti(s) + Mg^{+2}(aq)$

$Ti^{+2}(aq) + 2e^- \rightarrow Ti(s) \quad E° = -1.63\ V$

$Mg^{+2}(aq) + 2e^- \rightarrow Mg(s) \quad E° = -2.38\ V$

a) 144.73 kJ
b) 144.73 J
c) −144.73 J
d) −144.73 kJ
e) None of the above

Answer: (d)

$\Delta E° = 0.75$
$\Delta G° = -nF\Delta E° = -2 \times 96487 \times (0.75) = -144730\ J = -144.73\ kJ$

17. Which of the following metals would you expect to corrode more readily than Al?

a) Ag
b) Hg
c) Sn
d) Cd
e) Mg

Answer: (e)

Mg is more active than Al.

18. The standard reduction potential for $PbO_2 \rightarrow Pb^{+2}$ is 1.46 V. The standard reduction potential for $Fe^{+3} \rightarrow Fe^{+2}$ is +0.77 V. What is the standard cell voltage for the reaction $4H^+ + PbO_2 + 2Fe^{+2} \rightarrow 2Fe^{+3} + Pb^{+2} + 2H_2O$?

a) −0.08 V
b) +0.69 V
c) +2.33 V
d) −0.69 V
e) −2.33 V

Answer: (b)

$PbO_2 \rightarrow Pb^{+2}$ E = 1.46
$Fe^{+2} \rightarrow Fe^{+3}$ E = −0.77

1.46 − 0.77 = 0.69 V

19. Which of the following compounds includes an element with an oxidation number of +5?

a) ClO_4^-
b) MnO_4^-
c) NO_2^-
d) SO_3^{-2}
e) NO_3^-

Answer: (e)

a) ClO_4^-: +7 and −2
b) MnO_4^-: +7 and −2
c) NO_2^-: +3 and −2
d) SO_3^{-2}: +4 and −2
e) NO_3^-: +5 and −2

20. Which of the following metals does NOT react with water to produce hydrogen?

a) Zn
b) Li
c) Ca
d) Na
e) Rb

Answer: (a)

Even though Zn has a higher reduction potential than hydrogen, it does not react with water molecules. It does form a protective, water insoluble zinc hydroxide, $Zn(OH)_2$, which is layered with dissolved hydroxide ions.

21. In the electrolysis of an aqueous solution of $Cu(NO_3)_2$, which of the following is expected to occur?
    a) Formation of O_2 at the anode
    b) Formation of H_2 at the cathode
    c) Deposition of copper metal on the anode
    d) Formation of hydroxide ions at the cathode
    e) Formation of H^+ at the cathode

Answer: (a)

When comparing NO_3^- and OH^-, OH^- is more easily oxidized to O_2 at the anode. When comparing Cu^{2+} and H^+, Cu^{2+} is more easily reduced at the cathode.

22. Sodium metal cannot be electrolyzed from an aqueous Na_2SO_4 solution because
    a) the voltage needed is too high for any available instrument to achieve.
    b) water is reduced to O_2 before Na^+ to Na.
    c) Na^+ has a high reduction potential that keeps it from being reduced.
    d) H^+ has a more favorable reduction potential than Na^+.
    e) Na^+ does electrolyze, but it immediately reacts with water again.

Answer: (d)

$Na^+ + e^- \rightarrow Na \quad E^o = -2.71$

$2H^+ + 2e^- \rightarrow H_2 \quad E^o = 0$

23. Which of the following elements has the largest number of possible oxidation states?
    a) Fe
    b) Cl
    c) Ca
    d) Mn
    e) Na

Answer: (b)

Fe: 0, +2, +3
Cl: −1, 0, +1, +3, +5, +7
Ca: 0, +2
Mn: 0, +2, +4, +5, +7
Na: 0, +1

24. A metal is electrolyzed in an aqueous solution by using an electrical current of 1.23 A for 2½ hours and then 3.37 g of metal is deposited. In a separate experiment, 2 moles of electrons are used for the reduction of the metal. Which of the following is this metal?
    a) Al
    b) Ni
    c) Sn
    d) Mg
    e) Au

Answer: (b)

$1.23 \times 2.5 \times 60 \times 60 = 11070$ C

$\frac{11070}{2 \times 96487} = 0.05737$ moles

$\frac{3.37}{0.05737} = 58.7(Ni)$

It is Ni.

25. A galvanic cell is set up under nonstandard state conditions, and E_{cell} is measured as −0.16 V. Which of the following is true about this system?
    a) The galvanic cell is set up incorrectly because of the negative value of E_{cell}.
    b) If the contents of the two cells are mixed, the reaction will proceed in the forward direction.
    c) The reaction is definitely nonspontaneous.
    d) If the contents of the two cells are mixed, the reaction will proceed in the reverse direction.
    e) The reaction is definitely a spontaneous reaction.

Answer: (d)

If E_{cell} is a negative value, the reaction will proceed in the reverse direction spontaneously.

26. Which of the following compounds includes an element that has the same oxidation number as the chlorine in sodium chlorate, $NaClO_3$?
    a) $K_3Fe(CN)_6$
    b) $KMnO_4$
    c) $Al(NO_3)_3$
    d) $(NH_4)_2SO_4$
    e) $KClO_4$

Answer: (c)

$NaClO_3$: Cl is +5.
$K_3Fe(CN)_6$: Fe is +3.
$KMnO_4$: Mn is +7.
$Al(NO_3)_3$: N is +5.
$(NH_4)_2SO_4$: S is +6.
$KClO_4$: Cl is +7.

27. Which of the following is NOT true of a net ionic equation?
    a) All of the non-reacting ions have been canceled out.
    b) It shows the actual reactants in an equation.
    c) It allows the chemist to substitute reactants in a logical manner.
    d) It is used to determine which compounds are insoluble.
    e) It must have the charges as well as the atoms balanced.

Answer: (d)

(d) is not true. Compounds may be weak acids or bases.

28. What is the oxidation number of the underlined symbol in the compound $K_2\underline{Cr}O_4$?
    a) +1
    b) +2
    c) +4
    d) +5
    e) +6

Answer: (e)

4 × 2 (from O) − 2 × 1 (from K) = +6

29. What is the oxidation number of the underlined symbol in the compound $Na_2\underline{S}_2O_4$?
    a) +1
    b) +2
    c) +3
    d) +4
    e) +6

Answer: (c)

4 × 2 *(from O)* – 2 × 1 *(from Na)* = +6/2 = +3

30. What is the oxidation number of the underlined symbol in the compound $Mg(\underline{H}CO_3)_2$?
    a) +1
    b) +2
    c) +4
    d) +5
    e) +6

Answer: (a)

The H ion almost always has a charge of +1.

Relationship Analysis Questions

1.	When a piece of Al is dropped into a 1 M solution of $MgCl_2$, elemental Mg appears.	Al is more readily oxidized than Mg.	FF
2.	$Al^{3+} + 3e^- \rightarrow Al$ is a correctly balanced oxidation reaction.	$Al^{3+} + 3e^- \rightarrow Al$ correctly demonstrates conservation of mass and conservation of charge.	FT
3.	Elemental sodium is a good reducing agent.	An atom of elemental sodium readily gives up its valence electron.	TTCE
4.	An electrolytic cell makes a nonspontaneous redox reaction occur.	An electrolytic cell uses an external current to drive a redox reaction.	TTCE
5.	An ionic solid is a good conductor of electricity.	An ionic solid is composed of positive and negative ions joined together by electrostatic forces.	FT
6.	In an electrolytic cell, the anode becomes positive and the cathode becomes negative.	Anions migrate to the anode and cations migrate to the cathode.	TT
7.	Voltaic cells harness the energy of redox reactions.	In a voltaic cell, electron flow occurs through the salt bridge.	TF
8.	Oxidation and reduction occur together.	In redox reactions, electrons must be gained and lost.	TTCE

	Statement	Reason	
9.	Bromine is a stronger oxidizing agent than chlorine.	Bromine has a large atomic radius.	FT
10.	The Cu^{+2} ion needs to be oxidized to form Cu metal.	Oxidation is when an element gains electrons.	FF
11.	The anions migrate to the cathode in an electrochemical reaction.	Positively charged ions are attracted to the negatively charged cathode.	FT
12.	The standard reduction potential for $Ag^+ + e^- \rightarrow Ag$ is half of that of $2Ag^+ + 2e^- \rightarrow 2Ag$.	Standard potential is dependent on the number of electrons transferred.	FF

Chapter 14 Carbon and Hydrocarbons

I. Allotropes of Carbon and Organic Compounds

i. Diamond is the hardest substance found on Earth. It has an extremely high melting point (≈ 4000 °C). Diamond is an excellent conductor of heat but a very poor conductor of electricity.

ii. Graphite contains layers of carbon atoms, with each layer made up of strong covalent bonds. However, only weak forces exist between layers, therefore the layers can easily slide over each other. The sliding of these layers gives graphite its softness for writing and its lubricating properties.

Carbon Bonding and the Diversity of Organic Compounds

i. Carbon is the only element that can form a massive number of different compounds because each carbon atom can form four chemical bonds to other atoms, and is the right size to fit these atoms around it.
ii. Carbon can form chains or rings of single, double, and even triple covalent bonds with itself.
iii. Carbon can bond to other elements such as H, O, N, S, and the halogens to create a huge number of molecules.
iv. A molecule with the same chemical formula but a different geometrical arrangement makes an organic compound with a different shape and hence with different properties. These different compounds are called **isomers**.

Structural isomers are molecules that have the same formula, but their atoms are bonded together in a different order. For example,

C_4H_{10} Butane	C_4H_{10} 2-methylpropane
$CH_3-CH_2-CH_2-CH_3$	$CH_3-CH-CH_3$ with CH_3 on the middle C

Geometric isomers are the isomers in which the order of atom bonding is the same, but the arrangement of atoms in space is different. In order for an isomer to exist, there must be a double or triple bond in the molecule to prevent free rotation around a bond which has two different groups attached.

trans (same side) 1,2-dichloroethene cis (opposite) 1,2-dichloroethene

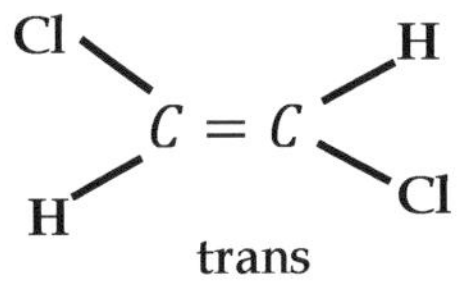

Cl, H on left C = C H, Cl (trans); Cl, H on left C = C Cl, H (cis)

trans 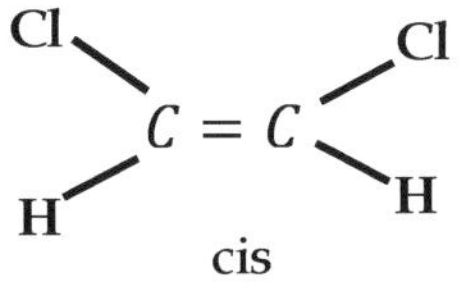 cis

Saturated Hydrocarbons

These are hydrocarbons in which each atom in the molecule forms four single covalent bonds with other atoms.

i. Alkanes contain only single bonds and have the following formula:

$$C_nH_{2n+2}$$

The First 8 Alkanes		
# of Carbons	Name	Formula (C_nH_{2n+2})
1	Methane	CH_4
2	Ethane	C_2H_6
3	Propane	C_3H_8
4	Butane	C_4H_{10}
5	Pentane	C_5H_{12}
6	Hexane	C_6H_{14}
7	Heptane	C_7H_{16}
8	Octane	C_8H_{18}

ii. **Cycloalkanes** are the alkanes where the carbon atoms are arranged in a ring, or cyclic structures.

Unsaturated Hydrocarbons contain at least one double or triple bond in the molecule forms.

i. Alkenes are the hydrocarbons that contain double bonds. The simplest form of the alkene is ethene, also known as ethylene (C_2H_4).

H H
C = C
H H

Ethene

ii. Alkynes are the hydrocarbons with triple covalent bonds. The simplest form of the alkyne is ethyne, also known as acetylene (C_2H_2).

$$H - C \equiv C - H$$

Ethyne

iii. Aromatic compounds are the hydrocarbons that contain benzene (C_6H_6) and its derivatives.

H
H C H
C C
C C
H C H
H

Benzene

Section Practice

1. Coke is produced from bituminous coal by
   a) cracking.
   b) synthesis.
   c) substitution.
   d) destructive distillation.
   e) oxidation.

Answer: (d)

Coke is the solid carbonaceous material derived from destructive distillation bituminous coal.

2. The "lead" in a lead pencil is a
   a) bone black.
   b) graphite and clay.
   c) lead oxide.
   d) lead peroxide.
   e) lead metal.

Answer: (b)

A pencil is made of graphite and clay.

3. Which of the following precipitates will be formed when carbon dioxide is bubbled into limewater?
   a) $CaCl_2$
   b) H_2CO_3
   c) CaO
   d) $CaCO_3$
   e) $CaSO_4$

Answer: (d)

$Ca(OH)_2(aq) + CO_2(g) \rightarrow CaCO_3(s) + H_2O(l)$

4. Carbon atoms usually
   a) lose 4 electrons.
   b) gain 4 electrons.
   c) form 4 covalent bonds.
   d) share the 2 electrons in the first principal energy level.
   e) form double bonds with oxygen.

Answer: (c)

Carbon can either lose or gain 4 electrons to form 4 covalent bonds.

5. Alloys are mixtures of metallic substances. Which of the following pairs are matched INCORRECTLY?
   a) Brass - copper and zinc
   b) Steel - iron and copper
   c) Bronze - copper, zinc, and others
   d) Pewter - tin, copper, bismuth, and antimony
   e) Sterling silver - silver and copper

Answer: (b)

Steel actually consists of iron and carbon

6. A student performed an experiment and a gas was produced. After the gas was collected and tested with a burning splint, a loud popping noise was heard. Which of the following gases was produced?
   a) Hydrogen
   b) Oxygen
   c) Carbon dioxide
   d) Chlorine
   e) Methane

Answer: (a)

Hydrogen explodes in the presence of oxygen.

7. The following statements about carbon dioxide are true EXCEPT?
   a) It can be prepared by the addition of acid to $CaCO_3$.
   b) It is used in fire extinguishers.
   c) It dissolves in water at room temperature.
   d) It sublimes rather than melts at 20 °C and 1 atm pressure.
   e) It is a product of photosynthesis in plants.

Answer: (e)

O_2 is a product of photosynthesis in plants.

8. The normal electron configuration for ethyne (acetylene) is
   a) H : C : : C : H
   b) H : C : C : H
   c) H·C : : : C·H
   d) H : C : : : C : H
   e) H : C : C : H

Answer: (d)

Ethyne has a triple bond.

9. Ethene is the first member of the
   a) alkane series.
   b) alkyne series.
   c) saturated hydrocarbons.
   d) unsaturated hydrocarbons.
   e) aromatic hydrocarbons.

Answer: (d)

Ethene has a double bond and is the first member of the unsaturated hydrocarbons.

10. Which is the first and simplest alkane?
   a) Ethane
   b) Methane
   c) C_2H_2
   d) Methene
   e) CCl_4

Answer: (b)

CH_4, methane, is the simplest alkane.

11. Compounds that have the same composition but differ in structural formulas
    a) are used for substitution products.
    b) are called polymers.
    c) are usually alkanes.
    d) have the same properties.
    e) are called isomers.

Answer: (e)

Definition of isomer.

12. Which of the following statements is true of ethene?
    a) Both carbon atoms are sp^2 hybridized and the molecule is planar.
    b) Both carbon atoms are sp^2 hybridized and all bond angles are approximately 109.5°.
    c) One carbon atom is sp hybridized while the other is sp^2.
    d) Both carbon atoms are sp^3 hybridized and all bond angles are approximately 109.5°.
    e) Both carbon atoms are sp hybridized and the molecule is planar.

Answer: (a)

Ethene has a double bond and both carbon atoms are sp^2 hybridized.

Molecular geometry of sp^2 hybridized is triangular planar.

13. Compounds that have the same composition but differ in structural formulas
    a) are used for substitution products.
    b) are called polymers.
    c) are usually alkanes.
    d) have the same properties.
    e) are called isomers.

Answer: (e)

Definition of isomer.

14. Which of the following is the formula for a noncyclic, saturated hydrocarbon?
    a) C_7H_{12}
    b) C_7H_{14}
    c) C_7H_{16}
    d) C_7H_{18}
    e) C_7H_{12}

Answer: (c)

A noncyclic, saturated hydrocarbon has the formula of C_nH_{2n+2}.

15. Which of the following organic structures is propane?
    a) $CH_3-CH_2-CH_3$
    b) $CH_3-CO-OH$
    c) $CH_3-O-CH_2-CH_3$
    d) $CH_3-CH_2-NH_2$
    e) $CH_3-CO-CH_3$

Answer: (a)

Propane has the formula of C_3H_8.

II. Functional Groups and Classes of Organic Compounds

Functional Group

An atom or group of atoms that is responsible for the specific properties of an organic compound.

i. **Alcohols** contain one or more hydroxyl (−OH) groups in the molecule.

$$C_nH_{2n+1}(OH)$$

ii. **Alkyl halides** are organic compounds in which one or more hydrogen atoms are substituted for halogen atoms.

$$C_nH_{2n+1}Cl$$

iii. **Ethers** are organic compounds which have two hydrocarbon groups bonded to the same oxygen.

R–O–R' (Ethers)

iv. **Aldehydes** are organic compounds with a carbonyl group attached to a carbon atom at the end of a carbon-atom chain.

R–C(=O)–H (Aldehydes)

v. **Ketones** are organic compounds with a carbonyl group attached to carbon atoms within the chain.

R–C(=O)–R' (Ketones)

vi. **Carboxylic acids** are organic compounds with a carboxyl functional group.

R–C(=O)–OH (Carboxylic Acid)

vii. **Esters** are organic compounds with carboxylic acid groups in which the hydrogen of the hydroxyl group has been replaced by an alkyl group.

R–C(=O)–OR' (Esters)

Section Practice

1. Which of the following functional groups of the organic compound is ester?
   a) –CO–
   b) –COOH
   c) –CHO–
   d) –O–
   e) –COO–

Answer: (e)

Organic ester:

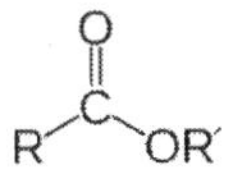

$$R-\overset{\displaystyle O}{\overset{\|}{C}}-OR'$$

2. Which of the following organic structures is ethanoic acid?
   a) $CH_3-CH_2-CH_3$
   b) $CH_3-CO-OH$
   c) $CH_3-O-CH_2-CH_3$
   d) $CH_3-CH_2-NH_2$
   e) $CH_3-CO-CH_3$

Answer: (b)

Organic acid: $R-COOH$

$CH_3-CO-OH$ *is ethanoic acid.*

3. Which of the following organic structures is methyl propyl ether?
   a) $CH_3-CH_2-CH_3$
   b) $CH_3-CO-OH$
   c) $CH_3-O-CH_2-CH_2-CH_3$
   d) $CH_3-CH_2-NH_2$
   e) $CH_3-CO-CH_3$

Answer: (c)

Organic ether: $R-O-R'$

Methyl: CH_3-

Propyl: $CH_3-CH_2-CH_2-$

4. Which of the following structures contains a ketone group?
   a) $CH_3-CH_2-CH_3$
   b) $CH_3-CO-OH$
   c) $CH_3-O-CH_2-CH_2-CH_3$
   d) $CH_3-CH_2-NH_2$
   e) $CH_3-CO-CH_3$

Answer: (e)

Organic ketone: $R-CO-R'$

5. Which of the following compounds is INCORRECTLY matched to the functional group that it contains?
   a) CH_3COOH hydroxyl
   b) CH_3OH hydroxyl
   c) $CH_3CH_2NH_2$ amine
   d) CCl_3COOH carboxylic acid
   e) C_6H_5COOH carboxylic acid

Answer: (a)

CH_3COOH *is a carboxylic acid.*

6. Which of the following is the functional group of organic ether?
   a) R –OH
   b) R–O–R′
   c) R–CO–R′
   d) R–COOH
   e) R–OH

Answer: (b)

Organic ether: R – O – R′

7. Which of the following structures is the third member of the alkyne series?
   a) H–C≡C–H
   b) $H-C{\equiv}C-CH_3$
   c) $H-C{\equiv}C-CH_2CH_3$
   d) H–C≡C–C≡C–H
   e) $H-C-C-CH{=}C-H_2$

Answer: (c)

Alkyne series have one triple bond in their structure.

8. The functional group shown below represents a(n)

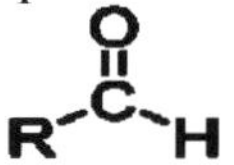

   a) alcohol
   b) ether
   c) aldehyde
   d) ketone
   e) organic acid derivative

Answer: (c)

Aldehyde: $R-C(=O)-H$

9. A triple bond may best be described as
   a) Two sigma bonds and one pi bond.
   b) Two sigma bonds and two pi bonds.
   c) One sigma bond and two pi bonds.
   d) Three sigma bonds.
   e) Three pi bonds.

Answer: (c)

A triple bond contains one sigma bond and two pi bonds.

III. Organic Reactions

Common Organic Chemical Reactions:

i. **A substitution reaction** is when one or more atoms replace another atom or group of atoms in a molecule.

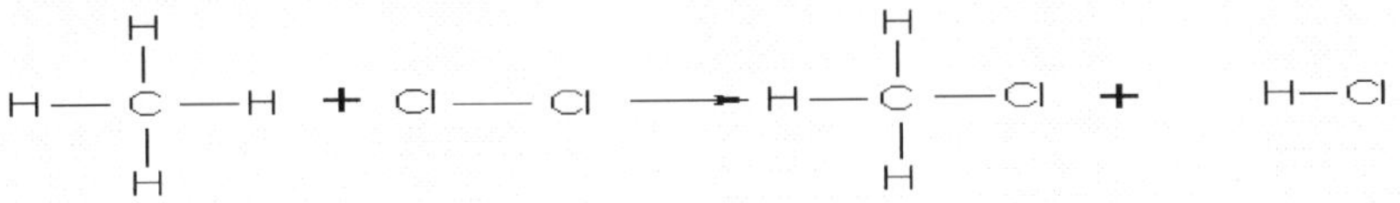

Methane chlorine → chloromethane + hydrogen chloride

ii. **An addition reaction** is when an atom or molecule is added to an unsaturated molecule and increases the saturation of the molecule.

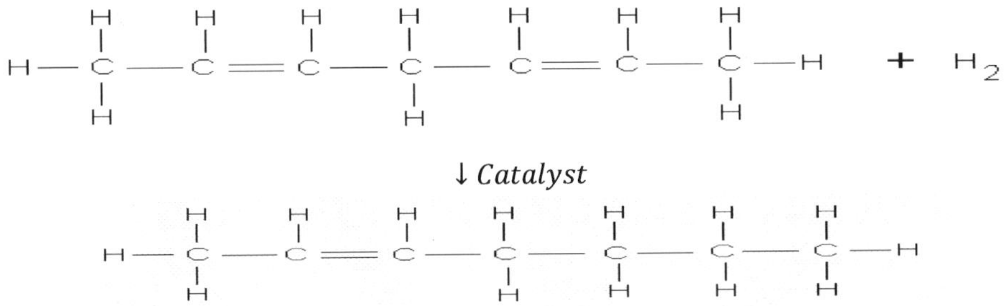

↓ *Catalyst*

iii. **A condensation reaction** is when an alcohol reacts with a carboxylic acid and produces an ester and water.

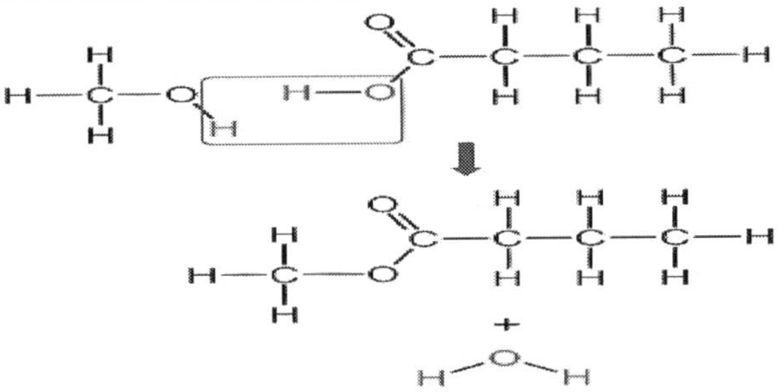

iv. **An alcohol oxidation reaction** is when alcohols burn in oxygen to produce carbon dioxide and water. In organic chemistry, oxidation can mean either adding oxygen or removing hydrogen. The three types of alcohol oxidations are:

1. Primary alcohol → aldehyde → carboxylic acid
2. Secondary alcohol → ketone → no further oxidation
3. Tertiary alcohol → not oxidized.

$R-CH_2-O-H \longrightarrow R-\overset{\overset{\large O}{\|}}{C}-OH$

Primary alcohol → Carboxylic acid

$R-CH_2-O-H \longrightarrow R-\overset{\overset{\large O}{\|}}{C}-H$

Primary alcohol → Aldehyde

$R-CH(OH)-R' \longrightarrow R-\overset{\overset{\large O}{\|}}{C}-R'$

Secondary alcohol → Ketone

Section Practice

1. The production of alkanes from alkenes is accomplished by
   a) burning in the presence of water.
   b) distillation.
   c) methylation.
   d) catalytic hydrogenation.
   e) hydrolysis.

Answer: (d)

Adding hydrogens to alkenes produces the corresponding alkanes.

2. The organic acid that can be made from ethanol is
   a) acetic acid.
   b) formic acid.
   c) C_3H_7OH.
   d) found in bees and ants.
   e) butanoic acid.

Answer: (a)

Oxidation of ethanol results in the formation of acetic acid.

3. An ester can be prepared by the reaction of
   a) two alcohols.
   b) an alcohol and an aldehyde.
   c) an alcohol and an organic acid.
   d) an organic acid and an aldehyde.
   e) an acid and a ketone.

Answer: (c)

An alcohol reacts with an organic acid to produce an ester.

4. Slight oxidation of a primary alcohol gives a(n)
   a) ketone.
   b) organic acid.
   c) ether.
   d) aldehyde.
   e) ester.

Answer: (d)

Slight oxidation of a primary alcohol produces an aldehyde. Further oxidation results in the formation of carboxylic acids.

5. When methane, CH_4, burns in excess oxygen, what are the products?
   a) CH_4O_2
   b) $CO + H_2O$
   c) $CO + CH_2OH$
   d) $CO_2 + H_2O$
   e) $CO_2 + 2H_2$

Answer: (d)

$CH_4 + O_2 \rightarrow CO_2 + H_2O$

Chapter 14 Carbon and Hydrocarbons SAT Questions

1. Hydrocarbons containing only single bonds between the carbon atoms are called?
   a) Alkenes
   b) Alkynes
   c) Aromatics
   d) Alkanes
   e) Ketones

Answer: (d)

Alkane's series contains only single bonds.

2. The melting and boiling points of hydrocarbons are determined by
   a) ion-dipole attraction.
   b) dipole-dipole attraction .
   c) London forces.
   d) hydrogen bonding.
   e) ionic bonding.

Answer: (c)

The main intramolecular forces of hydrocarbons are London forces.

3. Which of the following organic structures is ethylamine?
   a) $CH_3-CH_2-CH_3$
   b) $CH_3-CO-OH$
   c) $CH_3-O-CH_2-CH_2-CH_3$
   d) $CH_3-CH_2-NH_2$
   e) $CH_3-CO-CH_3$

Answer: (d)

Ethylamine: $C_2H_5 - NH_2$

4. Which of the following hydrocarbons would be expected to have the highest boiling point?
   a) CH_4
   b) C_3H_8
   c) C_4H_{10}
   d) C_5H_{12}
   e) C_6H_{14}

Answer: (e)

For non-polar compounds, the higher the molar mass is, the higher the boiling point.

5. Which of the following compounds contains the greatest percentage of oxygen by weight?
   a) $C_3H_6O_5Cl$
   b) $C_3H_6O_2$
   c) $C_5H_{10}O_5$
   d) $C_4H_8O_3$
   e) All are equal.

Answer: (c)

$C_5H_{10}O_5$ *has the highest percentage of oxygen by weight.*

6. The atomic structure of the alkane series contains hybrid orbitals designated as
   a) sp
   b) sp^2
   c) sp^3
   d) sp^3d^2
   e) sp^4d^3

Answer: (c)

Alkane series contain only single bonds. Therefore, their bonding structures contain only sp^3 hybrid orbitals.

7. Which of the following statements is the best expression for the sp^3 hybridization of carbon electrons?
   a) The new orbitals are one **s** orbital and three **p** orbitals.
   b) The **s** electron is promoted to the **p** orbitals.
   c) The **s** orbital is deformed into a **p** orbital.
   d) Four new and equivalent orbitals are formed.
   e) The **s** orbital electron loses energy to fall back into a partially filled **p** orbital.

Answer: (d)

The sp^3 hybridization of carbon electrons contains four identical sigma bonds.

8. Hybridization of the carbon atom indicated by (*) in $CH_3 - C^*H_2 - CH_2$, $C^*H = CH_2$, and $CH_3 - C^* \equiv CH$ is ______, ______, and ______, respectively.
   a) sp^3, sp^2, sp
   b) sp^3, sp, sp^2
   c) sp, sp^2, sp^3
   d) sp, sp^3, sp^2
   e) sp^2, sp, sp^3

Answer: (a)

A single bond, a double bond, and a triple bond have respectively sp^3, sp^2, and sp hybridization.

9. The addition of HBr to 2-butene produces
   a) 1-bromobutane.
   b) 2-bromobutane.
   c) 1, 2-dibromobutane.
   d) 2, 3-dibromobutane.
   e) No reaction.

Answer: (b)

$CH_3CH=CHCH_3 + HBr \rightarrow CH_3CHBrCH_2CH_3$

10. $CH_3CH_2C(=O)NH_2$ is called a(n)?
    a) Amine
    b) Amide
    c) Ketone
    d) Aldehyde
    e) Ester

Answer: (b)

$R - CONH_2$ is an amide.

11. In general, _____ are the most reactive hydrocarbons.
    a) alkanes
    b) alkenes
    c) alkynes
    d) cycloalkanes
    e) olefins

Answer: (c)

Triple bonds are more active than double bonds and single bonds.

12. The name of $CH_3 - CH = C = CH - CH - CH = CH - CH_3$ is?
    a) 2, 3, 5 - octatriene
    b) 2, 5, 6 - octatriene
    c) 2, 3, 6 - octatriene
    d) 3, 5, 6 - octatriene
    e) 3, 4, 7 - octatriene

Answer: (c)

Double bonds are located at carbon number 2, 3 and 6. It is an octatriene.

Relationship Analysis Questions

1.	The double and single bonds in benzene are subject to resonance.	Benzene has delocalized pi electrons that stabilize its structure.	TTCE
2.	The hybrid orbital form of carbon in acetylene is believed to be the sp form.	C_2H_2 is a linear compound with a triple bond between the carbons.	TTCE
3.	Ethane is considered to be a saturated hydrocarbon.	Ethene has a triple bond.	TF
4.	Ethylene (C_2H_4) has higher carbon-carbon bond energy than acetylene.	Ethylene contains a double bond and acetylene has only a single bond between the carbons.	FF
5.	Normal butyl alcohol and 2-butanol are isomers.	Isomers vary in the number of neutrons within the nucleus of the atom.	TF
6.	Benzene is a poor electrolyte in water solution.	Benzene does not ionize.	TTCE
7.	Benzene (C_6H_6) can be drawn as a series of resonance structures.	Benzene's bonds are hybrids of single and double bond character.	TTCE
8.	An organic compound with the molecular formula C_4H_{10} can exist as two compounds.	N-butane and 2-methylpropane are isomers that have the molecular formula of C_4H_{10}.	TTCE

	Statement I	Statement II	
9.	The reaction of $CaCO_3$ and HCl goes to completion.	Reactions that form a precipitate go to completion.	TT
10.	Butene can be converted into butane.	The addition of hydrogen gas with an alkene will form an alkane.	TTCE
11.	A molecule of ethyne is linear.	The carbon atoms in ethyne are sp hybridized.	TTCE
12.	Carbon is a nonmetal.	Carbon atoms can bond with each other.	TTCE
13.	CH_3CH_2-OH and CH_3-O-CH_3 are isomers.	CH_3CH_2-OH and CH_3-O-CH_3 have the same molecular formula but different structures.	TTCE
14.	DNA is a polymer.	DNA has many smaller units bonded to create longer chains.	TTCE

Chapter 15 Nuclear Chemistry

Nuclear vs. Chemical Reactions

i. Chemical reactions break and form bonds between atoms. In these reactions, the elements involved remain the same. On the other hand, nuclear reactions change the nuclei of atoms and transform them to new elements.
ii. Different isotopes of an element typically have similar reactivities in a chemical reaction but very different reactivities in a nuclear reaction.
iii. The rate of a nuclear reaction is not affected by temperature, pressure, or addition of a catalyst.
iv. Much larger quantities of energy are associated with nuclear reactions. For example, the combustion of 1.0 g of CH_4 releases 56 kJ of energy while nuclear transformation of 1.0 g ^{235}U releases 8.2×10^7 kJ of energy.

I. Atomic Structure

The common subatomic particles of all atoms are protons (p), neutrons (n), and electrons (e^-).

Particle	Mass	Charge
Proton, p^+	1.67×10^{-27} kg	+1
Neutron, n	1.67×10^{-27} kg	0
Electron, e^-	9.11×10^{-31} kg	−1

Nucleus

i. Protons and neutrons in the nucleus are called nucleons.
ii. The nucleus is the atom's center of mass and holds all of the positive charges.
iii. An atom is identified by its atomic number and mass number.
iv. The atomic number of an element is equal to the number of protons in the nucleus.
v. The mass number is equal to the number of protons plus the number of neutrons in the nucleus.

Isotopes are atoms with the same number of protons but different numbers of neutrons, such as ^{42}Ca and ^{44}Ca. The upper left number is the mass number of the atom. Because atoms of the element have the same number of protons, they must have different numbers of neutrons.

Section Practice

1. Radioactive changes differ from ordinary chemical changes because radioactive changes
   a) involve changes in the nucleus.
   b) are explosive.
   c) absorb energy.
   d) release energy.
   e) rearrange atoms.

Answer: (a)

Chemical reactions only transfer electrons and change bonds between atoms. Nuclear reactions involve changes in the nucleus.

2. Pierre and Marie Curie discovered
   a) oxygen.
   b) hydrogen.
   c) chlorine.
   d) radium.
   e) uranium.

Answer: (d)

Pierre and Marie Curie discovered radium.

3. How many protons are in the nucleus of an atom with atomic number 32?
   a) 4
   b) 32
   c) 36
   d) 42
   e) 73

Answer: (b)

Atomic Number = Number of Protons in the Nucleus

4. Atoms of ^{235}U and ^{238}U differ by three
   a) electrons.
   b) isotopes.
   c) neutrons.
   d) protons.
   e) positron.

Answer: (c)

Isotopes have the same number of protons but different neutrons.

5. Isotopes of uranium have different
   a) atomic numbers.
   b) atomic masses.
   c) numbers of electrons.
   d) numbers of protons.
   e) numbers of positrons.

Answer: (b)

The atomic mass, the number of protons plus neutrons, differs between two isotopes.

II. Nuclear Reactions and Radioactive Decay

A balanced nuclear equation demonstrates conservation of atomic number and mass number.

Σ mass number on the left = Σ mass number on the right

Σ atomic number on the left = Σ atomic number on the right

$$^{238}_{92}U \xrightarrow{\alpha\ decay} {}^{234}_{90}Th + {}^{4}_{2}He$$

Example: What is the missing product in the following nuclear reaction?

$^{63}_{28}Ni \rightarrow [^{63}_{29}Cu] + X$

Answer: $^{63}_{28}Ni \rightarrow [^{63}_{29}Cu] + {}^{0}_{-1}\beta$

Types of radioactive decay particles:

$^{4}_{2}He$	$^{1}_{0}n$	$^{0}_{-1}e$	$^{0}_{1}e$	$^{1}_{1}p$
α particle	neutron	β particle	positron	proton

Types of radioactive decay are listed below:

i. Alpha Decay

$$^{238}_{92}U \xrightarrow{\alpha\ decay} {}^{234}_{90}Th + {}^{4}_{2}He$$

ii. Beta Decay

$$^{40}_{19}K \xrightarrow{\beta\ decay} {}^{40}_{20}Ca + {}^{0}_{-1}e$$

iii. Positron Emission

$$^{13}_{7}N \xrightarrow{\beta^{+} emission} {}^{13}_{6}C + {}^{0}_{1}e$$

iv. Electron Capture

$$^{51}_{24}Cr + {}^{0}_{-1}e \xrightarrow{e^{-}\ capture} {}^{51}_{23}V$$

v. Gamma Decay

$$^{206}_{82}Pb^{*} \xrightarrow{\gamma\ deacy} {}^{206}_{82}Pb + {}^{0}_{0}\gamma$$

The **half−life** of the radioactive material is the amount of time it takes for half of the material to decay.

One common problem is to solve for the amount of material left after radioactive decay given its half-life. Solve with the following steps:

i. Calculate n, the number of years divided by the half-life of the material.

ii. Multiply the initial amount of radioactive material by $(\frac{1}{2})^{n}$.

For example, if a 100 g radioactive material has a half-life ($t_{\frac{1}{2}}$) of 2 years, then after 6 years, which is equal to 3 half-lives, this radioactive material will have $100 \times \left(\frac{1}{2}\right)^{\frac{6}{2}} = 12.5$ g left.

$$100 \text{ g of materials} \xrightarrow{2\ years} 50 \text{ g left} \xrightarrow{2\ years} 25 \text{ g left} \xrightarrow{2\ years} 12.5 \text{ g left}$$

It takes 6 years to go from 100 grams of radioactive materials to 12.5 grams.

Isotopic Dating

Radioactive isotopes can be used to estimate the age of various items.

i. ^{235}U, with a half-life of 4.5 billion years, is used to determine the age of a rock.
ii. ^{14}C, with a half-life of 5730 years, is used to determine the ages of organic materials in archeological sites.
iii. ^{3}H, with a half-life of 12.26 years, is used to determine the age of wines.
iv. Carbon-14 (^{14}C) is produced in the upper atmosphere. It is useful for dating objects between 500 and 50,000 years old.

Section Practice

1. Radioisotope injections for medicinal diagnostic purposes normally have
   a) short half-lives and are quickly eliminated from the body.
   b) short half-lives and are slowly eliminated from the body.
   c) long half-lives and are quickly eliminated from the body.
   d) long half-lives and are slowly eliminated from the body.
   e) no radiation isotopes.

Answer: (a)

Radioisotopes should not stay inside the body too long.

2. Iodine-131 is used to diagnose thyroid disorders because it is absorbed by the thyroid gland and
   a) has a very short half-life.
   b) has a very long half-life.
   c) emits alpha radiation.
   d) emits gamma radiation.
   e) emits beta radiation.

Answer: (a)

Radioisotopes that are injected into the body should have a short half-life.

3. Which of the following elements is used for dating archaeological discoveries?
   a) carbon-12
   b) carbon-13
   c) carbon-14
   d) carbon-15
   e) carbon-16

Answer: (c)

Radiocarbon dating is a dating method that uses C-14, a radioactive isotope of carbon.

4. Which of the following particles has a negative charge?
   a) A lithium ion
   b) An alpha particle
   c) An aluminum ion
   d) A beta particle
   e) A gamma ray

Answer: (d)

A beta particle is another name for an electron.

5. When $^{226}_{88}\text{Ra}$ undergoes a natural transmutation reaction, it emits
   a) an alpha particle.
   b) a beta particle.
   c) a proton.
   d) a neutron.
   e) a gamma ray.

Answer: (a)

$^{226}_{88}Ra \rightarrow {}^{4}_{2}He + {}^{222}_{86}Rn$

6. Which of the following equations represents alpha decay?
   a) $^{116}_{49}In \rightarrow {}^{116}_{50}Sn + \text{X}$
   b) $^{234}_{90}TH \rightarrow {}^{234}_{91}Pa + \text{X}$
   c) $^{38}_{19}K \rightarrow {}^{38}_{18}Ar + \text{X}$
   d) $^{222}_{86}Rn \rightarrow {}^{218}_{84}Po + \text{X}$
   e) $^{206}_{82}Pb^{*} \rightarrow {}^{206}_{82}Pb + \text{X}$

Answer: (d)

By balancing atomic mass and numbers, x is a $^{4}_{2}He$, an alpha particle.

7. Given the nuclear reaction $^{14}_{7}N + {}^{4}_{2}He \rightarrow {}^{1}_{1}H + \text{X}$, which of the following isotopes is represented by the X when the equation is correctly balanced?
   a) $^{17}_{8}O$
   b) $^{18}_{8}O$
   c) $^{17}_{9}O$
   d) $^{18}_{9}O$
   e) $^{19}_{9}O$

Answer: (a)

By balancing atomic mass and atomic numbers, we get that x is $^{17}_{8}O$.

8. In the equation: X → $^{226}_{88}R$ + $^{4}_{2}He$, what is X?
   a) $^{222}_{86}Th$
   b) $^{230}_{90}Th$
   c) $^{231}_{90}Th$
   d) $^{222}_{86}Rn$
   e) $^{230}_{90}Rn$

Answer: (b)

By balancing atomic mass and numbers, we get that x is $^{230}_{90}Th$.

9. The half-life of a radioactive isotope is 20.0 minutes. What is the total amount of a 1.00-gram sample of this isotope remaining after 1.00 hour?
   a) 0.500 g
   b) 0.333 g
   c) 0.250 g
   d) 0.125 g
   e) 0.0625 g

Answer: (d)

1 hour = 3 half-lives

$(\frac{1}{2})^3 \times 1 = 0.125\ g$

10. In the reaction $^{6}_{3}Li$ + $^{1}_{0}n$ → $^{4}_{2}He$ + X, what is X?
   a) $^{2}_{1}H$
   b) $^{3}_{1}H$
   c) $^{3}_{2}$He
   d) $^{4}_{2}He$
   e) $^{2}_{2}He$

Answer: (b)

By balancing atomic mass and numbers, x is $^{3}_{1}H$.

11. An 80 milligram sample of a radioactive isotope decays to 5 milligrams in 32 days. What is the half-life of this element?
   a) 8 days
   b) 10 days
   c) 12 days
   d) 16 days
   e) 32 days

Answer: (a)

$\frac{5}{80} = \frac{1}{16} = (\frac{1}{2})^4$

32 days is equal to 4 half-life times. The half-life of this element is 8 days.

III. Fission vs. Fusion

Fission occurs when a nucleus splits into two smaller nuclei and releases energy.

i. Fission is usually initiated by some sort of bombardment, i.e. neutrons hitting ^{235}U.

$$ {}^{0}_{1}n + {}^{235}_{92}U \rightarrow {}^{91}_{36}Kr + {}^{142}_{56}Ba + 2{}^{0}_{1}n $$

ii. A chain reaction can continue because more neutrons are created in the reaction above.

iii. The amount of material required to get a self-sustained chain reaction is called the critical mass.

iv. The speed of the nuclear fission is controlled in the nuclear reactors of a power plant using control rods, such as graphite, that absorb and regulate the neutron flow.

Fusion is the process in which light nuclei gain fuse together and release energy.

$$ {}^{1}_{1}H + {}^{1}_{1}H \rightarrow {}^{2}_{1}H + {}^{0}_{1}e $$

$$ {}^{1}_{1}H + {}^{2}_{1}H \rightarrow {}^{3}_{2}He $$

$$ {}^{3}_{2}H + {}^{3}_{2}H \rightarrow {}^{4}_{2}H + 2{}^{1}_{1}H $$

$$ {}^{3}_{2}H + {}^{1}_{1}H \rightarrow {}^{4}_{2}H + {}^{0}_{1}n $$

i. *Fusion* powers the Sun and stars and requires minimum temperatures of about 100 million K.

ii. Fusion is attractive as a potential alternative power source because hydrogen isotopes are plentiful, and fusion products are nonradioactive.

Section Practice

1. Which of the following represents the reaction ${}^{2}_{1}H$ + ${}^{2}_{1}H \rightarrow {}^{4}_{2}He$ + Energy?
   a) Fission
   b) Fusion
   c) Artificial transmutation
   d) Alpha decay
   e) Beta decay

Answer: (b)

Fusion: Smaller nuclei fuse together to become heavier nuclei.

2. Which of the following equations represents nuclear fusion?
   a) ${}^{14}_{6}C \rightarrow {}^{14}_{7}N + {}^{0}_{-1}e$
   b) ${}^{27}_{13}Al + {}^{4}_{2}He \rightarrow {}^{30}_{15}P + {}^{1}_{0}n$
   c) ${}^{235}_{82}U + {}^{1}_{0}n \rightarrow {}^{139}_{56}Ba + {}^{94}_{36}Kr + 3\,{}^{1}_{0}n$
   d) ${}^{2}_{1}H + {}^{3}_{1}H \rightarrow {}^{4}_{2}He + {}^{1}_{0}n$
   e) ${}^{14}_{6}C \rightarrow {}^{14}_{7}N + {}^{0}_{-1}e$

Answer: (d)

Fusion: Smaller nuclei fuse together to become heavier nuclei.

3. Which of the following statements best describes what happens in a fission reaction?
   a) Heavy nuclei split into lighter nuclei.
   b) Light nuclei form into heavier nuclei.
   c) Energy is released and less stable elements are formed.
   d) Energy is absorbed and more stable elements are formed.
   e) Heavy nuclei combine with neutrons to form heavier nuclei.

Answer: (a)

Fission: Heavy nuclei split into mid-weight elements and release energy in the process.

4. In a hydrogen bomb, hydrogen is converted into
   a) uranium.
   b) helium.
   c) barium.
   d) plutonium.
   e) carbon.

Answer: (b)

Hydrogen bombs undergo a nuclear fusion reaction.

5. Consider the following nuclear reaction $^{235}_{92}U + ^{1}_{0}n \rightarrow ^{138}_{56}Ba + ^{95}_{36}Kr + 3\,^{1}_{0}n$ + Energy. This equation can best be described as
   a) a fission reaction.
   b) a fusion reaction.
   c) natural decay.
   d) an endothermic reaction.
   e) beta decay.

Answer: (a)

Splitting a heavy particle into two medium size particles is a nuclear fission reaction.

Chapter 15 Nuclear Chemistry SAT Questions

1. The structure of an alpha particle is the same as a(n)
   a) lithium atom.
   b) hydrogen nucleus.
   c) neon atom.
   d) helium nucleus.
   e) oxygen nucleus.

Answer: (d)

An alpha particle is a helium nucleus.

2. Which type of radiation would be attracted to the positive electrode in an electric field?
   a) e_{-1}^{0}
   b) ${}_{1}^{1}H$
   c) ${}_{2}^{3}He$
   d) ${}_{0}^{1}n$
   e) e_{1}^{0}

Answer: (a)

Negatively charged particles are attracted to the positive electrode in the electric field. A beta particle, e_{-1}^{0}, carries negative charge.

3. Given the equation ${}_{6}^{14}C \rightarrow {}_{7}^{14}N$ + X, what is X?
   a) An alpha particle
   b) A beta particle
   c) A neutron
   d) A proton
   e) A positron

Answer: (b)

Balance atomic masses and atomic numbers.
Atomic Mass = 14 – 14 = 0
Atomic Number = 6 – 7 = –1
X is a beta particle.

4. A carbon-14 atom spontaneously decays to form a nitrogen-14 atom. This change took place because
   a) a transmutation occurred without particle emission.
   b) a transmutation occurred with particle emission.
   c) nitrogen-14 has an unstable nucleus.
   d) carbon-14 has a stable nucleus.
   e) None of the above

Answer: (b)

Carbon-14 has an unstable nucleus, and thus undergoes radioactive decay to form a stable nitrogen-14 nucleus. In the process, it emits a beta particle.

5. A positively charged particle has great difficulty penetrating a target nucleus because the target nucleus has
   a) a positive charge which repels the particle.
   b) a negative charge which attracts the particle.
   c) the protection of surrounding electrons.
   d) a very high binding energy.
   e) many neutron particles.

Answer: (a)

A nucleus is positively charged and repels other positively charged particles.

6. Which of the following listed particles can be accelerated by an electric field?
   a) Alpha particles, beta particles, and neutrons
   b) Alpha particles, beta particles, and protons
   c) Alpha particles, protons, and neutrons
   d) Beta particles, protons, and neutrons
   e) Alpha particles, beta particles, and gamma particles

Answer: (b)

All the charged particles can be accelerated by electric fields.

7. What is the primary result of a fission reaction?
   a) Conversion of mass to energy
   b) Conversion of energy to mass
   c) Binding together of two heavy nuclei
   d) Binding together of two light nuclei
   e) Releasing extra neutrons

Answer: (a)

Fission: heavy nuclei gain stability when they fragment into mid-weight elements. Tiny amounts of mass are lost in the process, which results in large amounts of energy released.

8. The course of a chemical reaction can be traced by using
   a) polar molecules.
   b) diatomic molecules.
   c) stable isotopes.
   d) radioisotopes.
   e) colored ions.

Answer: (d)

Only radioisotopes can be traced easily.

9. The use of radioactive isotopes has produced promising results in the treatment of certain types of
   a) cancer.
   b) heart disease.
   c) pneumonia.
   d) diabetes.
   e) bird flu.

Answer: (a)

Radioactive isotopes have been used to treat cancers.

10. The emission of a beta particle results in a new element with the atomic number
    a) increased by 1.
    b) increased by 2.
    c) decreased by 1.
    d) decreased by 2.
    e) no change.

Answer: (a)

A beta particle has -1 atomic number. Therefore, the emission of a beta particle results in a new element with the atomic number increased by 1.

Relationship Analysis Questions

	Statement	Reason	Answer
1.	Neutrons are used as the "bullet" that initiates the fusion of ${}^{235}_{92}U$.	Capture of the neutron by the ${}^{235}_{92}U$ nucleus causes an unstable condition that leads to its disintegration.	FT
2.	The sum of the products' masses from nuclear fusion does not equal the sum of the reactants' masses.	In nuclear fusion, the mass deficit is converted to energy.	TTCE
3.	Isotopes can be separated by gaseous diffusion.	The isotopes differ only in atomic mass.	TTCE
4.	The transmutation decay of ${}^{238}_{92}U$ can be shown as ${}^{238}_{92}U \rightarrow {}^{234}_{90}Th + {}^{4}_{2}He$.	The transmutation of ${}^{238}_{92}U$ is accompanied by the release of a beta particle.	TF
5.	The most penetrating type of nuclear radiation is γ rays.	γ ray is the radioactive particle with the highest mass.	TF
6.	${}^{4}_{2}He$ is the correct symbol for an alpha particle.	An alpha particle is a Helium-3 nucleus.	TF
7.	Alpha particles are the heaviest type of radiation decay.	Alpha emission particles consist of 2 protons and 2 neutrons.	TTCE
8.	Radiation and radioisotopes can have beneficial uses.	Radioisotopes and radiation can be used for radio dating, radiotracers, and food preservation.	TTCE

Chapter 16 Chemistry Laboratory

I. Common Laboratory Equipment

Erlenmeyer flasks and beakers are used for mixing, transporting, and reacting, but not for accurate measurements. The volumes stamped on the sides are only accurate to about 5% of the actual volume.

Graduated cylinders are useful for measuring liquid volumes with a higher accuracy of about 1%. They are for general use, not for quantitative analysis. If greater accuracy is needed, pipets or volumetric flasks are used instead. To measure the volume of a liquid, read the bottom of the meniscus. The reading is 36.6 mL, as shown in the figure on the right.

A **burette** is used to deliver precisely measured amounts of solution with variable volumes. Burettes are used primarily for titration to deliver one reactant until the precise endpoint of the reaction is reached.

A **pipet** is used to measure small amounts of solution very accurately. A pipet bulb is used to draw solution into the pipet.

A volumetric flask is used to very accurately make a solution of fixed volume.

A titration is a method of analysis that will allow you to determine the precise endpoint of a reaction and the precise quantity of reactant in the titration flask. A burette is used to deliver the second reactant to the flask and an indicator or pH meter is used to detect the endpoint of the reaction.

Section Practice

1. A student is performing an experiment where a blue salt is being heated to dryness in order to determine the percentage of water in the salt. Which of the following pieces of laboratory equipment would be used to help determine this percentage?

   I. A crucible and cover
   II. Tongs
   III. A triple beam balance

   a) II only
   b) III only
   c) I and III only
   d) II and III only
   e) I, II, and III

Answer: (e)

All of them are needed for this process. A crucible with a cover is needed to contain the salt while it is heated, and tongs are needed to pick up the hot crucible. Finally, a triple beam balance is needed to measure the mass before and after the water is evaporated

2. If a 35.25-mL sample is needed, then the best piece of glassware to use is a
   a) burette.
   b) beaker.
   c) graduated cylinder.
   d) volumetric flask.
   e) pipet.

Answer: (a)

Beakers and graduated cylinders are used to measure volume with low precision. Volumetric flasks and pipets are used to measure a specific volume, such as 10 ml, exactly.

3. Which of the following instruments would be best suited for use in a volumetric analysis to calculate the molarity of a base when titrated with a known acid?
   a) Graduated cylinder
   b) Pipette
   c) 250 mL beaker
   d) Burette
   e) Triple beam balance

Answer: (d)

Use a burette for the titration process.

4. Which of the following would be considered to be unsafe in a laboratory setting?
   a) Using a test tube holder to handle a hot test tube
   b) Tying one's long hair back before experimenting
   c) Wearing open-toed shoes
   d) Pouring liquids while holding the reagent bottles over the sink
   e) Working under a fume hood

Answer: (c)

Open-toed shoes should not be worn in the chemistry lab.

5. Which of the following(s) should never be done in a laboratory setting?
   I. Eat and drink in the laboratory.
   II. Push a thermometer through a rubber stopper.
   III. Remove your goggles to take a better look at a reaction.
   a) I only
   b) II only
   c) III only
   d) I and III only
   e) I, II, and III

Answer: (d)

I and III are prohibited in the lab.

II. Common Lab Techniques

Massing Solids

When obtaining the mass of solid chemicals, always use some type of weighing paper to protect the pan of the balance. Be careful not to include the mass of the weighing paper when determining the amount of solid obtained.

Measuring Liquids

When measuring out a particular volume of a liquid, you must choose an instrument that will measure as accurately as possible. For small quantities, it would be appropriate to use a pipette or burette. For larger quantities, a graduated cylinder might be appropriate. Remember that beakers are never accurate measuring instruments! Always measure the volumes of liquids using the bottom of the meniscus.

Filtering

When filtering a solid from a mixture by gravity filtration, always weigh the filter paper. Then fold it into the shape of the funnel, place it in, and wet it down to hold it in place before beginning the filtering process. After filtering, the solid on the filter paper must be dried and weighed. The initial weight of the filter paper is subtracted to find the mass of the solid obtained. The liquid that comes through the filter paper is known as the filtrate.

Solution Color

Many solutions in chemistry also have color, which is often the result of unpaired electrons. Metal ions are often colored.

Ions	Solution colors
Cu^{2+}	Blue
Fe^{3+}	Yellow to orange (rusty)
Ni^{2+}	Green
MnO_4^-	Purple
CrO_4^{-2}	Yellow
$Cr_2O_7^{-2}$	Orange

Colors of Transition Metal Ions

- $CoCl_2 \cdot 6H_2O$, Co^{2+} = red
- Cr_2O_3, Cr^{3+} = orange
- CrO_3, Cr^{6+} = yellow
- $Fe(NO_3)_3 \cdot 9H_2O$, Fe^{3+} = pale yellow (in 6 M of HCl)

- $FeSO_4 \cdot 7H_2O$, Fe^{2+} = pale green (in 6 M of HCl)
- $Ni(NO_3)_2 \cdot 6H_2O$, Ni^{2+} = green
- $CuSO_4 \cdot 5H_2O$, Cu^{2+} = blue
- $KMnO_4$, Mn^{7+} = pinkish-purple
- $MnSO_4 \cdot H_2O$, Mn^{2+} = pale pink
- $Zn(NO_3)_2 \cdot 6H_2O$, Zn^{2+} = colorless

Flame Color

One way to identify elements is to perform a flame test. This involves burning the solid and noting any changes in the color of the fire. When the electrons are heated, they get excited into higher energy levels, away from the nucleus. As they fall back towards the nucleus, they release energy often in the form of visible light. This creates the color you see in the fire. Some of the most common colors of flames are listed below. You may recognize many of these from fireworks displays!

Ion	Flame color
Li^+, Sr^{2+}, Ca^{2+}	Red
Na^+	Yellow
K^+	Purple (pink)
Ba^{2+}	Light green
Cu^{2+}	Blue-green
Fe^{3+}	Gold

Section Practice

1. Which of the following ions gives a bright yellow color in a flame test?
   a) Sodium ion
   b) Silver ion
   c) Bromide ion
   d) Sulfide ion
   e) Ammonium ion

Answer: (a)

Sodium ions produce a yellow flame when burned.

2. A very fine precipitate is best isolated by
   a) distillation.
   b) filtration.
   c) vacuum filtration.
   d) centrifugation.
   e) drying.

Answer: (d)

A very fine particle is extremely difficult to precipitate in the normal processes. Use centrifugation to separate very fine particles.

3. Which of the following ions can be identified by a characteristic odor?

   I. Sodium ion
   II. Silver ion
   III. Bromide ion
   IV. Sulfide ion
   V. Ammonium ion

   a) I only
   b) II and III only
   c) III only
   d) IV and V only
   e) V only

Answer: (d)

Sulfide and ammonium ions have special odors.

4. Which of the following is the LEAST effective when attempting to dissolve a solid?
   a) Adding the solid slowly to the solvent
   b) Grinding the solid to small particles
   c) Drying the solid
   d) Vigorous stirring or shaking
   e) Warming the solution

Answer: (c)

It is kind of obvious that drying the solid will not help.

5. Qualitative analysis is performed on a colored solution. Addition of HCl results in a white precipitate that dissolves completely in hot water. The original solution probably contains
   a) a transition metal ion and Ag^{+}.
   b) Pb^{+2} and no other cations.
   c) Pb^{+2} and possibly an alkali metal ion.
   d) Hg^{+2} and a transition metal ion.
   e) Pb^{+2} and a transit metal ion.

Answer: (e)

$PbCl_2$ dissolves in hot water. Many transition metal ion solutions are colored.

6. Which of the following laboratory techniques does NOT rely on a physical change in the components of a mixture?
   a) Chromatography
   b) Precipitation
   c) Filtering
   d) Distillation
   e) Evaporation

Answer: (b)

Precipitation is a chemical change.

III. Some Basic Laboratory Equipment Setups

The Setups for Collecting Gas

i. When gas is insoluble in water:

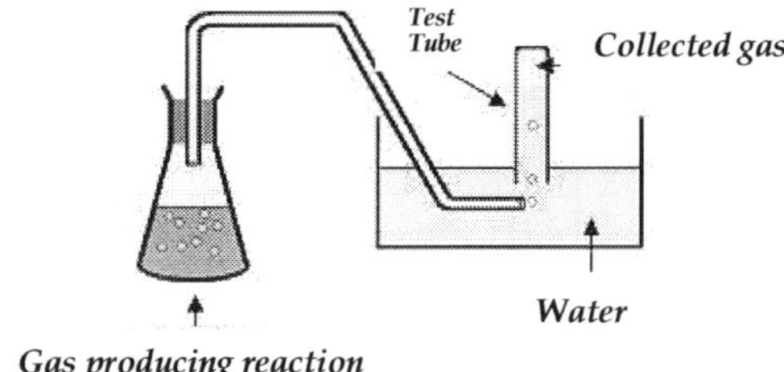

ii. When gas is soluble in water but more dense than air:

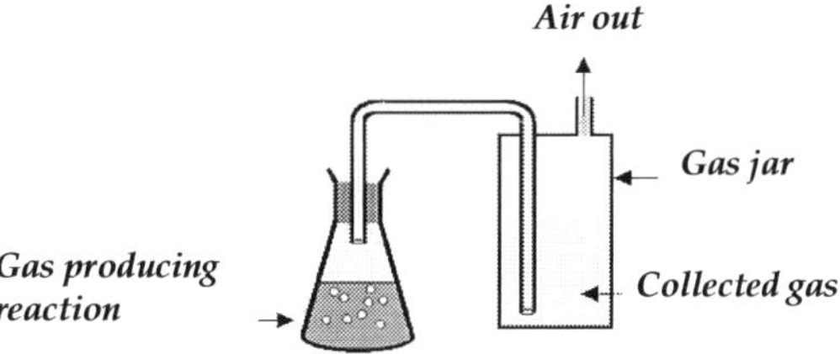

iii. When gas is soluble in water but lighter than air:

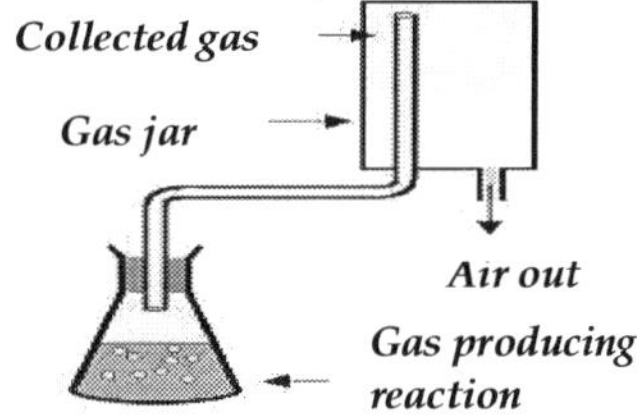

The Setups for Collecting Liquid

i. Distillation: separation by different boiling points

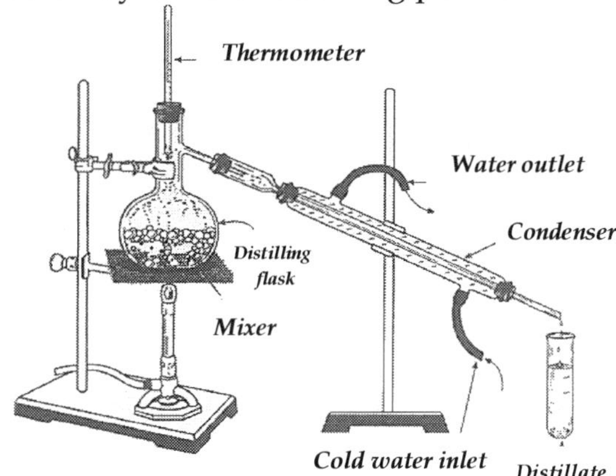

ii. Separation of two immiscible liquids: separation by different densities

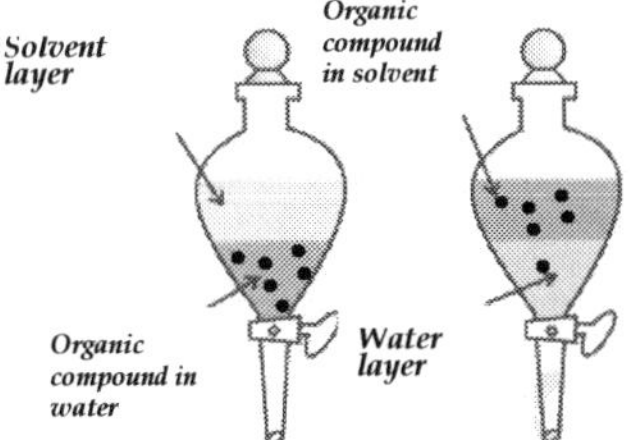

A separatory funnel used for laboratory scale extractions of two immiscible liquid phases

The Setups for Collecting Solids: filtration system with suction

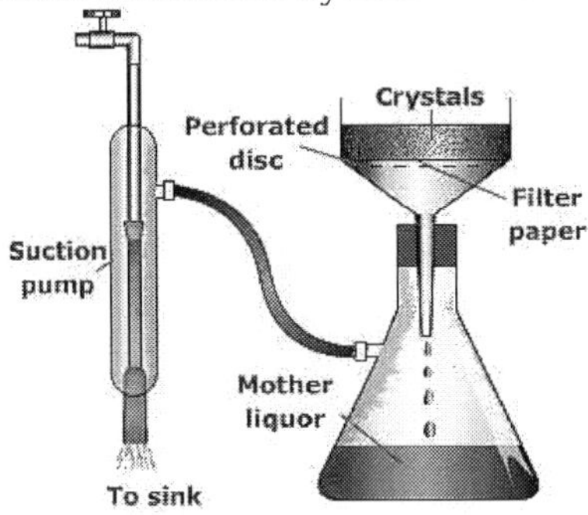

Section Practice

1. The most common method for determining the molarity of a solution of an acid is
    a) gravimetric analysis (weighing a precipitate).
    b) titration with a standard base.
    c) calculating the specific gravity of the acid.
    d) calculating the volume of gas evolved.
    e) determining the pH of the acid when the solution reacts with Mg metal.

Answer: (b)

Titration is the most common method to determine the molarity of the acid and base solutions.

2. Hydrogen sulfide is used to precipitate all of the following EXCEPT?
    a) Cu^{+2}
    b) Co^{+2}
    c) Ca^{+2}
    d) Fe^{+3}
    e) Cd^{+2}

Answer: (c)

CaS_2 dissolves in the water.

3. After a burette is filled for a titration, the bubble of air in the tip is dislodged. What will be the effect?
    a) Some error in measurement will result.
    b) The volume recorded will be too high.
    c) The calculated molarity of the sample will be too high.
    d) The mass of sample will be too low.
    e) All of the above will be true.

Answer: (e)

If the bubble comes out, the reading of final volume will be higher than the actual values. Therefore, the volume recorded will be higher and the calculated molarity of the sample will be higher than the actual values.
The mass of sample will be lower than expected based on calculations

4. Which of the following mixtures would best be separated by gravity filtration?
    a) A solid precipitate in a liquid solution
    b) A mixture of oil and water
    c) A mixture of solid iron with solid sulfur
    d) Carbon dioxide gas bubbles in a soft drink
    e) A mixture of dyes in a felt-tip pen

Answer: (a)

Use filtration to separate a solid from a liquid.

5. Methane is collected by
    a) upward displacement of air.
    b) displacement of water.
    c) downward displacement of air.
    d) displacement of mercury.
    e) filtration.

Answer: (b)

Methane is insoluble in water. Therefore, displacement of water is used to collect methane gas.

6. Which of the following ions is commonly a part of a white precipitate that dissolves in ammonia?
    a) Sodium ion
    b) Silver ion
    c) Bromide ion
    d) Sulfide ion
    e) Ammonium ion

Answer: (b)

AgCl is a white precipitate in water that dissolves in ammonia solution to form complex ions.
$AgCl + 2NH_3 \rightarrow Ag(NH_3)^+ + Cl^-$

IV. Analyzing Data

Accuracy and Precision

i. **Accuracy** is the nearness of a measurement to its accepted value.
ii. **Precision** is the agreement between two or more measurements that have been made in the same way.
   1. You can be precise without being accurate.
   2. Systematic errors can cause results to be precise but not accurate.

Calculating Percent Error:

$$\%\ \boldsymbol{Error} = \frac{|\boldsymbol{Experimental\ Value - True\ Value}|}{\boldsymbol{True\ Value}} \times \mathbf{100\%}$$

Errors in Measurement

i. Some error or uncertainty exists in all measurements. No measurement is known to have an infinite number of decimal places.
ii. All measurements should include every digit known with certainty plus the first digit that is uncertain - these are called the significant figures.

Significant Figures

To count the number of significant figures for an integer, start from the first non-zero digit on the right and count digits leftwards until you reach the last digit. Do the same thing for decimals except counting from left to right.

i. The result of adding and subtracting with significant figures must have the same number of decimal places as the measurement with the fewest decimal places.
ii. The result of multiplication and division with significant figures must have the same number of significant figures as the measurement with the fewest significant figures.
iii. Conversion factors have no uncertainty factor and do not contribute to limitations in calculations.

Examples: How many significant figures are in the following numbers?

1) 1200
   Answer: The number 1200 has 2 significant figures because it has 2 digits from right to the left after a non-zero digit.

2) 0.0231
   Answer: The number 0.0231 has 3 significant figures because it has 3 digits from left to the right after a non-zero digit.

3) 9.010×10^{-2}
   Answer: The number 9.010×10^{-2} has 4 significant figures because it has 4 digits from left to the right after a non-zero digit.

Examples: Unit conversions:

a. 1.2 mg = _____ g
b. 6.3 cm = _____ mm
c. 5.12 m = _____ cm
d. 32 °C = _____ K
e. 6.11 mL = _____ L
f. 1 km = _____ mm
g. 1.03 kg = _____ g
h. 0.003 g = _____ kg
i. 22.4 L = _____ mL
j. 10,013 cm = _____ km

a. 0.0012 g
b. 630 mm
c. 512 cm
d. 305 K
e. 0.00611 L
f. 1×10^{6} *mm*
g. 1030 g
h. 3×10^{-6}
i. 22400 mL
j. 0.010013 km

Section Practice

1. Which of the following is appropriate when constructing a graph of experimental data?
   a) Drawing a line that connects each data point.
   b) Plotting the independent variable on the y-axis.
   c) Drawing a straight line that passes through the data points.
   d) Extending the best-fit line beyond the last data point to the edge of the graph.
   e) Scaling the axes so that the data fills the graph as completely as possible.

Answer: (e)

Axes need to be scaled to fit the data ranges.

2. If an error is made during an experiment, the appropriate action is to
   a) stop the experiment and start over again.
   b) make a note of the error in the notebook and finish the experiment.
   c) tear the page(s) out of the notebook.
   d) adjust the results to correct for the error.
   e) continue the experiment.

Answer: (a)

Experimental procedures need to be conducted without errors.

3. A student mixes 10.0 mL of 0.10 M $AgNO_3$ with excess copper metal. The reaction should produce 0.107 grams of silver. However, the student obtains a mass of 0.150 grams of silver. Possible explanations for this yield >100% might include:

   I. The student did not subtract the mass of the filter paper before recording results.
   II. The student did not thoroughly dry the sample before massing.
   III. The copper metal did not react completely.

   a) I only
   b) II only
   c) I and II only
   d) I and III only
   e) I, II, and III

Answer: (c)

I and II will increase the yields of this experiment, whereas III will decrease the yields of this experiment.

Chapter 16 Chemistry Laboratory SAT Questions

1. A 1.00 M solution of NaOH is prepared by weighing exactly 40.0 g of NaOH and adding exactly 1000 mL of distilled water at room temperature. Which of the following is most likely to be the largest source of error using the above procedure?
   a) The wrong method is used to prepare the mixture.
   b) The room temperature is not 25 °C.
   c) The glassware is incorrectly calibrated.
   d) NaOH absorbs water in the atmosphere.
   e) Carbon dioxide in the water neutralizes some of the NaOH.

Answer: (d)

It takes time to weigh exactly 40.0 g of NaOH. Because NaOH absorbs water easily, by the time you finish, NaOH will have already absorbed some of the water from the air.

2. The vapor pressure of a liquid is measured at several temperatures. When a graph of the data is made,
   a) temperature, the dependent variable, belongs on the x-axis.
   b) pressure, the dependent variable, belongs on the y-axis.
   c) $\frac{1}{T}$ belongs on the x-axis because of Raoult's law.
   d) mole fraction, the independent variable, belongs on the x-axis.
   e) the temperature must be in Kelvin units.

Answer: (b)

Temperature is input data, so it is the independent variable and pressure is the dependent variable.

3. Safety glasses are NOT needed for which of the following lab procedures?
   a) Weighing samples
   b) Boiling water
   c) Distilling alcohol
   d) Pre-lab write-ups
   e) Titrations

Answer: (d)

Safety glasses need to be worn all the time in the lab.

4. Which of the following dissolves in both acids and bases?
   a) CaO
   b) CO_2
   c) $Al(OH)_3$
   d) AgCl
   e) As_2O_3

Answer: (c)

$Al(OH)_3$ dissolves in acid solution because OH- ions are taken out of the solution through neutralization. $Al(OH)_3$ dissolves in base solution to form the complex ion $Al(OH)_4^-$.

5. A 25.0 mL sample of a monoprotic acid is titrated to the endpoint with 20.0 mL, 0.20 M NaOH and the molarity of the acid was calculated as 0.16 M. After the titration is complete, it is observed that the burette is not clean and droplets of solution can be seen on the inside of the burette. What can be deduced about the molarity of the unknown acid?
   a) The calculation is wrong, and the molarity is really 0.250 M.
   b) The recorded volume of NaOH is low, and the molarity too high.
   c) The recorded volume of NaOH is high, and the molarity is too high.
   d) The recorded volume of NaOH is low, and the molarity is too low.
   e) The recorded volume of NaOH is high, and the molarity is too low.

Answer: (c)

The volume reading of NaOH is too high. Therefore the calculated molarity of acid solution is too high.

6. A solution is acidic and a noticeable odor can be observed. Which of the following is the most likely source of the odor?
   a) CH_4
   b) NH_3
   c) CO_2
   d) H_2S
   e) H_2

Answer: (d)

H_2S and NH_3 both have noticeable odors. However, NH_3 is a base and H_2S is an acid.

7. The salt $CrCl_3$ may be prepared in the pure form by
   a) reacting Cr metal with an excess of HCl gas.
   b) reacting NaCl with an excess of Cr_2Q_3.
   c) reacting 3 moles of HCl with 1 mole of $Cr(OH)_3$.
   d) reacting 1 mole of Na_2CrO with 3 moles of HCl.
   e) All of the above

Answer: (c)

The salt, $CrCl_3$, can be prepared by neutralization reactions.

8. The process of separating components of a mixture by making use of the difference in their boiling points is called
   a) destructive distillation.
   b) displacement.
   c) fractional distillation.
   d) filtration.
   e) chromatography.

Answer: (c)

Fractional distillation uses the boiling point difference of compounds to separate components in a mixture.

9. In a neutralization reaction performed in the lab, a student mixed 0.20 M NaOH with 0.10 M HCl until the reaction was complete. After the liquid left in the container was dried, which of the following statements must be true?
   I. The student produced a salt and water. All of that was left in the container was the salt.
   II. The total mass of the products in the evaporating dish at the end of the experiment had a lower mass than before heating.
   III. The student was left with an ionic bonded, white, crystalline solid.
   a) I only
   b) II only
   c) I and II only
   d) I and III only
   e) I, II, and III

Answer: (e)

$NaOH + HCl \rightarrow NaCl + H_2O$

A neutralization reaction will produce salt and water. After drying, only the salt will be left in the container.

10. A sample is brought into a laboratory and mixed with an equal volume of a preservative solution. The 5.00 mL sample is diluted to 100 mL, and the concentration of chloride ions in the diluted solution is found to be 3×10^{-3} M. What is the chloride concentration in the sample?
   a) 6.0×10^{-2} M
   b) 6.0×10^{-3} M
   c) 1.5×10^{-4} M
   d) 7.5×10^{-5} M
   e) 1.2×10^{-1} M

Answer: (e)

The volume of the sample is increased by 40 times, since it is doubled and then multiplied by $\frac{100}{5}$. Thus the chloride concentration is decreased by 40 times.

$40 \times 3 \times 10^{-3} = 1.2 \times 10^{-1}\ M$

11. Which of the following statements is the most probable explanation for colored solutions?
   a) The dissolved compound contains oxygen.
   b) The dissolved compound contains metals.
   c) The dissolved compound is ionically bonded with water.
   d) The dissolved compound contains transition metals with unpaired electrons.
   e) The dissolved compound contains electron configurations that are isoelectronic with the noble gases.

Answer: (d)

Transition-metal compounds are often colored. The color results from the transition of electrons between the two closely spaced d orbitals.

12. Which of the following is the most dangerous procedure in the laboratory setting?
    a) Pouring acids and bases into the sink
    b) Wearing goggles
    c) Pushing glass tubing, thermometers, or glass thistle tubes through a rubber cork
    d) Pointing the mouth of a test tube that is being heated away from you and others
    e) Knowing where the fire extinguisher and eyewash stations are located

Answer: (c)

Pushing glass tubing, thermometers, or glass thistle tubes through a rubber cork is a dangerous procedure because the glass might break.

Pouring acids and bases over the sink is harmful to the environment but not as dangerous as pushing glass tubing.

Relationship Analysis Questions

1.	NH_3 can best be collected by water displacement.	NH_3 is a polar substance.	FT
2.	3000 kilograms is equal to 3 grams.	The prefix kilo- means "one thousandth".	FF
3.	The number 5,007 has three significant figures.	Zeroes between non-zero digits are significant.	FT

Ten SAT Chemistry Subject Mock Tests

Periodic Table of the Elements

1 H 1.00794																	2 He 4.002602
3 Li 6.941	4 Be 9.012182											5 B 10.811	6 C 12.0107	7 N 14.00674	8 O 15.9994	9 F 18.9984	10 Ne 20.1797
11 Na 22.98977	12 Mg 24.3050											13 Al 26.981538	14 Si 28.0855	15 P 30.97376	16 S 32.065	17 Cl 35.453	18 Ar 39.948
19 K 39.0983	20 Ca 40.078	21 Sc 44.95591	22 Ti 47.867	23 V 50.9415	24 Cr 51.9961	25 Mn 54.93805	26 Fe 55.845	27 Co 58.9332	28 Ni 58.6934	29 Cu 63.546	30 Zn 65.409	31 Ga 69.723	32 Ge 72.64	33 As 74.9216	34 Se 78.96	35 Br 79.904	36 Kr 83.798
37 Rb 85.4678	38 Sr 87.62	39 Y 88.90585	40 Zr 91.225	41 Nb 92.90638	42 Mo 95.94	43 Tc [98]	44 Ru 101.07	45 Rh 102.9055	46 Pd 106.42	47 Ag 107.8682	48 Cd 112.411	49 In 114.818	50 Sn 118.710	51 Sb 121.760	52 Te 127.60	53 I 126.9045	54 Xe 131.293
55 Cs 132.90545	56 Ba 137.327	71 Lu 174.967	72 Hf 178.49	73 Ta 180.9479	74 W 183.84	75 Re 186.207	76 Os 190.23	77 Ir 192.217	78 Pt 195.078	79 Au 196.96655	80 Hg 200.59	81 Tl 204.3833	82 Pb 207.2	83 Bi 208.980	84 Po [209]	85 At [210]	86 Rn [222]
87 Fr [223]	88 Ra [226]	103 Lr [262]	104 Rf [261]	105 Db [262]	106 Sg [266]	107 Bh [264]	108 Hs [269]	109 Mt [268]	110 Ds [271]	111 Rg [272]	112 Uub [285]		114 Uuq [289]				

57 La 138.9055	58 Ce 140.116	59 Pr 140.90765	60 Nd 144.24	61 Pm [145]	62 Sm 150.36	63 Eu 151.964	64 Gd 157.25	65 Tb 158.9253	66 Dy 162.50	67 Ho 164.930	68 Er 167.259	69 Tm 168.934	70 Yb 173.04
89 Ac [227]	90 Th 232.038	91 Pa 231.0359	92 U 238.0289	93 Np [237]	94 Pu [244]	95 Am [243]	96 Cm [247]	97 Bk [247]	98 Cf [251]	99 Es [252]	100 Fm [257]	101 Md [258]	102 No [259]

Use This Periodic Table With All The Mock Tests.

You May Not Use A Calculator On These Tests.

85 Questions (60 Minutes)

SAT Chemistry Subject Test Raw Score Conversion Table

Raw Score	Scaled Score	Raw Score	Scaled Score	Raw Score	Scaled Score
80 and up	800	49	600	18	420
79	800	48	590	17	410
78	790	47	590	16	410
77	780	46	580	15	400
76	770	45	580	14	390
75	770	44	570	13	390
74	760	43	560	12	380
73	760	42	560	11	370
72	750	41	550	10	360
71	740	40	550	9	360
70	740	39	540	8	350
69	730	38	540	7	350
68	730	37	530	6	340
67	720	36	520	5	340
66	710	35	520	4	330
65	700	34	510	3	330
64	700	33	500	2	320
63	690	32	500	1	320
62	680	31	490	0	310
61	680	30	490	-1	310
60	670	29	480	-2	300
59	660	28	480	-3	300
58	660	27	470	-4	290
57	650	26	470	-5	280
56	640	25	460	-6	280
55	640	24	450	-7	270
54	630	23	450	-8	270
53	620	22	440	-9	260
52	620	21	440	-10	260
51	610	20	430		
50	600	19	420		

Raw Scores = Round of (Total number of correct answers − $\frac{1}{4}$ × Total number of wrong answers)

There are no deductions for blank answers. Use this conversion table for all the mock tests to calculate your SAT scaled scores in Chemistry subject test.

SAT Chemistry Subject Test No. 1

PART A

Directions: Each set of lettered choices below refers to the numbered statements or questions immediately following it. Select the one lettered choice that best fits each statement and then fill in the corresponding circle on the answer sheet. A given choice may be used once, more than once, or not at all in each set.

Note: For all questions involving solutions, assume that the solvent is water unless otherwise stated. Throughout the test the following symbols have the definitions specified unless otherwise noted.

H = enthalpy	T = temperature	L = liter(s)
M = molar	V = volume	mL = milliliter(s)
n = number of moles	atm = atmosphere(s)	mm = millimeter(s)
P = pressure	g = gram(s)	mol = mole(s)
R = molar gas constant	J = joule(s)	V = volt(s)
S = entropy	kJ = kilojoule(s)	

Questions 1–4 refer to the following topics and relationships:

a) Allotropes
b) Amphiprotic
c) Isoelectronic
d) Isomers
e) Isotopes

1. Refers to two or more species having the same electron configuration
2. Compounds having identical molecular formula with the atoms arranged differently
3. The term that would apply to C-12 and C-14
4. Would describe the relationship between $O_2(g)$ and $O_3(g)$

Questions 5–8 refer to the following topics and relationships:

a) Alpha particle
b) Beta particle
c) Neutron
d) Gamma ray
e) Positron

5. The particle that has the highest energy
6. The particle that has the greatest mass
7. The particle acts as the "bullet" in the nuclear fission reaction.
8. The particle which has the same mass but opposite charge as an electron

Questions 9–12 refer to the following topics and relationships:

a) H_2
b) CO_2
c) H_2O
d) NaCl
e) CH_2CH_2

9. It has the molecular geometric shape of triangular planar.
10. It has a bond formed from the transfer of electrons completely.
11. It has an atom that is sp hybridized.
12. It is a polar molecule.

Questions 13–16 refer to the following topics and relationships:

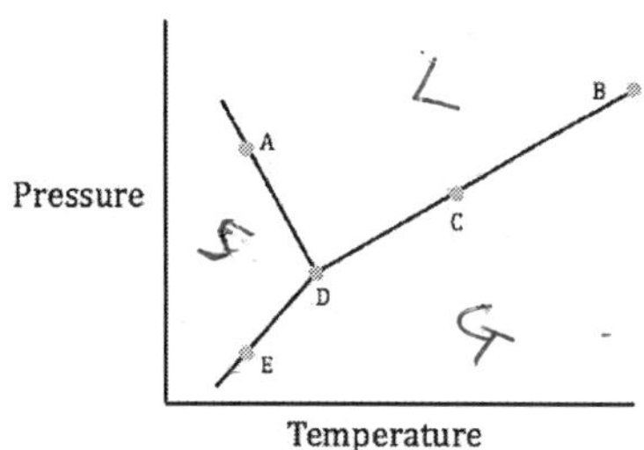

According to the phase diagram above:

13. Where is the critical point?
14. Where is the triple point?
15. Where is the boiling point?
16. Where is the sublimation point?

Questions 17–20 refer to the following topics and relationships:

a) A positive ΔH is used
b) A negative ΔH is used
c) A positive ΔG is used
d) A negative ΔG is used
e) A positive ΔS is used

17. to describe a spontaneous reaction
18. to describe an exothermic reaction
19. to describe a nonspontaneous reaction
20. to calculate free energy by multiplying temperature in the equation

Questions 21–24 refer to the following topics and relationships:

a) 0.010 molar KOH
b) 0.010 molar HNO_3
c) 0.010 molar $C_6H_{12}O_6$ (glucose)
d) 0.010 molar $Mg(OH)_2$
e) 0.010 molar H_2SO_4

These solutions use water as the solvent.

21. Which solution has the highest concentration of H_3O^+ ions?
22. Which solution has the highest pH?
23. Which solution has the lowest boiling point?
24. Which solution has a pH of 2?

PART B

Directions: Each question below consists of two statements, I in the left-hand column and II in the right-hand column. For each question, determine whether statement I is true or false and whether statement II is true or false and then fill in the corresponding T or F circles on your answer sheet. Fill in circle CE only if statement II is a correct explanation of the true statement I.

On the actual Chemistry Test, the following type of question must be answered on a special section (labeled "Chemistry") at the lower left-hand corner of your answer sheet. These questions will be numbered beginning with 101 and must be answered according to the following directions.

Examples:

	I		II
EX 1.	H_2SO_4 is a strong acid	BECAUSE	H_2SO_4 contains sulfer.
EX 2.	An atom of oxygen is electrically neutral	BECAUSE	an oxygen atom contains an equal number of protons and electrons.

SAMPLE ANSWERS

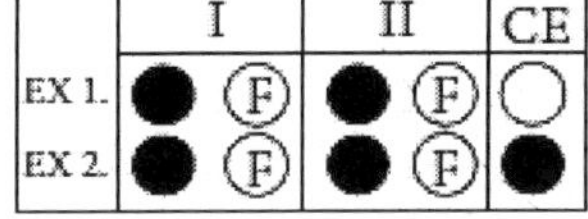

	Statement I		Statement II
101.	A voltaic cell spontaneously converts chemical energy into electrical energy	BECAUSE	A voltaic cell needs external electricity to work.
102.	When a piece of Al is dropped into a 1 M solution of $MgCl_2$, metal Mg appears	BECAUSE	Al is more readily oxidized than Mg.
103.	According to the equation $M_1V_1 = M_2V_2$, as the volume increases, the molarity decreases	BECAUSE	The solution is diluted by adding water to it.
104.	Both NO_3^- and CO_3^{-2} have planar geometric shapes	BECAUSE	Each ion has three equal bonds distributed equivalently in space.
105.	The $\Delta H_{reaction}$ of a particular reaction can be derived by the summation of the $\Delta H_{reaction}$ values of two or more reactions that, added together, give the $\Delta H_{reaction}$ of the particular reaction	BECAUSE	Hess's Law conforms to the First Law of Thermodynamics, which states that the total energy of the universe is a constant.

	Statement I		Statement II
106.	An aqueous solution of HI is considered to be a Brønsted-Lowry base	BECAUSE	HI(aq) can accept H^+ ions from another species.
107.	The alkane series are considered a homologous series	BECAUSE	Homologous series have the same functional group but differ in the formula by the addition of a fixed group of atoms.
108.	A chemical change involves changes in the composition and molecular structure of the reactants	BECAUSE	In a chemical reaction, bonds are broken and new substances and new bonds are formed.
109.	Nonmetallic oxides are usually acid anhydrides	BECAUSE	Nonmetallic oxides form acids when placed in water.
110.	Under the conditions of low pressure and high temperature, the ideal gas law is inaccurate	BECAUSE	Any deviation from the ideal gas law is due to the non-negligible volume of the molecules and the interactions between molecules.
111.	Atomic radius decreases as atomic number increases in a group	BECAUSE	Within a group, the higher the atomic number is, the smaller the atom.
112.	An element's nuclear charge is equal to the number of protons in the nucleus	BECAUSE	The only charged particles in the nucleus are neutrons.
113.	In a second order reaction with respect to reactant A, doubling [A] will quadruple the reaction rate.	BECAUSE	The rate equation is Rate = $k[A]^2$ for such a reaction.
114.	The reaction of hydrogen with oxygen that forms water is an exothermic reaction	BECAUSE	Water molecules have polar covalent bonds.
115.	In an equilibrium reaction, if the concentration of the reactants is increased, the forward reaction rate will increase	BECAUSE	When a stress is applied to a reaction at equilibrium, the equilibrium shifts in the direction that alleviates the stress.

PART C

Directions: Each of the questions or incomplete statements below is followed by five suggested answers or completions. Select the one that is best in each case and then fill in the corresponding circle on the answer sheet.

25. The relatively high boiling point of water is because of the
    a) hydrogen bonding.
    b) ionic bonding.
    c) metallic bonding.
    d) non-polar covalent bonding.
    e) polar covalent bonding.

26. In the reaction: ${}_{3}^{6}Li + {}_{0}^{1}n \rightarrow {}_{2}^{4}He +$ X, the species represented by X is
    a) ${}_{1}^{2}H$
    b) ${}_{1}^{3}H$
    c) ${}_{2}^{3}He$
    d) ${}_{2}^{4}He$
    e) γ ray

27. How many atoms are there in one mole of water?
    a) 1.807×10^{24}
    b) 3.476×10^{24}
    c) 1.171×10^{24}
    d) 1.204×10^{24}
    e) 2.414×10^{24}

28. Which of the following is/are TRUE?
    I. Adding a solute raises the vapor pressure and boiling point.
    II. The change in boiling and freezing point depends on the molality of solution.
    III. The number of solute particles in a solvent is an important factor in determining the boiling point elevation.
    a) I only
    b) II only
    c) I and II only
    d) II and III only
    e) I, II, and III

29. According to the phase diagram shown below, in what pressure range will the compound sublime?

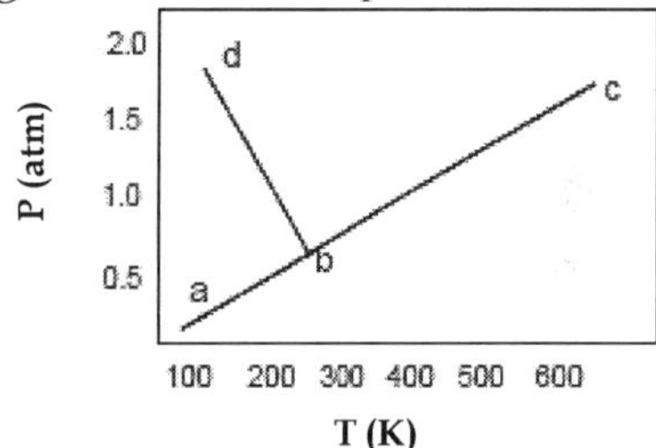

    a) Less than 0.5 atm
    b) Between 0.5 and 1.0
    c) Between 1.0 and 2.0
    d) Between 0.5 and 2.0
    e) This compound won't sublime.

30. The vapor pressure of a liquid is measured at several temperatures. When a graph of the data is made,
    a) temperature, the dependent variable, belongs on the x-axis.
    b) pressure, the dependent variable, belongs on the y-axis.
    c) $\frac{1}{T}$ belongs on the x-axis because of Raoult's law.
    d) mole fraction, the independent variable, belongs on the x-axis.
    e) the temperature must be in units of Kelvin.

31. Which of the following organic structures is propane?
    a) $CH_3-CH_2-CH_3$
    b) $CH_3-CO-OH$
    c) $CH_3-O-CH_2-CH_3$
    d) $CH_3-CH_2-NH_2$
    e) $CH_3-CO-CH_3$

32. What is the H_3O^+ concentration in a 1 M acetic acid solution ($K_a = 1.6 \times 10^{-5}$)?
    a) 1.6×10^{-5}
    b) 1.6×10^{-4}
    c) 1.3×10^{-2}
    d) 4.0×10^{-3}
    e) 2.0×10^{-3}

33. How many coulombs of electricity are required for the reduction of 1 mole of Al^{+3} to Al(s)? (The charge of one mole of electrons = 96,487 coulombs)
    a) 1 × 96,487 coulombs
    b) 2 × 96,487 coulombs
    c) 3 × 96,487 coulombs
    d) 3 coulombs
    e) 6.022×10^{23} coulombs

34. Which of the following statements describes the function of a catalytic *CO* converter in the car?
    a) To increase horsepower by burning more gasoline
    b) To absorb pollutants from the exhaust
    c) To complete the combustion of unburned gases
    d) To cool the exhaust gases
    e) To convert pollutants into water

35. $2HI(g) \leftrightarrow H_2(g) + I_2(g)$ $K_c = 0.25$
    According to the equation above, if 0.200 moles of HI is placed in a 1 0.0-L flask, how many moles of $I_2(g)$ will be in the flask when equilibrium is reached?
    a) 0.05
    b) 0.025
    c) 0.0125
    d) 0.005
    e) 0.0025

36. The ^{31}P isotope has how many electrons, protons, and neutrons, respectively?
    a) 15, 31, 15
    b) 15, 15,31
    c) 31, 15, 16
    d) 15, 15, 16
    e) 31, 31, 16

37. $\Delta H_{reaction}$ of −100 Kcal/mole indicates the reaction is
    a) endothermic
    b) unstable
    c) in need of a catalyst
    d) exothermic
    e) None of the above

38. Which of the following elements has the lowest electronegativity?
    a) Cesium
    b) Strontium
    c) Calcium
    d) Barium
    e) Potassium

39. Which of the following is the order of melting point for SiH_4, SiO_2, CI_4, NH_3, and PH_3 from lowest to highest?
    a) NH_3, PH_3, CH_4, SiH_4, SiO_2
    b) SiO_2, PH_3, NH_3, CH_4, SiH_4
    c) SiH_4, CH_4, NH_3, PH_3, SiO_2
    d) CH_4, SiH_4, PH_3, NH_3, SiO_2
    e) CH_4, SiH_4, SiO_2, NH_3, PH_3

40. When a gas with volume V at constant pressure is heated from 0 °C to 100 °C, the new volume is equal to?
   a) $\frac{0}{100}V$
   b) $\frac{100}{0}$V
   c) $\frac{273}{373}$V
   d) $\frac{373}{273}$V
   e) V

41. A 71.0 g sample of impure $CaCl_2$ is reacted with excess AgNO3: $2AgNO_3 + CaCl_2 \rightarrow 2AgCl + Ca(NO_3)_2$
If 14.3 g of AgCl precipitates, what is the percentage of chlorine in the sample?
   a) 2.5%
   b) 5.0%
   c) 6.5%
   d) 7.5%
   e) 8.5%

42. Calculate the enthalpy of formation of N(g) in the following reaction:
$N_2(g) \rightarrow 2N(g)$ ΔH=945.2kJ
   a) − 945.2kJ/mole
   b) 0.0 kJ/mole
   c) 472.6kJ/mole
   d) 945.2kJ/mole
   e) None of the above

43. What is the molarity of the solution when ten grams of sodium hydroxide are dissolved in 1 L of water?
   a) 0.25 M
   b) 0.5 M
   c) 1 M
   d) 1.5 M
   e) 4 M

44. Which of the following metals could be used for cathode protection of iron (Fe)?
   a) Sn
   b) Ni
   c) Ag
   d) Zn
   e) Hg

45. Which of the following electronic transitions requires the most energy?
   a) n = 1 to n = 2
   b) n = 5 to n = 2
   c) n = 2 to n = 3
   d) n = 4 to n = 1
   e) n = 5 to n = 1

46. The half-life of a radioactive isotope is 20.0 minutes. After one hour, how much of a 1.00 gram sample of this isotope will remain?
   a) 0.500 g
   b) 0.333 g
   c) 0.250 g
   d) 0.125 g
   e) 0.25 g

47. What is the X in the balanced equation shown below:
$$^{14}_{6}C \rightarrow \, ^{10}_{4}Be + X?$$
   a) $^{0}_{-1}\beta$
   b) $^{0}_{1}\beta$
   c) $^{4}_{2}He$
   d) $^{0}_{0}\gamma$
   e) $^{0}_{1}n$

48. Which of the following statements is/are true regarding the aqueous solution of HCN, $K_a = 4.9 \times 10^{-10}$ at 25 °C?
    I. At equilibrium, $[H^+] = [CN^-]$
    II. At equilibrium, $[H^+] =$ [HCN]
    III. HCN is a strong acid.
    a) I only
    b) II only
    c) I and II only
    d) II and III only
    e) I, II and III

49. Enthalpy is an expression for the
    a) heat content.
    b) energy state.
    c) reaction rate.
    d) activation energy.
    a. None of the above

50. A sample of the unstable isotope ^{20}Na is generated in the laboratory. Initially, 2.40 moles of the isotope are detected. After 0.30 seconds, 0.30 moles of ^{20}Na are detected. Which of the following is the half-life for this reaction?
    a) 0.10 seconds
    b) 0.15 seconds
    c) 0.20 seconds
    d) 0.25 seconds
    e) 0.30 seconds

51. Which of the following procedures increases the average kinetic energy?
    a) An increase in the reaction concentration
    b) An increase in temperature
    c) A decrease in pressure
    d) Adding catalysis into a reaction
    e) An increase in pH in solution

52. Which of the following is the name of $CH_3 - CH = C = CH - CH_2 - CH = CH - CH_3$?
    a) 2, 3, 5 - octatriene
    b) 2, 5, 6 - octatriene
    c) 2, 3, 6 - octatriene
    d) 3, 5, 6 - octatriene
    e) 3, 4, 7 - octatriene

53. In an electrolytic cell, which of the following acts as the anode?
    a) Zn(s)
    b) Cu^{2+}(aq)
    c) Zn^{2+}(aq)
    d) Cu(s)
    e) H_2O

54. Which of the following is a physical property of sugar?
    a) It dissolves in water.
    b) Its composition is carbon, hydrogen, and oxygen.
    c) It turns black by adding concentrated H_2SO_4.
    d) It can be decomposed with heat.
    e) It is a white crystalline solid.

55. Which of the following molecules does NOT have covalent bonds?
    a) HCl
    b) CCl_4
    c) H_2O
    d) CsF
    e) CO_2

56. Which of the following molecules is a polar molecule?
    a) BH_3
    b) NF_3
    c) C_2H_6
    d) SF_6
    e) CCl_4

57. A polluted pond contains 20.7 ppb of lead ions. What is the concentration of lead ions in molarity units?
    a) 1.0×10^{8} M
    b) 1.0×10^{-7} M
    c) 2.0×10^{-8} M
    d) 0.1 M
    e) 1.0×10^{-10} M

58. Which of the following groups is the least reactive family of elements?
    a) Alkali metals
    b) Alkaline Earth metals
    c) Noble gases
    d) Halogens
    e) Transition metals

59. Which of the following laws states that volume is inversely proportional to pressure?
    a) Boyle's law
    b) Charles' law
    c) Avogadro's law
    d) Ideal gas law
    e) Dalton's law

60. Which of the following bonds is the type of bond between atoms in a molecule of CO_2?
    a) Hydrogen bond
    b) Ionic bond
    c) Polar covalent bond
    d) Non-polar covalent bond
    e) Metallic bond

61. $2SO_3(g) \leftrightarrow 2SO_2(g) + O_2(g)\ \ \Delta H = 197\ kJ$
    Pure oxygen gas is added to the equilibrium reaction vessel. Which of the following changes will affect the quantities below once a new equilibrium is established?

	$[SO_3]$	$[SO_2]$	$[O_2]$	K_{eq}
a)	**Increase**	**Increase**	**Decrease**	
b)	**Decrease**	**Increase**	**Increase**	**Increase**
c)	**Increase**	**Decrease**	**Decrease**	**Decrease**
d)	**Increase**	**Decrease**	**Increase**	
e)	**Increase**	**Increase**	**Increase**	

62. For the reaction A + B $\leftrightarrow$ C + D, the equilibrium constant can be expressed as:
    a) $K_{eq} = \frac{[A][B]}{[C][D]}$
    b) $K_{eq} = \frac{[C][B]}{[A][D]}$
    c) $K_{eq} = \frac{[C][D]}{[A][B]}$
    d) $K_{eq} = \frac{[A][B]}{[C][D]}$
    e) $K_{eq} = \frac{C \times D}{A \times B}$

63. If 28 mL of nitrogen are reacted with 15 mL of hydrogen, what is the total volume of gas present after the reaction has occurred?
    a) 11 mL
    b) 17 mL
    c) 27 mL
    d) 33 mL
    e) 42 mL

64. What is the molar mass of a gas if 5.6 liters of this gas at STP have a mass of 12.5 g?
    a) 12.5 g/mole
    b) 25.0 g/mole
    c) 47.5 g/mole
    d) 50.0 g/mole
    e) 100 g/mole

65. H_2SO_4 is a strong acid because it is
    a) slightly ionized.
    b) unstable.
    c) an organic compound.
    d) highly ionized.
    e) None of the above

66. Which of the following consistently has the highest melting points?
    a) metals
    b) salts
    c) molecular crystals
    d) alkanes
    e) hydrogen bonded compounds

67. If one mole of H_2 is compressed from 10L to 7.5L at constant temperature, what happens to the gas pressure?
    a) It increases by 25%.
    b) It decreases by 25%.
    c) It increases by 33%.
    d) It increases by 50%.
    e) None of the above

68. How many moles of electrons are required to reduce 103.6 g of lead from Pb^{2+} to the metal?
    a) 0.5 moles
    b) 1 mole
    c) 2 moles
    d) 4 moles
    e) 8 moles

69. An aqueous solution with pH = 5 at 25°C has a hydroxide ion concentration of
    a) 1×10^{-11} M.
    b) 1×10^{-9} M.
    c) 1×10^{-7} M.
    d) 1×10^{-5} M.
    e) 1×10^{-3} M.

70. The addition of HBr to 2-butene will produce
    a) 1-bromobutane.
    b) 2-bromobutane.
    c) 1, 2-dibromobutane.
    d) 2, 3-dibromobutane.
    e) no reaction.

SAT Chemistry Subject Test No. 1 Keys

1. C	11. B	21. E	31. A	41. B	51. B	61. D
2. D	12. C	22. D	32. D	42. C	52. C	62. C
3. E	13. B	23. C	33. C	43. A	53. A	63. D
4. A	14. D	24. B	34. C	44. D	54. E	64. D
5. D	15. C	25. A	35. A	45. A	55. D	65. D
6. A	16. E	26. B	36. D	46. D	56. B	66. B
7. C	17. D	27. A	37. D	47. C	57. B	67. C
8. E	18. B	28. D	38. A	48. A	58. C	68. B
9. E	19. C	29. A	39. D	49. A	59. A	69. B
10. D	20. E	30. B	40. D	50. A	60. C	70. B

101.	TF	106.	FF	111.	FF
102.	FF	107.	TTCE	112.	TF
103.	TTCE	108.	TTCE	113.	TTCE
104.	TTCE	109.	TTCE	114.	TT
105.	TTCE	110.	FT	115.	TTCE

SAT Chemistry Subject Test No. 1 Answer to Part A

1 – 4 *Answer: (cdea)*
Allotropes: one or more forms of an elementary substance.

Amphiprotic: a substance that can both accept and donate a proton or H^+. It can act as an acid or a base.

Isoelectronic: elements or ions that have the same number of electrons.

Isomers: the molecules with the same formula but different structures.

Isotopes: the elements that have the same number of protons in each atom but differ in the number of neutron.

5 – 8 *Answer: (dace)*
The gamma particle has the highest energy.

The alpha particle has the greatest mass.

The neutrons act as the "bullet" in the nuclear fission reaction.

The positron has the same mass but opposite charge as an electron.

9 – 12 *Answer: (edbc)*
H_2: non-polar covalent bond
CO_2: sp ; linear
H_2O: sp^3 ; bent
NaCl: ionic compound
CH_2CH_2: sp^2 ; triangular planar

13 – 16 *Answer: (bdce)*
a) melting or freezing points
b) critical point
c) a boiling point
d) a triple point
e) a sublimation point

17 – 20 *Answer: (dbce)*
positive ΔH: endothermic reaction

negative ΔH: exothermic reaction

positive ΔG: nonspontaneous reaction

negative ΔG: spontaneous reaction

positive ΔS: increasing randomness
$\Delta G = \Delta H - T\Delta S$

21 – 24 *Answer: (edcb)*
0.010 molar KOH: $[OH^-] = 0.01$; pH = 12

0.010 molar HNO_3: $[H^+] = 0.01$; pH = 2

0.010 molar $C_6H_{12}O_6$ (glucose): nonelectrolytes; pH = 7

0.010 molar $Mg(OH)_2$: $[OH^-] = 0.02$; pH = 12.3

0.010 molar H_2SO_4: $[H^+] = 0.02$; pH = 1.7

SAT Chemistry Subject Test No. 1 Answer to Part C

25. *Answer: (a)*
Hydrogen bonding will increase boiling point.

26. *Answer: (b)*
By balancing atomic mass and numbers, x is $^{3}_{1}H$.

27. *Answer: (a)*
H_2O: *3 atoms in one molecule*
$3 \times 6.02 \times 10^{23} = 1.807 \times 10^{24}$

28. *Answer: (d)*
Adding a solute lowers the vapor pressure and raises the boiling point.

29. *Answer: (a)*
Sublimation line is segment ab. Pressure is less than 0.5 atm in segment ab.

30. *Answer: (b)*
Temperature is input data, so it is the independent variable and pressure is the dependent variable.

31. *Answer: (a)*
Propane has the formula of C_3H_8.

32. *Answer: (d)*
$HA \rightarrow H^+ + A^-$
$1-x \quad x \quad x$
$1.6 \times 10^{-5} = \frac{x^2}{1-x} \quad \rightarrow \quad x = 4.0 \times 10^{-3}$

33. *Answer: (c)*
$Al^{+3} + 3e^- \rightarrow Al$
1 mole of Al needs 3 moles of e^- *= 3F of C.*

34. *Answer: (c)*
To complete the combustion process

35. *Answer: (a)*
$2HI(g) \leftrightarrow H_2(g) + I_2(g)$
$0.2 \quad 0 \quad 0$
$0.2-2x \quad x \quad x$
$K = 0.25 = \frac{x^2}{(0.2-2x)^2} \quad \rightarrow \quad x = 0.05\ M$

36. *Answer: (d)*
P: 15 protons ; 15 electrons; 31 – 15 neutrons.

37. *Answer: (d)*
A reaction with a negative ΔH *is an exothermic reaction.*

38. *Answer: (a)*
Electronegativity increases across rows and decreases down columns.

39. *Answer: (d)*
SiO_2 *is a crystalline solid with the highest melting point.*
NH_3 *is a polar molecule. Its melting point should be higher than other non-polar compounds' melting points.*
For non-polar molecules, the greater the molar mass, the greater the melting point is.

40. *Answer: (d)*
$\frac{V1}{T1} = \frac{V2}{T2}$
$\frac{200}{273} = \frac{V2}{373}$
$V_2 = 200 \times \frac{373}{273}$
Temperature must be in Kelvins.

41. *Answer: (b)*
All the chlorine is from $CaCl_2$.
14.3 g of AgCl $= \frac{14.3}{143.5}$ *moles of Cl* $= \frac{14.3}{143.5} \times 35.5$
g of Cl = 3.55g of Cl
$\%\ Cl = \frac{3.55}{71} \times 100\% = 5\%$

42. *Answer: (c)*
The enthalpy of formation of $N_2(g)$ *in the standard state is zero.*
The enthalpy of formation of N(g) $= \frac{1}{2}(945.2) =$ *472.6 kJ/mole*

43. *Answer: (a)*
Molar Mass of NaOH = 40
$M = \frac{\frac{10}{40}}{1} = 0.25$

44. *Answer: (d)*
Zn has usually been used as sacrificial metal in cathode protection.

45. *Answer: (a)*
It requires energy to transfer electrons from lower to higher orbitals. The energy difference between orbital levels 1 and 2 is bigger than the energy difference between orbitals 2 and 3.

46. *Answer: (d)*
1 hour = 3 half-lives $\quad (\frac{1}{2})^3 \times 1 = 0.125\ g$

47. *Answer: (c)*
By balancing total mass and protons, it should be ${}^{4}_{2}He$.

48. *Answer: (a)*
$HCN \rightarrow H^+ + CN^-$
$[H^+] = [CN^-]$

49. *Answer: (a)*
Enthalpy is the heat content.

50. *Answer: (a)*
$\frac{2.4}{0.3} = 8 = 2^3$
3 half-lives have passed in 0.3 seconds.
One half-life is 0.1 seconds.

51. *Answer: (b)*
Molecules can move faster at the higher temperature.

52. *Answer: (c)*
Double bonds are located at carbon number 2, 3 and 6. It is an octatriene.

53. *Answer: (a)*
Oxidation occurs at the anode and reduction occurs at the cathode.
Zn is more active than Cu. Zn metal will be oxidized in the anode.

54. *Answer: (e)*
Sugar dissolved in water is a physical change. White crystalline solid is a physical property, not a chemical property.

55. *Answer: (d)*
CsF is an ionic compound.

56. *Answer: (b)*
NF_3 *has unshared paired electrons.*

57. *Answer: (b)*
20.7 ppb = 20.7 g of Pb in 10^9 *mL of solution*
The atomic weight of Pb = 207
$M = \frac{\frac{20.7}{207}}{\frac{10^9}{1000}} = 1.0 \times 10^{-7} M$

58. *Answer: (c)*
Noble gases, of course

59. *Answer: (a)*
Boyle's Law: The volume of a fixed mass of gas varies inversely with the pressure at a constant temperature.

60. *Answer: (c)*
Electronegativity difference $\approx 1 < 1.6 \rightarrow$ *polar covalent bonds*

61. *Answer: (d)*
Increase $[O_2]$ *will shift the equilibrium to the left but the overall* $[O_2]$ *will still increase.*

62. *Answer: (c)*
It is the definition of the equilibrium constant.

63. *Answer: (d)*
$N_2 + 3H_2 \rightarrow 2NH_3$
H_2 *is the limiting reactant.*
15 ml H_2 *uses 5 ml* N_2 *and produce 10 ml of* NH_3.
28 − 5 = 23 ml N_2 *left*
23 + 10 = 33 ml of total gas

64. *Answer: (d)*
$\frac{12.5}{5.6} \times 22.4 = 50$ *g/mole*

65. *Answer: (d)*
Strong acids ionize completely in aqueous solutions.

66. *Answer: (b)*
Melting points: ionic compounds > metals > hydrogen bonded compounds > molecular crystals

67. *Answer: (c)*
$P_1V_1 = P_2V_2$ $\quad 10 \times P_1 = 7.5 \times P_2$
$P2 = \frac{10}{7.5} \times P1$ $\quad P_2$ *increases 33% from* P_1.

68. *Answer: (b)*
$Pb^{2+} + 2e^- \rightarrow Pb$
One mole of lead needs two moles of electrons.
$\frac{103.6}{207.2} \times 2 = 1$ *mole of electrons*

69. *Answer: (b)*
$pOH = 14 - 5 = 9$
$pOH = -\log[OH^-] = 9$
$OH^- = 10^{-9}$

70. *Answer: (b)*
$CH_3CH{=}CHCH_3 + HBr \rightarrow CH_3CHBrCH_2CH_3$

SAT Chemistry Subject Test No. 2

PART A

Directions: Each set of lettered choices below refers to the numbered statements or questions immediately following it. Select the one lettered choice that best fits each statement and then fill in the corresponding circle on the answer sheet. A given choice may be used once, more than once, or not at all in each set.

Note: For all questions involving solutions, assume that the solvent is water unless otherwise stated. Throughout the test the following symbols have the definitions specified unless otherwise noted.

H = enthalpy	T = temperature	L = liter(s)
M = molar	V = volume	mL = milliliter(s)
n = number of moles	atm = atmosphere(s)	mm = millimeter(s)
P = pressure	g = gram(s)	mol = mole(s)
R = molar gas constant	J = joule(s)	V = volt(s)
S = entropy	kJ = kilojoule(s)	

Questions 1–4 refer to the following topics and relationships:

a) $Ag^+(aq) + Cl^-(aq) \rightarrow AgCl(s)$
b) $C_5H_{12(s)} + 8\ O_2(g) \rightarrow 5\ CO_2(g) + 6\ H_2O$
c) $NH_4^+(aq) + OH^-(aq) \rightarrow NH_3(g) + H_2O(l)$
d) $HC_2H_3O_2 + OH^-(aq) \rightarrow H_2O(l) + C_2H_3O2^-(aq)$
e) $CaCO_3(s) \rightarrow CaO(s) + O_2(g)$

1. It is a reaction that will decrease in entropy.
2. It is a combustion reaction.
3. It is an acid-base neutralization reaction.
4. It is a decomposition reaction.

Questions 5–8 refer to the following topics and relationships:

a) An increase in the reactant concentration
b) An increase in the temperature
c) A decrease in pressure
d) Adding catalysts to a reaction
e) pH value

5. Increases effective collisions without increasing average energy
6. Decreases activation energy
7. Increases average kinetic energy
8. The values that indicate an acidic or basic solutions

Questions 9–12 refer to the following topics and relationships:

a) Alpha particle
b) Beta particle
c) Neutron
d) Gamma ray
e) Positron

9. This particle has the greatest mass.

10. This particle has the same mass as an electron, but carries a positive charge.
11. This particle has the same mass and charge as an electron.
12. This particle is used as a "bullet" to start a nuclear fission chain reaction.

Questions 13–16 refer to the following topics and relationships:

a) Heisenberg Uncertainty Principle
b) Pauli Exclusion Principle
c) Schrodinger Wave Equation
d) Hund's Rule
e) Bohr model of the hydrogen atom

13. It states that no two electrons can have the same quantum number because they must have opposite spins.
14. It states that we cannot know the exact location of an electron in space.
15. It states that the electrons will occupy an orbital individually, with parallel spins, before pairing up.
16. It states that the energy changes of an electron are quantized.

Questions 17–20 refer to the following topics and relationships:

a) Alkali metals
b) Alkaline earth metals
c) Noble gases
d) Halogens
e) Transition metals

17. The least reactive family of elements
18. Consist of atoms that have valence electrons in a d subshell
19. Exist as diatomic molecules at room temperature
20. Members possess the lowest first ionization energy in their respective period.

Questions 21–24 refer to the following topics and relationships:

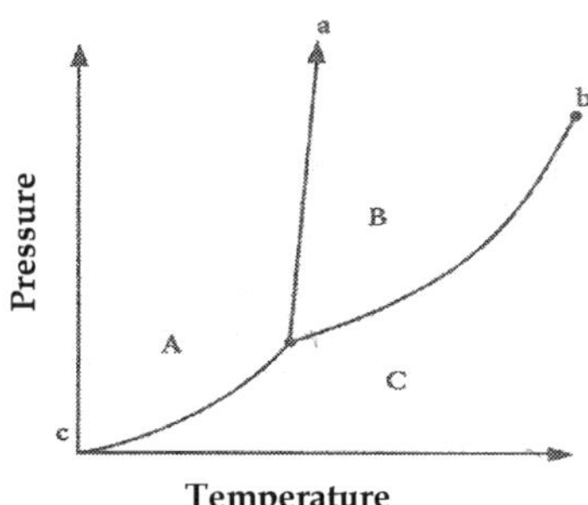

a) Sublimation
b) Deposition
c) Vaporization
d) Condensation
e) Melting

21. The process from phase A to phase B is called?
22. The process from phase B to phase C is called?
23. The process from phase A to phase C is called?
24. The process from phase C to phase A is called?

PART B

Directions: Each question below consists of two statements, I in the left-hand column and II in the right-hand column. For each question, determine whether statement I is true or false and whether statement II is true or false and then fill in the corresponding T or F circles on your answer sheet. Fill in circle CE only if statement II is a correct explanation of the true statement I.

On the actual Chemistry Test, the following type of question must be answered on a special section (labeled "Chemistry") at the lower left-hand corner of your answer sheet. These questions will be numbered beginning with 101 and must be answered according to the following directions.

Examples:

	I		II
EX 1.	H_2SO_4 is a strong acid	BECAUSE	H_2SO_4 contains sulfer.
EX 2.	An atom of oxygen is electrically neutral	BECAUSE	an oxygen atom contains an equal number of protons and electrons.

SAMPLE ANSWERS

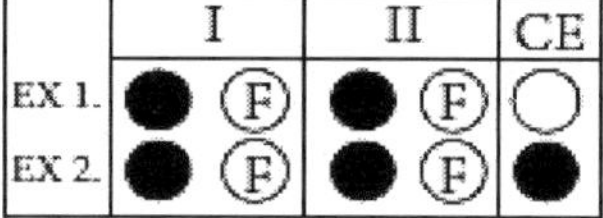

101.	$F_2 \rightarrow 2F^- + 2e^-$ is a correctly written half reaction	BECAUSE	This half reaction must demonstrate the proper conservation of masses and charges.
102.	Metals are good conductors of heat and electricity	BECAUSE	The positive nuclei are surrounded by a "sea" of electrons.
103.	Two electrons in the 2s subshell must have opposite spins	BECAUSE	The Pauli exclusion principle states that no two electrons in the same atom can have identical quantum numbers.
104.	The empirical formula of $C_6H_{12}O_6$ is CH_2O	BECAUSE	The empirical formula shows the lowest ratio of the elements present in the molecular formula.
105.	The temperature of a substance always increases as heat is added to the system	BECAUSE	The average kinetic energy of the particles in a system increases with an increase in temperature.

106. Sodium chloride is an example of ionic bonding BECAUSE Sodium and chlorine have the same electronegativity.

107. An organic compound with the molecular formula C_4H_{10} can exist as two compounds BECAUSE n-Butane and 2-methylpropane are isomers that have the molecular formula of C_4H_{10}.

108. A 1 N ("normal") solution of H_2SO_4 is the same as a 1 M ("molar") solution of H_2SO_4 BECAUSE Molarity refers to the moles of solute per liter of solution, whereas normality refers to the molarity of hydrogen ions.

109. Methane is defined as a compound BECAUSE Methane can be broken down chemically.

110. A saturated solution is not necessary concentrated BECAUSE Dilute and concentrated are terms that relate only to the relative amount of solute dissolved in the solvent.

111. A piece of zinc placed in a blue copper nitrate solution will displace the copper from the solution, producing copper metal and a colorless Zn^{+2} solution BECAUSE Copper is a much more active metal than zinc.

112. As ice absorbs heat and begins to melt, its temperature remains constant BECAUSE Changes of state bring about changes in a substance's potential energy, not in its kinetic energy.

113. Increasing the temperature of a reaction increases the reaction rate BECAUSE At higher temperatures, molecules or atoms tend to be further apart.

114. At equilibrium, the forward reaction and the reverse reaction stop. BECAUSE At equilibrium, the reactants and the products have reached the equilibrium concentrations.

115. A basic solution has more hydrogen ions than an acidic solution. BECAUSE At 25 °C, the product of $[H^+] \times [OH^-]$ equals 10^{-14}.

PART C

Directions: Each of the questions or incomplete statements below is followed by five suggested answers or completions. Select the one that is best in each case and then fill in the corresponding circle on the answer sheet.

25. Which of the following actions does NOT involve a chemical reaction?
    a) Combining atoms of elements to form a molecule
    b) Separation of the molecules in a mixture
    c) Breaking down compounds into elements
    d) Reacting with a compound and an element to form a new compound and a new element
    e) None of the above

26. Which of the following orbitals has the lowest energy?
    a) 2p
    b) 3s
    c) 3d
    d) 4s
    e) 3p

27. Which of the following correctly represents an excited state of scandium?
    a) $1s^2\ 2s^2\ 2p^6\ 3s^2\ 3p^6\ 3d^1\ 4s^2$
    b) $1s^2\ 2s^3\ 2p^5\ 3s^2\ 3p^6\ 3d^1\ 4s^2$
    c) $1s^2\ 2s^2\ 2p^6\ 3s^2\ 3p^6\ 3d^2\ 4s^1$
    d) $1s^2\ 2s^2\ 2p^6\ 3s^2\ 3p^6\ 3d^2\ 4s^2$
    e) $1s^2\ 2s^2\ 2p^6\ 3s^2\ 3p^6\ 3d^3\ 4s^2$

28. The Heisenberg uncertainty principle states that
    a) electrons have no momentum.
    b) the position of an electron is impossible to determine.
    c) the faster an electron moves, the more unreliable its energy.
    d) the momentum and the position of an electron cannot be precisely determined simultaneously.
    e) Einstein's theory of relativity is still unproved.

29. Which of the following groups makes oxides with the formula of X_2O?
    a) Alkali metals
    b) Alkaline earth metals
    c) Metalloids
    d) Halogens
    e) Rare earth metals

30. Which of the following is the order the elements S, Cl, and F in terms of increasing atomic radii?
    a) S, Cl, F
    b) Cl, F, S
    c) F, S, Cl
    d) F, Cl, S
    e) S, F, Cl

31. Which of the following molecules has/have sp^3 bonding?
    I. CBr_4
    II. PF_5
    III. NH_3
    IV. SO_3
    V. HCN
    a) I and III only
    b) II only
    c) III and V only
    d) IV only
    e) V only

32. Which of the following bonds holds a sample of barium iodide, BaI_2, together?
    a) Hydrogen bonds
    b) Ionic bonds
    c) Metallic bonds
    d) Non-polar covalent bonds
    e) Polar covalent bonds

33. Which of the following bonds allows many solids to conduct electricity?
    a) Hydrogen bonds
    b) Ionic bonds
    c) Metallic bonds
    d) Non-polar covalent bonds
    e) Polar covalent bonds

34. Which of the following molecules is incorrectly matched with its molecular geometry?
    a) SF_6 octahedral
    b) CH_4 tetrahedral
    c) SO_3 trigonal planar
    d) $SeCl_4$ tetrahedral
    e) PH_3 trigonal pyramidal

35. In the reaction $CaCO_3 + 2HCl \rightarrow H_2O + CO_2 + CaCl_2$, how many grams of $CaCO_3$ (molar mass of 100) are needed to produce 2.24 L of CO_2 at STP?
    a) 10.0
    b) 9.0
    c) 6.0
    d) 20.0
    e) 30.0

36. For $4NH_3(g) + 5O_2(g) \rightarrow 4NO(g) + 6H_2O(g)$, if you begin with 68.00 g of ammonia and 64.00 g of oxygen, how many moles of water will be produced?
    a) 2
    b) 2.4
    c) 1.2
    d) 0.6
    e) 43.2

37. What is the approximate percent composition by mass of the element oxygen in the compound $HClO_4$?
    a) 16%
    b) 35%
    c) 50%
    d) 64%
    e) 75%

38. What is the volume of a gas at STP that contains 6.02×10^{23} atoms and forms diatomic molecules?
    a) 11.2 L
    b) 22.4 L
    c) 33.6 L
    d) 67.2 L
    e) 1.06 L

39. Which of the following action(s) will always decrease the volume of a gas?
    I. Decreasing the pressure with the temperature held constant
    II. Increasing the pressure with a temperature decrease
    III. Increasing the temperature with a pressure increase
    a) I only
    b) II only
    c) I and III only
    d) II and III only
    e) I, II, and III

40. At STP a 11.2-L flask filled with N_2 has a mass of 450.0g. The N_2 in the flask is replaced with another gas, and the mass of the flask is then determined to be 478 g. What is the gas that replaced the N_2?
   a) Ne
   b) O_2
   c) Ar
   d) Kr
   e) Xe

41. Which of the following statements is NOT related to the kinetic molecular theory of gases?
   a) Gas molecules have no intermolecular forces.
   b) Gas particles are in random motion.
   c) The collisions between gas particles are elastic.
   d) Gas particles have no volume.
   e) The average kinetic energy is proportional to the temperature (°C) of the gas.

42. Which of the following forces is the weakest attractive force?
   a) Van der Waals
   b) Coordinate covalent bonding
   c) Covalent bonding
   d) Polar covalent bonding
   e) Ionic bonding

43. Above which of the following points can a liquid not exist?
   a) The triple point
   b) The critical point
   c) The eutectic point
   d) The boiling point
   e) The sublimation point

44. The structures of vitamins C and E are shown below. Which of the following statements is correct?

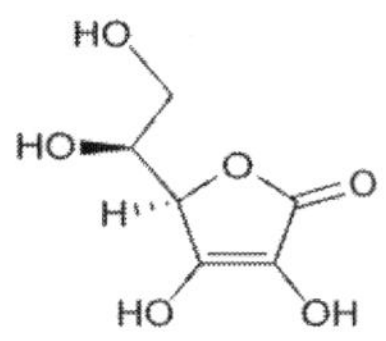

Vitamin C

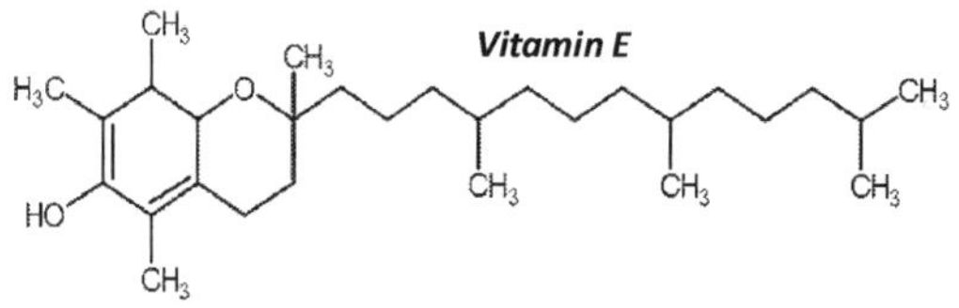

Vitamin E

   a) Vitamin E contains more polar bonds than vitamin C.
   b) The melting point of vitamin E is likely higher than that of vitamin C.
   c) Vitamin C should have excellent solubility in hexane.
   d) Vitamin C should have a higher solubility in water than vitamin E.
   e) Vitamin C can be described as a "fat-soluble" vitamin.

45. When NaCl crystal was added to a water solution of NaCl, the crystal seemed to remain unchanged. Its particles were
   a) dissolving into an unsaturated solution.
   b) exchanging places with others in the solution.
   c) causing the solution to become supersaturated.
   d) not going into solution in this static condition.
   e) None of the above

46. Which of the following compounds is expected to be the most soluble in hexane, C_6H_{14}?
   a) KCl
   b) C_2H_5OH
   c) C_6H_6
   d) H_2O
   e) $HC_2H_3O_2$

47. Which of the following aqueous solutions would probably have the highest boiling point?
    a) 0.100 m KOH
    b) 0.100 m Na_2SO_4
    c) 0.100 m $C_6H_{12}O_6$
    d) 0.200 m $CaCl_2$
    e) 0.200 m CH_3CH_2OH

48. Given $2Na_{(s)}+Cl_{2(g)} \rightarrow 2NaCl_{(s)}+822\ kJ$, how much heat is released if 0.5 mole of sodium reacts completely with chlorine?
    a) 205.5 kJ
    b) 411 kJ
    c) 822 kJ
    d) 1644 kJ
    e) 3288 kJ

49. Which of the following conditions will produce a spontaneous reaction?
    a) Low enthalpy values and high entropy values
    b) Low enthalpy values and low entropy values
    c) High enthalpy values and low entropy values
    d) High enthalpy values and high entropy values
    e) High temperatures and low pressures

50. Consider the following reaction at equilibrium at 25 °C:
    $N_2(g) + 3H_2(g) \rightarrow 2\ NH_3(g)\ \Delta G° = -33.3\ kJ$.
    Which of the following statements is NOT true?
    a) The quantity $\frac{[NH3]^2}{[N2][H_2]^3}$ is > 1 at equilibrium.
    b) $\Delta H°$ must be negative.
    c) The reaction is spontaneous under the conditions specified.
    d) $\Delta G°$ is independent of temperature.
    e) For the equilibrium $2NH_3(g) \rightarrow N_2(g) + 3H_2(g)$, we expect that $\Delta G° = 33.3$ kJ.

51. Step 1: $V^{3+} + Cu^{2+} \rightarrow V^{4+} + Cu^{+}$ (fast)
    Step 2: $Cu^{+} + Fe^{3+} \rightarrow Cu^{2+} + Fe^{2+}$ (slow)
    According to the reaction mechanisms above, which of the following ions is the reaction intermediate?
    a) Cu^{+}
    b) Cu^{2+}
    c) V^{3+}
    d) Fe^{3+}
    e) Fe^{2+}

52. $C_6H_6(l) + O_2(g) \rightarrow 6CO_2(g) + 3H_2O(l)$
    The above reaction represents the combustion of benzene. If a sample of benzene is burning at 0.25 mole/L−s, which of the following is the rate at which $CO_2(g)$ is being produced?
    a) 0.25 mole/L−s
    b) 0.75 mole/ L−s
    c) 1.5 mole/L−s
    d) 2.5 mole/L−s
    e) 3.0 mole/ L−s

53. What is the order of the reaction if a rate law is found to be $Rate = k[A]^2[B]$?
    a) First order
    b) Second order
    c) Third order
    d) Fourth order
    e) The rate order cannot be determined.

54. The solubility product of PbI_2 is 4×10^{-9}. What is the molar solubility of PbI_2 in pure water?
   a) 2.0×10^{-3}
   b) 1.0×10^{-3}
   c) 5.0×10^{-3}
   d) 1.0×10^{-4}
   e) 2.0×10^{-4}

55. If at a given temperature the equilibrium constant for the reaction $H_2 + Cl_2 \leftrightarrow 2HCl$ is K_p, the equilibrium constant for the reaction $HCl \leftrightarrow \frac{1}{2} H_2 + \frac{1}{2} Cl_2$ can be represented as?
   a) $\frac{1}{Kp^2}$
   b) K_p^2
   c) $\frac{1}{\sqrt{Kp}}$
   d) $\sqrt{K_p}$
   e) K_p^3

56. The value of the equilibrium constant, K_{eq}, is dependent on
   I. the temperature of the system.
   II. the concentration of the reactants.
   III. the concentration of the products.
   IV. the nature of the reactants and products.
   a) I and II only
   b) II and III only
   c) III and IV only
   d) I and IV only
   e) I, II, and IV only

57. A salt derived from a strong base and a weak acid will undergo hydrolysis and give a solution that will be a(n)
   a) basic solution.
   b) acidic solution.
   c) neutral solution.
   d) volatile solution.
   e) None of the above

58. Which of the following statements is not true for a solution at 25 °C that has a hydroxide concentration of 1.0×10^{-6} M?
   a) $K_w = 1 \times 10^{-14}$
   b) The solution is acidic.
   c) The solution is basic.
   d) The $[H^+]$ is 1×10^{-8} M.
   e) The pOH equals 6.0.

59. Which of the following ions is the strongest base?
   I. $Cu(NH_3)_4^{+2}$
   II. KOH
   III. HCO_3^-
   IV. CO_3^{-2}
   V. SO_3^{-2}
   a) I
   b) II
   c) III
   d) IV
   e) V

60. What is the pH of the solution, if 50.0 mL of 0.04 M HCl is mixed with 50.0 mL of 0.02 M NaOH solution?
   a) 4
   b) 10
   c) 2.7
   d) 2
   e) 12

61. $Cl_2(g)+2OH^-(aq) \rightarrow$
$Cl^-(aq)+OCl^-(aq)+H_2O$
Which of the following is/are true regarding the above reaction?
    I. Cl_2 undergoes both oxidation and reduction.
    II. The oxidation state of O in OCl^- is −1.
    III. OH^- is the reducing agent.
    a) I only
    b) II only
    c) II and III only
    d) I and III only
    e) I, II, and III

62. For a metal atom to replace another kind of metallic ion in a solution, the metal atom must be
    a) a good oxidizing agent.
    b) higher in the activity series than the metal in solution.
    c) lower in the activity series than the metal in solution.
    d) equal in activity to the metal in solution.
    e) None of the above

63. Which of following metals does NOT react with hydrochloric acid to produce hydrogen gas?
    a) Zn
    b) Fe
    c) Hg
    d) Na
    e) Mg

64. What is the oxidation number of the underlined symbol in the given formulas $\underline{P}O_4^{-3}$?
    a) +1
    b) +2
    c) +4
    d) +5
    e) +6

65. The organic acid that can be made from ethanol is
    a) acetic acid.
    b) formic acid.
    c) C_3H_7OH.
    d) CH_3COCH_3.
    e) butanoic acid.

66. Carbon atoms usually
    a) lose 4 electrons.
    b) gain 4 electrons.
    c) form 4 covalent bonds.
    d) share the 2 electrons in the first principal energy level.
    e) are negative ions.

67. Which of the following gases is known to shield the earth from harmful ultraviolet radiation?
    a) CO
    b) CO_2
    c) CFCs
    d) SO_2
    e) O_3

68. Which of the following conditions are required to form ${}^4_2He$ during the fusion reaction in the Sun?
    a) High temperature and low pressure
    b) High temperature and high pressure
    c) Low temperature and low pressure
    d) Low temperature and high pressure
    e) Any temperature and pressure

69. Which of the following equations represents a nuclear fusion?
   a) ${}^{14}_{6}C \rightarrow {}^{14}_{7}N + {}^{0}_{-1}e$
   b) ${}^{27}_{13}Al + {}^{4}_{2}He \rightarrow {}^{30}_{15}P + {}^{1}_{0}n$
   c) ${}^{235}_{82}U + {}^{1}_{0}n \rightarrow {}^{139}_{56}Ba + {}^{94}_{36}Kr + 3{}^{1}_{0}n$
   d) ${}^{2}_{1}H + {}^{3}_{1}H \rightarrow {}^{4}_{2}He + {}^{1}_{0}n$
   e) ${}^{116}_{49}In \rightarrow {}^{116}_{50}Sn + {}^{0}_{-1}e$

70. A student mixes a 0.10 M $AgNO_3$ aqueous solution with excess copper metal. The reaction should produce 0.2 grams of silver. However, the student obtains a mass of 0.22 grams of silver. Which of the following is/are the possible explanations for the yield > 100%?
   I. The student did not subtract the mass of the filter paper before recording results.
   II. The student did not thoroughly dry the sample before measuring the mass.
   III. The copper metal did not react completely.
   a) I only
   b) II only
   c) I and II only
   d) I and III only
   e) I, II, and III

SAT Chemistry Subject Test No. 2 Keys

1. A	11. B	21. E	31. A	41. E	51. A	61. A
2. B	12. C	22. C	32. B	42. A	52. C	62. B
3. D	13. B	23. A	33. C	43. B	53. C	63. C
4. E	14. A	24. B	34. D	44. D	54. B	64. D
5. A	15. D	25. B	35. A	45. B	55. C	65. A
6. D	16. E	26. A	36. B	46. C	56. D	66. C
7. B	17. C	27. C	37. D	47. D	57. A	67. E
8. E	18. E	28. D	38. A	48. A	58. B	68. B
9. A	19. D	29. A	39. B	49. C	59. D	69. D
10. E	20. A	30. D	40. D	50. D	60. D	70. C

101.	FT	106.	TF	111.	TF
102.	TTCE	107.	TTCE	112.	TTCE
103.	TTCE	108.	FT	113.	TT
104.	TTCE	109.	TTCE	114.	FT
105.	FT	110.	TTCE	115.	FT

SAT Chemistry Subject Test No. 2 Answer to Part A

1 – 4 *Answer: (abde)*
AgCl: a white precipitate

$C_5H_{12(s)} + 8O_2(g)$*: combustion reaction*

$NH_3(g) + H_2O(l)$*: weak basic solution*

$HC_2H_3O_2 + OH^-(aq)$*: acid-base neutralization reaction*

$CaCO_3(s)$*: decomposition reaction*

5 – 8 *Answer: (adbe)*
An increase in the reactant concentration will increase the collisions but not the temperature. The average kinetic energy does not change.

Adding catalysts to a reaction will decrease activation energy because of different pathways.

An increase in the temperature will increase average kinetic energy.

The pH scale indicates an acidic or basic solution.

9 – 12 *Answer: (aebc)*
Alpha particle: ^4_2He*; +2*
Beta particle: e^{-1}
Neutron: no charge
Gamma ray: a high energy light.
Positron: e^{+1}

13 – 16 *Answer: (bade)*
Remember the definitions

17 – 20 *Answer: (ceda)*
The least reactive family of elements is Noble gasfamily.

Consist of atoms that have valence electrons in a d subshell: Transition metals

The halogen family exists as diatomic molecules at room temperature, such as H_2*,* O_2*, and* N_2*.*

Alkali metals have the lowest first ionization energy in the period.

21 – 24 *Answer: (ecab)*
a) a solid phase
b) a liquid phase
c) a gas phase

Sublimation: from solid to gas
Deposition: from gas to solid
Vaporization: from liquid to gas
Condensation: from vapor to liquid
Freezing: from liquid to solid

SAT Chemistry Subject Test No. 2 Answer to Part C

25. *Answer: (b)*
    Chemical reactions will produce new substances. Only (b) does not produce a new substance.

26. *Answer: (a)*
    Energy level: $1s<2s<2p<3s<3p<4s<3d$

27. *Answer: (c)*
    Energy level: $1s<2s<2p<3s<3p<4s<3d$
    Ground state of Sc, $1s^2\ 2S^2\ 2p^6\ 3s^2\ 3p^6\ 3d^1\ 4s^2$, *excited to* $1s^2\ 2S^2\ 2p^6\ 3s^2\ 3p^6\ 3d^2\ 4s^1$

28. *Answer: (d)*
    Heisenberg uncertainty principle

29. *Answer: (a)*
    X ion should have a +1 charge. Alkali metals from +1 ion.

30. *Answer: (d)*
    Increase atomic radii down the column and decrease down the row.

31. *Answer: (a)*
    I. CBr_4 : sp^3
    II. PF_5 : dsp^3
    III. NH_3 : sp^3
    IV. SO_3 : sp^2
    V. HCN : sp

32. *Answer: (b)*
    Alkaline earth metals bond to halogen with ionic bonds.

33. *Answer: (c)*
    Metals conduct electricity in solid.
    Ionic compounds conduct electricity in an aqueous solution or molten state.

34. *Answer: (d)*
    $SeCl_4$ *is* dsp^3 *hybridized.*

35. *Answer: (a)*
    2.24 L of $CO_2 = \frac{2.24}{22.4}$ moles of $CO_2 = \frac{2.24}{22.4}$ moles of $CaCO_3$
    $\frac{2.24}{22.4} \times 100 = 10.0\ g$

36. *Answer: (b)*
    68.00 g ammonia $= \frac{68}{17} = 4$ moles
    64.00 g oxygen $= \frac{64}{32} = 2$ moles
    Oxygen is the limiting reactant.
    $O_2 : H_2O = 5 : 6 = 2 : x$
    $x = 2.4$ moles

37. *Answer: (d)*
    $\frac{4 \times 16}{1 + 35.5 + 4 \times 16} = 0.64 = 64\%$

38. *Answer: (a)*
    6.02×10^{23} atoms of diatomic molecules = 0.5 moles of gas $= \frac{22.4}{2} = 11.2$ L

39. *Answer: (b)*
    $\frac{P_1V_1}{T_1} = \frac{P_2V_2}{T_2}$
    Increasing pressure and decreasing temperature will decrease the volume of gas.

40. *Answer: (d)*
    Mass of $N_2 = \frac{11.2}{22.4} \times 28 = 14\ g$
    Mass of the bottle = 450 – 14 = 436 g
    Mass of the gas = 478 – 436 = 42.0 g
    Molar mass of the gas $= \frac{42}{14} \times 28 = 84\ g/mole$
    It is Kr gas.

41. *Answer: (e)*
    The average kinetic energy is proportional to the temperature (°K) of the gas.

42. *Answer: (a)*
    Van der Waals is a non-polar attractive force.

43. *Answer: (b)*
    This is the definition of critical point.

44. *Answer: (d)*
    Vitamin C has more hydrogen bonds than vitamin E.

45. *Answer: (b)*
    In a saturated solution, solid material continues to dissolve, and material that is in solution continues to crystallize. Dissolution and crystallization occur at the same rate.

46. *Answer: (c)*
Non-polar solvents dissolve non-polar solutes.

47. *Answer: (d)*
$\Delta T = i \times m \times Kb$
a). $i \times m = 0.2$
b). $i \times m = 0.3$
c). $i \times m = 0.1$
d). $i \times m = 0.6$
e). $i \times m = 0.2$

48. *Answer: (a)*
2 moles Na : 822 = 0.5 moles of Na : x
x = 205.5 kJ

49. *Answer: (c)*
$\Delta G = \Delta H - T\Delta S$
$\Delta G < 0$: $\Delta H < 0$ and $\Delta S > 0$ *Enthalpy is driven from high to low and entropy is driven from low to high.*

50. *Answer: (d)*
$\Delta G = \Delta G° + RTln(\frac{[NH3]^2}{[N2][H_2]^3})$
At equilibrium, $\Delta G = 0$
$0 = \Delta G° + RTln(\frac{[NH3]^2}{[N2][H_2]^3})$
$\frac{[NH3]^2}{[N2][H_2]^3} = exp(\frac{-\Delta G^o}{RT}) > 1$
$\Delta G^o = \Delta H^o - T\Delta S^o$
ΔS^o *is negative(less randomness).*
ΔH^o *must be negative to make* $\Delta G°$ *negative.*
The reaction is spontaneous because of its negative $\Delta G°$.
$\Delta G°$ *is a state function. Reversing a reaction will reverse its* $\Delta G°$.
$\Delta G°$ *is a temperature dependent function.*

51. *Answer: (a)*
Cu^+ *is a reaction intermediate and* Cu^{2+} *is a catalyst.*

52. *Answer: (c)*
$C_6H_6 : CO_2 = 1 : 6 = 0.25 : x$
$x = 1.5$

53. *Answer: (c)*
Order of the reaction: 2 + 1 = 3

54. *Answer: (b)*
$PbI_2 \rightarrow pb^{2+} + 2I^-$
$x \quad 2x$
$K = [x][2x]^2 = 4 \times 10^{-9}$
$x = 1.0 \times 10^{-3}$

55. *Answer: (c)*
$HCl \leftrightarrow \frac{1}{2}H_2 + \frac{1}{2}Cl_2$
$K_{eq} = (\frac{1}{K_p})^{1/2} = \frac{1}{\sqrt{Kp}}$

56. *Answer: (d)*
The value of the equilibrium constant, K, is dependent on the nature of the reactions and the temperature.

57. *Answer: (a)*
Strong Base + Weak Acid = Weak Basic Solution

58. *Answer: (b)*
$[OH^-][H^+] = 10^{-14}$
$[H^+] = \frac{10^{-14}}{10^{-6}} = 10^{-8}$
$pH = -log[10^{-8}] = 8 > 7$
This is a basic solution.
$pOH = 14 - 8 = 6$

59. *Answer: (d)*
The weakest acid has the strongest conjugate base ion.
H_2CO_3 *is the weakest acid among the answer choices.*

60. *Answer: (d)*
$\frac{50 \times 0.04 - 50 \times 0.02}{50 + 50} = 1 \times 10^{-2}$ *M of* $[H^+]$
$pH = -log(1 \times 10^{-2}) = 2$

61. *Answer: (a)*
Cl_2 *undergoes two different reactions here.*
$Cl_2 \rightarrow OCl^-$ *and its oxidation number changes from 0 to +1.*
$Cl_2 \rightarrow Cl^-$ *and its oxidation number changes from 0 to −1.*
Cl_2 *undergoes both oxidation and reduction.*

62. *Answer: (b)*
The higher in the activity series, the stronger the reduction agent is and the easier is to be oxidized from a metal to a positive ion.

63. *Answer: (c)*
Only Hg is a weaker reduction agent than H_2.

64. *Answer: (d)*
$4 \times 2 - 3 = 5$

65. *Answer: (a)*
Oxidation of ethanol results in the formation of acetic acid.

66. *Answer: (c)*
Carbon can either lose or gain 4 electrons to form 4 covalent bonds.

67. *Answer: (e)*
Ozone, O_3, can shield the earth from harmful ultraviolet radiation.

68. *Answer: (b)*
Nuclei fusion is dependent on high temperature and pressure.

69. *Answer: (d)*
Fusion: Light nuclei fuse together to become heavier nuclei.

70. *Answer: (c)*
Cases I and II will increase the yield of this experiment and case III will decrease the yield of this experiment.

SAT Chemistry Subject Test No. 3

PART A

Directions: Each set of lettered choices below refers to the numbered statements or questions immediately following it. Select the one lettered choice that best fits each statement and then fill in the corresponding circle on the answer sheet. A given choice may be used once, more than once, or not at all in each set.

Note: For all questions involving solutions, assume that the solvent is water unless otherwise stated. Throughout the test the following symbols have the definitions specified unless otherwise noted.

H = enthalpy	T = temperature	L = liter(s)
M = molar	V = volume	mL = milliliter(s)
n = number of moles	atm = atmosphere(s)	mm = millimeter(s)
P = pressure	g = gram(s)	mol = mole(s)
R = molar gas constant	J = joule(s)	V = volt(s)
S = entropy	kJ = kilojoule(s)	

Questions 1–4 refer to the following topics and relationships:

a) Solute
b) Solvent
c) Solubility
d) Aqueous solution
e) Solvation

1. It is defined as the substance present in a lesser amount in a solution.
2. It is the solution when solvent is water.
3. It is defined as the substance present in a greater quantity in a solution.
4. It is defined as the interaction between the solute and solvent molecules.

Questions 5–8 refer to the following topics and relationships:

a) Gamma decay
b) Nuclear fusion
c) Alpha decay
d) Positron emission
e) Nuclear fission

5. The nuclear reaction is responsible for the energy output of the sun.
6. The nuclear reaction results in no change in the mass number and atomic number of a nuclide.
7. The nuclear reaction is responsible for the energy output of nuclear power plant.
8. The nuclear reaction transmutes uranium-238 into thorium-234.

Questions 9–12 refer to the following topics and relationships:

a) $1s^22s^22p^63s^23P^6$
b) $1s^22s^22p^6$
c) $ls^22s^22p^63s^23p^64s^l$
d) $1s^2$
e) $ls^22s^22p^63p^1$

9. It is the electron configuration for the most stable sodium ion.
10. It is the electron configuration for an excited atom.
11. It is the electron configuration for potassium in its ground state.
12. It is the electron configuration for the noble gas with the highest first ionization energy.

Questions 13–16 refer to the following topics and relationships:

a) 0.01 M $MgCl_2$ aqueous solution
b) 0.01 M $HClO_4$ aqueous solution
c) 0.01 M NH_4OH aqueous solution
d) 0.01 M KOH aqueous solution
e) 0.01 M $LiNO_3$ aqueous solution

13. This solution has a pH of 12.
14. This solution has the highest boiling point temperature.
15. The solution is a weak basic solution.
16. This solution indicates a red flame when ionized with a Bunsen burner.

Questions 17–20 refer to the following topics and relationships:

a) Pyramidal
b) Trigonal, planar
c) Linear
d) Tetrahedral
e) Bent

From the choices above, choose the shape that best describes each of the following molecules:

17. CCl_4
18. BH_3
19. CO_2
20. H_2O

Questions 21–24 refer to the following topics and relationships:

a) K
b) Ca
c) Br
d) Kr
e) Zn

21. This element has the smallest atomic radii.
22. This element has the highest electronegativity.
23. This element has the largest second ionization energy.
24. This element has the highest melting point.

PART B

Directions: Each question below consists of two statements, I in the left-hand column and II in the right-hand column. For each question, determine whether statement I is true or false and whether statement II is true or false and then fill in the corresponding T or F circles on your answer sheet. Fill in circle CE only if statement II is a correct explanation of the true statement I.
On the actual Chemistry Test, the following type of question must be answered on a special section (labeled "Chemistry") at the lower left-hand corner of your answer sheet. These questions will be numbered beginning with 101 and must be answered according to the following directions.

Examples:

	I		II
EX 1.	H_2SO_4 is a strong acid	BECAUSE	H_2SO_4 contains sulfer.
EX 2.	An atom of oxygen is electrically neutral	BECAUSE	an oxygen atom contains an equal number of protons and electrons.

SAMPLE ANSWERS

	I		II		CE
EX 1.	●	Ⓕ	●	Ⓕ	○
EX 2.	●	Ⓕ	●	Ⓕ	●

101. A catalyst increases the rate of reaction BECAUSE It raises the energy of the products.

102. An emission of a β particle results in a decrease of the atomic number BECAUSE A β particle is an electron emitted from the nucleus.

103. Chloride ions, Cl^-, can be oxidized to produce chlorine gas BECAUSE Two chloride ions give up an electron to form Cl_2.

104. CO_2 is able to sublimate at atmospheric pressure BECAUSE Carbon dioxide's liquid form is impossible to produce.

105. Electrolytic cells require the input of energy BECAUSE Electrolytic cells have just one container, while voltaic cells have two.

106. Halogen molecules can exist as solids, liquids or gases at room temperature BECAUSE As the mass of a non-polar molecule increases, the dispersion forces between them increases.

	Statement I		Statement II
107.	If an acid is added to water with the original pH of 7, the concentration of hydroxide ions will increase	BECAUSE	The product of hydroxide ions and hydrogen ions is equal to 1.0×10^{-14} in all aqueous solutions at 25 °C.
108.	An exothermic reaction has the heat of formation with the minus sign	BECAUSE	The first law of Thermodynamics states that a negative heat of formation is associated with an exothermic reaction.
109.	Sodium chloride forms an aqueous solution of ions	BECAUSE	The sodium in NaCl has a +1 charge while the chlorine has a −1 charge. The compound is then hydrated by the water molecules.
110.	The 5s orbital is filled after the 4d orbital.	BECAUSE	The 5s orbital has a lower energy than the 4d orbital.
111.	The conjugate base of a weak acid is a strong base.	BECAUSE	Elements that are strong Brønsted-Lowry acids are not strong Brønsted-Lowry bases.
112.	The ideal gas law does not hold under low temperatures and high pressure	BECAUSE	Interactions between particles cannot be neglected under these conditions.
113.	The ion of a nonmetallic atom is larger in radius than the atom	BECAUSE	When a nonmetallic ion is formed, it gains electrons in the outer orbital, thus increasing the size of its electron cloud.
114.	The N-N bond distance in N_2 is shorter than the N-N bond distance in N_2H_4	BECAUSE	The atomic radius of H is smaller than the atomic radius of N.
115.	When the temperature of a reaction at equilibrium is increased, the equilibrium will shift to favor the endothermic direction.	BECAUSE	Endothermic reactions involve heat acting as a reactant. Le Chatelier's principle states that an equilibrium shift will occur to offset temperature changes.

PART C

Directions: Each of the questions or incomplete statements below is followed by five suggested answers or completions. Select the one that is best in each case and then fill in the corresponding circle on the answer sheet.

25. Which of the following changes is a physical change?
    a) Eggs rotting
    b) Iron turning white when heated
    c) Lighter fluid burning
    d) Bikes rusting
    e) None of the above

26. The inability of precisely determining the position and momentum of a subatomic particle is summarized by the
    a) Rydberg equation.
    b) Heisenberg uncertainty principle.
    c) Hund's rule.
    d) Pauli exclusion principle.
    e) Bohr model.

27. Which of the following statements is NOT consistent with the crystal properties of the substance?
    a) SiC is used to grind metal parts to shape.
    b) Tungsten is drawn into thin wires.
    c) Aluminum is used to cut glass.
    d) Graphite is used to lubricate locks.
    e) MgF_2 shatters when dropped.

28. The atom of bromine contains how many protons, neutrons and electrons?
    a) 35 p, 45 n, 35 e^-
    b) 35 p, 80 n, 35 e^-
    c) 45 p, 35 n, 45 e^-
    d) 80 p, 35 n, 80 e^-
    e) Neutrons cannot be determined unless an isotope is specified.

29. Which of the following species has the largest radius?
    a) Sr
    b) P
    c) Mg
    d) Al^{3+}
    e) Mg^{2+}

30. Which of the following groups consists of atoms that have valence electrons in a ***d*** subshell?
    a) Alkali metals
    b) Alkaline earth metals
    c) Noble gases
    d) Halogens
    e) Transition metals

31. What type of bonds can be formed when the electronegativity difference between two atoms is 2?
    a) Ionic
    b) Covalent
    c) Polar covalent
    d) Metallic
    e) Hydrogen bonding

32. For the following bond angles:
    I. HCH angle in CH_4
    II. HOH angle in H_2O
    III. HNH angle in NH_3

    Which of the following orders represents the bond angles I, II, and III in increasing order from the smallest to largest bond angles?
    a) I, II, III
    b) II, III, I
    c) I, III, II
    d) II, I, III
    e) III, II, I

33. Which of the following answers lists all of the bond angles contained in a sulfur hexafluoride molecule?
    a) 120°
    b) 180°
    c) 90° and 180°
    d) 90°, 120°, and 180°
    e) 109.5°

34. Which of following molecules is linear?
    I. CBr_4
    II. PF_5
    III. NH_3
    IV. SO_3
    V. HCN

    a) I
    b) II
    c) III
    d) IV
    e) V

35. What is the empirical formula for a compound containing 2.8 grams of N and 8 grams of O?
    a) N_2O_5
    b) N_2O_3
    c) NO_2
    d) NO
    e) N_2O

36. Which of the following reactions is the type of chemical reaction below:
    $Na_2SO_4 + ZnBr_2 \rightarrow ZnSO_4 + 2 NaBr$
    a) Single replacement
    b) Decomposition
    c) Double replacement
    d) Combustion
    e) Synthesis

37. For $4NH_3(g) + 5O_2(g) \rightarrow 4NO(g) + 6H_2O(g)$, if you begin with 17.00 g ammonia and excess oxygen, how many grams of water will be obtained?
    a) 6.7
    b) 13.5
    c) 20.1
    d) 27.0
    e) 40.5

38. Which of the following graphs presents the relationship between the pressure (y-axis) and the absolute temperature (axis-axis) of a given volume of gas?
    a)
    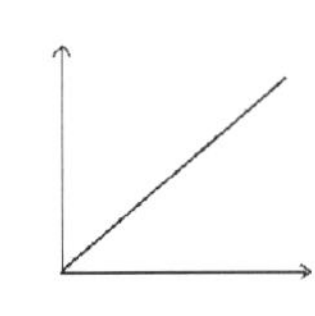
    b)

    c)
    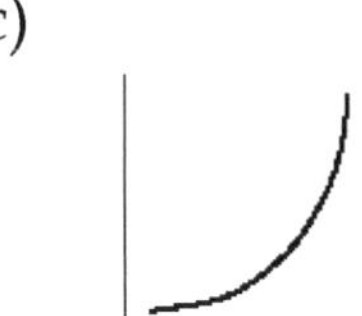
    d)
    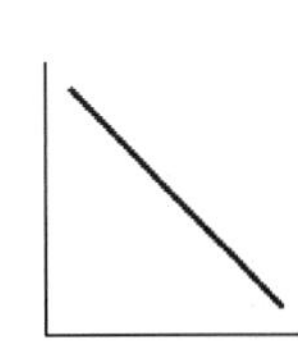

e)

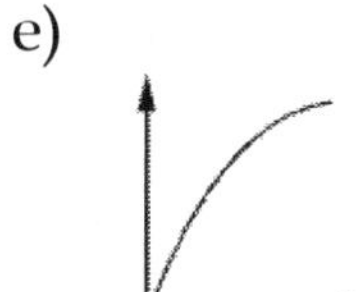

39. At 5 atm and 0 °C, how many moles are there in a 1.12 liter of O_2 gas?
    a) 0.5
    b) 0.25
    c) 0.0.2
    d) 0.125
    e) 0.1

40. What is the molecular formula for a gas of which the density is nearly equal to 2 g L^{-1} at STP?
    a) C_2H_6
    b) HF
    c) CH_4
    d) CO_2
    e) NH_3

41. Which of the following statements explains the effect of increasing the temperature on the pressure of the ideal gas by using kinetic molecular theory?
    a) The increase in force of the gas molecules colliding with the container walls
    b) The increase in rotational energy of the gas molecules
    c) The increase in average velocity of the gas molecules by the higher rate of collisions with the container walls
    d) An increase in the attractive forces among the gas molecules
    e) Both (a) and (c)

42. Which of the following statements is NOT true?
    a) CH_2O (formaldehyde) has a relatively high boiling point due to hydrogen bonding.
    b) $BaCl_2$ is an example of an ionic solid.
    c) Ionic solids are poor conductors of heat and electricity.
    d) The melting point of Fe is higher than that of $C_6H_{12}O_6$ (glucose).
    e) The melting point of diamond is higher than that of Cu (copper).

43. Under which of the following vapor pressure and temperature conditions would $CO_2(g)$ have the lowest solubility in water?
    a) 5.0 atm and 75 °C
    b) 1.0 atm and 75 °C
    c) 5.0 atm and 25 °C
    d) 1.0 atm and 25 °C
    e) 3.0 atm and 25 °C

44. Which of the following physical transformations occurs during sublimation?
    a) Gas to liquid
    b) Gas to solid
    c) Solid to liquid to gas
    d) Solid to gas
    e) Solid to liquid

45. How many grams of NaOH are needed to make a 100g of 5% solution?
    a) 2
    b) 5
    c) 20
    d) 40
    e) 95

46. What volume must 10.0 mL of 5.00 M HCl be diluted to in order to make a 0.500 M HCl solution?
    a) 1 mL
    b) 50 mL
    c) 100 mL
    d) 500 mL
    e) 1,000 mL

47. What is the molarity of a solution when 50.0 mL of 6.0 M HCl is diluted to a volume of 300.0 mL?
    a) 0.01 M
    b) 0.10 M
    c) 0.20 M
    d) 0.30 M
    e) 1.0 M

48. $CH_4(g) + 2O_2(g) \rightarrow CO_2(g) + 2H_2O(g) + 800$ kJ
    According to the above reaction, if one mole of $O_2(g)$ is consumed, how much energy is produced?
    a) 200 kJ
    b) 400 kJ
    c) 800 kJ
    d) 1200 kJ
    e) 1600 kJ

49. Which of the following statements is true?
    a) A reaction with a positive $\Delta S°$ will always be spontaneous.
    b) A reaction with a negative $\Delta H°$ will always be spontaneous.
    c) A reaction with a positive $\Delta S°$ and a negative $\Delta H°$ will always be spontaneous.
    d) A reaction with a negative $\Delta S°$ and a negative $\Delta H°$ will never be spontaneous.
    e) A reaction with a positive $\Delta S°$ and a positive $\Delta H°$ will never be spontaneous.

50. If a reaction has a negative free energy change,
    a) the reaction can occur spontaneously.
    b) the reaction can be used to do work by driving other reactions.
    c) the entropy must always be negative.
    d) Both a) and b)
    e) None of the above

51. Usually the reaction rate doubles for each 10 °C increase in temperature. Estimate the time it takes for a reaction to finish at 0 °C, if it takes 1 hour to finish at 50 °C.
    a) 5 hours
    b) 16 hours
    c) 32 hours
    d) 2 days
    e) 32 days

52. $2NO(g) + O_2(g) \rightarrow 2NO_2(g)$
    According to the reaction above, the data of the reaction rate is listed below.

Experiment	$[O_2]$	[NO]	Rate
1	0.02	0.05	0.038
2	0.02	0.1	0.152
3	0.08	0.1	0.608

Which of the following is the rate law for this reaction?
    a) Rate = $k[O_2]^2[NO]^2$
    b) Rate = $k[NO]^2$
    c) Rate = $k[O_2][NO]^2$
    d) Rate = $k[O_2][NO]$
    e) Rate = $k[O_2]^2$

53. A first order reaction has a half-life of 85 seconds. How many grams of the reactant are left after 255 seconds if the initial weight of the reactant is one gram?
   a) 1/2
   b) 1/4
   c) 1/8
   d) 1/3
   e) 7/8

54. $2NO_2(g) \leftrightarrow N_2O_4(g)$; $Kp = 10\ atm^{-1}$
According to the equation above, which of the following conditions will allow the reaction to proceed in the forward direction?

	$NO_2(g)$	$N_2O_4(g)$
a)	0.2 atm	0.4 atm
b)	380 mm Hg	380 mm Hg
c)	0.002 atm	0.001 atm
d)	38 mm Hg	76 mm Hg
e)	0.1 atm	0.5 atm

55. An increase in pressure for the reaction of $2HI(g) \leftrightarrow H_2(g) + I_2(g)$ would
   a) produce more I_{aq}^{-1}.
   b) produce more H_2.
   c) not affect the system.
   d) move the reaction to the right.
   e) move the reaction to the left.

56. In this closed container equilibrium reaction: A + B ↔ AB + Heat, how could the forward reaction rate be increased?
   I. Increasing [AB]
   II. Increasing [A]
   III. Reducing [AB]
   a) I only
   b) III only
   c) I and III only
   d) II and III only
   e) I, II, and III

57. Which of the following characteristics is associated with Lewis bases?
   a) They react with metal to produce hydrogen gas.
   b) They donate an unshared electron pair.
   c) They always contain the hydroxide ion in their structure.
   d) They taste sour.
   e) They are formed by the reaction of a nonmetal oxide and water.

58. Which of the following solutions has the lowest pH?
   a) NaCl (1M, 10 mL) and NaOH (1M, 10 mL)
   b) NaOAc (1M, 10 mL) and HOAc(1M, 10 mL)
   c) HNO_3 (1M, 10 mL) and $NaNO_3$ (1M, 10 mL)
   d) NH_3 (1M, 10 mL) and NH_4Cl (1M, 10 mL)
   e) NaCl (1M, 10 mL) and K_2SO_4 (1M, 10 mL)

59. The Cl^- in the aqueous solution is
   a) a strong acid.
   b) a strong base.
   c) a weak acid.
   d) a weak base.
   e) a salt (made from an acid and a base).

60. Which of the following salts will create an acidic solution when placed in water?
   a) Na_2SO_4
   b) K_2SO_4
   c) $NaNO_3$
   d) $Cu(NO_3)_2$
   e) $NH_4C_2H_3O_2$

61. A reaction has a very large equilibrium constant of 1×10^{23}. Which statement is NOT true about this reaction?
    a) The reaction will be very fast.
    b) The reaction will essentially run to completion.
    c) The reaction is spontaneous.
    d) The equilibrium constant will change if the temperature is changed.
    e) The products will react to yield very little reactant.

62. With a current of 9.65 A, how many minutes will be required to deposit 6.35 g of copper on a platinum electrode from a copper(II) nitrate solution? (The charge of one mole of electrons = 96,500 C)
    a) 16.7
    b) 33.3
    c) 66.6
    d) 1,000
    e) 2,000

63. Which of the following compounds/elements is NOT commonly produced by electrolysis?
    a) Na
    b) Al
    c) Fe
    d) O_2
    e) H_2

64. What is the oxidation number of Mn in $KMnO_4$?
    a) −7
    b) −3
    c) 0
    d) +3
    e) +7

65. The first and simplest alkane is
    a) Ethane
    b) Methane
    c) C_2H_2
    d) Methene
    e) CCl_4

66. The primary products of hydrocarbon combustion are
    a) water and carbon.
    b) water and carbon monoxide.
    c) water and carbon dioxide.
    d) hydrogen and carbon monoxide.
    e) hydrogen and carbon.

67. Radioactive isotopes produce good results in the treatment of
    a) Parkinson disease.
    b) cancer.
    c) heart disease .
    d) AIDS.
    e) common colds.

68. Which of the following statements describes a carbon-14 atom that has spontaneously decayed to form a nitrogen-14 atom?
    a) A transmutation occurred without particle emission.
    b) A transmutation occurred with particle emission.
    c) Nitrogen-14 has an unstable nucleus.
    d) Carbon-14 has a stable nucleus.
    e) Carbon-12 has an unstable nucleus.

69. The substance used as a moderator in a nuclear power plant reactor is
    a) marble.
    b) hydrogen.
    c) tritium.
    d) graphite.
    e) copper.

70. Which of the following instruments would be the best suited for use in a volumetric analysis to find the unknown molarity of base when titrated with a known acid?
    a) Graduated cylinder
    b) Pipette
    c) 250 mL beaker
    d) Burette
    e) Triple beam balance

SAT Chemistry Subject Test No. 3 Keys

1. A	11. C	21. D	31. A	41. E	51. C	61. A
2. D	12. D	22. C	32. B	42. A	52. C	62. B
3. B	13. D	23. A	33. C	43. B	53. C	63. C
4. E	14. A	24. B	34. E	44. D	54. B	64. E
5. B	15. C	25. B	35. A	45. B	55. C	65. B
6. A	16. E	26. B	36. C	46. C	56. D	66. C
7. E	17. D	27. C	37. D	47. E	57. B	67. B
8. C	18. B	28. E	38. A	48. B	58. C	68. B
9. B	19. C	29. A	39. B	49. C	59. D	69. D
10. E	20. E	30. E	40. D	50. D	60. D	70. D

101.	TF	106.	TTCE	111.	TT
102.	FT	107.	FT	112.	TTCE
103.	TTCE	108.	TF	113.	TTCE
104.	TF	109.	TTCE	114.	TT
105.	TT	110.	FT	115.	TTCE

SAT Chemistry Subject Test No. 3 Answer to of Part A

1 – 4 *Answer: (adbe)*
Solute: Present in a lesser amount in a solution

Solvent: present in a greater quantity in a solution

Aqueous solution: Solvent is water

Solvation: Interaction between the solute and solvent molecules

5 – 8 *Answer: (baec)*
The Sun undergoes nuclear fusion to provide the energy that earth needs.

Gammy decay releases r-ray, a high energy of electromagnetic wave, in the process.

Most of the nuclear power plant use nuclear fission of u-235 to produce energy.

$^{238}_{92}U \rightarrow {}^{234}_{90}Th + {}^{4}_{2}He$, *an alpha decay reaction*

9 – 12 *Answer: (becd)*
Na^+ has 10 electrons: $1s^22s^22p^6$
$ls^22s^22p^63s^1$ excited to $1s^22s^22p^63p^1$

13 – 16 *Answer: (dace)*
0.01 M $MgCl_2$: 3 ions; pH ≈ 7

0.01 M $HClO_4$: 2 ions; pH=2;

0.01 M NH_4OH: weak base

0.01 M KOH: 2 ions; pH = 12

0.01 M $LiNO_3$: 2 ions; pH ≈ 7; the flame color of Li^+ ion is red.

17 – 20 *Answer: (dbce)*
CCl_4: sp^3 4 bonds

BH_3: sp^2 3 bonds

CO_2: sp 2 bonds

H_2O: sp^3 3 bonds

21 – 24 *Answer: (dcab)*
Atomic radii decrease from left to right across a period.

Electronegativity increases from left to right across a period.

The largest 2nd ionization energy is alkali metals because they have only one valence electron.

Ca has the highest melting point.

SAT Chemistry Subject Test No. 3 Answer to Part C

25. *Answer: (b)*
Heating iron is a physical means.

26. *Answer: (b)*
It is Heisenberg's uncertainty principle.

27. *Answer: (c)*
Aluminum is a relatively soft metal.
Diamond is used to cut glass.

28. *Answer: (e)*
The atomic number of bromine is 35, so it has 35 protons and 35 electrons. But the number of neutrons can be different among different isotopes.

29. *Answer: (a)*
Sr has the highest principal quantum number.

30. *Answer: (e)*
Transition metals have valence electrons in a d shell.

31. *Answer: (a)*
Two atoms with an electronegativity difference greater than 1.6 will form ionic bonds.

32. *Answer: (b)*
I. HCH: 109.5°
II. HOH: 104.5°
III. HNH: 107°

33. *Answer: (c)*
Sulfur hexafluoride molecules have an octahedral geometric shape.

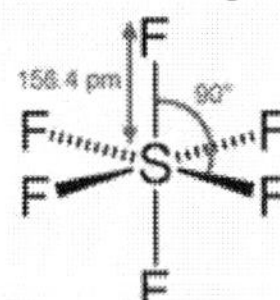

34. *Answer: (e)*
Only the SP molecular shape is linear.
I. $CBr_4 : sp^3$
II. $PF_5 : dsp^3$
III. $NH_3 : sp^3$
IV. $SO_3 : sp^2$
V. $HCN : sp$

35. *Answer: (a)*
$N : O = \frac{2.8}{14} : \frac{8}{16} = 2 : 5$

36. *Answer: (c)*
$AB + CD \rightarrow AC + BD$

37. *Answer: (d)*
$NH_3 : H_2O = 4 : 6 = \frac{17}{17} : \frac{x}{18}$
$x = \frac{6 \times 17 \times 18}{4 \times 17} = 27\,g$

38. *Answer: (a)*
Pressure and temperature are directly proportional to each other.
$\frac{P_1}{T_1} = \frac{P_2}{T_2}$

39. *Answer: (b)*
$5 \times \frac{1.12}{22.4} = 0.25$ *moles of* O_2

40. *Answer: (d)*
Molar Mass $= 22.4 \times 2 = 44.8$
The molar mass of CO_2 *is close to 44.*

41. *Answer: (e)*
Increasing temperature will increase the average velocity of gas molecules, therefore increasing the frequency and forces of the collisions.

42. *Answer: (a)*
CH_2O *does not have hydrogen bonds.*

43. *Answer: (b)*
The lower pressure and higher temperature will decrease the solubility of CO_2 *in water.*

44. *Answer: (d)*
Sublimation: from solid to gas

45. *Answer: (b)*
$5\% = \frac{x}{100} \times 100\%$
$x = 5\,g$

46. *Answer: (c)*
$10 \times 5 = x \times 0.5$
$x = 100$ *ml*

47. *Answer: (e)*
$50 \times 6 = 300 \times M$
$M = 1\,M$

48. *Answer: (b)*
2 moles of $O_2 : 800 = 1 : x$
$x = 400$ *Kj*

49. *Answer: (c)*
$\Delta G^o = \Delta H^o - T\Delta S^o$

50. *Answer: (d)*
Free energy: The energy that is available to do work (useful energy) depends on enthalpy and entropy. The reaction is a spontaneous reaction when ΔG^o *is negative.*

51. *Answer: (c)*
$50 - 0 = 50$
$1\ hour \times 2^{\frac{50}{10}} = 32\ hours$

52. *Answer: (c)*
[NO] double: rate 4x
$[O_2]$ *4 times: rate 4x*
$Rate = k[O_2][NO]^2$

53. *Answer: (c)*
$\frac{255}{85} = 3\ half\text{-}lives \rightarrow (\frac{1}{2})^3 = \frac{1}{8}$

54. *Answer: (b)*
$Q = \frac{N_2O_4}{NO_2^2}$;
Converting pressure to atm
a) $\frac{0.4}{0.2^2} = 10 = Kp$ *at equilibrium*
b) $\frac{\frac{380}{760}}{\left(\frac{380}{760}\right)^2} = 2 < 10$ *reaction moves forward*
c) $\frac{0.001}{0.002^2} = 250 > 10$; *shift left*
d) $\frac{76/760}{\left(\frac{38}{760}\right)^2} = 40 > 10$; *shift left*
e) $\frac{0.5}{0.1^2} = 50 > 10$; *shift left*

55. *Answer: (c)*
An increase in pressure will not change the equilibrium conditions because the number of gas molecules of reactant is equal to the number of gas molecules of products.

56. *Answer: (d)*
By increasing [A] and [B] or removing [AB], the reaction will shift to the right.

57. *Answer: (b)*
This is the definition of a Lewis base.

58. *Answer: (c)*
Strong acids and weak bases would result in the lowest pH values.

59. *Answer: (d)*
HCl is a strong acid, so its conjugate base, Cl^-*, is a weak base.*

60. *Answer: (d)*
Only the weak acidic ions or weak basic ions can be hydrolyzed.
Only Cu^{2+} *is a weak acidic ion among the choices.*

61. *Answer: (a)*
Reaction rates and the equilibrium constants are not directly related.

62. *Answer: (b)*
$Cu^{2+} + 2e^- \rightarrow Cu$
$6.35\ g\ of\ Copper = \frac{6.35}{63.5} = 0.1\ moles$
$0.1 \times 2 \times 96500 = 9.65 \times t \times 60$
$t = 33.3\ minutes$

63. *Answer: (c)*
Iron production involves iron ores in a carbothermic reaction (reduction with carbon) in a blast furnace at temperatures of about 2,000 ℃.

64. *Answer: (e)*
$O: -2$
$K: +1$
$Mn: 4(2) - 1 = 7$

65. *Answer: (b)*
CH_4*, methane, is the simplest alkane.*

66. *Answer: (c)*
$C_nH_m \rightarrow CO_2 + H_2O$

67. *Answer: (b)*
One medical use for radioactive isotopes is to treat cancers.

68. *Answer: (b)*
Carbon-14 has an unstable nucleus that decays to form a stable nitrogen-14 nucleus and emit a beta particle.

69. *Answer: (d)*
Graphite can absorb many neutrons, so it is a good control material for nuclear fission reactions.

70. *Answer: (d)*
Use a burette in the titration process.

SAT Chemistry Subject Test No. 4

PART A

Directions: Each set of lettered choices below refers to the numbered statements or questions immediately following it. Select the one lettered choice that best fits each statement and then fill in the corresponding circle on the answer sheet. A given choice may be used once, more than once, or not at all in each set.

Note: For all questions involving solutions, assume that the solvent is water unless otherwise stated. Throughout the test the following symbols have the definitions specified unless otherwise noted.

H = enthalpy	T = temperature	L = liter(s)
M = molar	V = volume	mL = milliliter(s)
n = number of moles	atm = atmosphere(s)	mm = millimeter(s)
P = pressure	g = gram(s)	mol = mole(s)
R = molar gas constant	J = joule(s)	V = volt(s)
S = entropy	kJ = kilojoule(s)	

Questions 1–4 refer to the following topics and relationships:

a) Sublimation
b) Deposition
c) Vaporization
d) Condensation
e) Freezing

1. It is the process of a substance going from solid to gas.
2. It is the process of a substance going from gas to solid.
3. It is the process of a substance going from liquid to gas.
4. It is the process of a substance going from gas to liquid.

Questions 5–8 refer to the following topics and relationships:

a) purple solution
b) brown-orange liquid
c) green gas
d) metal in liquid form at room temperature
e) yellow-orange when burned in a flame

5. Potassium permanganate is a
6. Sodium salt is a
7. Chlorine is a
8. Mercury is a

Questions 9–12 refer to the following topics and relationships:

a) Arrhenius acid
b) Arrhenius base
c) Lewis acid
d) Lewis base
e) Brønsted-Lowry acid

9. It yields hydroxide ions in solution.
10. It is the electron pair acceptor.
11. It is a proton donor.
12. NH_3 is a(n)

Questions 13–16 refer to the following topics and relationships:

a) Pipette
b) Manometer
c) Balance
d) Calorimeter
e) Galvanometer

Match the definitions given below with the appropriate piece of laboratory equipment.

13. Used to measure the pressure of liquids and gases
14. Used to measure small electric currents
15. Used to measure a specific volume of liquid
16. Used to measure heat

Questions 17–20 refer to the following topics and relationships:

a) CH_4
b) CO_2
c) NH_3
d) N_2
e) O_2

17. It is the natural gas used in the cooking and heating at home.
18. It has a triple bond.
19. It forms hydrogen bonds.
20. It is the gas form of the "dry ice."

Questions 21–24 refer to the following topics and relationships:

a) Halogens
b) Actinides
c) Transition metals
d) Group IA alkali metals
e) Noble gases

From the list above, choose the group of elements that best matches the following statements.

21. This group of elements has the lowest electron affinity within a period.
22. This group of elements is the most stable in the periodic table.
23. In general, this group of ionic solutions has many colors.
24. This group of elements has the largest electron affinities within a period.

PART B

Directions: Each question below consists of two statements, I in the left-hand column and II in the right-hand column. For each question, determine whether statement I is true or false and whether statement II is true or false and then fill in the corresponding T or F circles on your answer sheet. Fill in circle CE only if statement II is a correct explanation of the true statement I.
On the actual Chemistry Test, the following type of question must be answered on a special section (labeled "Chemistry") at the lower left-hand corner of your answer sheet. These questions will be numbered beginning with 101 and must be answered according to the following directions.
Examples:

	I		II
EX 1.	H_2SO_4 is a strong acid	BECAUSE	H_2SO_4 contains sulfer.
EX 2.	An atom of oxygen is electrically neutral	BECAUSE	an oxygen atom contains an equal number of protons and electrons.

SAMPLE ANSWERS

	I		II		CE
EX 1.	●	Ⓕ	●	Ⓕ	○
EX 2.	●	Ⓕ	●	Ⓕ	●

	I		II
101.	Water boils at a lower temperature at higher altitudes	BECAUSE	The vapor pressure of water is lower at higher altitudes.
102.	If two elements react exothermically to form a compound, the compound should be relatively stable	BECAUSE	The release of energy from a chemical reaction indicates that the relative stable compound formed is at a lower energy level than the reactants.
103.	The bond in an O_2 molecule is considered to be non-polar	BECAUSE	The oxygen atoms in an O_2 molecule share the bonding electrons equally.
104.	Alkali metals are strong oxidizing agents	BECAUSE	The one electron in alkali metals' valence shell is easily lost.
105.	Nuclear fusion in the sun converts hydrogen to helium with a release of energy	BECAUSE	Some mass is converted to energy in a solar fusion.
106.	Nitrogen gas will have a greater rate of effusion than oxygen gas	BECAUSE	Lighter and less dense gases travel faster than heavier and denser gases.

107. Long chain hydrocarbons are insoluble in water	BECAUSE	Like dissolves like. Water is a polar compound and long chain hydrocarbon is a non-polar compound.
108. Lithium is the most active metal in the first group of the periodic table	BECAUSE	Lithium has only one electron in the outer energy level.
109. K is considered to be a metal	BECAUSE	When K becomes an ion, its atomic radius increases.
110. Increasing the concentration of reactants will cause a reaction to proceed faster	BECAUSE	More reactants lower the activation energy of a reaction.
111. Hydrosulfuric acid is often used in qualitative tests	BECAUSE	$H_2S(aq)$ reacts with many metallic ions to give colored precipitates.
112. Gas-phase elements absorb or emit only specific wavelengths of visible light when excited by an electric current	BECAUSE	The energy levels that electrons can occupy in gas-phase atoms and molecules are continuous.
113. An equation where two gas molecules combine to form one gas molecule at equilibrium will increase the yield of the product when the pressure is increased	BECAUSE	Increased pressure always favors products.
114. A super saturated solution of glucose in boiling water crystallizes as it cools	BECAUSE	The solubility increases as the temperature decreases.
115. A basic solution has more hydrogen ions than acidic solution has	BECAUSE	The pH scale is equal to $-log[H^+]$.

PART C

Directions: Each of the questions or incomplete statements below is followed by five suggested answers or completions. Select the one that is best in each case and then fill in the corresponding circle on the answer sheet.

25. Which of the following properties is a physical property?
    a) Flammability
    b) Magnetism
    c) Changes when exposed to light
    d) Freezing
    e) All of the above

26. Which of the following is a neutral atom with the electron configuration of $1s^2 2s^2 2p^6 3s^2 3p^6 4s^2 3d^{10} 4p^6 5s^2 4d^{10} 5p^6$?
    a) highly reactive
    b) A noble gas
    c) A positively charged ion
    d) A transition metal
    e) A lanthanide element

27. Which of the following has valence electrons in the d orbitals?
    a) Na^+
    b) Al
    c) F
    d) Ti
    e) B

28. Which of the following types of electromagnetic radiation has the highest energy?
    a) Visible light
    b) Ultraviolet
    c) Microwave
    d) Infrared
    e) X rays

29. Which of the following statements is NOT true?
    a) Cl^- and Ar are isoelectronic.
    b) Cs is likely to exist in ionic compounds as Cs^{2+}.
    c) O is likely to exist in ionic compounds as O^{2-}.
    d) He and Ne are unlikely to participate in covalent bonding with other atoms.
    e) I^- and B^- are stable ions in solution.

30. Which of the following elements in group 1*A* of the periodic table has the greatest metallic character?
    a) H
    b) Li
    c) Na
    d) K
    e) Rb

31. The Lewis structure of the cyanide ion is similar to which of the following compounds?
    a) N_2
    b) O_2
    c) CO_2
    d) NO
    e) C_2H_2

32. What types of chemical bonds will be formed if two atoms have an electronegativity difference between 0.3 and 1.6?
    a) Ionic
    b) Covalent
    c) Polar covalent
    d) Metallic
    e) Hydrogen bonding

33. The bonds between the atoms in a nitrogen molecule are
    a) hydrogen bonds.
    b) ionic bonds.
    c) polar covalent bonds.
    d) pure covalent bonds.
    e) metallic bonds.

34. The bonds between the atoms in a calcium crystal are
    a) hydrogen bonds.
    b) ionic bonds.
    c) polar covalent bonds.
    d) pure covalent bonds.
    e) metallic bonds.

35. How many grams of SO_2 are there in a 5.60-L sample at STP?
    a) 32.0
    b) 16.0
    c) 12.0
    d) 6.0
    e) 3.0

36. A 0.200 g sample of a compound containing only carbon, hydrogen, and oxygen is burned, and 0.44 g of CO_2 and some of H_2O are collected. What is the percentage of the carbon in this compound?
    a) 80.0%
    b) 70.0%
    c) 60.0%
    d) 50.0%
    e) 40.0%

37. How many milligrams of Na_2SO_4 (molar mass = 142) are needed to prepare 100 mL of a solution that is 0.00100 M in Na^+ ions?
    a) 28.4
    b) 14,200
    c) 1.00
    d) 7.1
    e) 14.2

38. What will be the total pressure in a 2.24-L flask at 0 °C if it contains 0.016 moles of CO and 0.034 moles of CH_4?
    a) 31.4 mm Hg
    b) 380 mm Hg
    c) 0.041 mm Hg
    d) 935 mm Hg
    e) 1.23 atm

39. A gas is the least likely to behave ideally under which of the following condition(s)?
    I. High temperature
    II. Low temperature
    III. Low pressure
    a) I only
    b) II only
    c) I and III only
    d) II and III only
    e) I, II, and III

40. The rate of diffusion of hydrogen gas to the rate of diffusion of oxygen gas is
    a) ½ as fast.
    b) identical.
    c) twice as fast.
    d) four times as fast.
    e) eight times as fast.

41. Between gases CO and N_2, which of the following will be nearly identical at 25 °C and 1 atm?
    I. Average molecular speed
    II. Rate of effusion through a pinhole
    III. Density
    a) I only
    b) III only
    c) I and II only
    d) II and III only
    e) I, II, and III

42. Which of the following gases is governed by London dispersion forces?
    a) H_2
    b) CH_3OH
    c) CH_2Cl_2
    d) KCI
    e) CO

43. Which of the following compounds would you expect to have the highest boiling point?
    a) H_2Se
    b) H_2Te
    c) H_2O
    d) H_2S
    e) SiH_4

44. Which of following explains why a soda bottle fizzes when opened?
    a) Osmotic pressure
    b) Freezing-point depression
    c) Vapor pressure
    d) Raoult's law
    e) Henry's law

45. How many grams of HCl must be added to 500 mL of water to produce a solution that freezes at −1.86 °C? (molar freezing constant = 1.86 °C kg/mole)
    a) 4.6
    b) 9.1
    c) 18.3
    d) 36.5
    e) 73.0

46. What is the boiling point of water at the top of a mountain?
    a) = 100 °C
    b) > 100 °C since the pressure is less than at ground level
    c) < 100 °C since the pressure is less than at ground level
    d) > 100 °C since the pressure is greater than at ground level
    e) < 100 °C since the pressure is greater than at ground level

47. Calculate the approximate amount of heat necessary to raise the temperature of 50.0 grams of liquid water from 10.0 °C to 30.0 °C. (The specific heat of water liquid is 4.18 J/g°C.)
    a) 20 J
    b) 80 J
    c) 100 J
    d) 200 J
    e) 4,180 J

48. Which of the following processes involves no heat exchange?
    a) Isothermal process
    b) Isobaric process
    c) Adiabatic process
    d) Isometric process
    e) None of the above

49. 10g of liquid at 300 K is heated to 350 K. The liquid absorbs 6 kcal. What is the specific heat of the liquid?
    a) 6 cal/g°C
    b) 120 cal/g°C
    c) 12 cal/g°C
    d) 600 cal/g°C
    e) 60 cal/g°C

50. 4.00 g of CH_4 is burned in excess oxygen in a bomb calorimeter that has a heat capacity of 3000 J °C, A temperature increase of 7.0 °C is observed. What is the heat of this reaction?
    a) 21 kJ mol^{-1}
    b) 84.0 kJ
    c) −5.25 kJ
    d) −21.0 kJ
    e) −84.0 kJ g^{-1}

51. Which of the following statements is true?
   a) The rate of a reaction is always proportional to the concentration of the reactants.
   b) The activation energy of a reaction is constant with respect to temperature.
   c) The rate constant is constant with respect to temperature.
   d) A reaction with a large negative $\Delta G°$ will occur at a faster rate.
   e) For the second-order reaction $2A \rightarrow B + C$, we can calculate the value of the rate constant using a plot of ln[A] versus time.

52. Which of the following statements is NOT true about entropy?
   a) Entropy is a measure of the randomness in a system.
   b) The entropy of an amorphous solid is greater than that of a crystalline solid.
   c) The entropy of a spontaneous reaction cannot decrease.
   d) The entropy of an isolated system will spontaneously increase or remain constant.
   e) The entropy of a liquid is greater than that of a solid.

53. Consider the following reaction mechanism:

   Step 1: $M + X \rightarrow MX$

   Step 2: $MX + A \rightarrow D + X$

   The chemical species MX is a(n)
   a) catalyst.
   b) inhibitor.
   c) final product.
   d) reaction intermediate.
   e) None of the above

54. In an experiment, 0.0300 moles each of $SO_3(g)$, $SO_2(g)$, and $O_2(g)$ were placed in a 10.0 L flask at a certain temperature. When the reaction came to equilibrium, the concentration of $SO_2(g)$ in the flask was 2×10^{-3} M. What was the Kc for the reaction:

   $$2SO_2(g) + O_2(g) \leftrightarrow 2SO_3(g)$$

   a) 3.2×10^4
   b) 1.6×10^4
   c) 1.6×10^3
   d) 1.6×10^{-3}
   e) 3.2×10^{-3}

55. $$H_2(g) + Br_2(g) \leftrightarrow 2HBr(g)$$

   The concentrations of H_2, Br_2 and HBr are 0.05 M, 0.05 M, and 500.0 M, respectively. The equilibrium constant for the above reaction at 400 °C is 2.5×10^3. Is this system at equilibrium?
   a) Yes, the system is at equilibrium.
   b) No, the reaction must shift to the right in order to reach equilibrium.
   c) No, the reaction must shift to the left in order to reach equilibrium.
   d) It cannot be determined.
   e) The reaction will never be at equilibrium.

56. In the complex ion, $Cu(NH3)_4^{+2}$, the NH_3 is called a(n)
   a) cation.
   b) ligand.
   c) Lewis acid.
   d) anion.
   e) conjugate acid.

57. $H_2(g) + I_2(g) \rightarrow 2HI(g)$
According to the reaction above, if 1.00 g of HI is placed in a 2.00 L flask, which of the following is the LEAST important in determining the equilibrium constant?
   a) The temperature must remain constant at the desired value.
   b) Several measurements must be made to assure that the reaction is at equilibrium.
   c) Only one of the three concentrations needs to be accurately determined.
   d) All three concentrations must be accurately measured.
   e) The original mass and volume of the flask must be accurately measured.

58. A buffer is generated using NH_3 and NH_4Cl. Which of the following is/are true?
   I. Any buffers generated with the same $\frac{[NH_3]}{[NH_4Cl]}$ will have an identical pH.
   II. If $[NH_3] = [NH_4Cl]$, the pH will equal the PKa for NH_4^+.
   III. Any buffers generated with the same $\frac{[NH_3]}{[NH_4Cl]}$ will have an identical buffering capacity.
   a) I only
   b) II only
   c) I and II only
   d) I and III only
   e) I, II, and III

59. Which of the following statements is correct?
   a) $HClO_2$ is a stronger acid than $HClO_3$.
   b) HI is a weaker acid than HCl.
   c) CH_3COOH is a stronger acid than $CH_2BrCOOH$.
   d) HNO_3 is a stronger acid than HNO_2.
   e) H_3PO_4 is a stronger acid than $HClO_4$.

60. What is the pOH of a solution with $[H^+] = 0.001$ M?
   a) −3
   b) 1
   c) 3
   d) 11
   e) 14

61. Which of the following half-cell reactions describes the half-reaction at the anode in the diagram below?

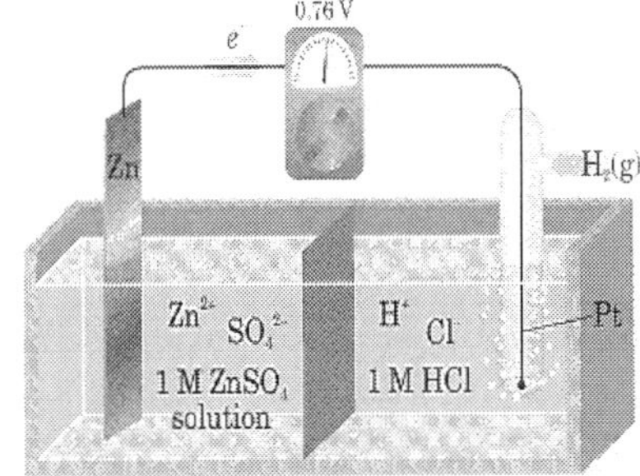

   a) $Zn \rightarrow Zn^{2+} + 2e^-$
   b) $H_2 \rightarrow 2H^+ + 2e^-$
   c) $2Cl^- \rightarrow Cl_2 + 2e^-$
   d) $SO_4^{-2} \rightarrow S + 2O_2 + 6e^-$
   e) $2H^+ + 2e^- \rightarrow H_2$

62. A metal is electrolyzed from ions with +2 charged in an aqueous solution by using an electrical current of 1 A for 9650 seconds, and 2.93 g of metal is deposited. Which of the following is this metal? (The charge of one mole electrons = 96,500 C)
   a) Al
   b) Ni
   c) Sn
   d) Mg
   e) Au

63. Which of the following statements is TRUE?
    a) The number of positive ions in solution equals the number of negative ions.
    b) The positive ions are called anions.
    c) The positive ions are called cathodes.
    d) The total positive charge equals the total negative charge in solution.
    e) None of the above

64. Balance the following half-reaction in the acid solution: $NO_3^- \rightarrow NH_4^+$. When balanced with the smallest whole-number coefficients possible, the sum of all the coefficients is
    a) 13.
    b) 14.
    c) 15.
    d) 21.
    e) 23.

65. Which of the following is the functional group of organic ether?
    a) R -OH
    b) R–O–R′
    c) R—CO—R′
    d) R—COOH
    e) R—OH

66. A triple bond is formed by
    a) two sigma bonds and one pi bond.
    b) two sigma bonds and two pi bonds.
    c) one sigma bond and two pi bonds.
    d) three sigma bonds.
    e) three pi bonds.

67. Hybridizations of the carbon atom indicated by (*) in, $CH_3-{}^*CH_2-CH_3C^*H=CH_2$, and $CH_3-{}^*C\equiv CH$ are?
    a) $sp^3, sp^2,$ and sp respectively
    b) $sp^3, sp,$ and sp^2 respectively
    c) $sp, sp^2,$ and sp^3 respectively
    d) $sp, sp^3,$ and sp^2 respectively
    e) $sp^2, sp^3,$ and sp respectively

68. Atoms of ^{235}U and ^{238}U differ in structure by three
    a) electrons.
    b) isotopes.
    c) neutrons.
    d) protons.
    e) alpha particles.

69. The production of alkanes from alkenes is accomplished by
    a) burning in the presence of water.
    b) distillation.
    c) methylation.
    d) catalytic hydrogenation.
    e) hydrolysis.

70. Which of the following ions can be identified by their characteristic odor?
    I. sodium ion
    II. silver ion
    III. bromide ion
    IV. sulfide ion
    V. ammonium ion
    a) I only
    b) II and III only
    c) III only
    d) IV and V only
    e) V only

SAT Chemistry Subject Test No. 4 Keys

1. A	11. E	21. D	31. A	41. E	51. B	61. A
2. B	12. D	22. E	32. C	42. A	52. C	62. B
3. C	13. B	23. C	33. D	43. C	53. D	63. D
4. D	14. E	24. A	34. E	44. E	54. B	64. E
5. A	15. A	25. B	35. B	45. B	55. C	65. B
6. E	16. D	26. B	36. C	46. C	56. B	66. C
7. C	17. A	27. D	37. D	47. E	57. D	67. A
8. D	18. D	28. E	38. B	48. C	58. C	68. C
9. B	19. C	29. B	39. C	49. C	59. D	69. D
10. C	20. B	30. E	40. D	50. D	60. D	70. D

101.	TF	106.	TTCE	111.	TTCE
102.	TTCE	107.	TTCE	112.	TF
103.	TTCE	108.	FT	113.	TF
104.	FT	109.	TF	114.	TF
105.	TTCE	110.	TF	115.	FT

SAT Chemistry Subject Test No. 4 Answer to Part A

1 – 4 *Answer: (abcd)*
Sublimation: from solid to gas
Deposition: from gas to solid
Vaporization: from liquid to gas
Condensation: from vapor to liquid
Freezing: from liquid to solid

5 – 8 *Answer: (aecd)*
Potassium permanganate: a purple solution
sodium salt: colorless solution
chlorine: a green gas
mercury: a liquid metal in room temperature

9 – 12 *Answer: (bced)*
Arrhenius acid: provide H^+
Arrhenius base: provide OH^-
Lewis acid: accept e^-
Lewis base: provide e^-
Brønsted-Lowry acid: provide proton

13 – 16 *Answer: (bead)*
Pipette: to measure a specific volume of liquid with a high level of accuracy
Manometer: to measure the air pressure by using a column of liquid
Balance: to measure the weight of the sample
Calorimeter: to measure the heat of chemical reactions or physical changes
Galvanometer: to detect an electric current in a circuit

17 – 20 *Answer: (adcb)*
CH_4*: the major component of the natural gas*
CO_2*: can be pressurized into a solid as dry ice*
NH_3*: N – H, O – H and Cl – H can form hydrogen bonds*
N_2*: N≡N*

21 – 24 *Answer: (deca)*
Electron affinity: increasing from left to right in the same period.
Most stable elements are noble gases.
Because of the d-orbitals, transition metals normally have colors in their ionic solutions.

SAT Chemistry Subject Test No. 4 Answer to Part C

25. *Answer: (b)*
 Magnetism is a physical property.
 Freezing is a physical change.

26. *Answer: (b)*
 Noble gases have full p orbitals.

27. *Answer: (d)*
 Ti is in the transition metal family.

28. *Answer: (e)*
 The higher the frequency and the shorter the wave length, the higher the energy of the light is.

29. *Answer: (b)*
 Cs has only one valence electron, so it most likely forms Cs^{+1}.

30. *Answer: (e)*
 Metallic character increases because as you move down a group, it becomes easier for elements to lose electrons.

31. *Answer: (a)*
 CN^- *and* N_2 *have the same electron structure.*

32. *Answer: (c)*
 $1.7 - 0.3 = 1.4 < 1.6$
 Polar covalent bond

33. *Answer: (d)*
 Two nitrogen atoms have the same electronegativity.

34. *Answer: (e)*
 Calcium is a metallic element.

35. *Answer: (b)*
 $\frac{5.6}{22.4} \times (32 + 2 \times 16) = 16\ g$

36. *Answer: (c)*
 $0.44\ g$ *of* $CO_2 = \frac{0.44}{44}$ *moles of* $CO_2 = .0.01$ *moles of C = .12 grams of C*
 $\%\ of\ C = \frac{.12}{.2} \times 100\% = 60\%$

37. *Answer: (d)*
 $0.1 \times 0.001 = 0.0001$ *moles of* $Na^+ = \frac{0.0001}{2}$ *moles Of* Na_2SO_4
 $= \frac{0.0001}{2} \times 142\ g = 0.0071\ g = 7.1\ mg$ *of* Na_2SO_4

38. *Answer: (b)*
 Compare to STP conditions: $\frac{p_1 v_1}{n1} = \frac{p_2 v_2}{n_2}$
 $\frac{760 \times 22.4}{1} = \frac{p_2 \times 2.24}{0.016 + 0.034}$; $p_2 = 380\ mmHg$

39. *Answer: (c)*
 The further apart the gas particles, the more ideal.

40. *Answer: (d)*
 Rate of Diffusion of Oxygen to Hydrogen
 $= \sqrt{2} : \sqrt{32} = 1 : 4$

41. *Answer: (e)*
 The molar masses of CO and N_2 *are very close. Therefore, their density, effusion rate, and average kinetic energy are very close when they are at the same temperature.*

42. *Answer: (a)*
 Non-polar molecules only have London forces.

43. *Answer: (c)*
 Because of hydrogen bonding, water has an abnormally high boiling point.

44. *Answer: (e)*
 Henry's law: At a constant temperature, the amount of a given gas that dissolves in a liquid is directly proportional to the partial pressure of that gas in equilibrium with that liquid.

45. *Answer: (b)*
 Molar mass of HCl is 36.5.
 $\Delta T_f = 2 \times 1.86 \times \frac{\frac{x}{36.5}}{0.5} = 1.86$
 $x = 9.1\ g$

46. *Answer: (c)*
 The lower the pressure, the lower the boiling point is.

47. *Answer: (e)*
 $Q = MC\Delta T$
 $= 50 \times 4.18 \times (30 - 10) = 4180\ J$

48. *Answer: (c)*
 An adiabatic process involves no heat transfer.

49. *Answer: (c)*
$Q = mc\Delta T$
$C = \frac{6000}{10 \times (350 - 300)} = 12\ cal/g\,°C$

50. *Answer: (d)*
$Q = Cp \times \Delta T = 7 \times 3000 = 21\ kJ$
It is an exothermic process because of the increasing temperature in the system. Q is a negative value.

51. *Answer: (b)*
The activation energy required for a chemical reaction is temperature independent.
The value of $\Delta G°$ is only associated with the equilibrium conditions, but not the kinetics conditions.
For the second-order reaction:
$R = -kA^2$
$\frac{dA}{dt} = -kA^2;$
$\frac{dA}{A^2} = -kdt$
$\frac{1}{A} - \frac{1}{A_0} = kt$

52. *Answer: (c)*
Gibbs free energy change is the indication of a spontaneous or nonspontaneous reaction.

53. *Answer: (d)*
MX is a reaction intermediate because it disappears from the final equation (cancels out when you add the two steps together).

54. *Answer: (b)*
$2SO_2(g) + O_2(g) \leftrightarrow 2SO_3(g)$
0.003 0.003 0.003
$0.003 - 2x$ $0.003 - x$ $0.003 + 2x$
$0.003 - 2x = 2 \times 10^{-3}$
$x = 0.0005$
$K = \frac{[0.003 + 0.001]^2}{[0.003 - 0.001]^2[0.003 - 0.0005]}$
$K = 1.6 \times 10^4$

55. *Answer: (c)*
$Kc = \frac{[HBr]^2}{[H_2][Br_2]} = \frac{500^2}{0.05 \times 0.05} = 1 \times 10^8 > 2.5 \times 10^3$
It is not at equilibrium, so the reaction must shift to the left.

56. *Answer: (b)*
A ligand is an ion that binds to a central metal atom to form a complex ion.

57. *Answer: (d)*
By applying the stoichiometry rules, only one of the three concentrations needs to be accurately determined.

58. *Answer: (c)*
$NH_4^- \rightarrow NH_3 + H^+$
$pH = pKa - \log\frac{NH3}{NH4^-}$

59. *Answer: (d)*
HNO_3 is a strong acid.

60. *Answer: (d)*
$[H^+] = 0.001\ M = 10^{-3}$
$[OH^-] = \frac{10^{-14}}{10^{-3}} = 10^{-11}$
$pOH = -\log[OH^-] = 11$

61. *Answer: (a)*
Anode: electrode where oxidation occurs

62. *Answer: (b)*
$\frac{9650}{2 \times 96500} = 0.05\ moles$
$\frac{2.93}{0.05} = 58.6\ (Ni)$
It is Ni.

63. *Answer: (d)*
An anion has a negative charge and a cation has a positive charge.
The total of negative charges equals the total of positive charges in solutions.

64. *Answer: (e)*
$10H^+ + NO_3^- + 8e^- \rightarrow NH_4^+ + 3H_2O$

65. *Answer: (b)*
Organic ether: $R-O-R'$

66. *Answer: (c)*
A triple bond contains one sigma bond and two pi bonds.

67. *Answer: (a)*
A single bond, a double bond, and a triple bond sp^3, sp^2, and sp hybridization

68. *Answer: (c)*
Isotopes have the same number of protons but different neutrons.

69. *Answer: (d)*
Adding hydrogen to alkenes produces the corresponding alkanes.

70. *Answer: (d)*
Sulfide and ammonium ions have special odors.

SAT Chemistry Subject Test No. 5

PART A

Directions: Each set of lettered choices below refers to the numbered statements or questions immediately following it. Select the one lettered choice that best fits each statement and then fill in the corresponding circle on the answer sheet. A given choice may be used once, more than once, or not at all in each set.

Note: For all questions involving solutions, assume that the solvent is water unless otherwise stated. Throughout the test the following symbols have the definitions specified unless otherwise noted.

H = enthalpy	T = temperature	L = liter(s)
M = molar	V = volume	mL = milliliter(s)
n = number of moles	atm = atmosphere(s)	mm = millimeter(s)
P = pressure	g = gram(s)	mol = mole(s)
R = molar gas constant	J = joule(s)	V = volt(s)
S = entropy	kJ = kilojoule(s)	

Questions 1–4 refer to the following topics and relationships:

a) Br_2 and Hg
b) Cl_2 and F_2
c) $NH4^+$ and H_3O^+
d) Fe and Co
e) Diamond and graphite

1. These two compounds are in the liquid phase at room temperature.
2. These two compounds have colorful ionic solutions in water.
3. These two compounds are allotropes of each other.
4. These two compounds are good oxidizing agents.

Questions 5–8 refer to the following topics and relationships:

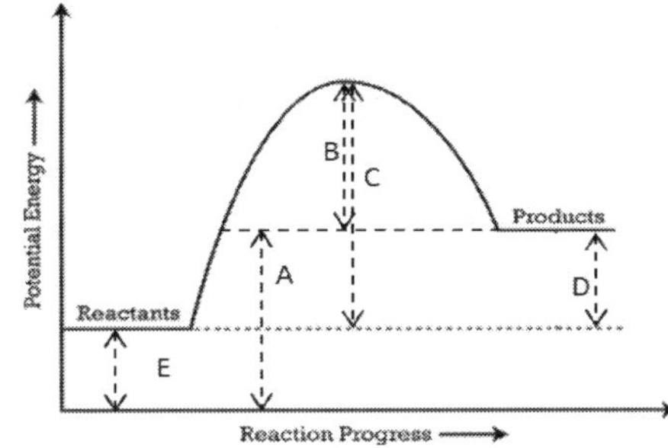

a) A
b) B
c) C
d) C − B
e) C + E

5. It is the activation energy of the forward reaction.
6. It is the activation energy of the reverse reaction.
7. It is the heat of the reaction for the forward reaction.
8. It is the potential energy of the activated complex.

Questions 9–12 refer to the following topics and relationships:

a) $NaC_2H_3O_2$
b) $HC_2H_3O_2$
c) KBr
d) NH_3
e) HCl

9. It will form a yellow precipitate in Ag^+ aqueous solution.
10. It is a salt that will undergo hydrolysis to form a basic solution.
11. It will form a coordinate covalent bond with a hydronium ion.
12. It is a weak acid.

Questions 13–16 refer to the following topics and relationships:

a) Is a polar covalent compound.
b) Is a non-polar covalent compound.
c) Is a network covalent bond.
d) Is an ionic compound.
e) Is a metallic substance.

13. KCI
14. HC1(g)
15. C_2H_6
16. Na

Questions 17–20 refer to the following topics and relationships:

a) C_2H_2
b) C_2H_4
c) C_4H_{10}
d) C_6H_6
e) $C_6H_{12}O_6$

17. It is an aromatic compound.
18. Its C atoms are sp hybridized.
19. It contains only single bonds.
20. It is a water soluble solid at room temperature.

Questions 21–24 refer to the following topics and relationships:

a) Distillation
b) Chromatography
c) Fractional crystallization
d) Filtration
e) Titration

Which statements refer to the above laboratory procedures?

21. To separate a precipitate from a filtrate using a porous substance
22. To separate a mixture of liquids based on differences in their boiling points
23. To determine the unknown concentration of a known acid
24. To separate a mixture of dissolved solids by evaporation according to individual solubility

PART B

Directions: Each question below consists of two statements, I in the left-hand column and II in the right-hand column. For each question, determine whether statement I is true or false and whether statement II is true or false and then fill in the corresponding T or F circles on your answer sheet. Fill in circle CE only if statement II is a correct explanation of the true statement I.

On the actual Chemistry Test, the following type of question must be answered on a special section (labeled "Chemistry") at the lower left-hand corner of your answer sheet. These questions will be numbered beginning with 101 and must be answered according to the following directions.

Examples:

	I		II
EX 1.	H_2SO_4 is a strong acid	BECAUSE	H_2SO_4 contains sulfer.
EX 2.	An atom of oxygen is electrically neutral	BECAUSE	an oxygen atom contains an equal number of protons and electrons.

SAMPLE ANSWERS

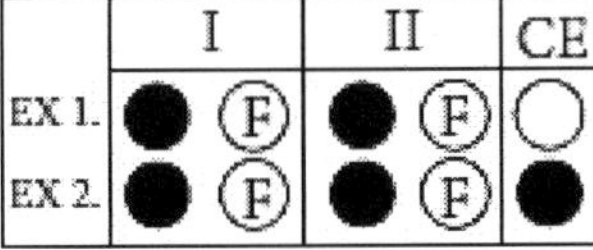

101. ΔS will be positive in value when vaporization occurs BECAUSE Vaporization increases the order of the molecules from liquid to gas phase.

102. In the system $N_2(g) + O_2(g) \leftrightarrow 2NO(g)$, decreasing the pressure will not cause a shift in position of the equilibrium BECAUSE There is no net change in the number of moles of gas from one side of the reaction to another.

103. For an element with an atomic number of 17, the most stable oxidation number is +1 BECAUSE The outer energy level of the halogen family has a tendency to add one electron to itself.

104. The atomic number of a neutral atom that has a mass of 39 and 19 electrons is 19 BECAUSE The number of protons in a neutral atom is equal to the number of electrons.

105. The first ionization energy for an atom is greater than the second ionization energy BECAUSE The closer an electron is to the nucleus, the more difficult it is to remove.

106. Alpha particles are able to pass through a thin sheet of gold foil	BECAUSE	The atom is mainly empty space.
107. When volumes of 1.0 M HCl and 1.0 M NaOH are mixed, the resulting mixture is theoretically safe to drink	BECAUSE	The acid and the base form a neutral salt.
108. An increase in temperature will cause a gas to expand	BECAUSE	Temperature and volume have a direct relationship.
109. Powdered zinc will react faster with HCl than one larger piece of zinc of the same mass	BECAUSE	Powdered zinc has less surface area than one larger piece of zinc of the same mass.
110. When HCl gas and NH_3 gas come into contact, a white smoke forms	BECAUSE	NH_3 and HCl react to form a white solid, ammonium chlorate.
111. An exothermic reaction has a positive ΔH value	BECAUSE	Heat must be added to the reaction for the reaction to occur.
112. HCl is considered to be an acid	BECAUSE	HCl is a proton donor.
113. The addition of H_2 to ethene will form an unsaturated compound called ethane	BECAUSE	Ethane has as many hydrogen atoms bonded to the carbon atoms as possible.
114. The weakest of the bonds between molecules are coordinate covalent bonds	BECAUSE	Coordinate covalent bonds represent the weak attractive force between the electrons of one molecule to the positively charged nucleus of another.
115. 1 M NaCl(aq) will have a higher boiling point than 1 M $CaCl_2$(aq)	BECAUSE	1 mole of NaCl yields 3 moles of ions in solution.

PART C

Directions: Each of the questions or incomplete statements below is followed by five suggested answers or completions. Select the one that is best in each case and then fill in the corresponding circle on the answer sheet.

25. $2H_2O_2(g) \leftrightarrow 2\,H_2O(g) + O_2(g)$
After the equilibrium shown above is established, some pure H_2O vapor is injected into the reaction vessel at constant temperature. When equilibrium is reestablished, which of the following has a lower value compared to its value at the original equilibrium?
    a) K_{eq}
    b) $[H_2O_2]$
    c) $[H_2O]$
    d) $[O_2]$
    e) The total pressure in the reaction vessel

26. $2NaN_3(s) \rightarrow 2Na(s) + 3N_2(g)$
According to the reaction above, what mass of NaN_3 is required to inflate a 22.4 L air bag to a pressure of 1.5 atm at 0 °C?
    a) 8.50 g
    b) 16.5 g
    c) 33.0 g
    d) 48.0 g
    e) 65.0 g

27. $2NO(g) + O_2(g) \rightarrow 2NO_2(g)$
The reaction between nitrogen monoxide and oxygen is shown above. One proposed mechanism is the following:
Step 1: $NO(g) + O_2(g) \rightarrow NO_2(g) + O(g)$ (slow)
Step 2: $NO(g) + O(g) \rightarrow NO_2(g)$ (fast)
Which of the following rate expressions best agrees with this possible mechanism?
    a) Rate = k [NO] [O]
    b) Rate = k [NO] $[O_2]$
    c) Rate = k $[NO]^2$ $[O_2]$
    d) Rate = k [NO] / $[O_2]$
    e) Rate = k [NO]/ [O]

28. A 600 mL container holds 2 moles O_2, 3 moles H_2, and 1 mole He. The total pressure within the container is 760 torr. What is the partial pressure of O_2?
    a) 127 torr
    b) 253 torr
    c) 380 torr
    d) 507 torr
    e) 760 torr

29. A compound that dissolves in water that barely conducts electrical current will probably be
    a) a strong electrolyte.
    b) an ionic salt.
    c) a strong acid.
    d) a strong base.
    e) None of the above

30. A metallic oxide placed in water would most likely yield
    a) an acid.
    b) a base.
    c) a metallic anhydride.
    d) a basic anhydride.
    e) None of the above

31. Using the information given in the reaction equations below, calculate the heat of formation for 1 mole of carbon monoxide.
$2C(s) + 2O_2 \rightarrow 2CO_2$ $\Delta H = -787$ kJ
$2CO + O_2 \rightarrow 2CO_2$ $\Delta H = -566$kJ
    a) −221 kJ/mol
    b) −410 kJ/mol
    c) −110 kJ/mol
    d) 410 kJ/mol
    e) 221 kJ/mol

32. A sample of argon occupies 50 L at standard temperature. Assuming constant pressure, what volume will the gas occupy if the temperature is doubled?
    a) 25 L
    b) 50 L
    c) 100 L
    d) 200 L
    e) 2,500 L

33. According to the activity chart of metals, which metal would react most vigorously in a dilute acid solution?
    a) Zinc
    b) Iron
    c) Aluminum
    d) Magnesium
    e) Silver

34. After a burette is filled for a titration, the bubble of air in the tip is not dislodged. What will the effect be?
    a) No error will result if the bubble is not dislodged.
    b) The volume recorded will be too high if the bubble is dislodged.
    c) The calculated molarity of the sample will be too high if the bubble is dislodged.
    d) The mass of the sample will be too low if the bubble is dislodged.
    e) All of the above

35. An electron-dot notation consists of the symbol representing the element and an arrangement of dots which represent
    a) the atomic number.
    b) the atomic mass.
    c) the number of neutrons.
    d) the electrons in the outermost energy level.
    e) None of the above

36. An ester can be prepared by reacting
    a) two alcohols.
    b) an alcohol and an aldehyde.
    c) an alcohol and an organic acid.
    d) an organic acid and an aldehyde.
    e) an acid and a ketone.

37. An increase in pressure will change the equilibrium by
    a) shifting the reaction to the side resulting in a smaller volume results.
    b) shifting the reaction to the side resulting in a larger volume results.
    c) favoring the endothermic reaction.
    d) favoring the exothermic reaction.
    e) None of the above

38. An aqueous solution contains equal volumes of the following pairs of solutions. Which of the following solutions has the pH > 9?
    a) NaCl (1M) and NaOH(1M)
    b) NaOAc (1M) and HOAC(1M)
    c) HNO_3 (1M) and $NaNO_3$ (1M)
    d) NH_3 (1M) and NH_4Cl (1M)
    e) NaCl (1M) and K_2SO_4 (1M)

39. Boron found in nature has an atomic weight of 10.8 and is made up of the isotopes ^{10}B (mass 10.0 amu) and ^{11}B (mass 11.00 amu). What percentage of naturally occurring boron is made up of ^{10}B and ^{11}B respectively?
    a) 30 : 70
    b) 25 : 75
    c) 20 : 80
    d) 15 : 85
    e) 10 : 90

40. Consider diamond and graphite. Which of the following statements is true?
    a) Graphite has a higher melting point than that of diamond.
    b) Differences in composition account for the different properties of graphite and diamond.
    c) Amorphous solids are likely to have higher melting points than their crystalline counterparts.
    d) Introducing an impurity into a crystalline material will increase the observed melting point.
    e) The carbon atoms in diamond are sp^3-hybridized.

41. Consider the reaction below. $C_2H_5OH(l) + 3O_2(g) \rightarrow 2CO_2(g) + 3H_2O(l)$ $\Delta H = -1.40 \times 10^3$ kJ
    When a 46.00 gram sample of ethanol is burned with excess oxygen, how much heat is released?
    a) 0.995 kJ
    b) 5.1×10^2 kJ
    c) 1.40×10^3 kJ
    d) 2.80×10^3 kJ
    e) 5,000 kJ

42. When the equation $Cu(s) + NO_3^-(aq) + H^+(aq) \rightarrow Cu^{2+}(aq) + NO_2(g) + H_2O(l)$ is balanced, what is the coefficient of H^+?
    a) 1
    b) 2
    c) 3
    d) 4
    e) 5

43. How many grams of CO_2 will be produced by the reaction of 100 g of $CaCO_3$ with excess HCl?
    a) 22 g
    b) 44 g
    c) 79 g
    d) 110 g
    e) 132 g

44. How many moles are in 4.5 grams of water?
    a) 1.25×10^{-24}
    b) 3.75×10^{-2}
    c) 1.25×10^{-2}
    d) 1.25×10^{24}
    e) 2.5×10^{-1}

45. Which of the following has the lowest boiling point if an equal number of moles of each are dissolved in 1 kg of distilled water?
    a) NaF
    b) MCl_3
    c) $Mg(C_2H_3O_2)_2$
    d) CH_3CH_2COOH
    e) Glucose

46. In neutralizing 500 mL of 1.0 M HCl with 500 mL of 1.0 M NaOH, the temperature of the solution rises 5.0 °C. Given that the density of the solution is 1.0 g/mL and the specific heat of the solution is 4.184 J/g °C, calculate the approximate energy released from this experiment.
   a) 20 J
   b) 1,000 J
   c) 4,200 J
   d) 2.1×10^4 J
   e) 1.0×10^4 kJ

47. A solution comprising of 100 mL of 1 M HCl and 100 mL of 5 M NaCl is mixed. What is the final molarity of the chloride (Cl^- ion)?
   a) 0.5 M
   b) 2 M
   c) 3 M
   d) 4 M
   e) 5 M

48. One of the reasons why a double displacement reaction will go to completion is that
   a) a product is soluble.
   b) a product is given off as a gas.
   c) the products can react with each other.
   d) the products are miscible.
   e) None of the above

49. The sp^2 hybridization will be found in carbon in which of the following compounds?
   a) CH_4
   b) C_2H_4
   c) C_2H_6
   d) CH_3OH
   e) CH_3OCH_3

50. The important considerations in deciding if a reaction will be spontaneous are
   a) stability and state of reactants.
   b) energy gained and heat evolved.
   c) exothermic energy and randomness of the products.
   d) endothermic energy and randomness of the products.
   e) endothermic energy and structure of the products.

51. The law of conservation of mass states that
   a) in a chemical reaction, the final mass of the products is always greater than the starting mass of the reactants.
   b) matter can be created and destroyed but does not change forms.
   c) in a chemical reaction, efforts should be made to preserve rare elements without changing them.
   d) the mass of all substances present before a change equals the mass of all substances remaining after the change.
   e) None of the above

52. The molecule with the largest dipole moment is
   a) C_2H_2
   b) CH_2Cl_2
   c) BF_3
   d) CH_3CH_2OH
   e) HF

53. The number of protons in the nucleus of an atom with the atomic number 32 is
    a) 4
    b) 32
    c) 42
    d) 73
    e) 64

54. The order of the elements in the periodic table is based on
    a) the number of neutrons.
    b) the radius of the atom.
    c) the atomic number.
    d) the atomic weight.
    e) the number of oxidation states.

55. The rate of reaction will be large if
    a) ΔG^o is a large negative number.
    b) ΔS^o is a large negative number.
    c) ΔH° is a large negative number.
    d) K_{eq} is a large positive number.
    e) None of the above

56. The standard reduction potential for $PbO_2 \rightarrow Pb^{+2}$ is +1.46 V. The standard reduction potential for $Fe^{+3} \rightarrow Fe^{+2}$ is +0.77 V. What is the standard cell voltage for the reaction: $4H^+ + PbO_2 + 2Fe^{+2} \rightarrow 2Fe^{+3} + Pb^{+2} + 2H_2O$?
    a) −0.08 V
    b) +0.69 V
    c) +2.33 V
    d) −0.69V
    e) −2.33 V

57. Which of the following species contains only one π bond?
    a) BeF_2
    b) NH_3
    c) CH_4
    d) CH_2CH_2
    e) CCl_4

58. What is the correct name for the compound of V_2O_5?
    a) Divanadium pentoxide
    b) Vanadic oxide
    c) Vanadium(V) oxide
    d) Vanadium(V) pentoxide
    e) Vanadous oxide

59. What is the molar mass of $Al(NO_3)_3$?
    a) 165.00
    b) 56.99
    c) 213.00
    d) 88.99
    e) 184.99

60. What weight of $KClO_3$ (molar mass = 122.5) is needed to make 200 mL of a 0.150 M solution of this salt?
    a) 2.73 g
    b) 3.68 g
    c) 27.3 g
    d) 164 g
    e) 3.69 kg

61. When ammonium oxalate, $(NH_4)_2C_2O_4$, is dissolved in water, the ions formed are
    a) $2N^{3-}(aq) + 8H^+ + 2C^{4+}(aq) + 4O^{2-}(aq)$
    b) $(NH_4)^{2+}(aq) + C_2O_4^{-2}(aq)$
    c) $2NH_4^+(aq) + C_2O_4^{-2}(aq)$
    d) $NH_4^{+2}(aq) + C_2O_4^{-2}(aq)$
    e) $2NH_4^+(aq) + 2CO_2^-(aq)$

62. When the electrons are shared unequally by two atoms, the bond is said to be
   a) covalent.
   b) polar covalent.
   c) network covalent.
   d) ionic.
   e) metallic.

63. In a 0.20 M aqueous solution, lactic acid ($HC_3H_5O_3$) is 2% dissociated. What is the closet value of K_a for this acid?
   a) 4×10^{-5}
   b) 6×10^{-5}
   c) 8×10^{-5}
   d) 1.6×10^{-4}
   e) 2.0×10^{-4}

64. Which of the following equations represents an alpha decay?
   a) ${}^{116}_{49}In \rightarrow {}^{116}_{50}Sn + X$
   b) ${}^{234}_{90}TH \rightarrow {}^{234}_{91}Pa + X$
   c) ${}^{38}_{19}K \rightarrow {}^{38}_{18}Ar + X$
   d) ${}^{222}_{86}Rn \rightarrow {}^{218}_{84}Po + X$
   e) ${}^{27}_{13}Al + {}^{4}_{2}He \rightarrow {}^{30}_{15}P + X$

65. Which of the following atoms has the largest second ionization energy?
   a) Mg
   b) Cl
   c) S
   d) Ca
   e) Na

66. Which of the following compounds includes an element with an oxidation number of +5?
   a) ClO_4^-
   b) MnO_4^-
   c) NO_2^-
   d) SO_3^{-2}
   e) NO_3^-

67. Which of the following elements has the greatest number of *p* electrons in the outermost shell?
   a) C
   b) Si
   c) Fe
   d) Cl
   e) Ar

68. Which of the following sets of materials would make the best buffer solution?
   a) H_2O, 1 M NaOH, 1 M H_2SO_4
   b) H_2O, 1 M CH_3COOH, 1 M $NaCH_3COO^-$
   c) H_2O, 1 M CH_3COOH, 6 M $Na^+CH_3COO^-$
   d) H_2O, 1 M CH_3COOH, 1 M NaOH
   e) None of the above

69. Which of the following would cause the light to glow when dissolved in water and placed in conductivity apparatus?
   a) Table salt
   b) Ethyl alcohol
   c) Sugar
   d) Glycerin
   e) None of the above

70. Which of the following organic structures is ethylamine?
   a) $CH_3-CH_2-CH_3$
   b) $CH_3-CO-OH$
   c) $CH_3-O-CH_2-CH_2-CH_3$
   d) $CH_3-CH_2-NH_2$
   e) $CH_3-CO-CH_3$

SAT Chemistry Subject Test No. 5 Keys

1. A	11. D	21. D	31. C	41. C	51. D	61. C
2. D	12. B	22. A	32. C	42. D	52. E	62. B
3. E	13. D	23. E	33. D	43. B	53. B	63. C
4. B	14. A	24. C	34. E	44. E	54. C	64. D
5. C	15. B	25. D	35. D	45. E	55. E	65. E
6. B	16. E	26. E	36. C	46. D	56. B	66. E
7. D	17. D	27. B	37. E	47. C	57. D	67. E
8. E	18. A	28. B	38. A	48. B	58. C	68. B
9. C	19. C	29. E	39. C	49. B	59. C	69. A
10. A	20. E	30. B	40. E	50. C	60. B	70. D

101. TF
102. TTCE
103. FT
104. TTCE
105. FT
106. TTCE
107. TTCE
108. TTCE
109. TF
110. TF
111. FF
112. TTCE
113. FT
114. FF
115. FF

SAT Chemistry Subject Test No. 5 Answer to Part A

1−4 *Answer: (adeb)*
Br_2 and Hg: only liquid metal and nonmetal element

Cl_2 and F_2: The halogen family has the highest electronegativity. They are good oxidizing agents.

Fe and Co are transition metals. Fe^{3+} aqueous solution is yellow. Co^{2+} aqueous solution is pink.

Diamond and graphite are the element carbon in two different forms.

5−8 *Answer: (cbde)*
The activated complex represents the structure of the system as it exists at the peak of the activation energy curve.

Activation energy: potential energy difference between the activated complex and the reactant.

The heat of reaction is equal to the potential energy of product minus the potential energy of reactant.

9−12 *Answer: (cadb)*
AgCl: white precipitates

AgBr: yellow precipitates

$NH_3 + H^+ \rightarrow NH_4^+$

$HC_2H_3O_2$: acetic acid, vinegar; weak acid

$NaC_2H_3O_2$, a weak basic salt, is from strong basic and weak acidic solution.

13−16 *Answer: (dabe)*
KCl: ionic compound

HC1(g): polar covalent compound

C_2H_6: non-polar covalent compound

Na: a metal

17−20 *Answer: (dace)*
C_2H_2 : HC≡CH; sp; linear

C_2H_4 : CH_2=CH_2; sp^2 ; triangular planar

C_4H_{10} : $CH_3 - CH_2 - CH_2 - CH_3$; sp^3 ;

C_6H_6: aromatic compound

$C_6H_{12}O_6$: Glucose, water soluble.

21−24 *Answer: (daec)*
Distillation: separation of two liquids based on their boiling point difference.

Chromatography: separation of two liquids or gases based on different moving speeds in mobile and stationary phases.

Fractional crystallization: separation of two solids based on their solubility.

Filtration: separation of liquids and solids.

Titration: use acid-base reactions to determine the concentrations of acids or bases.

SAT Chemistry Subject Test No. 5 Answer to Part C

25. *Answer: (d)*
    The reaction shifts to the left.

26. *Answer: (e)*
    The molar volume of N_2 at 1atm (℃) is 22.4 liters.
    The number of mole at 1.5 atm (℃) and 22.4 liters of N2 is 1.5 moles.
    1 Mole of $N_2 = \frac{2}{3}$ moles of NaN_3
    $1.5 \times \frac{2}{3} \times (23 + 3 \times 14) = 65\ grams$

27. *Answer: (b)*
    The 1st step is the rate determining step.
    $R = k[NO][O_2]$

28. *Answer: (b)*
    Partial pressure of $O_2 = \frac{2}{2+3+1} \times 760 = 253.3$ torr

29. *Answer: (e)*
    All of them can conduct electrical current in an aqueous solutions.

30. *Answer: (b)*
    metallic oxide + water = base
    nonmetal oxide + water = acid

31. *Answer: (c)*
    $2C + O_2 \rightarrow 2CO$
    $\Delta H = -787 - (-566) = -221\ kJ$
    1 mole of CO will need $\frac{-221}{2}$ kJ = – 110.5 kJ.

32. *Answer: (c)*
    Volume and temperature are directly proportional to each other.
    $50 \times 2 = 100\ L$

33. *Answer: (d)*
    Magnesium is the most active metal among the selections.

34. *Answer: (e)*
    If the bubble is dislodged, the reading of the final volume will be higher than the actual values. Therefore, the volume recorded will be higher and the calculated molarity of the sample will be higher than the actual values. The mass of the sample will be lower than calculated values.

35. *Answer: (d)*
    Valence electrons

36. *Answer: (c)*
    Alcohol reacts with organic acid to produce an ester.

37. *Answer: (e)*
    Dependent on how the pressure has been changed. For example, if the pressure is changed by adding an inert gas, no change will result.

38. *Answer: (a)*
    A strong base plus a neutral salt solution becomes a strong base solution.

39. *Answer: (c)*
    x: % of ^{10}B
    y: % of ^{11}B
    $10.8 = \frac{10.0x + 11.0y}{x + y}$
    $10.8x + 10.8y = 10.0x + 11.0y$
    $0.8x = 0.2y, \quad x : y = 1 : 4 = 20 : 80$

40. *Answer: (e)*
    Diamond: sp^3, 3D network covalent bonds
    Graphite: sp^2, 2D covalent bonds

41. *Answer: (c)*
    46.00 grams of ethanol = $\frac{46}{12 \times 2 + 5 + 16 + 1} = 1$ mole
    $\Delta H = -1.40 \times 10^3\ kJ$

42. *Answer: (d)*
    $Cu(s) + 2NO_3^-(aq) + 4H^+(aq) \rightarrow Cu^{2+}(aq) + 2NO_2(g) + 2H_2O(l)$

43. *Answer: (b)*
    $CaCO_3 + 2HCl \rightarrow CaCl_2 + CO_2 + H_2O$
    100 g CaCO3 = 1 mole of $CaCO_3$
    1 mole of $CaCO_3$ = 1 mole of CO_2 = 44 g of CO_2

44. *Answer: (e)*
    The molar mass of water is 18 g/mole.
    $\frac{4.5}{18} = 0.25$

45. *Answer: (e)*
    $\Delta T = i \times m \times Kb$
    a). i = 2; b). i = 4; c). i = 3; d). i >1; e). i = 1

46. *Answer: (d)*
Total Mass = (500 + 500) × 1 = 1000 g
$Q = mc\Delta T = 1000 \times 4.2 \times 5 = 2.1 \times 10^4\ J$

47. *Answer: (c)*
$M_1V_1 + M_2V_2 = (V_1+V_2)\ M$
$M = \frac{100 \times 1 + 100 \times 5}{200} = 3M$

48. *Answer: (b)*
Continuing to remove the product will let the reaction proceed to completion.

49. *Answer: (b)*
The alkene series contains a double bond with sp^2 *hybridization.*
Ethylene has a double bond and sp^2 *hybridization.*

50. *Answer: (c)*
Gibbs free energy change is an indication of spontaneous or nonspontaneous reaction.
$\Delta G = \Delta H - T\Delta S$

51. *Answer: (d)*
Conservation of mass: The total mass is always the same before and after changes.

52. *Answer: (e)*
HF has the largest difference in electronegativity.
BF_3 *has 0 dipole moment.*

53. *Answer: (b)*
Atomic Number = Number of Protons in the Nucleus

54. *Answer: (c)*
The arrangement of the periodic table is based on atomic number.

55. *Answer: (e)*
All of them are related to equilibrium conditions which have nothing to do with kinetics.

56. *Answer: (b)*
$PbO_2 \rightarrow Pb^{+2}$ $E = 1.46$
$Fe^{+2} \rightarrow Fe^{+3}$ $E = -0.77$
$1.46 - 0.77 = 0.69$

57. *Answer: (d)*
Whatever has a double bond will have a π bond.
$CH_2{=}CH_2$

58. *Answer: (c)*
Transition metals use Roman numeral corresponding to their oxidation states.

59. *Answer: (c)*
$27 + (14 + 3 \times 16) \times 3 = 213$

60. *Answer: (b)*
$0.15\ M = \frac{\frac{x}{122.5}}{0.2},\quad x = 3.68\ g$

61. *Answer: (c)*
$(NH_4)_2C_2O_4 \rightarrow NH_4^+ + C_2O_2^{-2}$

62. *Answer: (b)*
Shared electrons are a covalent bond.

63. *Answer: (c)*
$HC_3H_5O_3 \rightarrow C_3H_5O_3^- + H^+$
$0.2 - x \quad x \quad x$
$x = 0.02 \times 0.2 = 0.004,\quad K_a = \frac{0.004^2}{0.2 - 0.004} \approx 8 \times 10^{-5}$

64. *Answer: (d)*
By balancing atomic mass and numbers, x is ${}^4_2He$*, an alpha particle.*

65. *Answer: (e)*
The element that has only one valence electron will have the largest 2nd *ionization energy.*

66. *Answer: (e)*
a) ClO_4^-: +7 and −2
b) MnO_4^-: +7 and −2
c) NO_2^-: +3 −2
d) SO_3^{-2}: +4; −2
e) NO_3^-: +5; −2

67. *Answer: (e)*
Noble gases have full p orbitals.

68. *Answer: (b)*
A good buffer solution needs the same concentration of weak acid or base and its conjugate salt

69. *Answer: (a)*
An electrolyte, such as salt, will conduct electric current in the solution.

70. *Answer: (d)*
Ethylamine: $C_2H_5 - NH_2$

SAT Chemistry Subject Test No 6.

PART A

Directions: Each set of lettered choices below refers to the numbered statements or questions immediately following it. Select the one lettered choice that best fits each statement and then fill in the corresponding circle on the answer sheet. A given choice may be used once, more than once, or not at all in each set.

Note: For all questions involving solutions, assume that the solvent is water unless otherwise stated. Throughout the test the following symbols have the definitions specified unless otherwise noted.

H = enthalpy	T = temperature	L = liter(s)
M = molar	V = volume	mL = milliliter(s)
n = number of moles	atm = atmosphere(s)	mm = millimeter(s)
P = pressure	g = gram(s)	mol = mole(s)
R = molar gas constant	J = joule(s)	V = volt(s)
S = entropy	kJ = kilojoule(s)	

Questions 1–4 refer to the following topics and relationships:

a) −2
b) −1
c) 0
d) 1
e) 2

1. is the oxidation number of O in H_2O_2
2. is the oxidation number of F in NF_3
3. is the oxidation number of O in O_3
4. is the oxidation number of Mg in magnesium phosphate

Questions 5–8 refer to the following topics and relationships:

a) H_2
b) SO_2
c) CO
d) HCl
e) O_3

5. A product of the incomplete combustion of hydrocarbons.
6. A gas produced by the heating of sodium chlorate
7. Can be found in acid rain
8. Screens out a large fraction of the ultraviolet rays of the sun

Questions 9–11 refer to the following topics and relationships:

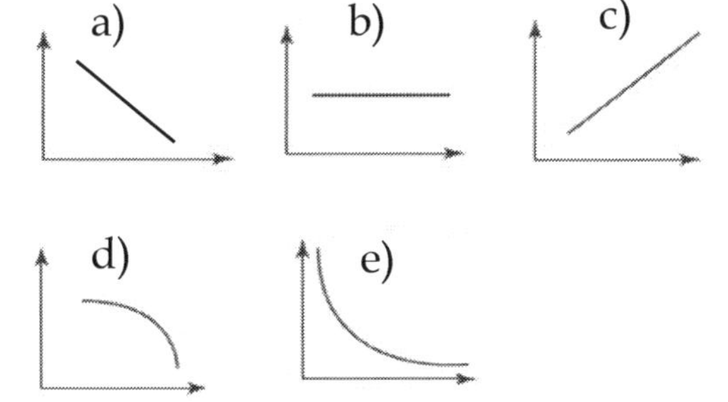

9. The graph of volume (x-axis) vs. pressure (y-axis) for a gas at constant temperature
10. The graph of pressure (x-axis) vs. temperature (y-axis) for a gas at constant volume
11. The graph of volume (x-axis) vs. temperature (y-axis) for a gas at constant pressure

Questions 12–14 refer to the following topics and relationships:

a) Reduction potential
b) Ionization energy
c) Electronegativity
d) Heat of formation
e) Activation energy

12. This is the energy needed to remove an electron from a gaseous atom in its ground state.
13. This is the energy change that accompanies the combining of elements in their natural states to form a compound.
14. This is the minimum energy needed for molecules to react and form compounds.

Questions 15–18 refer to the following topics and relationships:

a) A molecule
b) A mixture of compounds
c) An isotope
d) An isomer
e) An acid

15. An atom with the same number of protons as another atom of the same element but a different number of neutrons
16. The smallest particle in a chemical element or compound that has the chemical properties of that element or compound
17. A substance made by combining two or more different materials in such a way that no chemical reaction occurs
18. Same molecular formula but different geometry structure

Questions 19–21 refer to the following topics and relationships:

a) Heisenberg's Uncertainty Principle
b) Pauli Exclusion Principle
c) Schrodinger Wave Equation
d) Hund's Rule
e) Bohr model of the hydrogen atom

19. We cannot know the exact location of an electron in space.
20. No two electrons can have the same quantum number because they must have opposite spins.
21. The electrons will occupy an orbital individually, with parallel spins, before pairing up.

Questions 22–25 refer to the following topics and relationships:

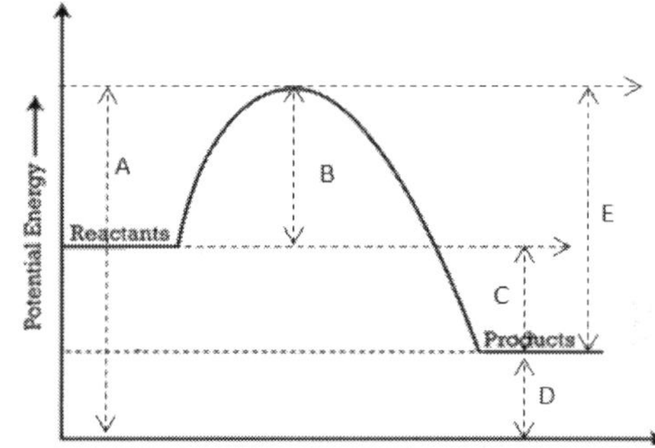

22. The heat of the reaction for the forward reaction
23. The activation energy of the forward reaction
24. The activation energy of the reverse reaction
25. The potential energy of the products

PART B

Directions: Each question below consists of two statements, I in the left-hand column and II in the right-hand column. For each question, determine whether statement I is true or false and whether statement II is true or false and then fill in the corresponding T or F circles on your answer sheet. Fill in circle CE only if statement II is a correct explanation of the true statement I.

On the actual Chemistry Test, the following type of question must be answered on a special section (labeled "Chemistry") at the lower left-hand corner of your answer sheet. These questions will be numbered beginning with 101 and must be answered according to the following directions.

Examples:

	I		II
EX 1.	H_2SO_4 is a strong acid	BECAUSE	H_2SO_4 contains sulfer.
EX 2.	An atom of oxygen is electrically neutral	BECAUSE	an oxygen atom contains an equal number of protons and electrons.

SAMPLE ANSWERS

	I		II		CE
EX 1.	●	Ⓕ	●	Ⓕ	○
EX 2.	●	Ⓕ	●	Ⓕ	●

	I		II
101.	A liquid can boil at different temperatures	BECAUSE	The atmospheric (or surrounding) pressure can vary.
102.	Adding more reactants will speed up a reaction	BECAUSE	The reactants will collide less frequently.
103.	The empirical formula of the $C_6H_{12}O_6$ is CH_2O	BECAUSE	The empirical formula shows the lowest ratio of the elements present in the molecular formula.
104.	The double and single bonds in benzene are subject to resonance	BECAUSE	Benzene has delocalized pi electrons that stabilize its structure.
105.	HCl is an Arrhenius acid	BECAUSE	HCl will provide hydronium ions in the solution.
106.	Bromine has an atomic mass close to 80	BECAUSE	About 50% of all bromine atoms are ^{79}Br and the other 50% are ^{81}Br.

107.	The bond length in N_2 is shorter than NO_3	BECAUSE	N_2 violates the octet rule.
108.	Propane can be decomposed chemically	BECAUSE	Propane is a compound that is made up of simpler elements.
109.	A reaction will be spontaneous if ΔH is negative and ΔS is positive	BECAUSE	ΔG will be negative when there is a decrease in enthalpy and an increase in entropy.
110.	KNO_3 will not dissolve in water	BECAUSE	All chlorides are soluble in water.
111.	Under the same temperature and pressure, CO_2 is heavier than CO	BECAUSE	CO_2 is a non-polar molecule and CO is a polar molecule.
112.	The electrolysis of potassium iodide, KI, produces electrical energy	BECAUSE	Electrolytic cells convert chemical energy into electrical energy.
113.	The molecular shape of ethyne is linear	BECAUSE	The carbon atoms in ethyne are sp hybridized.
114.	320 calories or 1.34×10^3 joules of heat will melt 4 grams of ice at 0 °C	BECAUSE	The heat of fusion of water is 80 calories per gram or 3.34×10^2 joules per gram.
115.	When a Li atom reacts and becomes an ion, the Li atom can be considered a reducing agent.	BECAUSE	The Li atom lost an electron and was oxidized.

PART C

Directions: Each of the questions or incomplete statements below is followed by five suggested answers or completions. Select the one that is best in each case and then fill in the corresponding circle on the answer sheet.

26. Consider the system below at equilibrium. Which of the following changes will shift the equilibrium to the right?

$$H_2 + N_2 \rightarrow NH_3 + 92.94 \text{ kJ}$$

I. Increasing the temperature
II. Decreasing the temperature
III. Increasing the pressure on the system

a) I only
b) II only
c) III only
d) I and III only
e) II and III only

27. Which of the following physical properties can be determined if the unit cell and its dimensions are found by x−ray diffraction?

a) Heat capacity
b) Heat of fusion
c) Boiling and melting points
d) Vapor pressure
e) Density

28. Which of the following half-cell reactions describes what is happening at the anode in the diagram below?

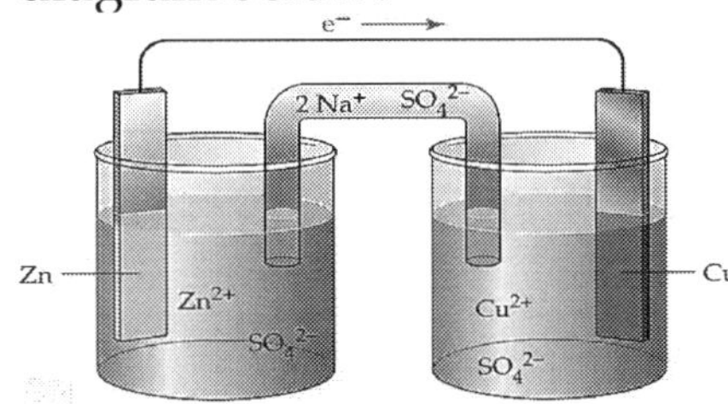

a) $Zn \rightarrow Zn^{2+} + 2e^-$
b) $H_2 \rightarrow 2H^+ + 2e^-$
c) $2Cl^- \rightarrow Cl_2 + 2e^-$
d) $SO_4^- \rightarrow S + 2O_2 + 6e^-$
e) $2H^+ + 2e^- \rightarrow H_2$

29. Which of the following statements is inconsistent with the concept of isotopes of the same element?

a) Isotopes have the same number of protons.
b) Isotopes have the same atomic number.
c) Isotopes differ in mass number.
d) Isotopes differ in number of neutrons present.
e) Isotopes differ in their nuclear charge.

30. $F_2 + 2e^- \rightarrow 2F^-(aq)$ E° = +1.87 V;
$Ca^{+2} + 2e^- \rightarrow Ca(s)$ E° = −2.76 V

When the above half-reactions are combined in a galvanic cell, which species will be reduced and which will be oxidized?

a) F^- will be oxidized and Ca^{+2} will be reduced.
b) Ca^{+2} will be oxidized and F_2 will be reduced.
c) Ca(s) will be oxidized and F_2 will be reduced.
d) F_2 will be oxidized and Ca(s) will be reduced.
e) None of the above

31. The energy of a system can be
    a) Easily changed into mass.
    b) transformed into a different form.
    c) measured only in terms of potential energy.
    d) measured only in terms of kinetic energy.
    e) None of the above

32. When 50 grams of water is heated from 273 K to 373 K, the water
    a) absorbs 21,000 joules of heat.
    b) absorbs 377 Joules of heat.
    c) releases 5,220 Joules of heat.
    d) absorbs 242 Joules of heat.
    e) releases 90 Joules of heat.

33. Which of the following is/are the product(s) of a Lewis acid reacting with a Lewis base?

    I. $Cu(NH_3)_4^{+2}$
    II. KOH
    III. HCO_3^-
    IV. CO_3^{-2}
    V. SO_3^{-2}

    a) I and II only
    b) II only
    c) I and III only
    d) IV only
    e) IV and V only

34. Which of the following was used to determine the charge of the electron?
    a) Gold foil experiment
    b) Deflection of cathode rays by electric and magnetic fields
    c) Oil drop experiment
    d) Electrolysis
    e) Mass spectrometer

35. Which of the following will increase the average kinetic energy?
    a) An increase in the reaction concentration
    b) An increase in temperature
    c) A decrease in pressure
    d) A catalysis
    e) An increase of pH

36. When a fixed amount of gas has its Kelvin temperature and pressure doubled, the new volume of the gas is
    a) four times greater than its original volume.
    b) twice its original volume.
    c) unchanged.
    d) one-half its original volume.
    e) one-fourth its original volume.

37. The freezing point depression constant for water is 1.86 °C/m. When 100 g of a compound is dissolved in 1000 g of H_2O, the freezing point is −5.0 °C. Which of the following is the identity of this compound?
    a) $Mg(NO_3)_2$
    b) KCl
    c) Na_2SO_4
    d) HCOOH
    e) HF

38. Which of the following accepts a proton?
    a) A Brønsted acid
    b) A Brønsted base
    c) A strong acid
    d) A weak base
    e) A buffer

39. Which of the following is not part of the atomic theory?
    a) Compounds are made up of combinations of atoms.
    b) All atoms of a given element are alike.
    c) All matter is composed of atoms.
    d) A chemical reaction involves the rearrangement of atoms.
    e) The atom is mainly empty space.

40. Which of the following bonds is expected to be the most polar?
    a) C−Si
    b) C−N
    c) O−C
    d) S−C
    e) H−C

41. A substance that can be further simplified using ordinary means may be either a(n)
    a) element or compound.
    b) element or mixture.
    c) mixture or compound.
    d) mixture or atom.
    e) atom or element.

42. Which section shows melting in the figure below?

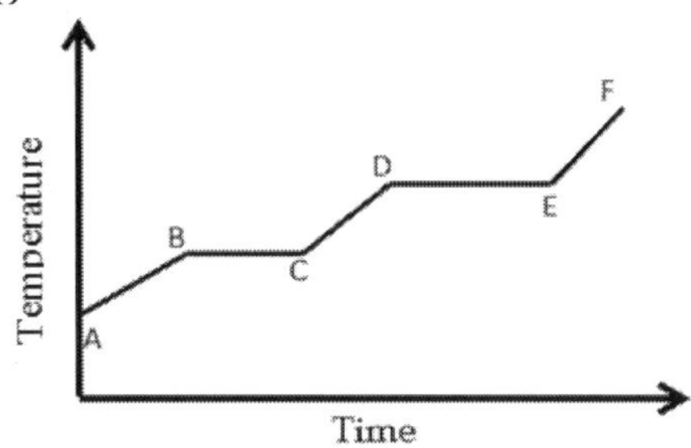

The heating curve of a pure substance

    a) AB
    b) BC
    c) CD
    d) DE
    e) E

43. Which of the following elements is in the halogen group?
    a) Sodium
    b) Strontium
    c) Uranium
    d) Bromine
    e) Bismuth

44. A titration experiment is conducted in which 15 mL of a 0.015 M $Ba(OH)_2$ solution is added to 30 mL of an HCl solution of unknown concentration and titration is complete. What is the approximate concentration of the HCl solution?
    a) 0.015 M
    b) 0.03 M
    c) 1.5 M
    d) 2.5 M
    e) 3.0 M

45. At a given temperature, if the equilibrium constant for the reaction, $H_2 + Cl_2 \leftrightarrow 2HCl$, is K_p, the equilibrium constant for the reaction, $HCl \leftrightarrow \frac{1}{2}H_2 + \frac{1}{2}Cl_2$ can be represented as
    a) $\frac{1}{Kp^2}$.
    b) Kp^2.
    c) $\frac{1}{\sqrt{Kp}}$.
    d) $\sqrt{K_p}$.
    e) Kp^3 .

46. In which of the following pairs is the first element expected to have a higher electronegativity than the second?
    a) O, P
    b) Cs, Rb
    c) I, Br
    d) AI, P
    e) Sb, As

47. Which of the following could act as amphoteric acids/bases pairs?
    I. $HCl + H_2O \rightarrow H_3O^{+1} + Cl^{-1}$ and $H_2O + NH_3 \rightarrow OH^{-1} + NH_4^+$
    II. $HS^- + HCl \rightarrow Cl^- + H_2S$ and $HS^- + NH_3 \rightarrow NH_4^+ + s^{-2}$
    III. $HCl + NaOH \rightarrow NaCl + H_2O$ and $NaCl + H_2O \rightarrow HCl + NaOH$
    a) I only
    b) II only
    c) III only
    d) I and II only
    e) I and III only

48. What is the empirical formula for a compound containing 0.28 grams of N_2 and 0.48 grams of O_2 ?
    a) N_2O_5
    b) N_2O_3
    c) NO_2
    d) NO
    e) N_2O

49. A 5% solution of NaCl means that in 100 g of solution there is
    a) 5 g of NaCl.
    b) 5.85 g of NaCl.
    c) 10 g of NaCl.
    d) 90 g of NaCl.
    e) 95 g of NaCl.

50. Given the following thermochemical data:
    $N_2O_4(g) \rightarrow 2NO_2(g)$ $\Delta H° = +57.93$ kJ
    $2NO(g) + O_2(g) \rightarrow 2NO_2(g)$ $\Delta H° = -113.1$ kJ
    Determine the heat of the reaction
    $2NO(g) + O_2(g) \rightarrow N_2O_4(g)$
    a) 171.07 kJ
    b) −55.21 kJ
    c) −171.03 kJ
    d) +55.21 kJ
    e) −85.54 kJ

51. Which of the following solutions would probably have the highest boiling point?
    a) 0.100 m KOH
    b) 0.100 m Na_2SO_4
    c) 0.100 m $C_6H_{12}O_6$
    d) 0.200 m CaC12
    e) 0.200 m CH_3CH_2OH

52. When the equation $Br_2 + SO_2 + H_2O \rightarrow H_2SO_4 + HBr$ is balanced, the lowest whole number coefficient of HBr is
    a) 1
    b) 2
    c) 3
    d) 4
    e) 5

53. A sample of gas is trapped in a manometer and the stopcock is opened as shown below. The level of mercury moves to a new height. If the pressure of the gas inside the manometer is 780 torr, what is the atmospheric pressure in this case?

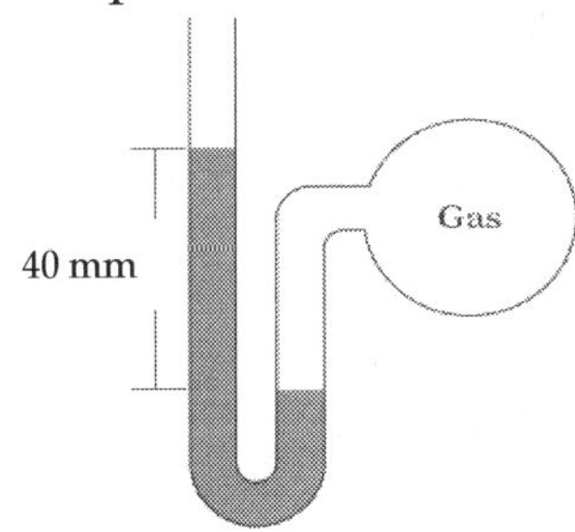

    a) 820 torr
    b) 780 torr
    c) 750 torr
    d) 740 torr
    e) 700 torr

54. The activated complex is a compound that is
    a) stable and has low potential energy.
    b) stable and has high potential energy.
    c) unstable and has low potential energy.
    d) unstable and has high potential energy.
    e) one of the reactants.

55. When 3.45 moles of $C_6H_{13}Cl$ and 1.26 moles of C_5H_{12} are mixed, which of the following is needed to calculate the molarity of this solution?
    a) The density of the solution
    b) The densities of $C_6H_{13}Cl$ and C_5H_{12}
    c) The temperature
    d) The molar masses of $C_6H_{13}Cl$ and C_5H_{12}
    e) The volumes of $C_6H_{13}Cl$ and C_5H_{12}

56. Which of the following functional groups does not contain a carbonyl group?
    a) Aldehydes
    b) Ketones
    c) Esters
    d) Ethers
    e) Carboxylic acids

57. Which of the following particles has a negative charge?
    a) A lithium ion
    b) An alpha particle
    c) An aluminum ion
    d) A beta particle
    e) A gamma ray

58. The following reactions are known to occur spontaneously:

    $Cu + 2Ag^{+} \rightarrow Cu^{+2} + 2Ag$

    $Zn + 2Ag^{+} \rightarrow Zn^{+2} + 2Ag$

    $Zn + Cu^{+2} \rightarrow Zn^{+2} + Cu$

    The activity series of the metal for the three elements as reducing agents is
    a) Cu > Ag > Zn.
    b) Zn > Cu > Ag.
    c) Ag > Cu > Zn.
    d) Ag > Zn > Cu.
    e) Zn > Ag > Cu.

59. What type of chemical reaction is this?

    $3H_2SO_4 + 2Ga(OH)_3 \rightarrow 6H_2O + 1Ga_2(SO_4)_3$

    a) Single replacement
    b) Decomposition
    c) Double replacement
    d) Combustion
    e) Synthesis

60. The correct form of the solubility product for silver chromate, Ag_2CrO_4, is
    a) $[Ag^{+}]^2[CrO_4^{-2}]$.
    b) $[Ag^{+}][CrO_4^{-2}]$.
    c) $[Ag^{+}][CrO_4^{-2}]^2$.
    d) $[Ag^{+}]^2[CrO_4^{-2}]^4$.
    e) $[Ag]^2[CrO_4^{-2}]$.

61. In a neutralization reaction performed in the lab, a student mixed 0.20 M NaOH with 0.10 M HCl until the reaction was complete. After the liquid left in the container was dried, which of the following statements must be true?

    I. The student produced a salt and water. All of that was left in the container was the salt.
    II. The total mass of the products in the evaporating dish at the end of the experiment had a lower mass than before heating.
    III. The student was left with an ionically bonded, white, crystalline solid.

    a) I only
    b) II only
    c) I and II only
    d) I and III only
    e) I, II, and III

62. Which of the following statements is incorrect regarding balanced equations?
    a) $C + O_2 \rightarrow CO_2$ is balanced and is a synthesis reaction.
    b) $CaCO_3 \rightarrow CaO + CO_2$ is balanced and is a decomposition reaction.
    c) $Na + Cl_2 \rightarrow NaCl$ is not balanced, but demonstrates a synthesis reaction.
    d) $KI + Pb(NO_3)_2 \rightarrow PbI_2 + KNO_3$ is balanced and demonstrates a double replacement reaction.
    e) $2H_2O \rightarrow 2H_2 + O_2$ is balanced and demonstrates a single replacement reaction.

63. Which of the following molecular shapes is/are trigonal planar?
    I. BF_3
    II. $CH_2=CH_2$
    III. Cyclopropane
    a) I only
    b) II only
    c) III only
    d) I and II only
    e) I, II, and III

64. A triple bond may best be described as
    a) two sigma bonds and one pi bond.
    b) two sigma bonds and two pi bonds.
    c) one sigma bond and two pi bonds.
    d) three sigma bonds.
    e) three pi bonds.

65. Enthalpy is an expression for the
    a) heat content.
    b) energy state.
    c) reaction rate.
    d) activation energy.
    e) equilibrium state.

66. When the enthalpy is positive and the entropy is negative,
    a) the free energy is always negative.
    b) the free energy is negative at low temperatures.
    c) the free energy is negative at high temperatures.
    d) the free energy is never negative.
    e) the system is at equilibrium.

67. Which of the following concerning PCl_5 and PCl_3 is/are true?
    I. PCl_3 has a net dipole moment, whereas PCl_5 does not.
    II. The geometry of PCl_3 is trigonal planar.
    III. Both PCl_3 and PCl_5 use higher energy d orbitals for bonding.
    a) I only
    b) II and III only
    c) I and III only
    d) I and II only
    e) I, II, and III

68. What is the mass of 1 L of a gas at STP (molar mass = 224 g/mole)?
    a) 10.0 g
    b) 20.0 g
    c) 30.5 g
    d) 44.0 g
    e) 224.0 g

69. Which of the following acids is capable of dissolving gold?
    a) Hydrochloric
    b) Nitric
    c) Sulfuric
    d) A combination of a) and b)
    e) A combination of a) and c)

70. What is the normality of a 2M solution of phosphoric acid, H_3PO_4, for an acid-base titration?
    a) 0.67
    b) 2
    c) 3
    d) 6
    e) None of the above

SAT Chemistry Subject Test No. 6 Keys

1. B	11. C	21. D	31. B	41. C	51. D	61. E
2. B	12. B	22. C	32. A	42. B	52. B	62. D
3. C	13. D	23. B	33. C	43. D	53. D	63. D
4. E	14. E	24. E	34. C	44. A	54. D	64. C
5. C	15. C	25. D	35. B	45. C	55. A	65. A
6. D	16. A	26. E	36. C	46. A	56. D	66. D
7. B	17. B	27. E	37. B	47. D	57. D	67. A
8. E	18. D	28. A	38. B	48. B	58. B	68. A
9. E	19. A	29. E	39. E	49. A	59. C	69. D
10. C	20. B	30. C	40. C	50. C	60. A	70. D

101.	TTCE	106.	TTCE	111.	TT
102.	TF	107.	TF	112.	FF
103.	TTCE	108.	TTCE	113.	TTCE
104.	TTCE	109.	TTCE	114.	TTCE
105.	TTCE	110.	FF	115.	TTCE

SAT Chemistry Subject Test No. 6 Answer to Part A

1 – 4 *Answer: (bbce)*
In peroxides the oxidation number of each oxygen atom is 1−.
After reacting, fluorine will have an oxidation number of 1−.
In a compound made up entirely of a single element, each atom will have an oxidation number of 0.

Magnesium is a group 2 metal and will have an oxidation state of 2.

5 – 8 *Answer: (cdbe)*
When hydrocarbons containing C and H do not have enough oxygen to combust with $O_2(g)$ completely, the product will be CO, carbon monoxide.

$2NaClO_3 \rightarrow 2NaCl + O_2(g)$

SO_2 found in the upper atmosphere is dissolved in water molecules to form sulfurous acid (corrosive acid rain).

The ozone (O_3) in the stratosphere absorbs ultraviolet rays from the Sun.

9 – 11 *Answer: (ecc)*
This graph shows the volume decreasing as the pressure is increased and the temperature is held constant.

This graph shows the pressure increasing as the temperature is increased and the volume is held constant.

This graph shows the volume increasing as the temperature is increased and the pressure is held constant.

12 – 14 *Answer: (bde)*
Ionization energy is defined as the energy needed to remove an electron from the ground state of the isolated gaseous atom or ion.
The heat of formation is the energy change caused by the difference in the initial energy and final energy of the system when elements in their standard state react to form a compound.
The activation energy is defined as the minimum energy required for molecules to react. This is true for both exothermic and endothermic reactions.

15 – 18 *Answer: (cabd)*
Question 15 is the definition of an isotope.
Question 16 is the definition of any molecule.
Question 17 is the definition of a mixture.
Question 18 is the definition of isomer.

19 – 21 *Answer: (abd)*
Heisenberg's Uncertainty Principle: We can never simultaneously know the exact position and the exact speed of an object.

Pauli Exclusion Principle: No two electrons can have the same four electronic quantum numbers.

Schrodinger Wave Equation: A partial differential equation describes how the wave function of a physical system evolves over time.

Hund's Rule: The electrons will occupy an orbital individually, with parallel spins, before pairing up.

Bohr model of the hydrogen atom: an atom consisting of a small, positively-charged nucleus orbited by negatively-charged electrons.

22 – 25 *Answer: (cbed)*
The heat of the reaction is the heat liberated between the level of potential energy of the reactants and that of the products. This is quantity (C) on the diagram.

The activation energy of the forward reaction is the energy needed to begin the reaction.

For the reverse reaction to occur, an activation energy equal to the sum of (B) + (C) is needed. This is shown by (E).

The potential energy of the products is the total of the original potential energies of the products shown by (D).

SAT Chemistry Subject Test No. 6 Answer to Part C

26. *Answer: (e)*
Decreasing the temperature and increasing the pressure will shift the equilibrium to the right.

27. *Answer: (e)*
Volume and density can be determined.

28. *Answer: (a)*
Anode: electrode where oxidation occurs.

29. *Answer: (e)*
Because isotopes are the same element with different mass numbers, they will have the same number of protons and the same nuclear charge.

30. *Answer: (c)*
Ca(s) will be oxidized and F_2 *will be reduced.*

31. *Answer: (b)*
Energy can be easily transferred between forms.

32. *Answer: (a)*
Use the equation $q = mc\Delta T$ *to find the amount of heat absorbed by the sample of water.*
(50 grams)(4.2 J/g K)(100) = 21,000 joules.

33. *Answer: (c)*
Cu^{2+} *and* NH_3 *can act as a Lewis acid or base.*

34. *Answer: (c)*
Millikan's oil drop experiment determined the charge of an electron.

35. *Answer: (b)*
Molecules can move faster at the higher temperature.

36. *Answer: (c)*
Combined gas law: $\frac{P_1V_1}{T_1} = \frac{P_2V_2}{T_2}$

37. *Answer: (b)*
$\Delta T_f = i \times 1.86 \times \frac{\frac{100}{M}}{1} = 5$
$\frac{M}{i} = 37.2$
KCl gives an i = 2 and a molar mass of 74.5.

38. *Answer: (b)*
Brønsted Theory

39. *Answer: (e)*
All the statements are included in the atomic theory except for the empty space concept of the atom. Rutherford concluded this in his gold foil experiment.

40. *Answer: (c)*
O has the highest electronegativity; therefore O−C has the biggest difference in electronegativity among pairs of atoms.

41. *Answer: (c)*
A mixture can be simplified by physical means. A compound can be simplified by chemical means.

42. *Answer: (b)*
BC is melting and DE is vaporizing.

43. *Answer: (d)*
Bromine belongs to the halogen family.

44. *Answer: (a)*
$N_1V_1 = N_2V_2$
$0.015 \times 2 \times 15 = N_2 \times 30$
$N_2 = 0.015\ N = 0.015M$

45. *Answer: (c)*
$HCl \leftrightarrow \frac{1}{2} H_2 + \frac{1}{2} Cl_2$
$Keq = (\frac{1}{K_p})^{1/2} = \frac{1}{\sqrt{Kp}}$

46. *Answer: (a)*
Electronegativity decreases from top to bottom in the same family and from left to right in the same period.

47. *Answer: (d)*
In reaction I, the water acts like an acid and a base. In reaction II, the HS^{-1} *ion acts like an acid and a base. Reaction III shows neutralization and hydrolysis, but not amphoteric acid/base.*

48. *Answer: (b)*
$\frac{0.28}{14} : \frac{0.48}{16} = 2 : 3$

49. *Answer: (a)*
$5\% = \frac{x}{100} \times 100\%$
$x = 5g$

50. *Answer: (c)*
$Total\ Reaction = Reaction\ 2 - Reaction\ 1$
$Total\ \Delta H = -113.1 - 57.93 = -171.03\ kJ$

51. *Answer: (d)*
$\Delta T = i \times m \times Kb$
a). $i \times m = 0.2$
b). $i \times m = 0.3$
c). $i \times m = 0.1$
d). $i \times m = 0.6$
e.) $i \times m = 0.2$

52. *Answer: (b)*
$Br_2 + SO_2 + 2H_2O \rightarrow H_2SO_4 + 2HBr$

53. *Answer: (d)*
The atmospheric pressure is 40 mm lower than the pressure of the gas. 780 – 40 = 740 torr.

54. *Answer: (d)*
The activated complexes are unstable (hence why they are usually intermediate compounds) and have high potential energy.

55. *Answer: (a)*
To calculate the molarity of a solution, the volume information will be needed. Density information can be used to calculate volume of this solution.

56. *Answer: (d)*
A carbonyl group is characterized as C==O. Ethers have an oxygen atom but the oxygen has only single bonds, R – O – R.

57. *Answer: (d)*
A beta particle is an electron.

58. *Answer: (b)*
Reducing agents will be oxidized.
Zn > Cu > Ag

59. *Answer: (c)*
$AB + CD \rightarrow AC + BD$

60. *Answer: (a)*
$Ag_2CrO_4 \rightarrow 2Ag^+ + CrO_4^{-2}$
Pure solids are not part of the equation of equilibrium constant.

61. *Answer: (e)*
$NaOH + HCl \rightarrow NaCl + H_2O$
A neutralization reaction will produce salt and water. After drying, only the salt will be left in the container.

62. *Answer: (d)*
This reaction is not balanced. It should be $2KI + Pb(NO_3)_2 \rightarrow PbI_2 + 2KNO_3$. *Also, this reaction is classified as a double replacement.*

63. *Answer: (d)*
The sp^2 hybridization of the two carbon atoms in ethane and the six valence electrons preferred by boron creates a trigonal planar molecular geometry. Cyclopropane has all single bonds in its molecule and will have sp^3 hybridized carbon atoms.

64. *Answer: (c)*
A triple bond contains one sigma bond and two pi bonds.

65. *Answer: (a)*
Enthalpy is the heat content.

66. *Answer: (d)*
$\Delta G = \Delta H - T\Delta S$
A positive number minus a negative number results in a positive number.

67. *Answer: (a)*
PCl_3 molecule has a pyramidal shape.
Both PCl_3 and PCl_5 use p orbitals for bonding.

68. *Answer: (a)*
$\frac{1}{22.4} \times 224 = 10.0\ g$

69. *Answer: (d)*
Aqua regia, three parts of hydrochloric acid and one part of nitric solution, can dissolve gold.

70. *Answer: (d)*
H_3PO_4 can release $3H^+$.
$N = 3 \times M = 3 \times 2 = 6$

SAT Chemistry Subject Test No. 7

PART A

Directions: Each set of lettered choices below refers to the numbered statements or questions immediately following it. Select the one lettered choice that best fits each statement and then fill in the corresponding circle on the answer sheet. A given choice may be used once, more than once, or not at all in each set.

Note: For all questions involving solutions, assume that the solvent is water unless otherwise stated. Throughout the test the following symbols have the definitions specified unless otherwise noted.

H = enthalpy	T = temperature	L = liter(s)
M = molar	V = volume	mL = milliliter(s)
n = number of moles	atm = atmosphere(s)	mm = millimeter(s)
P = pressure	g = gram(s)	mol = mole(s)
R = molar gas constant	J = joule(s)	V = volt(s)
S = entropy	kJ = kilojoule(s)	

Questions 1–3 refer to the following topics and relationships:

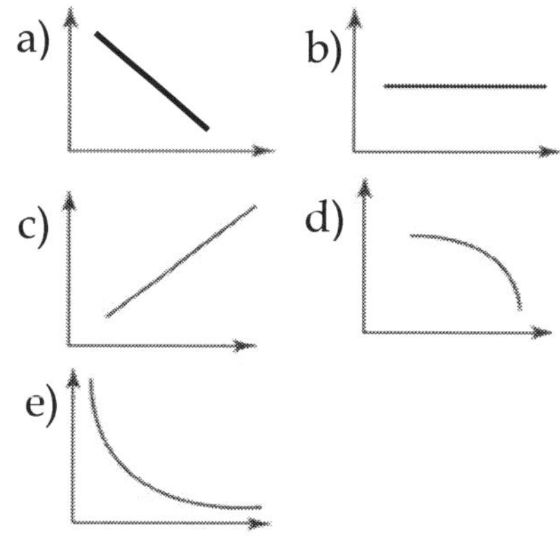

1. The graph represents the relationship of gas volume (y-axis) to temperature (x-axis), with pressure held constant.
2. The graph represents the relationship of gas volume (y-axis) to pressure (x-axis), with temperature held constant.
3. The graph represents the relationship of the solubility of a given gas (y-axis) to the partial pressure of that gas (x-axis).

Questions 4–7 refer to the following topics and relationships:

a) The process of solid to gas
b) The process of gas to solid
c) The process of liquid to gas
d) The process of liquid to solid
e) The process of solid to liquid

4. is called sublimation
5. is called deposition
6. is called vaporization
7. is called freezing

Questions 8–11 refer to the following topics and relationships:

a) Isomers
b) Cations
c) Element
d) Isotope
e) Molecule

8. The smallest matter cannot be broken down chemically.
9. An atom loses electrons to form
10. An atom of the same element that differs by the number of neutrons
11. Same molecular formula but different geometric structure

Questions 12–15 refer to the following topics and relationships:

a) 1*s*
b) 3*s*
c) 4*s*
d) 2*p*
e) 3*d*

12. Contains the valence electrons in the ground state of the calcium atom
13. Contains a filled orbital of electrons in the ground state of helium
14. The electron configurations of the transition metals
15. The electron configuration of the element with the highest electronegativity

Questions 16–18 refer to the following topics and relationships:

a) Barometer
b) pH meter
c) Calorimeter
d) Voltaic cell
e) Electrolytic cell

16. Requires an external current to make a redox reaction spontaneous
17. Measure the heat of reactions
18. Measure the gas pressure

Questions 19–21 refer to the following topics and relationships:

a) Alkali metals
b) Alkaline earth metals
c) Transition metals
d) Halogens
e) Noble gases

19. Contain elements in the solid, liquid, and gas phases at room temperature and 1 atm
20. Need to lose two electrons to form a stable octet
21. Will have the highest first ionization energy

Questions 22–25 refer to the following topics and relationships:

a) Hydrogen bond
b) Ionic bond
c) Network covalent bond
d) Non-polar covalent bond
e) Metallic bond

22. The type of bond between alkali metals and halogen atoms
23. The type of bond between the atoms in a nitrogen molecule
24. The type of bond among the diamond atoms
25. The type of bond that relates to the high boiling point of water

PART B

Directions: Each question below consists of two statements, I in the left-hand column and II in the right-hand column. For each question, determine whether statement I is true or false and whether statement II is true or false and then fill in the corresponding T or F circles on your answer sheet. Fill in circle CE only if statement II is a correct explanation of the true statement I.

On the actual Chemistry Test, the following type of question must be answered on a special section (labeled "Chemistry") at the lower left-hand corner of your answer sheet. These questions will be numbered beginning with 101 and must be answered according to the following directions.
Examples:

	I		II
EX 1.	H_2SO_4 is a strong acid	BECAUSE	H_2SO_4 contains sulfer.
EX 2.	An atom of oxygen is electrically neutral	BECAUSE	an oxygen atom contains an equal number of protons and electrons.

SAMPLE ANSWERS

	I		II		CE
EX 1.	●	Ⓕ	●	Ⓕ	○
EX 2.	●	Ⓕ	●	Ⓕ	●

	I		II
101.	Helium will have fewer dispersion forces among its atoms than the other noble gases	BECAUSE	As the mass of non-polar atoms and molecules increases, dispersion forces increase.
102.	NaCl has a higher melting point than KCl	BECAUSE	Na is smaller than K.
103.	The Gibbs free-energy equation can be used to predict the solubility of a solute	BECAUSE	The solubility of most salts increases as temperature increases.
104.	Copper is an oxidizing agent in the reaction with silver nitrate solution	BECAUSE	Copper loses electrons in a reaction with silver ions.
105.	1 M NaCl(aq) will have a higher boiling point than that of 1 M $CaCl_2$(aq)	BECAUSE	1 mole of NaCl yields 3 moles of ions in solution.
106.	Isotopes have different atomic numbers	BECAUSE	Isotopes must have different numbers of electrons.

107.	A catalyst accelerates a chemical reaction	BECAUSE	A catalyst lowers the activation energy of the reaction.
108.	HCl is considered to be an acid	BECAUSE	HCl is a proton acceptor.
109.	The burning of a piece of paper is a physical change	BECAUSE	Once burned, the chemical properties of the paper remain the same.
110.	Warmer air rises	BECAUSE	The density of gases decreases with increasing temperature.
111.	An ionic solid is a good conductor of electricity	BECAUSE	An ionic solid is composed of positive and negative ions joined together by electrostatic forces.
112.	Nitrogen has five valence electrons	BECAUSE	The electron configuration for nitrogen is $1s^22s^22p^6$.
113.	Powdered zinc reacts faster with acid than a larger piece of zinc	BECAUSE	Powdered zinc has a greater surface area.
114.	According to the KMT, collisions between gas particles and the walls of a container are elastic	BECAUSE	Gas molecules are considered volume-less particles, with no intermolecular forces, in constant random motion.
115.	SiO_2 is a solid and CO_2 is gaseous	BECAUSE	SiO_2 is a network covalent and CO_2 is a molecular covalent compound.

PART C

Directions: Each of the questions or incomplete statements below is followed by five suggested answers or completions. Select the one that is best in each case and then fill in the corresponding circle on the answer sheet.

26. If the pH of a solution changes from 6 to 5, which of the following statements is true?
    a) The pH of the solution now is one time more acidic than before.
    b) The solution now has 10 times more hydroxide ions than before.
    c) The pH of the solution is now 10 times more acidic than before.
    d) The solution is more basic now than before.
    e) The concentration of hydronium ion in the solution has decreased.

27. To what volume must the 10.0 mL of 5.00 M HCl be diluted in order to make a 0.500 M HCl solution?
    a) 1 mL
    b) 50 mL
    c) 100 mL
    d) 500 mL
    e) 1,000 mL

28. Consider the following reaction at equilibrium at 25 °C:
    $N_2(g) + 3H_2(g) \rightarrow 2NH_3(g)$ $\Delta G° = -33.3$ kJ
    Which of the following is NOT true?
    a) The quantity $\frac{[NH_3]^2}{[N2][H_2]^3}$ is >1 at equilibrium.
    b) $\Delta H°$ must be negative.
    c) The reaction is spontaneous under the conditions specified.
    d) $\Delta G°$ is independent of temperature.
    e) For the equilibrium $2NH_3(g) \rightarrow N_2(g) + 3H_2(g)$, we expect that $\Delta G° = 33.3$ kJ.

29. Balance the equation $C_2H_6 + O_2 \rightarrow CO_2 + H_2O$ by using the lowest whole number coefficients. What is the sum of the coefficients?
    a) 4
    b) 9
    c) 19
    d) 15
    e) 11

30. Which of the following statements about intramolecular bonding is correct?
    a) Van der Waals forces exist between polar molecules.
    b) Dipoles are the result of the equal sharing of electrons.
    c) Cu(s) is a network solid.
    d) Hydrogen bonds exist between the molecules of HCl.
    e) NaCl(aq) has attractions between the molecules and the ions.

31. In the equation: X $\rightarrow {}^{226}_{88}Ra + {}^{4}_{2}He$, what is X?
    a) ${}^{222}_{86}Th$
    b) ${}^{230}_{90}Th$
    c) ${}^{231}_{90}Th$
    d) ${}^{222}_{86}Rn$
    e) ${}^{230}_{90}Rn$

32. Which pair of elements is expected to have the most similar properties?
    a) Potassium and lithium
    b) Sulfur and phosphorus
    c) Silicon and carbon
    d) Strontium and barium
    e) Fluorine and iodine

33. The dissociation percentage of an ionic solution can be best estimated by using which of the following?
    I. Osmotic pressure
    II. Freezing-point depression
    III. Vapor pressure
    IV. Raoult's law
    V. Henry's law
    a) I and III only
    b) II only
    c) III and V only
    d) IV only
    e) V only

34. An element with an atomic number of 26 has how many electrons in the 3d orbital?
    a) 0
    b) 2
    c) 6
    d) 8
    e) 10

35. Which of the following statements about the process of gas collection is FALSE?
    a) Carbon dioxide can be collected by an upward displacement of air.
    b) The presence of ammonia can be tested by placing red litmus paper at the mouth of the collection glassware.
    c) Ammonia can be collected by water displacement.
    d) Hydrogen gas can be collected by water displacement.
    e) The presence of carbon dioxide can be tested by a lit match.

36. The half-life of a radioactive isotope is 10.0 minutes. What is the total amount of a 1.00-gram sample of this isotope remaining after 0.5 hours?
    a) 0.500 g
    b) 0.333 g
    c) 0.250 g
    d) 0.125 g
    e) 0.0625 g

37. Using the bond dissociation energies as seen in the table below, calculate the change in the heat of reaction of $2H_2 + O_2 \rightarrow 2H_2O$.

Bonds	Bond Dissociation Energies in kJ/mole
H–H	435
O–H	462
O–O	145

    a) −118 kJ
    b) +118 kJ
    c) −91 kJ
    d) −1,042 kJ
    e) −833 kJ

38. A synthesis reaction will occur spontaneously after the activation energy is provided if the heat of formation of the product is
    a) large and negative.
    b) small and negative.
    c) large and positive.
    d) small and positive.
    e) All of the above

39. According to the equation, $4Fe + 3O_2 \rightarrow 2Fe_2O_3$, how many grams of Fe_2O_3 can be formed from 558 grams of Fe and an excess of oxygen?
    a) 200 grams
    b) 300 grams
    c) 400 grams
    d) 600 grams
    e) 800 grams

40. What functional groups are present in the compound below?

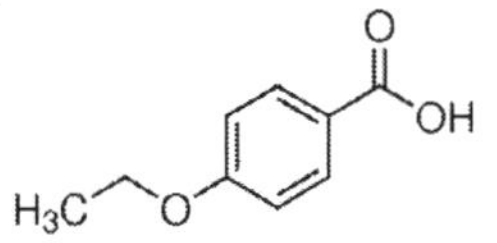

    (structure: H_3C–CH_2–O–C_6H_4–C(=O)OH)

    a) Ester and ether
    b) Ester and amine
    c) Ester and carboxylic acid
    d) Ether and carboxylic acid
    e) Ether and ketone

41. What is the potential of the reaction below based on the given half-reaction potentials?

    $2Fe^{2+} + Cl_2 \rightarrow 2Fe^{3+} + 2Cl^-$

    $Fe^{3+} + e^- \rightarrow Fe^{2+}$ E = 0.77 V

    $Cl_2 + 2e^- \rightarrow 2Cl^-$ E = 1.36 V

    a) 0.18 V
    b) 0.59 V
    c) 1.05 V
    d) 2.13 V
    e) 2.90 V

42. Which of the following is true?
    a) The Bohr model applies to ^4He.
    b) The spectrum of hydrogen in the visible region of the electromagnetic spectrum is continuous.
    c) The electron is in the most stable state in its smallest allowed orbit.
    d) The electron in a hydrogen atom may circulate in either a circular or elliptical orbit.
    e) To remove an electron from the
    n = 2 level, the absorption of more energy than removal of a ground-state electron is required.

43. Which of the following is a homogeneous mixture?
    a) KI(aq)
    b) Fe(s)
    c) CO_2(g)
    d) NH_3(l)
    e) NaCl(s)

44. What is the pOH of a solution with $[H^+] = 0.001$ M?
    a) −3
    b) 1
    c) 3
    d) 11
    e) 14

45. Which of the following is the LEAST likely to have allotropes?
    a) S
    b) P
    c) H
    d) Se
    e) Sn

46. $CH_4(g) + 2O_2(g) \rightarrow CO_2(g) + 2H_2O(l)$ According to the equation above, how many grams of methane gas were burned if 67.2 liter of carbon dioxide gas are produced in the reaction? (Assume STP.)
    a) 16 grams
    b) 48 grams
    c) 3 grams
    d) 132 grams
    e) 22.4 grams

47. $A + B \rightarrow 2C \quad \Delta H = -500\ kJ$
$D + 2B \rightarrow E \quad \Delta H = -700\ kJ$
$2D + 2A \rightarrow F \quad \Delta H = +50\ kJ$
According to the reactions shown above, find the heat of reaction for $F + 6B \rightarrow 2E + 4C$.
   a) +450 kJ
   b) −1,100 kJ
   c) +2,350 kJ
   d) −350 kJ
   e) −2,450 kJ

48. If the pressure of a gas sample is doubled at constant temperature, the volume will be
   a) 4 times of the original.
   b) 2 times of the original.
   c) ½ of the original.
   d) ¼ of the original.
   e) ⅛ of the original.

49. When molten NaBr is electrolyzed, which reaction occurs at the anode?
   a) $Na^{+1} + e^- \rightarrow Na(s)$
   b) $2Br^{-2} \rightarrow Br_2 + 2e^-$
   c) $Na(s) \rightarrow Na^{+1} + 1e^-$
   d) $Br_2 \rightarrow Br^- + 2e-$
   e) $Br_2 + 2e^- \rightarrow 2Br^{-1}$

Questions 50 – 51 refer to the following information:

$A(g) + B(g) \rightarrow$ Products

Experiment	*[A] mole/L*	*[B] mole/L*	*Initial Rate (M/s)*
1	0.06	0.01	0.04
2	0.03	0.01	0.04
3	0.03	0.02	0.08

50. Based on the reaction and rate data above, what is the order of the reaction with respect to B?
   a) 0
   b) 1
   c) 2
   d) 3
   e) 4

51. Based on the reaction and rate data above, what is the rate constant?
   a) 0
   b) 1
   c) 2
   d) 3
   e) 4

52. Which compound will be insoluble in water?
   I. Ammonium ion
   II. Calcium ion
   III. Bromide ion
   IV. Iron(III)
   V. Phosphate ion
   a) I and V only
   b) III and I only
   c) II and III only
   d) III and IV only
   e) IV and V only

53. The pH of a solution that has a hydrogen ion concentration of 1×10^{-4} M is
   a) 4
   b) −4
   c) 10
   d) −10
   e) 1×10^{-4}

54. Which of the following is colored in an aqueous solution?
   I. $Cu(NH_3)_4^{+2}$
   II. KOH
   III. HCO_3^-
   IV. CO_3^{-2}
   V. SO_3^{-2}
   a) I
   b) II
   c) III
   d) IV
   e) V

55. Order the following, from highest to lowest, with respect to their boiling points.

I. CF_4
II. $CaCl_2$
III. ICl

a) I, II, III
b) I, III, II
c) II, III, I
d) III, II, I
e) III, I, II

56. How much heat is required to raise the temperature of 100 grams of water from 280 K to 340 K?

a) 5,270 J
b) 355 J
c) 259 J
d) 15,100 J
e) 25,200 J

57. What is the $\Delta G°$ for the following reaction equation (Faraday's constant is ***F*** C/mol)?

$Ti^{2+}(aq) + Mg(s) \rightarrow Ti(s) + Mg^{+2}(aq)$
$Ti^{+2}(aq) + 2e^- \rightarrow Ti(s)$ $E° = -1.63$ V
$Mg^{+2}(aq) + 2e^- \rightarrow Mg(s)$ $E° = -2.38$ V

a) 1 ***F*** J
b) 1.5 ***F*** J
c) -1 ***F*** J
d) −1.5 ***F*** J
e) −2 ***F*** J

58. Which of the following methods can be chosen to determine the molecular mass of large biomolecules?

a) Osmotic pressure
b) Freezing-point depression
c) Vapor pressure
d) Raoult's law
e) Henry's law

59. Which of the following gases is/are found in the acid rain?

I. CFCs
II. Methane
III. Carbon dioxide

a) I only
b) II only
c) III only
d) I and III only
e) I, II, and III

60. What is the units of the equilibrium constant, Kc, for the following reaction: $CH_4(g) + 3O_2(g) \rightarrow CO_2(g) + 2H_2O(g)$?

a) M^{-2}
b) M^2
c) M
d) M^{-1}
e) M^3

61. Which of the following reactions does not form a precipitate?

a) $Ag^{+1} + Cl^{-1}$
b) $Pb^{+2} + 2I^{-1}$
c) $Ca^{+2} + CO_3^{-2}$
d) $Hg^{+2} + 2Br^{-1}$
e) $Na^{+1} + OH^{-1}$

62. Which of the following half reactions is correctly balanced?

a) $MnO_4^{-1} \rightarrow Mn^{+2} + 4H_2O$
b) $Cu + 2Ag^{+1} \rightarrow 2Ag + Cu^{+2}$
c) $H_2 + OH^{-1} \rightarrow 2H_2O$
d) $Pb^{+2} + 2e^- \rightarrow Pb$
e) $2F^- + 2e^- \rightarrow F_2$

63. Which of the following statements is true regarding the percent composition by mass in $C_6H_{12}O_6$?

a) Carbon is 6.7% by mass.
b) Oxygen is 53.3% by mass.
c) Hydrogen is 12% by mass.
d) Carbon is 72% by mass.
e) Carbon is 20% by mass.

64. Which of the following compounds is incorrectly classified?
    a) NaF electrolyte
    b) CH_3OH weak electrolyte
    c) $Mg(C_2H_3O_2)_2$ electrolyte
    d) CH_3CH_2COOH weak electrolyte
    e) glucose nonelectrolyte

65. The functional group shown below represents a(n)

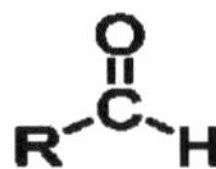

    a) alcohol.
    b) ether.
    c) aldehyde.
    d) ketone.
    e) organic acid derivative.

66. The ratio of the rate of diffusion of oxygen to hydrogen is
    a) 1 : 2
    b) 1 : 4
    c) 1 : 8
    d) 4 : 1
    e) 1 : 32

67. On the basis of this heating curve, which of the following statements is correct about the substance?

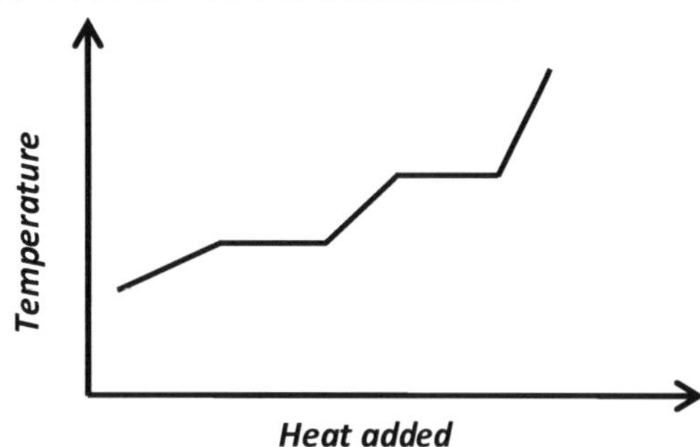

    a) The substance can be cooled easily.
    b) The gas is a metastable state.
    c) The substance must be a salt that dissociates on heating.
    d) The density of the liquid is greater than that of the solid.
    e) The specific heat can be determined if the mass is known.

68. Which of the following molecules has the most pi bonds?
    a) CBr_4
    b) PF_5
    c) NH_3
    d) SO_3
    e) HCN

69. The K_w of water is equal to
    a) 1×10^{-7}.
    b) 1×10^{-17}.
    c) 1×10^{-14}.
    d) 1×10^{-1}.
    e) 2×10^{-7}.

70. The equilibrium expression, $K = [CO_2]$, represents the reaction of
    a) $C(s) + O_2(g) \leftrightarrow CO_2(g)$.
    b) $CO(g) + \frac{1}{2} O_2(g) \leftrightarrow CO_2(g)$.
    c) $CaCO_3(s) \leftrightarrow CaO(s) + CO_2(g)$.
    d) $CO_2(g) \leftrightarrow C(s) + O_2(g)$.
    e) $CaO(s) + CO_2(g) \leftrightarrow CaCO_3(s)$.

SAT Chemistry Subject Test No. 7 Keys

1. C	11. A	21. E	31. B	41. B	51. E	61. E
2. E	12. C	22. B	32. D	42. C	52. E	62. D
3. C	13. A	23. D	33. B	43. A	53. A	63. B
4. A	14. E	24. C	34. C	44. D	54. A	64. B
5. B	15. D	25. A	35. C	45. C	55. C	65. C
6. C	16. E	26. C	36. D	46. B	56. E	66. B
7. D	17. C	27. C	37. E	47. E	57. D	67. E
8. C	18. A	28. D	38. A	48. C	58. A	68. E
9. B	19. D	29. C	39. E	49. B	59. C	69. C
10. D	20. B	30. E	40. D	50. B	60. D	70. C

101.	TTCE	106.	FF	111.	FT
102.	TT	107.	TTCE	112.	TF
103.	FT	108.	TF	113.	TTCE
104.	FT	109.	FF	114.	TTCE
105.	TF	110.	TTCE	115.	TTCE

SAT Chemistry Subject Test No. 7 Answer to Part A

1 – 3 *Answer: (cec)*

The volume of a gas increases as temperature increases, provided that pressure remains constant. This is a direct proportion. Heating a balloon is a good example.

The volume of a gas decreases as the pressure increases, provided that the temperature is held constant. This is shown by the inversely proportional curve in c). Pressure increase in a closed cylinder is a good example.

Henry's law: At a constant temperature, the amount of a given gas that dissolves in a liquid is directly proportional to the partial pressure of that gas in equilibrium with that liquid.

4 – 7 *Answer: (abcd)*

The changing of a solid to a gas without a liquid phase is called sublimation.

Deposition is the changing of a gas to a solid without a liquid phase.

Vaporization of a liquid will cause the liquid to enter the gas phase.

Freezing a liquid will turn the liquid into a solid.

8 – 11 *Answer: (cbda)*

Elements cannot be broken down chemically.

Cations are ions that are positive in charge.

Isotopes are atoms of the same element that have a different number of neutrons.

Isomers are molecules with the same chemical formula but different chemical structures.

12 – 15 *Answer: (caed)*

The 1s orbital is filled with two electrons in the lithium atom.

The helium atom has a filled 1s orbital.

The electron configurations of the transition metals are in the d-orbitals.

The element with the highest electronegativity is F, 2p.

16 – 18 *Answer: (eca)*

Electrolytic cells use an electric current to drive a redox reaction.

Calorimeters are used to measure the heat of formation.

Barometers are used to measure the air pressure.

19 – 21 *Answer: (dbe)*

Fluorine and chlorine are gases at STP, while bromine is a liquid and iodine is a solid.

The alkali earth metals have a valence electron configuration of s^2 and need to lose two electrons to form a stable ion.

Noble gases have the highest first ionization energies in the period.

22 – 25 *Answer: (bdca)*

Alkali metal and halogen form ionic bonds.

A diatomic molecule always has non-polar covalent bonds.

Diamond has network covalent bonds.

Water has abnormal boiling points because of its hydrogen bonds.

SAT Chemistry Subject Test No. 7 Answer to Part C

26. *Answer: (c)*
$pH = -\log[H^+]$
When pH changes by a value of 1.0, the $[H^+]$ changes by a factor of 10.
Because the pH value dropped, the solution has become more acidic.

27. *Answer: (c)*
$10 \times 5 = x \times 0.5$
$x = 100\ ml$

28. *Answer: (d)*
$\Delta G = \Delta G° + RTln(\frac{[NH_3]^2}{[N_2][H_2]^3})$
At equilibrium, $\Delta G = 0$
$0 = \Delta G° + RTln(\frac{[NH_3]^2}{[N_2][H_2]^3})$
$\frac{[NH_3]^2}{[N_2][H_2]^3} = exp(\frac{-\Delta G^o}{RT}) > 1$
$\Delta G^o = \Delta H^o - T\Delta S^o$
ΔS^o *is negative (less randomness).*
ΔH^o *must be negative to make* $\Delta G°$ *a negative.*
The reaction is spontaneous because of its negative $\Delta G°$.
$\Delta G°$ *is a state function. Reversing a reaction will reverse its* $\Delta G°$.
$\Delta G°$ *is a temperature dependent function.*

29. *Answer: (c)*
$2C_2H_6 + 7O_2 \rightarrow 4CO_2 + 6H_2O$.

30. *Answer: (e)*
When ions are dissolved in water to make a solution, there is an attraction between the polar water molecules and the charged ions. This is called the molecule-ion attraction.

31. *Answer: (b)*
By balancing atomic mass and numbers, we get that x is ${}^{230}_{90}Th$.

32. *Answer: (d)*
Strontium and barium are the same family and close to each other.

33. *Answer: (b)*
Using freezing-point depression can determine ion pairing in a electrolytic solution.

34. *Answer: (c)*
$[Ar]4s^23d^6$ *has 26 electrons.*

35. *Answer: (c)*
Ammonia is a polar molecule and will dissolve in a polar substance like water. This means that water displacement is a poor method for the collection of ammonia.

36. *Answer: (d)*
0.5 hour = 3 half-lives
$(\frac{1}{2})^3 \times 1 = 0.125\ g$

37. *Answer: (e)*
$[2(H-H) + 1(O-O)] - [4(H-O)]$
$[2(435) + 1(145)] - [4(462)]$
$= [870 + 145] - [1,848]$
$= [1,015] - [1,848] = -833\ kJ$

38. *Answer: (a)*
$\Delta G = \Delta H - T\Delta S$
When ΔG *is negative, the reaction will occur spontaneously. A large, negative* ΔH *is needed to make* ΔG *a negative value.*

39. *Answer: (e)*
558 grams of Fe (atomic mass = 55.8) is 10 moles of iron. If 10 moles of Fe react, then according to the balanced equation, 5 moles of Fe_2O_3 *should be produced. 5 moles of* Fe_2O_3 *(molar mass = 160) is 800 grams.*

40. *Answer: (d)*
$R-O-CH_3$ *and* $R'-COOH$ *are present in the compound.*

41. *Answer: (b)*
$1.36 - 0.77 = 0.59V$

42. *Answer: (c)*
The Bohr model only applies to the hydrogen atom.
The spectrum of hydrogen in the visible region is discontinuous.
(c) is correct.
The electron in hydrogen goes in a circular orbit.
The removal of a ground-state electron needs more energy.

43. *Answer: (a)*
By definition, an aqueous solution must be homogeneous. The KI(aq) is a homogeneous solution of water and KI.

44. *Answer: (d)*
$[H^+] = 0.001\ M = 10^{-3}$
$[OH^-] = \frac{10^{-14}}{10^{-3}} = 10^{-11}$
$pOH = -\log[OH^-] = 11$

45. *Answer: (c)*
H_2 *is a gas.*

46. *Answer: (b)*
67.2 liters of carbon dioxide equals 3 moles of carbon dioxide. Because carbon dioxide and methane are in a 1 : 1 ratio, for each mole of carbon dioxide produced, 1 mole of methane was reacted. This means that 3 moles of methane were burned. Because the molar mass of methane is 16 g/mol, 3 moles of methane would weigh 48 grams.

47. *Answer: (e)*
$A + B \rightarrow 2C \quad \Delta H = -500\ kJ$
$D + 2B \rightarrow E \quad \Delta H = -700\ kJ$
$2D + 2A \rightarrow F \quad \Delta H = +50\ kJ$
$F + 6B \rightarrow 2E + 4C\ \Delta H = 2(-500) + 2(-700) - (+50) = -2450\ kJ$

48. *Answer: (c)*
$P_1V_1 = P_2V_2$
The pressure and the volume are inversely proportional to each other.

49. *Answer: (b)*
Remember the mnemonic device, "An Ox," and that oxidation occurs at the anode. This means that the half reaction at the anode will show a loss of electrons. The negatively charged bromine ions will serve this purpose. The half reaction must also be written correctly.

50. *Answer: (b)*
The reaction rate quadruples when the concentration of B doubles.
$R \propto [B]^2$ *,it is a 2nd order reaction with respect to [B].*

51. *Answer: (e)*
Doubling [A], the rate of the reaction is the same.
Doubling [B], the rate of the reaction is also doubled.
$R = k[B]$
$0.04 = 0.01 \times k$
$k = 4$

52. *Answer: (e)*
Iron(III) phosphate is insoluble in water.

53. *Answer: (a)*
$[H^+] = 10^{-4}$
$pH = -\log[10^{-4}] = 4$

54. *Answer: (a)*
$Cu(NH_3)_4^{+2}$ *has blue color in the aqueous solution.*

55. *Answer: (c)*
Boiling point: ionic bonds > polar covalent bond > non – polar covalent bond

56. *Answer: (e)*
The amount of heat absorbed by water can be calculated using the equation $q = mc\Delta T$ *= (100 grams)(4.2J/g K)(60 K) =25200 J.*

57. *Answer: (d)*
$\Delta E^o = 0.75$
$\Delta G^\circ = -nF\Delta E^o = -2 \times F \times (0.75) = -1.5F$

58. *Answer: (a)*
Osmotic Pressure $(\pi) = MRT$
M: molarity of the solution
R: gas constant
T: temperature in K
From molarity in the solution, we can determine the molar mass of the solute.

59. *Answer: (c)*
Carbon dioxide and water can react to produce carbonic acid. CFCs are responsible for causing a hole in the ozone layer and methane is a greenhouse gas that can trap heat on earth.

60. *Answer: (d)*
$Kc = \frac{[H_2O]^2[CO_2]}{[CH_4][O_2]^3} = \frac{1}{M}$

61. *Answer: (e)*
Halides of lead, mercury, and silver will form precipitates, so choices A, B, and D are all precipitates. Calcium carbonate is also a solid. Sodium hydroxide is soluble in water.

62. *Answer: (d)*
The reaction Pb2+ + 2e – .Pb shows conservation of mass and charge. Notice that choice B is not a half reaction; it is a full redox reaction that is properly balanced.

63. *Answer: (b)*
The total mass of this compound is 180. The oxygen makes up 96 of the 180, which is about 53%.

64. *Answer: (b)*
CH_3OH is a nonelectrolyte compound.

65. *Answer: (c)*

Aldehyde: 

66. *Answer: (b)*
The rate of diffusion of oxygen to hydrogen is equal to $\sqrt{2} : \sqrt{32} = 1 : 4$.

67. *Answer: (e)*
The specific heat of the substance can be determined by the slope and amount of mass.

68. *Answer: (e)*
HC≡N
One triple bond has 2 pi bonds.

69. *Answer: (c)*
$H_2O_{(l)} \rightarrow H^+ + OH^-$
At 25 °C in pure water, $[H+] = [OH-] = 10^{-7}$
$K_w = [1 \times 10^{-7}]^2 = 1 \times 10^{-14}$

70. *Answer: (c)*
Pure solids are not part of the equation of equilibrium constant.

SAT Chemistry Subject Test No 8.

PART A

Directions: Each set of lettered choices below refers to the numbered statements or questions immediately following it. Select the one lettered choice that best fits each statement and then fill in the corresponding circle on the answer sheet. A given choice may be used once, more than once, or not at all in each set.

Note: For all questions involving solutions, assume that the solvent is water unless otherwise stated. Throughout the test the following symbols have the definitions specified unless otherwise noted.

H = enthalpy	T = temperature	L = liter(s)
M = molar	V = volume	mL = milliliter(s)
n = number of moles	atm = atmosphere(s)	mm = millimeter(s)
P = pressure	g = gram(s)	mol = mole(s)
R = molar gas constant	J = joule(s)	V = volt(s)
S = entropy	kJ = kilojoule(s)	

Questions 1–4 refer to the following topics and relationships:

a) $PV = nRT$
b) $P_1V_1 = P_2V_2$
c) $\frac{V_1}{T_1} = \frac{V_2}{T_2}$
d) $\Delta T_b = i \times k_b \times m$
e) $\Delta E = Q + w$

1. This equation represents Boyle's Law.
2. This equation represents the 1st law of thermodynamics.
3. This equation represents the ideal gas law.
4. This equation represents Charles's Law.

Questions 5–8 refer to the following topics and relationships:

a) A buffer solution
b) A pH indicator
c) Arrhenius acid
d) The Brønsted-Lowry acid
e) Amphoteric substance

5. Exhibits different colors in acidic and basic solutions.
6. A solution that can be added a strong acid or base to the solution without causing a large change in the pH scale.
7. The chemical compound that provides hydrogen ions, H^+, in an aqueous solution.
8. An oxide of an element that can act as either an acid or a base.

Questions 9–11 refer to the following topics and relationships:

a) $1s^2$
b) $1s^22s^22p^63s^23p^64s^23d^{10}4p^5$
c) $1s^22s^22p^63s^23p^64s^2$
d) $1s^22s^22p^63s^23p^64s^1$
e) $1s^22s^22p^5$

9. The electron configuration for a non-metal liquid element at STP
10. The electron configuration for an element with the highest electronegativity
11. The electron configuration for the noble gas with the highest first ionization energy

Questions 12–14 refer to the following topics and relationships:

a) Alpha particle
b) Beta particle
c) Neutron
d) Gamma ray
e) Positron

12. This particle has the greatest mass.
13. This particle has the highest energy.
14. This particle has the same mass but opposite charge of an electron.

Questions 15–18 refer to the following topics and relationships:

a) H_2
b) CO_2
c) H_2O
d) NaCl
e) CH_2CH_2

15. This molecule contains just one sigma bond.
16. This molecule has a bond formed from the transfer of electrons.
17. This molecule has an atom that is *sp* hybridized.
18. This molecule is a polar molecule.

Questions 19–22 refer to the following topics and relationships:

a) The critical point in the phase diagram
b) The triple point in the phase diagram
c) The point of the highest potential energy in the reaction coordinate diagram
d) The freezing point
e) The boiling point

19. The point where the substance is indistinguishable between liquid and gaseous states.
20. The point where solid, liquid, and gas phases exist simultaneously.
21. The point where vapor pressure of a liquid is equal to the pressure of the surroundings.
22. The point where the activated complex exists.

Questions 23–25 refer to the following topics and relationships:

a) Alkali metals
b) Alkaline earth metals
c) Transition metals
d) Halogens
e) Noble gases

23. The most stable group of elements
24. A group containing elements in the solid, liquid, and gas phases at STP conditions.
25. A group with the strongest reducing agent.

PART B

Directions: Each question below consists of two statements, I in the left-hand column and II in the right-hand column. For each question, determine whether statement I is true or false and whether statement II is true or false and then fill in the corresponding T or F circles on your answer sheet. Fill in circle CE only if statement II is a correct explanation of the true statement I.

On the actual Chemistry Test, the following type of question must be answered on a special section (labeled "Chemistry") at the lower left-hand corner of your answer sheet. These questions will be numbered beginning with 101 and must be answered according to the following directions.

Examples:

	I		II
EX 1.	H_2SO_4 is a strong acid	BECAUSE	H_2SO_4 contains sulfer.
EX 2.	An atom of oxygen is electrically neutral	BECAUSE	an oxygen atom contains an equal number of protons and electrons.

SAMPLE ANSWERS

	I		II		CE
EX 1.	●	(F)	●	(F)	○
EX 2.	●	(F)	●	(F)	●

	I		II
101.	According to the kinetic molecular theory, the particles of a gas are in random motion above absolute zero	BECAUSE	The velocity of the gas molecule varies inversely with the temperature of the gas.
102.	1, 1-dichloropropane and 1, 2-dichloropropane are constitutional isomers	BECAUSE	Both compounds contain one double bond.
103.	The activation energy of the forward reaction must be equal to the activation energy of the reverse reaction	BECAUSE	At equilibrium, the rates of the forward and reverse reactions are equal.
104.	Water is a good solvent for ionic and/or polar covalent substances	BECAUSE	Water shows hydrogen bonding between oxygen atoms.
105.	Water has a surprisingly high boiling point compared to the compound SO_2	BECAUSE	During boiling, covalent bonds between O and H are broken.

106.	The volume of a gas at 100 °C and a pressure of 600 torr will be less than at STP conditions	BECAUSE	To calculate the relationship among volume, pressure, and temperature, use $\frac{V_1P1}{T_1} = \frac{V_2P_2}{T2}$.
107.	Absolute zero is equal to -273 degrees Celsius	BECAUSE	C = K + 273.
108.	The most penetrating nuclear radiation is γ-rays	BECAUSE	γ-ray is the highest mass radioactive particle.
109.	A nonspontaneous redox reaction occurs in an electrolytic cell	BECAUSE	An electrolytic cell uses an external current to drive a redox reaction.
110.	N_2 has non-polar covalent bonds	BECAUSE	There is an equal sharing of electrons between nitrogen atoms.
111.	The maximum number of electrons allowed in the third principal energy level is 18	BECAUSE	The maximum number of electrons allowed in a principal energy level n equals $2n^2$.
112.	Cl^{-1} is the conjugate base of HCl	BECAUSE	A conjugate base is formed once a Brønsted-Lowry acid accepts a proton.
113.	At STP conditions, ammonia gas, NH_3, has a lower density than argon gas, Ar	BECAUSE	At STP conditions, all ideal gases have the same molar volume of 22.4 liters.
114.	Magnesium has a lower melting point than Aluminum	BECAUSE	Al has one unpaired electron on its 3d orbital.
115.	Fluorine has the highest electronegativity out of all the elements	BECAUSE	Fluorine has the greatest electron affinity.

PART C

Directions: Each of the questions or incomplete statements below is followed by five suggested answers or completions. Select the one that is best in each case and then fill in the corresponding circle on the answer sheet.

26. An indicator has a K_a of 1×10^{-6}. The conjugate acid shows up red and the conjugate base shows up yellow. At what pH will the solution be red?
    a) 5.2
    b) 5.5
    c) 4.0
    d) 6.0
    e) 6.4

27. A reaction at equilibrium may be forced to completion by
    a) adding a catalyst.
    b) increasing the pressure.
    c) increasing the temperature.
    d) removing the products from the reaction mixture as they are formed.
    e) decreasing the reactant concentration.

28. Which of the following statements is FALSE?
    a) H_2 has just one sigma bond.
    b) HCl has just one sigma bond.
    c) H–C≡C–H has four pi bonds and three sigma bonds.
    d) $CH_2=CH_2$ has five sigma bonds and one pi bond.
    e) H_2O has two sigma bonds and two lone pairs.

29. How many moles of hydrogen sulfide are contained in a 35.0 g sample of this gas?
    a) 1.03 moles
    b) 2.06 moles
    c) 6.18 moles
    d) 9.45 moles
    e) 11.3 moles

30. The value of the equilibrium constant, K, is dependent on which of the following?
    I. The temperature of the system.
    II. The concentration of the reactants.
    III. The concentration of the products.
    IV. The nature of the reactants and products.
    a) I, II only
    b) II, III only
    c) III, IV only
    d) I and IV only
    e) I, II, and IV

31. The cathode in an electrochemical cell is the electrode that is
    a) always negative.
    b) always positive.
    c) always neutral.
    d) the electrode at which reduction takes place.
    e) None of the above

32. Which of the following has the highest pH?
    a) 0.1 M HCl
    b) 0.2 M $HC_2H_3O_2$
    c) 0.1 M Na_2CO_3
    d) 0.2 M NaCl
    e) 0.5 M $NaC_2H_3O_2$

33. For an ideal gas, which of the following quantities will be pressure dependent?
    I. Enthalpy
    II. Entropy
    III. Gibbs free energy
    a) I only
    b) II only
    c) I and II only
    d) II and III only
    e) I, II and III

34. At 25°C, which of the following is not true for a solution that has a hydroxide concentration of 1.0×10^{-6} M?
    a) $K_w = 1 \times 10^{-14}$
    b) The solution is acidic.
    c) The solution is basic.
    d) The $[H^+]$ is 1×10^{-8} M.
    e) The pOH equals 6.0.

35. Which of the following instruments would be best suited for use in a volumetric analysis to calculate the molarity of a base when titrated with a known acid?
    a) Graduated cylinder
    b) Pipette
    c) 250 mL beaker
    d) Burette
    e) Triple beam balance

36. An ideal gas in a closed inflexible container has a pressure of 6 atm and a temperature of 27 °C. What will be the new pressure at −73 °C?
    a) 2 atm
    b) 3 atm
    c) 4 atm
    d) 8 atm
    e) 9 atm

37. If 171 grams of sucrose (molecular mass = 342 g) are dissolved in 1,000 grams of water, what will be the freezing point of this solution?
    a) −0.93 °C
    b) −1.86 °C
    c) −3.72 °C
    d) −6.58 °C
    e) None of the above

38. Hydrocarbons containing only single bonds between the carbon atoms are called
    a) Alkenes
    b) Alkynes
    c) Aromatics
    d) Alkanes
    e) Ketones

39. $CaSO_4(s) \rightarrow Ca^{+2}(aq) + SO_4^{-2}(aq)$
    According to the equation above, which of the following statements is true when the sodium sulfate is added to a saturated solution of $CaSO_4$?
    a) The solubility of the calcium sulfate will decrease.
    b) The concentration of calcium ions will increase.
    c) The reaction will shift to the right.
    d) The Ksp value will change.
    e) The equilibrium will shift to compensate for the decrease in sulfate ions.

40. The correct name for N_2O_3 is
    a) dinitrogen tetroxide.
    b) dinitrogen trioxide.
    c) dinitrogen oxide.
    d) trinitrogen dioxide.
    e) nitric anhydride.

41. Heating 10 grams of water from 4 °C to 14 °C requires
    a) 10 cal.
    b) 14 cal.
    c) 100 cal.
    d) 140 cal.
    e) None of the above

42. Chemical properties of elements are defined by the
    a) electrons.
    b) ionization energy.
    c) protons.
    d) neutrons.
    e) electronegativity.

43. Which of the following is/are true regarding the aqueous dissociation of HCN, $K_a = 4.9 \times 10^{-10}$ at 25 °C?
    I. At equilibrium, $[H^+] = [CN^-]$
    II. At equilibrium, $[H^+] = [HCN]$
    III. HCN is a strong acid.
    a) I only
    b) II only
    c) I and II only
    d) II and III only
    e) I, II and III

44. Substance Z has three common isotopes: **Z**-24, **Z**-25, and **Z**-26. If the relative abundances of these isotopes are 40%, 50%, and 10%, respectively, what is the atomic mass of substance X?
    a) 24.5
    b) 24.7
    c) 24.9
    d) 25.0
    e) 25.1

45. A self-sustaining fission chain reaction depends upon the release of
    a) protons.
    b) neutrons.
    c) electrons.
    d) alpha particles.
    e) energy.

46. An unknown compound contains the elements C, H, and O. It is known to contain 48% C and 4.0% H by mass. The molar mass of this compound has been determined in the lab to have a value of 200. The molecular formula for this compound is
    a) $C_2H_3O_2$
    b) $C_4H_6O_4$
    c) $C_4H_4O_3$
    d) $C_8H_3O_6$
    e) $C_8H_8O_6$

47. The following redox reaction occurs in an acidic solution: $Ce^{+4} + Bi \rightarrow Ce^{+3} + BiO^{+1}$. What is the coefficient before Ce^{+4} when the equation is fully balanced?
    a) 1
    b) 2
    c) 3
    d) 6
    e) 9

48. Which of the following process(es) would have a positive value of the changed entropy?
    I. The expansion of the universe
    II. The condensation of a liquid
    III. A food fight in a school cafeteria
    a) I only
    b) II only
    c) III only
    d) II and III only
    e) I and III only

49. Which of the following is expected to have the most electron affinity?
    a) Cl
    b) S
    c) O
    d) Li
    e) H

50. Given the equation ${}^{14}_{6}C \rightarrow {}^{14}_{7}N + X$, which of the following particles is represented by the letter X?
    a) An alpha particle
    b) A beta particle
    c) A neutron
    d) A proton
    e) A positron

51. If an exothermic process is spontaneous, which of the following statements must be true?
    a) ΔG must be positive.
    b) ΔS must be positive.
    c) ΔS must be negative.
    d) The temperature must be over 500K.
    e) ΔG must be negative.

52. When going from $1s^2 2s^2 2p^6 3s^2 3p^6 4s^1$ to $1s^2 2s^2 2p^6 3s^2 3p^5 4s^2$, an electron would
    a) absorb energy.
    b) emit energy.
    c) relax to the ground state.
    d) bind to another atom.
    e) undergo no change in energy.

53. A 600 mL container holds 2 moles of O_2, 3 moles of H_2, and 1 mole of He. The total pressure within the container is 760 torr. What is the partial pressure of O_2?
    a) 127 torr
    b) 253 torr
    c) 380 torr
    d) 507 torr
    e) 760 torr

54. Aluminum reacts with sulfur gas to form aluminum sulfide. If 27.0 g of aluminum are reacted in excess sulfur, what is the theoretical yield of aluminum sulfide?
    a) 50 g
    b) 75 g
    c) 125 g
    d) 150 g
    e) 175 g

55. Which of the following must be measured in order to calculate the molality of a solution?
    I. Mass of the solute
    II. Mass of the solvent
    III. Total volume of the solution
    a) I only
    b) I and III only
    c) II and III only
    d) I and II only
    e) I, II, and III

56. Which of the following pairs of substances can be broken down chemically?
    a) Ammonia and iron
    b) Helium and argon
    c) Methane and water
    d) Potassium and lithium
    e) Water and carbon

57. What is the pH of a solution with a hydroxide ion concentration of 0.00001 M?
    a) −5
    b) −1
    c) 5
    d) 9
    e) 14

58. Which of the following aqueous solutions is expected to have the highest boiling point?
    a) 1.5 m $FeCl_2$
    b) 3.0 m CH_3OH
    c) 2.5 m $C_6H_{12}O_6$
    d) 2.5 m NaCl
    e) 1.0 m $CaCl_2$

59. The standard reduction potential of $Cr^{+3}(aq) + 3e^- \rightarrow Cr(s)$ is 0.74V. The standard reduction potential of $Cl_2(g) + 2e^- \rightarrow 2Cl^-(aq)$ is 1.36V. Based on the information given, it must be true that
    a) Cl_2 is more easily oxidized than Cr^{+3}, so Cl_2 is a better oxidizing agent than Cr^{+3}.
    b) Cl_2 is more easily oxidized than Cr^{+3}, so Cl_2 is a better reducing agent than Cr^{+3}.
    c) Cl_2 is more easily reduced than Cr^{+3}, so Cl_2 is a better reducing agent than Cr^{+3}.
    d) Cl_2 is more easily reduced than Cr^{+3}, so Cl_2 is a better oxidizing agent than Cr^{+3}.
    e) None of the above

60. A rate law is found to be: Rate = $k[A]^2[B]^2$. The order of the reaction is
    a) first order.
    b) second order.
    c) third order.
    d) fourth order.
    e) not able to be determined.

61. $C_{30}H_{62}$ is a non-polar compound that is a solid at room temperature. Water is highly hydrogen bonded but it is a liquid because
    a) water molecules are very light.
    b) water molecules ionize easily.
    c) London dispersion forces build up a large dipole moment across the 62 hydrogen atoms in $C_{30}H_{62}$ and lead to attractive forces that exceed that of water's hydrogen bonds.
    d) $C_{30}H_{62}$ is so large that it cannot melt easily.
    e) $C_{30}H_{62}$ has a lower melting point if dissolved in non-polar hexane.

62. Add 200 mL of pure water into a 500 mL of a 0.2 M solution. What is the new molarity of this solution?
    a) 0.50 M
    b) 0.28 M
    c) 0.70 M
    d) 0.14 M
    e) 0.40 M

63. With a current of 9.65 A, how many minutes will be required to deposit 6.35 g of copper on a platinum electrode from a copper(II) nitrate solution? (The charge of one mole of electrons = 96,500 C)
    a) 16.7
    b) 33.3
    c) 66.6
    d) 1,000
    e) 2,000

64. Ethene is the first member of the
    a) alkane series.
    b) alkyne series.
    c) saturated hydrocarbons.
    d) unsaturated hydrocarbons.
    e) aromatic hydrocarbons.

65. How many grams of CH_4 produce 425.6 kcal in the reaction below:
$CH_4 + 2O_2 \rightarrow CO_2 + 2H_2O + 212.8$ kcal
    a) 8 g
    b) 16 g
    c) 24 g
    d) 32 g
    e) 64 g

66. Which of the following demonstrate(s) a negative ΔS?
    I. Freezing water into ice
    II. Lining up people into single file
    III. Boiling a liquid

    a) I only
    b) II only
    c) I and II only
    d) I and III only
    e) II and III only

67. Which of the following statements is FALSE?
    a) Reduction involves a gain of electrons.
    b) Batteries are galvanic cells.
    c) A spontaneous reaction always has a positive $E°_{cell}$.
    d) Electrolysis reactions always produce a gas at least in one of the electrodes.
    e) Galvanic cells can be used to determine equilibrium constants.

68. According to the chemical kinetic theory, a reaction can occur
    a) if the reactants collide with the proper orientation.
    b) if the reactants possess sufficient energy of collision.
    c) if the reactants are able to form a correct transition state.
    d) All of the above
    e) Only a) and b) are correct.

69. Which of the following factors will contribute to a decrease in oxygen in the water of a lake?
    a) Decreasing salinity (salt concentration)
    b) Increasing acidity due to acid rain
    c) Increasing temperature
    d) Increasing surface tension of the water
    e) Increasing atmospheric pressure

70. Which of the following molecules is a non-polar molecule but has polar intramolecular bonds?
    a) H_2
    b) H_2O
    c) NH_3
    d) NaCl
    e) CO_2

SAT Chemistry Subject Test No. 8 Keys

1. B	11. A	21. E	31. D	41. C	51. E	61. C
2. E	12. A	22. C	32. C	42. A	52. A	62. D
3. A	13. D	23. E	33. D	43. A	53. B	63. B
4. C	14. E	24. D	34. B	44. B	54. B	64. D
5. B	15. A	25. A	35. D	45. B	55. D	65. D
6. A	16. D	26. C	36. C	46. D	56. C	66. C
7. C	17. B	27. D	37. A	47. C	57. D	67. D
8. E	18. C	28. C	38. D	48. E	58. D	68. D
9. B	19. A	29. A	39. A	49. A	59. D	69. C
10. E	20. B	30. D	40. B	50. B	60. D	70. E

101. TF
102. TF
103. FT
104. TF
105. TF
106. TTCE
107. TF
108. TF
109. TTCE
110. TTCE
111. TTCE
112. TF
113. TTCE
114. TF
115. TTCE

SAT Chemistry Subject Test No. 8 Answer to Part A

1 – 4 *Answer: (beac)*
Boyle's Law states that volume decreases as the pressure is increased, when the temperature is held constant.

1st law of thermodynamics: energy conservation. $\Delta E = Q + w$

Ideal gas law: $PV = nRT$

Charles's Law states that volume increases as the temperature is increased, when the pressure is held constant.

5 – 8 *Answer: (bace)*
Color change is the function of indicators.

Buffers resist changes in pH.

It is the definition of Arrhenius acids.

This is the definition of amphoteric substances.

9 – 11 *Answer: (bea)*
Br_2 *is a non-metal liquid element at STP.*

The noble gas with the highest first ionization energy is helium.

F_2 *has the highest electronegativity among all elements.*

12 – 14 *Answer: (ade)*
Alpha particle: He_2^4

Gamma ray has the highest energy.

Positron has the same mass but opposite charge of an electron.

15 – 18 *Answer: (adbc)*
H_2 *contains only a single bond.*
Ionic bond is formed from the transfer of electrons.
CO_2 *has sp hybridized bonds.*
Only water molecules are polar molecules.

19 – 22 *Answer: (abec)*
Definition of the critical point in phase diagram.

The triple point on a phase diagram shows the temperature and pressure needed for a solid, liquid, and gas to exist at the same time.

The boiling point of a liquid is the temperature in which the vapor pressure of a liquid is equal to the atmospheric pressure.

The activated complex on the reaction coordinate diagram has the highest potential energy.

23 – 25 *Answer: (eda)*
The noble gas is the most stable group of elements in the periodic table.

Only halogens have elements that contain solid, liquid, and gas phases STP conditions.

Alkali metals are the strongest reducing agents.

SAT Chemistry Subject Test No. 8 Answer to Part C

26. *Answer: (c)*
pH > pka + 1 = color of the conjugate base
pH < pka – 1 = color of the conjugate acid
pka = log[1 × 10^{-6}] = 6
A pH < 6 – 1 will be red.

27. *Answer: (d)*
Removing the products from the reaction will keep shifting equilibrium to the right.

28. *Answer: (c)*
A triple bond between the carbon atoms has two pi bonds and one sigma bond. The total is two pi bonds and three sigma bonds.

29. *Answer: (a)*
Molar Mass of H_2S = 34
$\frac{35}{34}$ = 1.03 moles

30. *Answer: (d)*
The value of the equilibrium constant, K, is dependent on the nature of the reactants and the temperature.

31. *Answer: (d)*
Oxidation occurs at the anode and reduction occurs at the cathode.

32. *Answer: (c)*
The strongest base has the highest pH value. Na_2CO_3 is the strongest base here.

33. *Answer: (d)*
Because there is no attractive force between ideal gas molecules, ideal gas enthalpy is not dependent on system pressure.

34. *Answer: (b)*
$[OH^-][H^+] = 10^{-14}$
$[H^+] = \frac{10^{-14}}{10^{-6}} = 10^{-8}$
$pH = -\log[10^{-8}] = 8 > 7$
This is a basic solution.
pOH = 14 – 8 = 6

35. *Answer: (d)*
Use a burette in the titration process.

36. *Answer: (c)*
$\frac{P1}{T1} = \frac{P2}{T2}$
$\frac{6}{273+27} = \frac{P2}{273-73}$
P2 = 4 atm

37. *Answer: (a)*
$\Delta T_f = 1.86 \times \frac{\frac{171}{342}}{1} = 0.93\ ℃$

38. *Answer: (d)*
Alkane's series contain only single bonds.

39. *Answer: (a)*
Adding sodium sulfate to the solution increases the concentration of sulfate ion in the solution, driving the reverse reaction. This is called the common ion effect and more of the solid calcium sulfate will be made. If the solid is being formed, that means that it is not dissolving and the solubility has decreased.

40. *Answer: (b)*
Need to specify number of nitrogen and oxygen.

41. *Answer: (c)*
Heat capacity of water is 1 cal/gram ℃.
10 × 1 × (14 – 4) = 100 cal

42. *Answer: (a)*
Chemical reactions are all about sharing or transferring electrons.

43. *Answer: (a)*
$HCN \rightarrow H^+ + CN^-$
$[H^+] = [CN^-]$

44. *Answer: (b)*
Multiply the mass numbers by their abundances:
(24)(0.4) + 25 × .5 + 26 × 0.1 = 24.7

45. *Answer: (b)*
A chain reaction that can continue with external supply of neutrons.

46. *Answer: (d)*
$\frac{48}{12}:\frac{4}{1}:\frac{48}{16} = 4:4:3$
$(12 \times 4 + 4 \times 1 + 16 \times 3) \times n = 200$
$N = 2$
$C_8H_8O_6$

47. *Answer: (c)*
$3Ce^{+4} + Bi + H_2O \rightarrow 3Ce^{+3} + BiO^{+1} + 2H^{+1}$
The coefficient for the cesium ions is 3.

48. *Answer: (e)*
The positive value for the change in entropy means that there will be more disorder. An expanding universe and a food fight are sure signs of more disorder.

49. *Answer: (a)*
Halogen has the most negative value for its electron affinity.

50. *Answer: (b)*
Atomic Mass = $14 - 14 = 0$
Atomic Number = $6 - 7 = -1$
It is a beta particle.

51. *Answer: (e)*
$\Delta G = \Delta H - T\Delta S$
A spontaneous reaction of ΔG *is a negative number.*
An exothermic process of ΔH *is a negative value, too.*
ΔS *can be either a negative or positive value.*

52. *Answer: (a)*
Electrons moving up to a higher level always require energy.

53. *Answer: (b)*
Partial Pressure of $O_2 = \frac{2}{2+3+1} \times 760 = 253.3$ *torr*

54. *Answer: (b)*
$2Al + 3S \rightarrow Al_2S_3$
$Al : Al_2S_3 = 2:1 = \frac{27}{27} : \frac{x}{27 \times 2 + 32 \times 3}$
$x = \frac{150 \times 27}{27 \times 2} = 75\ g$

55. *Answer: (d)*
Molality is equal to the number of moles of solute dissolved in the mass of the solvent.

56. *Answer: (c)*
Compounds can be broken down chemically, while elements cannot. Methane and water are examples of compounds.

57. *Answer: (d)*
$[OH^-] = 10^{-5}$
$[H^+] = \frac{10^{-14}}{10^{-5}} = 10^{-9}$
$pH = -\log(10^{-9}) = 9$

58. *Answer: (d)*
2.5 molal NaCl will be, in effect, 5.0 molal because 1 mole of sodium chloride yields 2 moles of ions. This is the highest concentration of any of the choices and will have the greatest effect on the boiling and freezing points of water.

59. *Answer: (d)*
Cl_2 *is more easily reduced than* Cr^{+3}, *and* Cl_2 *is thus a better oxidizing agent than* Cr^{+3}.

60. *Answer: (d)*
Order of the reaction: $2 + 2 = 4$

61. *Answer: (c)*
Bigger molecules tend to be more difficult to melt because of a bigger effect from London dispersion forces.

62. *Answer: (d)*
The initial volume, V_1, *is 500 mL and the initial molarity,* M_1, *is 0.2 M. The new volume,* V_2, *is 700 mL because 200 mL of water were added to the original 500 mL. Using the equation* $M_1V_1 = M_2V_2$, *substitute and find that* $(0.2)(500) = (M_2)(700)$. M_2 *is 0.14 M.*

63. *Answer: (b)*
$Cu^{2+} + 2e^- \rightarrow Cu$
6.35 g of Copper $= \frac{6.35}{63.5} = 0.1$ *moles*
$0.1 \times 2 \times 96500 = 9.65 \times t \times 60$
$t = 33.3$ *minutes*

64. *Answer: (d)*
Ethene has a double bond and is the first member of the unsaturated hydrocarbons.

65. *Answer: (d)*
1 mole : 212.8 = x : 425.6
$x = 2$ *moles of* $CH_4 = 32$ *g of* CH_4

66. *Answer: (c)*
A negative sign for entropy means more order (or less chaos and less disorder). Ice is more orderly than water. Lining up is a more orderly state.

67. *Answer: (d)*
In an electrolytic cell, the less active metal ions, such as $CuSO_4$ or $Ag_2(SO_4)$, can deposit metal at the cathode. No gas has been produced in those cases.

68. *Answer: (d)*
All of them are true.

69. *Answer: (c)*
The solubility of the oxygen is decreased when temperature is increased.

70. *Answer: (e)*
Water, ammonia, and carbon dioxide all have polar bonds. Because it is a symmetrical molecule, carbon dioxide will counterbalance the dipole forces and be a non-polar molecule.

SAT Chemistry Subject Test No. 9

PART A

Directions: Each set of lettered choices below refers to the numbered statements or questions immediately following it. Select the one lettered choice that best fits each statement and then fill in the corresponding circle on the answer sheet. A given choice may be used once, more than once, or not at all in each set.

Note: For all questions involving solutions, assume that the solvent is water unless otherwise stated. Throughout the test the following symbols have the definitions specified unless otherwise noted.

H = enthalpy	T = temperature	L = liter(s)
M = molar	V = volume	mL = milliliter(s)
n = number of moles	atm = atmosphere(s)	mm = millimeter(s)
P = pressure	g = gram(s)	mol = mole(s)
R = molar gas constant	J = joule(s)	V = volt(s)
S = entropy	kJ = kilojoule(s)	

Questions 1–4 refer to the following topics and relationships:

a) Halogens
b) The carbon group
c) Transition metals
d) Alkali metals
e) Noble gases

1. Some of its elements show the properties of both metals and non-metals.
2. Has the greatest 1st ionization energy
3. Has the greatest electronegativity
4. Produces hydrogen gas when reacts with water

Questions 5–8 refer to the following topics and relationships

a) Non-polar covalent substance
b) Polar covalent substance
c) Network covalent substance
d) Ionic substance
e) Metallic network

5. Quartz, $SiO_2(s)$
6. NaCl(g)
7. $CH_4(g)$
8. $NH_3(g)$

Questions 9–11 refer to the following topics and relationships:

a) $Q = m \times C \times \Delta T$
b) $Q = H_v \times m$
c) $\Delta E = Q + W$
d) $P_1V_2 = P_2V_2$
e) $P_a = P_{total} \times X_a$

9. Boyle's Law
10. Thermodynamics 1st Law
11. Used to find energy gained or lost during a particular phase change

Questions 12–15 refer to the following topics and relationships:

a) Nuclear fusion
b) Nuclear fission
c) Le Chatelier's principle
d) Pauli Exclusion Principle
e) Graham's Law of Diffusion

12. The main process that generates energy at nuclear power plant
13. The main process that generates energy in the Sun
14. The ratio of the rate of movement of hydrogen gas to the rate of oxygen gas is 4 : 1.
15. A reaction at equilibrium will proceed in a direction that relieves the stress placed on the reaction.

Questions 16–19 refer to the following topics and relationships:

a) Mole
b) Avogadro's law
c) Molar mass
d) Freezing point
e) Molarity

16. Unit of "moles of solute per liter of solution"
17. Unit of "each 12 g of carbon-12"
18. Unit of "grams per mole of a molecule"
19. Unit of "6.02×10^{23} molecules/ mole"

Questions 20–22 refer to the following topics and relationships:

a) Red
b) Purple
c) Orange
d) Green
e) Blue

20. The color of $KMnO_4$ solution
21. The color of Copper(II) sulfate solution
22. The color of Ni^{+2} ion in water solution

Questions 23–25 refer to the following topics and relationships:

a) Arrhenius acid
b) Arrhenius base
c) Lewis acid
d) Lewis base
e) Brønsted-Lowry acid

23. It is an electron pair acceptor.
24. It yields hydroxide ions, the only negative ions in solution.
25. It is a proton donor.

PART B

Directions: Each question below consists of two statements, I in the left-hand column and II in the right-hand column. For each question, determine whether statement I is true or false and whether statement II is true or false and then fill in the corresponding T or F circles on your answer sheet. Fill in circle CE only if statement II is a correct explanation of the true statement I.

On the actual Chemistry Test, the following type of question must be answered on a special section (labeled "Chemistry") at the lower left-hand corner of your answer sheet. These questions will be numbered beginning with 101 and must be answered according to the following directions.

Examples:

	I		II
EX 1.	H_2SO_4 is a strong acid	BECAUSE	H_2SO_4 contains sulfer.
EX 2.	An atom of oxygen is electrically neutral	BECAUSE	an oxygen atom contains an equal number of protons and electrons.

SAMPLE ANSWERS

	I		II		CE
EX 1.	●	Ⓕ	●	Ⓕ	○
EX 2.	●	Ⓕ	●	Ⓕ	●

	I		II
101.	When the heat of formation of a compound is negative, ΔH is negative	BECAUSE	A negative enthalpy change indicates that a reaction is exothermic.
102.	In the Rutherford experiment, most of the alpha particles were able to pass through a thin sheet of gold foil	BECAUSE	An atom is mainly empty space.
103.	Electrolyzing 90 grams of water will yield 80 grams of H_2 and 10 grams of O_2	BECAUSE	Water is composed of hydrogen and oxygen in a ratio of 1 : 8 by mass.
104.	The radius of a cation is less than that of its atom	BECAUSE	The nucleus of a cation has less positive charge than the electron cloud.
105.	BF_3 is a Lewis acid	BECAUSE	The central atom B has only three bonding electrons.
106.	A solution of KBr will conduct electricity.	BECAUSE	KBr will not form ions in solution.

	Statement I		Statement II
107.	SF_6 is a non-polar molecule	BECAUSE	S atom is sp^3d^2 hybridized.
108.	A gas heated from 20 °C to 80 °C at constant pressure will increase its volume	BECAUSE	As Charles's Law states, if the pressure remains constant, the volume varies directly with temperatures.
109.	At room temperature, Cl_2 is a gas, but Br_2 is a liquid	BECAUSE	Cl_2 and Br_2 are both diatomic elements.
110.	Alkali metal sodium is much more reactive than Cu	BECAUSE	Sodium can easily lose its valence electrons.
111.	Ethene is defined as a compound	BECAUSE	Ethene can be broken down chemically.
112.	As you go from left to right across the periodic table, the elements tend to become more metallic in character	BECAUSE	As you go from left to right across the periodic table, the elements tend to lose electrons more easily.
113.	Excited mercury atoms will give off light energy	BECAUSE	As the excited electrons return to their ground state, they emit energy in the form of light.
114.	The rate of diffusion of hydrogen gas compared with that of helium gas is 1 : 4.	BECAUSE	The rate of diffusion of gases varies inversely to the square root of the molecular mass.
115.	ΔS will be positive in value during the melting process.	BECAUSE	Melting increases the order of the molecules from the solid to liquid phase.

PART C

Directions: Each of the questions or incomplete statements below is followed by five suggested answers or completions. Select the one that is best in each case and then fill in the corresponding circle on the answer sheet.

26. Based on the information below, what will be the change of enthalpy of the reaction when chlorine gas and hydrogen gas react to form hydrogen chloride?

	Bond Dissociation Energies in kJ/mole
Cl−Cl	240
H−Cl	430
H−H	435

a) +245 kJ/mole
b) +185 kJ/mole
c) −185 kJ/mole
d) −1105 kJ/mole
e) +1105 kJ/mole

27. A buffer is generated using NH_3 and NH_4Cl. Which of the following is/are true?
    I. Any buffers generated with the same $\frac{[NH_3]}{[NH_4Cl]}$ ratio will have an identical pH.
    II. If $[NH_3] = [NH_4Cl]$, the pH will equal the pKa of NH_4^+.
    III. Any buffers generated with the same $\frac{[NH_3]}{[NH_4Cl]}$ ratio will have an identical buffering capacity.

a) I only
b) II only
c) I and II only
d) I and III only
e) I, II, and III

28. Which of the following has the strongest carbon-carbon bond?
a) C_2H_2
b) C_2H_4
c) C_2H_6
d) C_2H_8
e) C_2H_{10}

29. Which of the following is the LEAST likely to be a metalloid?
a) As
b) Hg
c) Ge
d) Si
e) Sb

30. Which letter shows the enthalpy change (ΔH) of the reaction?

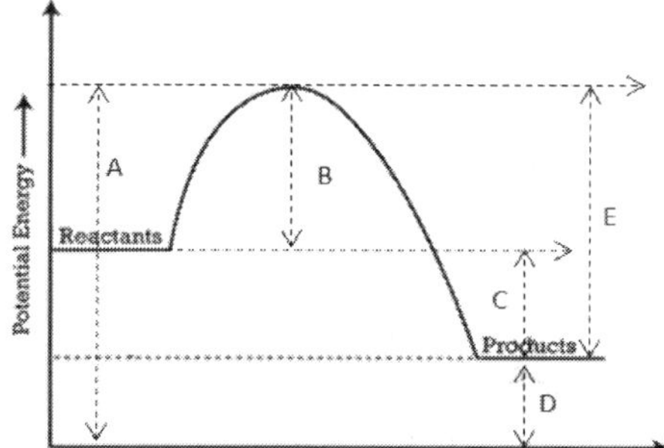

31. Which of the following conclusions CANNOT be made regarding the phase change of a pure substance from solid to liquid?
a) It involves a change in potential energy.
b) It involves no change in temperature.
c) It involves a change in kinetic energy.
d) It involves a change in entropy.
e) It may occur at different temperatures for different compounds.

32. $2Na + Cl_2 \rightarrow 2NaCl$
According to the equation above, if the reaction starts with 5.0 moles of Na and 3.0 moles of Cl_2, then which of the following statements is true?
   a) Cl_2 is the excess reagent and 5.0 moles of NaCl will be produced.
   b) Na is the excess reagent and 2.5 moles of NaCl will be produced.
   c) There will be an excess of 2.0 moles of Na.
   d) Na is the limiting reagent and 2.0 moles of NaCl will be produced.
   e) Cl is the excess reagent and 2.0 moles of NaCl will be produced.

33. Which of the following statements regarding significant figures is FALSE?
   a) Zeros can be significant.
   b) When multiplying, the answer is determined by the number of significant figures.
   c) When adding, the answer is determined by the number of decimal places.
   d) When dividing, the answer is determined by the number of decimal places.
   e) The number 50,004 has five significant figures.

34. There will be ______ if methane, CH_4, rather than ethane, CH_3CH_3, is the gas used under comparable conditions.
I. increased volume
II. increased temperature
III. increased average kinetic energy
IV. increased effusion rate
V. increased pressure
   a) I and III only
   b) II only
   c) III and V only
   d) IV only
   e) V only

35. What is the H_3O^+ concentration of a 0.100 M acetic acid solution ($K_a = 4 \times 10^{-5}$)?
   a) 2×10^{-6}
   b) 4×10^{-6}
   c) 2×10^{-4}
   d) 2×10^{-3}
   e) 4×10^{-3}

36. What is the sum of the coefficients of the following equation when it is balanced?
$C_6H_{12}O_6 + O_2 \rightarrow CO_2 + H_2O$
   a) 20
   b) 38
   c) 21
   d) 19
   e) 18

37. Which of the following reactions shows a decrease in entropy?
   a) $C(s) + 2H_2(g) \rightarrow CH_4(g)$
   b) $H_2O(g) \rightarrow H_2(g) + \frac{1}{2}O_2(g)$
   c) $2NI_3(s) \rightarrow N_2(g) + 3I_2(g)$
   d) $2O_3(g) \rightarrow 3O_2(g)$
   e) None of the above

38. $BaCl_2$ dissociates in water to release one Ba^{2+} ion and two Cl^- ions. If a HCl solution is added to this solution,
   a) $[Ba^{2+}]$ increases.
   b) $[OH^-]$ increases.
   c) $[Ba^{2+}]$ remains constant.
   d) $[H^+]$ decreases.
   e) the number of moles of un-dissociated $BaCl_2$ increases.

39. When ΔG, free energy, is zero,
    a) the free energy is always negative.
    b) the free energy is negative at low temperatures.
    c) the free energy is negative at high temperatures.
    d) the free energy is never negative.
    e) the system is at equilibrium.

40. Which is the most appropriate method for determining the molar mass of a newly discovered enzyme?
    a) Freezing-point depression
    b) Osmotic pressure
    c) Boiling-point depression
    d) Gas density
    e) Vapor pressure

41. Which of the following aqueous solutions has a molarity of 1.0 M?
    a) 73 grams of HCl dissolved to make 2.0 liters of solution
    b) 360 grams of $C_6H_{12}O_6$ dissolved to make 1.5 liters of solution
    c) 94 grams of K_2O dissolved to make 0.75 liters of solution
    d) 24 grams of LiOH dissolved to make 1.25 liters of solution
    e) 40 grams of HF dissolved to make 2.50 liters of solution

42. Which of the following is/are necessary for successful collisions to occur?

    I. Favorable geometry
    II. Sufficient energy
    III. Large ΔH

    a) I only
    b) I and II only
    c) II and III only
    d) I and III only
    e) I, II, and III

43. At 0 °C, how much heat is released by freezing a sample of 16 grams water into ice?
    a) 16 J
    b) 4,368 J
    c) 18,258 J
    d) 350 J
    e) 5,334 J

44. What type of chemical reaction is the following reaction?

$$1C_4H_8 + 6O_2 \rightarrow 4CO_2 + 4H_2O$$

    a) Single replacement
    b) Decomposition
    c) Double replacement
    d) Combustion
    e) Synthesis

45. In order to produce aluminum, large amounts of electricity are used to perform the ____of aluminum oxide.
    a) Nernst equation
    b) spontaneous reaction
    c) reduction
    d) oxidation
    e) electrolysis

46. In an experiment, 0.0300 moles each of $SO_3(g)$, $SO_2(g)$, and $O_2(g)$ were placed in a 10.0 L flask at a certain temperature. When the reaction reached equilibrium, the concentration of $SO_2(g)$ in the flask was 1×10^{-3} M. What is K_c for the following reaction:

$$2SO_2(g) + O_2(g) \leftrightarrow 2SO_3(g)$$

    a) 2.5×10^{-3}
    b) 1.25×10^{4}
    c) 5.0×10^{4}
    d) 1.25×10^{6}
    e) 5.0×10^{6}

47. Which sample has atoms that are arranged in a crystal structure?
    a) NaCl(l)
    b) K_2SO_4(s)
    c) Fe(l)
    d) $HClO_3$(aq)
    e) HCl(g)

48. Which of the following conditions is required to form ${}^{4}_{2}He$ during the fusion reaction in the Sun?
    a) High temperature and low pressure
    b) High temperature and high pressure
    c) High temperature and any pressure
    d) Low temperature and low pressure
    e) Low temperature and high pressure

49. According to the diagram below, segment *bc* is

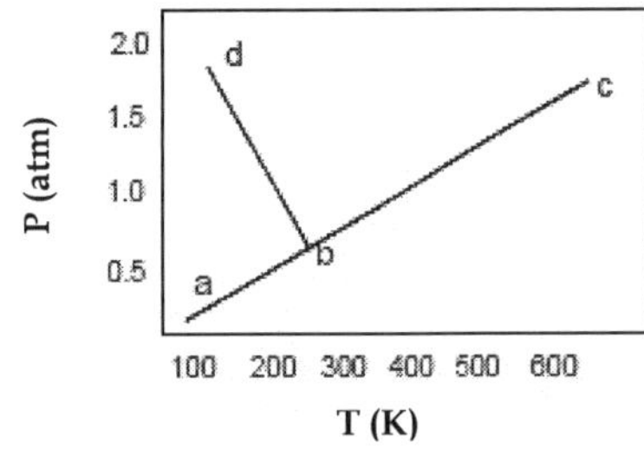

    a) condensation.
    b) melting.
    c) evaporation.
    d) sublimation.
    e) boiling.

50. What is the correct formula for iron(III) sulfate?
    a) $FeSO_4$
    b) $Fe_2(SO_4)_3$
    c) $Fe(SO_4)_3$
    d) Fe_3SO_4
    e) $Fe_3(SO_4)_2$

51. The decomposition of gaseous hydrogen iodide is shown below:

$$2HI(g) \leftrightarrow H_2(g) + I_2(g)$$

What is the equilibrium expression for this reaction?
    a) $[H_2]^2[I_2]$
    b) $[H_2]$
    c) $[H_2][I_2]/[HI]^2$
    d) $[H^2][I^2]^2$
    e) $[H_2]^2[I_2]^2$

52. Aqueous solutions contain 1:1 mole ratios of the following pairs of substances. Assume all concentrations are 1 M. The solution with the lowest pH is
    a) NaCl and NaOH solution.
    b) NaOAc and HOAc solution.
    c) HNO_3 and $NaNO_3$ solution.
    d) NH_3 and NH_4Cl solution.
    e) NaCl and K_2SO_4 solution.

53. Which of the following compounds is not paired with their correct name?
    a) $FeCl_2$ / iron(II) chloride
    b) K_2O / potassium oxide
    c) NO_2 / nitrogen dioxide
    d) PCl_3 / potassium trichloride
    e) NH_4Cl / ammonium chloride

54. Which of the following electronic configurations corresponds to that of a noble gas?
    a) $1s^2, 2s^2, 2p^6, 3s^2, 3p^6, 4s^1$
    b) $1s^2, 2s^2, 2p^6, 3s^2, 3p^4$
    c) $1s^2, 2s^2, 2p^6, 3s^2, 3p^6$
    d) $1s^2, 2s^2, 2p^6, 3s^1$
    e) 1s, 2s, 2p, 3s, 3p

55. What is the oxidation number of the underlined symbol in the given formulas <u>Ca</u>CO_3?
   a) +1
   b) +2
   c) +4
   d) +5
   e) +6

56. Which of the following CANNOT be either a Lewis acid or a Lewis base?
   a) CH_4
   b) Cu^{+2}
   c) CO
   d) Fe^{+3}
   e) NH_3

57. Determine the empirical formula for a compound that is 25% hydrogen and 75% carbon.
   a) CH
   b) CH_2
   c) CH_4
   d) C_2H_8
   e) C_4H

58. The name of $CH_3 - CH = C = CH - CH - CH = CH - CH_3$ is?
   a) 2, 3, 5 - octatriene
   b) 2, 5, 6 - octatriene
   c) 2, 3, 6 - octatriene
   d) 3, 5, 6 - octatriene
   e) 3, 4, 7 - octatriene

59. Which of the following choices correctly describes the solubility of potassium chloride (KCl)?
   a) Solubility in CCl_4 > Solubility in CH_3CH_2OH > Solubility in H_2O
   b) Solubility in H_2O > Solubility in CH_3CH_2OH > Solubility in CCl_4
   c) Solubility in CH_3CH_2OH > Solubility in CCl_4 > Solubility in H_2O
   d) Solubility in H_2O > Solubility in CCl_4 > Solubility in CH_3CH_2OH
   e) None of the above

60. Which of the following is defined as the space occupied by matter?
   a) Density
   b) A solid
   c) Volume
   d) Weight
   e) Matter

61. Which of the following describe(s) water?
   I. Solvent for polar solutes
   II. Polar molecule
   III. Good conductor of electricity
   a) I, II and III
   b) I and II only
   c) II and III only
   d) I only
   e) III only

62. For a metal atom to replace another kind of metallic ion in a solution, the metal atom must be
   a) a good oxidizing agent.
   b) higher in the activity series than the metal in a solution.
   c) lower in the activity series than the metal in a solution.
   d) equal in activity to the metal in a solution.
   e) lower in solubility in a solution.

63. As you go from left to right across a period on the periodic table, there is a decrease in
   a) first ionization energy.
   b) nuclear charge.
   c) electronegativity.
   d) the ability to gain electrons.
   e) metallic character.

64. In the diagram shown below, which letter represents the potential energy of the products minus the potential energy of the reactants?

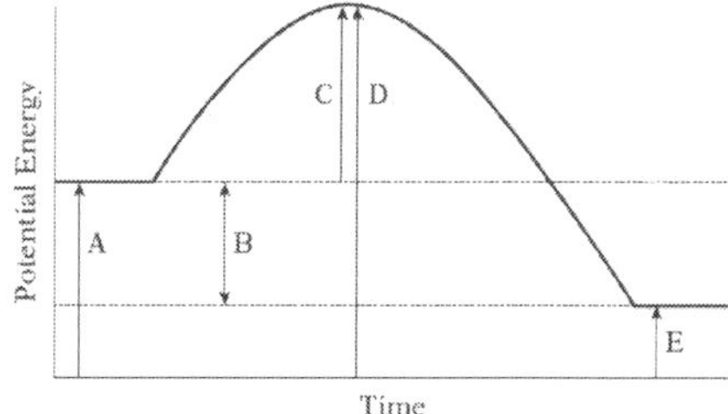

   a) B
   b) D
   c) A
   d) E
   e) C

65. Which of the following reactions presents the Lewis acids and bases?
   a) $HCl + NaOH \rightarrow HOH + NaCl$
   b) $H_2O + NH_3 \rightarrow OH^{-1} + NH_4^+$
   c) $NH_3 + BF_3 \rightarrow NH_3BF_3$
   d) $HI + KOH \rightarrow H_2O + KI$
   e) $H^+ + OH^{-1} \rightarrow H_2O$

66. The molarity of a solution which is composed of 80.00 g of sodium hydroxide dissolved in 2.0 L of solution is
   a) 1.0 M.
   b) 2.0 M.
   c) 4.0 M.
   d) 40.0 M.
   e) 160.0 M.

67. What volume would 16 g of molecular oxygen gas occupy at STP?
   a) 5.6 L
   b) 11.2 L
   c) 22.4 L
   d) 33.6 L
   e) 44.8 L

68. For the reaction below, indicate which element is reduced and which element is oxidized.

$$2Cu(NO_3)_2 \rightarrow 2CuO + 4NO_2 + O_2$$

	Oxidized	Reduced
a)	Nitrogen	Oxygen
b)	Copper	Oxygen
c)	Copper	Nitrogen
d)	Nitrogen	Copper
e)	Oxygen	Nitrogen

69. Which of the following principles is NOT a part of Dalton's atomic theory?
   a) Atoms are the smallest, indivisible particles in nature.
   b) Chemical reactions are simple rearrangements of atoms.
   c) Atoms follow the law of multiple proportions.
   d) Each atom of an element is identical to every other atom of that element.
   e) All matter is composed of atoms.

70. Isotopes of uranium have different
   a) atomic numbers.
   b) atomic masses.
   c) numbers of electrons.
   d) numbers of protons.
   e) numbers of positron.

SAT Chemistry Subject Test No. 9 Keys

1. B	11. B	21. E	31. C	41. A	51. C	61. B
2. E	12. B	22. D	32. A	42. B	52. C	62. B
3. A	13. A	23. C	33. D	43. E	53. D	63. E
4. D	14. E	24. B	34. D	44. D	54. C	64. A
5. C	15. C	25. E	35. D	45. E	55. B	65. C
6. D	16. E	26. C	36. D	46. B	56. A	66. A
7. A	17. A	27. C	37. A	47. B	57. C	67. B
8. B	18. C	28. A	38. E	48. B	58. C	68. E
9. D	19. B	29. B	39. E	49. E	59. B	69. C
10. C	20. B	30. C	40. B	50. B	60. C	70. B

101. TTCE
102. TTCE
103. FT
104. TF
105. TTCE
106. TF
107. TT
108. TTCE
109. TT
110. TTCE
111. TTCE
112. FF
113. TTCE
114. FT
115. TF

SAT Chemistry Subject Test No. 9 Answer to Part A

1 – 4 *Answer: (bead)*
Si and Ge in the carbon group are metalloids.

Noble gases have greatest 1st ionization energy.

Halogens have greatest electronegativity.

Alkali metals react with water to produce hydrogen gas.

5 – 8 *Answer: (cdab)*
Quartz is a network covalent substance.

NaCl is an ionic substance.

CH_4 is a non-polar covalent substance.

NH_3 is a polar covalent substance.

9 – 11 *Answer: (dcb)*
Boyle's Law: $PV = k$

Thermodynamics 1st Law: energy conservation, $\Delta E = Q + W$.
Energy transfer during phase changes, $Q = H_v \times m$

Energy transfer during the temperature changes, $Q = m \times C \times \Delta T$

12 – 15 *Answer: (baec)*
Power plants use nuclear fission to generate energy.

Sun use nuclear fusion to generate huge energy.

Graham's Law of Diffusion:

$$\frac{Effusion\ Rate\ of\ Gas\ A}{Effusion\ Rate\ of\ Gas\ B} = \frac{\sqrt{M_B}}{\sqrt{M_A}}$$

Le Chatelier's principle: A reaction at equilibrium will proceed in a direction that relieves the stress put into the reactions.

16 – 19 *Answer: (eacb)*
Molarity is defined as moles of solute/liter of solution.
1 Mole = 12 g of carbon-12
Molar mass: the mass of 1 mole of a substance.

Avogadro's law: one mole contains 6.02×10^{23} molecules.

20 – 22 *Answer: (bed)*
Copper sulfate is a blue salt that forms blue solutions.

Chlorine is a green gas.

Permanganate ions will form a dark purple solution.

The color of Ni^{+2} ions in water is green

23 – 25 *Answer: (cbe)*
Lewis acids and bases are defined as electron pair acceptors and donors, respectively.

Arrhenius bases yield hydroxide ions as negative ions in solution.

While the Arrhenius definition of an acid says that an acid yields hydronium ions, the only positive ions in solution, the Brønsted-Lowry definition says that acids are proton donors.

SAT Chemistry Subject Test No. 9 Answer to Part C

26. *Answer: (c)*
[1(H – H) +1(Cl – Cl)] – [2(H – Cl)] : [435 +240] – [2(430)] = 675 – 860 = – 185 kJ.

27. *Answer: (c)*
$NH_4^- \rightarrow NH_3 + H^+$
$pH = pKa - log\frac{NH_3}{NH_4^-}$

28. *Answer: (a)*
A triple bond is stronger than either a double bond or a single bond.

29. *Answer: (b)*
Mercury is a transition metal.

30. *Answer: (c)*
ΔH = Energy of Products – Energy of Reactants = C

31. *Answer: (c)*
Phase changes of a pure substance are changes of their potential energy, not the kinetic energy.

32. *Answer: (a)*
5.0 moles of sodium will require only 2.5 moles of chlorine gas because twice as much sodium is consumed in the reaction as chlorine (as seen in the balanced equation). This means that sodium is the limiting reagent and chlorine is in excess. If all 5.0 moles of the sodium are used up, then 5.0 moles of NaCl will be produced because of their 1 : 1 ratio in the balanced equation.

33. *Answer: (d)*
When multiplying and dividing, the final answer contains the same number of significant figures as the number with the fewest significant figures.

34. *Answer: (d)*
Methane has a higher effusion rate than ethane.

35. *Answer: (d)*
$HA \rightarrow H^+ + A^-$
$0.1 - x \quad x \quad x$
$4 \times 10^{-5} = \frac{x^2}{0.1-x} \approx \frac{x^2}{0.1}$
$x = 2 \times 10^{-3}$

36. *Answer: (d)*
$C_6H_{12}O_6 + 6O_2 \rightarrow 6CO_2 + 6H_2O$
1+6 + 6 + 6 = 19

37. *Answer: (a)*
$C(s) + 2H_2(g) \rightarrow CH_4(g)$
The number of gas molecules in the products is less than the number of gas molecules in the reactants.

38. *Answer: (e)*
By adding the Cl^- to the solution, the solubility of $BaCl_2$ will be reduced.

39. *Answer: (e)*
When ΔG, free energy, is zero, the system is at equilibrium.

40. *Answer: (b)*
Osmotic pressure can determine the molar mass of an enzyme.

41. *Answer: (a)*
The equation for calculating the molarity of a solution is moles of solute / total liters of solution. Because 73 grams of HCl (molar mass is 36.5) is 2 moles of HCl dissolved to make 2.0 liters of solution in total, the solution will be 1.0 M.

42. *Answer: (b)*
Sufficient energy and good orientation are necessary for successful collisions to occur.

43. *Answer: (e)*
This calculation requires using the heat of fusion of water. The equation is $q = H_{fm}$. Substitution gives q = (333.6 J/g)(16 grams) = 5,334 joules of heat.

44. *Answer: (d)*
Combines with oxygen to produce water and carbon dioxide.

45. *Answer: (e)*
The electrolysis of aluminum oxide produces aluminum metal.

46. *Answer: (b)*
$2SO_2(g) + O_2(g) \leftrightarrow 2SO_3(g)$
$0.003M \quad 0.003M \quad 0.003M$
$0.003 - 2x \quad 0.003 - x \quad 0.003 + 2x$
$0.003 - 2x = 1 \times 10^{-3} \quad x = 0.001$
$K = \frac{[0.003 + 0.002]^2}{[0.003 - 0.002]^2[0.003 - 0.001]}$
$K = 1.25 \times 10^4$

47. *Answer: (b)*
Only solids have their atoms set in a fixed position. This allows for a regular geometric pattern, such as the lattice in $Na_2SO_4(s)$, to be formed.

48. *Answer: (b)*
Nuclei fusion needs high temperature and pressure to be initiated.

49. *Answer: (e)*
Segment bc separates liquid and vapor.
Boiling only occurs when the heating curve crosses segment bc, but evaporation can occur at any temperature and pressure.

50. *Answer: (b)*
The Roman numeral III means that the iron ion has a charge of 3+. Sulfate has a charge of 2-. Using the crisscross method and using parentheses for the polyatomic ion, the correct formula is $Fe_2(SO_4)_3$.

51. *Answer: (c)*
This is the definition of equilibrium constant.

52. *Answer: (c)*
Strong acids and weak bases in a solution would result in the lowest pH values.

53. *Answer: (d)*
Although it does use the prefix "tri-" correctly for a covalent compound, PCl_3 is phosphorus trichloride.

54. *Answer: (c)*
Noble gases fill up p orbitals.

55. *Answer: (b)*
$3 \times 2 - 4 = 2$

56. *Answer: (a)*
Molecules without any pairs of electrons cannot be either a Lewis acid or a Lewis base.
CH_4 does not have any unshared pairs of electrons.

57. *Answer: (c)*
$C : H = \frac{75}{12} : \frac{25}{1} = 1 : 4$; *it is a CH_4 molecule.*

58. *Answer: (c)*
Double bonds are located at carbon number 2, 3 and 6. It is an octatriene.

59. *Answer: (b)*
Ionic compounds dissolve easily in water and other polar solvents.

60. *Answer: (c)*

61. *Answer: (b)*
Pure water cannot conduct electricity easily.

62. *Answer: (b)*
The higher in the activity series, the stronger the reduction agent is, and the easier it is to be oxidized from a metal to a positive ion.

63. *Answer: (e)*
Going from left to right across period 2, the elements become more nonmetallic and there is a decrease in the metallic character.

64. *Answer: (a)*
The potential energy of the products minus the potential energy of the reactants is the heat of reaction, which is designated by "B" on the diagram.

65. *Answer: (c)*
The Lewis definition of acids states that acids are electron pair acceptors, while bases are electron pair donors. Choices a), d), and e) show the Arrhenius definition, whereas choice b) shows the Brønsted-Lowry definition.

66. *Answer: (a)*
The Molar Mass of NaOH = 40
$M = \frac{\frac{80}{40}}{2} = 1\ M$

67. *Answer: (b)*
16 g of Oxygen $= \frac{16}{32} = 0.5$ *moles*
$0.5 \times 22.4 = 11.2\ L$

68. *Answer: (e)*
Cu^{2+} keeps the same oxidation number.
The oxidation number of N changes from +5 to +4 (reduced).
The oxidation number of O changes from -2 to 0 (oxidized).

69. *Answer: (c)*
Atoms do not follow the law of multiple proportions.

70. *Answer: (b)*
The atomic mass, the number of protons plus neutrons, differs between two isotopes.

SAT Chemistry Subject Test No. 10

PART A

Directions: Each set of lettered choices below refers to the numbered statements or questions immediately following it. Select the one lettered choice that best fits each statement and then fill in the corresponding circle on the answer sheet. A given choice may be used once, more than once, or not at all in each set.

Note: For all questions involving solutions, assume that the solvent is water unless otherwise stated. Throughout the test the following symbols have the definitions specified unless otherwise noted.

H = enthalpy	T = temperature	L = liter(s)
M = molar	V = volume	mL = milliliter(s)
n = number of moles	atm = atmosphere(s)	mm = millimeter(s)
P = pressure	g = gram(s)	mol = mole(s)
R = molar gas constant	J = joule(s)	V = volt(s)
S = entropy	kJ = kilojoule(s)	

Questions 1–4 refer to the following topics and relationships:

a) Br_2 and Hg
b) Cl_2 and F_2
c) NH_4^+ and H_3O^+
d) Li and Na
e) Diamond and graphite

1. These two compounds are in the liquid phase at room temperature.
2. These two compounds are non-polar covalent molecules.
3. These two compounds have network covalent bonds.
4. These two compounds are good reducing agents.

Questions 5–7 refer to the following topics and relationships:

a) $\Delta E°$ is positive
b) $\Delta S°$ is negative
c) $\Delta G°$ is positive
d) $K_{eq} \ll 1$
e) $K_a \gg 1$

5. Indicates a strong acid
6. A reaction is nonspontaneous
7. Less chaos, disorder, and randomness

Questions 8–10 refer to the following topics and relationships:

a) 6.02×10^{23} molecules
b) 44.8 liters
c) 3.5 moles
d) 1.0 grams
e) 3.01×10^{23} atoms

8. 0.5 moles of H_2 at STP
9. 32 grams of O_2 at STP
10. 1.6 grams of CH_4 at STP

Questions 11–13 refer to the following topics and relationships:

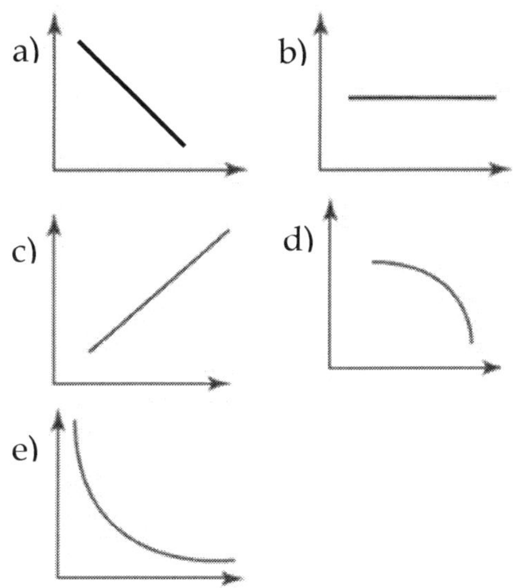

11. Demonstrates the relationship between pressure (x-axis) and volume (y-axis) in Boyle's Law
12. Demonstrates the relationship between temperature (x-axis) and volume (y-axis) in Charles' Law
13. Demonstrates the relationship between temperature (x-axis) and pressure (y-axis) in Gay Lussac's Law

Questions 14–17 refer to the following topics and relationships:

a) Brownian movement
b) Litmus paper reaction
c) Phenolphthalein reaction
d) Hydrogen bonding
e) Tyndall Effect

14. The light scattering by particles in a colloid or particles in a fine suspension solution
15. The random motion of particles suspended in a fluid resulting from their collision
16. The pink color in a basic solution
17. Water creates stronger than normal surface tension.

Questions 18–21 refer to the following topics and relationships:

a) Purple color
b) Brown-orange color
c) Green color
d) Silver-gray color
e) Yellow-orange color

18. The color of mercury metal
19. The color of potassium permanganate solution
20. The flame color of sodium
21. The color of chlorine gas

Questions 22–25 refer to the following topics and relationships:

a) Alkali metals
b) Halogen
c) Noble gases
d) The carbon group
e) Transition metals

22. This group of elements is the least likely involved in the chemical reactions.
23. This group of elements reacts with water to release hydrogen.
24. This group of elements contains elements in gaseous, liquid, and solid states, in STP conditions.
25. Some of its elements show both the properties of both metals and non-metals.

PART B

Directions: Each question below consists of two statements, I in the left-hand column and II in the right-hand column. For each question, determine whether statement I is true or false and whether statement II is true or false and then fill in the corresponding T or F circles on your answer sheet. Fill in circle CE only if statement II is a correct explanation of the true statement I.

On the actual Chemistry Test, the following type of question must be answered on a special section (labeled "Chemistry") at the lower left-hand corner of your answer sheet. These questions will be numbered beginning with 101 and must be answered according to the following directions.

Examples:

	I		II
EX 1.	H_2SO_4 is a strong acid	BECAUSE	H_2SO_4 contains sulfer.
EX 2.	An atom of oxygen is electrically neutral	BECAUSE	an oxygen atom contains an equal number of protons and electrons.

SAMPLE ANSWERS

	I		II		CE
EX 1.	●	(F)	●	(F)	○
EX 2.	●	(F)	●	(F)	●

	I		II
101.	The element with an electron configuration of [He]$2s^1$ has a larger atomic radius than fluorine	BECAUSE	The element of [He]$2s^1$ has a greater nuclear charge than fluorine.
102.	Cl^- is the conjugate base of HCl	BECAUSE	A conjugate base is formed when an acid gains a proton.
103.	An electrolytic cell makes a nonspontaneous redox reaction	BECAUSE	An electrolytic cell uses an external current to push a redox reaction.
104.	An exothermic reaction has a negative ΔH	BECAUSE	In an exothermic reaction, the products have less potential energy than the reactants.
105.	CCl_4 is a polar molecule	BECAUSE	The dipoles for CCl_4 show counterbalance and symmetry.
106.	When 2 liters of oxygen gas react with 2 liters of hydrogen completely, the limiting reactant is the oxygen	BECAUSE	The coefficients in balanced equations of gaseous reactions give the volume relationships of the reaction gases.

	Statement I		Statement II
107.	At constant temperature, the relationship between pressure and volume is considered to be an inverse relationship for an ideal gas	BECAUSE	As pressure increases on a gas, the volume of the gas will decrease.
108.	A catalyst will change the heat of reaction	BECAUSE	A catalyst will lower the potential energy of the activated complex in a reaction.
109.	Propane is considered to be a saturated hydrocarbon	BECAUSE	Propene has a triple bond.
110.	Water is a polar substance	BECAUSE	The sharing of the bonding electrons in water is unequal.
111.	NH_3 can best be collected by water displacement.	BECAUSE	NH_3 is a polar substance.
112.	Molten KCl conducts electricity	BECAUSE	KCl has metallic bonding.
113.	Increasing the concentration of reactants will cause a reaction to proceed faster	BECAUSE	More reactants will lower the activation energy of a reaction.
114.	The oxidation state of Cr in $Al_2(Cr_2O_7)_3$ is +3	BECAUSE	As a neutral compound, the sum of oxidation numbers of all the atoms must equal zero.
115.	An 0.5 m of NaCl(aq) solution will freeze at a temperature below 272K	BECAUSE	As a solute is added to a solvent, the boiling point increases while the freezing point decreases.

PART C

Directions: Each of the questions or incomplete statements below is followed by five suggested answers or completions. Select the one that is best in each case and then fill in the corresponding circle on the answer sheet.

26. What is the molar mass of ethanol (C_2H_5OH)?
    a) 34.2
    b) 38.9
    c) 46.1
    d) 45.1
    e) 62.1

27. The shape of a PCl_3 molecule is described as
    a) bent.
    b) trigonal pyramidal.
    c) linear.
    d) trigonal planar.
    e) tetrahedral.

28. What is the general formula of the compound of alkaline earth metal oxide?
    a) M_2O
    b) MO
    c) MO_2
    d) M_2O_3
    e) M_3O_2

29. Which of the following is used to determine cell voltages when standard state conditions are not present?
    I. Nernst equation
    II. spontaneous reaction
    III. reduction
    IV. oxidation
    V. electrolysis
    a) I
    b) II
    c) III
    d) IV
    e) V

30.
$$A + B \rightarrow 2C \quad \Delta H = +150 \text{ kcal}$$
$$C \rightarrow 2D + 2E \quad \Delta H = -450 \text{ kcal}$$
$$F \rightarrow 4D + 4E \quad \Delta H = +725 \text{ kcal}$$
    According to the reactions above, what is the heat of reaction for $A + B \rightarrow F$?
    a) −1475 kcal
    b) +25 kcal
    c) −1025 kcal
    d) +325 kcal
    e) +300 kcal

31. Which of the following statements is true?
    a) Water has bent molecular geometry and one lone pair of electrons.
    b) Ammonia has trigonal pyramidal molecular geometry and two lone pairs of electrons.
    c) Methane has trigonal planar molecular geometry.
    d) Carbon dioxide is linear because it has one single bond and one triple bond.
    e) The carbon atoms in ethane are sp^3 hybridized.

32. When methane, CH_4, burns in excess oxygen, what would the product(s) be?
    a) CH_4O_2
    b) $CO + H_2O$
    c) $CO + CH_2OH$
    d) $CO_2 + H_2O$
    e) $CO_2 + 2H_2$

33. $2A(g) + B(g) + Heat \rightarrow 3C(g) + D(g)$ According to the equation above, what could be done to the reaction to shift the equilibrium to the right?
    a) Increase the concentration of D.
    b) Increase the concentration of C.
    c) Increase the temperature.
    d) Increase the pressure.
    e) Remove B from the reaction.

34. The standard reduction potential of $Cu^{+2}(aq)$ is +0.34 V. What is the oxidation potential of Cu(s)?
    a) +0.68 V
    b) +0.34 V
    c) - 0.34 V
    d) - 0.68 V
    e) None of the above

35. Sodium metal cannot be electrolyzed from an aqueous Na_2SO_4 solution because
    a) the voltage needed is too high for any available instrument to achieve.
    b) water is reduced to O_2 first.
    c) Na^+ has a high reduction potential that keeps it from being reduced.
    d) H^+ has a more favorable reduction potential than Na^+.
    e) Na^+ does electrolyze, but it immediately reacts with water again.

36. Which of the following solutions is expected to be the weakest electrolyte?
    a) HCl(aq)
    b) HF(aq)
    c) NaOH(aq)
    d) KI(aq)
    e) $HClO_4$(aq)

37. How many grams of Na_2SO_4 can be produced by reacting 98 g H_2SO_4 with 40 g NaOH?
    a) 18 g
    b) 36 g
    c) 71 g
    d) 142 g
    e) 150 g

38. An atom has the following ionization energies:

    $I_1 = 589.8$ kJ/mole
    $I_2 = 1145.4$ kJ/mole
    $I_3 = 4912.4$ kJ/mole
    $I_4 = 6491$ kJ/mole

    These values most likely correspond to which of the following elements?
    a) Ne
    b) Li
    c) I
    d) Ca
    e) Al

39. Which of the following substances is used as a moderator in a nuclear reactor?
    a) Marble
    b) Hydrogen
    c) Tritium
    d) Graphite
    e) Diamond

40. When an equal number of moles of each are mixed, which of the following can be used to prepare a buffer solution?

    I. $Cu(NH_3)_4^{+2}$
    II. KOH
    III. HCO_3^-
    IV. CO_3^{-2}
    V. SO_3^{-2}

    a) I and II only
    b) II and III only
    c) III and IV only
    d) IV and V only
    e) V and I only

41. An ideal gas has a volume of 10 L at 20 °C and 750 mm Hg. Which of the following expressions is needed to determine the volume of the same amount of gas at STP?
    a) 10 × (750/760) × (0/20)
    b) 10 × (750/760) × (293/273)
    c) 10 × (760/750) × (0/20)
    d) 10 × (760/750) × (273/293)
    e) 10 × (750/760) × (273/293)

42. Given $2Na(s) + Cl_2(g) \rightarrow 2NaCl(s)$ + 820 kJ, how much heat is released if 0.5 moles of sodium reacts completely with chlorine?
    a) 205.0 kJ
    b) 411 kJ
    c) 822 kJ
    d) 1,644 kJ
    e) 3,288 kJ

43. What is ΔH_{rxn} for the decomposition of 1 mole of sodium chlorate? (ΔH_f values are as follows: $NaClO_3(s)$ = −85.7 kcal/mole; NaCl(s) = −98.2 kcal/mole; $O_2(g)$ = 0 kcal/mole)
    a) −183.9 kcal
    b) −91.9 kcal
    c) +45.3 kcal
    d) +22.5 kcal
    e) −12.5 kcal

44. A solution is prepared in which $[Sr^{+2}] = [Ba^{+2}] = 4.0 \times 10^{-4}$ M. NaF is slowly added to the solution at 25 °C. The Ksp for BaF_2 is 2.4×10^{-5} and the Ksp for SrF_2 is 7.9×10^{-9} at 25 °C. Which of the following is true?
    I. The first compound that will precipitate is SrF_2.
    II. There is a concentration of F^- at which SrF_2 will precipitate but not BaF_2.
    III. There is no concentration of F^- at which SrF_2 and BaF_2 will both precipitate.
    a) I only
    b) II only
    c) I and II only
    d) II and III only
    e) I, II, and III

45. Which of the following pieces of glassware requires a careful reading of the meniscus?
    a) Watch glass
    b) Burette
    c) Beaker
    d) Flask
    e) Funnel

46. The valence electrons in the main group are
    a) all electrons in an atom beyond the preceding noble gas.
    b) all outermost electrons in a sublevel.
    c) s and any p electrons in the highest energy level or shell.
    d) electrons in the last unfilled sublevel.
    e) any electrons that can ionize.

47. How many milliliters of 1.5 M HCl are needed to titrate 30.0 mL of 1.0 M NaOH?
    a) 10.00 mL
    b) 30.00 mL
    c) 20.00 mL
    d) 35.00 mL
    e) 40.00 mL

48. Which of the following compounds is insoluble in water?
    a) $Ca(OH)_2$
    b) Fe_2S_3
    c) Na_2CO_3
    d) H_2SO_3
    e) $AuCl_3$

49. One reason for a double displacement reaction to go to completion is that
    a) a product is soluble.
    b) a product is given off as a gas.
    c) the products can react with each other.
    d) the products are miscible.
    e) the products are a strong acid.

50. Which of the following is true of an electrolytic cell?
    a) An electric current causes an otherwise non-spontaneous chemical reaction to occur.
    b) Reduction occurs at the anode.
    c) A spontaneous electrochemical reaction produces an electric current.
    d) The electrode to which the electrons flow is where oxidation occurs.
    e) None of the above

51. A gas at STP that contains 6.02×10^{23} atoms and forms diatomic molecules will occupy
    a) 11.2 L.
    b) 22.4 L.
    c) 33.6 L.
    d) 67.2 L.
    e) 1.06 quarts.

52. The collision theory explains the reaction rates of chemical reactions using which of the following?
    I. Activation energy
    II. Molecule orientation
    III. Potential energy curve
    IV. Frequency
    V. Activated complex
    a) I and III only
    b) II only
    c) I, II, and IV only
    d) IV only
    e) I, III, and V only

53. The units of work are given as L atm. To convert L atm to the metric unit of joules, we need to know
    a) Avogadro's constant.
    b) Planck's constant.
    c) the universal gas law constant in units of J mol^{-1} K^{-1}.
    d) gravity constant.
    e) All of the above

54. Which of the following statements is FALSE?
    a) The empirical formula for butyne is C_2H_3.
    b) The empirical formula for ammonia is NH_3.
    c) The empirical formula of CH_2O is $C_6H_{12}O_6$.
    d) Ionic compounds are written as empirical formulas.
    e) The empirical and molecular formulas for methane are the same.

55. Which of the following organic structures is propane?
    a) $CH_3-CH_2-CH_3$
    b) $CH_3-CO-OH$
    c) $CH_3-O-CH_2-CH_3$
    d) $CH_3-CH_2-NH_2$
    e) $CH_3-CO-CH_3$

56. What is the pH of a 0.100 M solution of K_2HPO_4? (For H_3PO_4, $pK_1 = 2.15$, $pK_2 = 7.20$, $pK_3 = 12.35$)
    a) 1.00
    b) 13.00
    c) 9.78
    d) 6.67
    e) 4.10

57. An electron with the four quantum numbers 3, 2, −1, −½ may be the electron in an unfilled sublevel of
   a) Ti.
   b) Co.
   c) Pd.
   d) Fe.
   e) Ag.

58. Which of the following substances would dissociate completely when placed into excess amounts of distilled water?
   a) C_2H_5OH
   b) $HC_2H_3O_2$
   c) $LiNO_3$
   d) $Mg(OH)_2$
   e) All of these will dissociate completely in water.

59. Which of the following indicate(s) a basic solution?
   I. Litmus paper turns blue.
   II. Phenolphthalein turns pink.
   III. Hydronium ion concentration is greater than hydroxide ion concentration.
   a) I only
   b) II only
   c) III only
   d) I and II only
   e) I, II, and III

60. Based on the relationship of entropy to the degree of disorder of a system, which of the following processes may represent a decrease in entropy?
   I. The freezing of water
   II. The vaporization of water
   III. Sublimation (vaporization) of dry ice, solid CO_2
   IV. The extraction of Mg and pure water from seawater
   a) I and II only
   b) II and IV only
   c) I and IV only
   d) III only
   e) II and III only

61. Which two items are most closely related to each other?
   I. Osmotic pressure
   II. Freezing-point depression
   III. Vapor pressure
   IV. Raoult's law
   V. Henry's law
   a) I and III
   b) II and V
   c) III and IV
   d) IV and V
   e) V and I

62. Which of the following is the most likely to increase the rate of a reaction?
   a) Decreasing the temperature
   b) Increasing the volume of the reaction vessel
   c) Reducing the activation energy
   d) Decreasing the concentration of the reactant in the reaction vessel
   e) Reducing the pressure

63. Sodium carbonate (Na_2CO_3) is the least soluble in which of the following liquids?
   a) CH_3OH
   b) CF_3COOH
   c) H_2O
   d) $CH_3(CH_2)_4CH_3$
   e) $CHCl_3$

64. Which of the following solution(s) has/have a concentration of 1.0 M?
    I. 40 grams of sodium hydroxide is dissolved to make 1 liter of solution.
    II. 111 grams of calcium chloride is dissolved to make 1 liter of solution.
    III. 119 grams of potassium bromide is dissolved to make 1 liter of solution.
    a) I only
    b) III only
    c) I and III only
    d) II and III only
    e) I, II, and III

65. The emission of a beta particle results in a new element with the atomic number
    a) increased by 1.
    b) increased by 2.
    c) decreased by 1.
    d) decreased by 2.
    e) no change.

66. Which of the following is the acid anhydride of a monoprotic acid?
    a) CaO
    b) SO_3
    c) FeO
    d) CO_2
    e) N_2O_5

67. How many phosphine molecules are in two moles of phosphine?
    a) 1.807×10^{24}
    b) 3.476×10^{24}
    c) 1.171×10^{24}
    d) 1.204×10^{24}
    e) 2.414×10^{24}

68. Which of the following is a physical property?
    a) Flammability
    b) Magnetism
    c) A color change in clothes due to exposure to light
    d) Freezing
    e) Burning

69. Which molecule(s) below exhibit(s) resonance?
    I. AsF_5
    II. HNO_3
    III. SO_2
    a) I only
    b) II only
    c) II and III only
    d) III and IV only
    e) I, II, and III

70. All of the following may determine the molar masses. Which one requires ideal solution for the accurate results?
    a) Freezing-point depression
    b) Boiling-point elevation
    c) Osmotic pressure
    d) Vapor pressure
    e) Gas density

SAT Chemistry Subject Test No. 10 Keys

1. A	11. E	21. C	31. E	41. E	51. A	61. C
2. B	12. C	22. C	32. D	42. A	52. C	62. C
3. E	13. C	23. A	33. C	43. E	53. C	63. D
4. D	14. E	24. B	34. C	44. C	54. C	64. E
5. E	15. A	25. D	35. D	45. B	55. A	65. A
6. C	16. C	26. C	36. B	46. C	56. C	66. E
7. B	17. D	27. B	37. C	47. C	57. B	67. D
8. D	18. D	28. B	38. D	48. B	58. E	68. B
9. A	19. A	29. A	39. D	49. B	59. D	69. C
10. E	20. E	30. A	40. C	50. A	60. C	70. D

101. TF
102. TF
103. TTCE
104. TTCE
105. FT
106. FT
107. TTCE
108. FT
109. TF
110. TTCE
111. FT
112. TF
113. TF
114. FT
115. TTCE

SAT Chemistry Subject Test No. 10 Answer to Part A

1 – 4 *Answer: (abed)*
Bromine and mercury are liquids at room temperature.

Cl_2 and F_2 are non-polar covalent molecules.

Diamond and graphite have network covalent bonds.

Li and Na are good reducing agents.

5 – 7 *Answer: (ecb)*
The larger the K_a, the stronger acid or electrolyte is.

If ΔG is positive, the reaction is nonspontaneous.

If ΔS is negative, there is less entropy.

8 – 10 *Answer: (dae)*
0.5 moles of H_2 will have 1 gram of mass.

32 grams of O_2 = 1 mole = 6.02×10^{23} molecules.

1.6 grams of CH_4 = 0.1 moles = $0.1 \times 6.02 \times 10^{23} \times 5$ atoms = 3.01×10^{23} atoms.

11 – 13 *Answer: (ecc)*
As the pressure of a gas increases, the volume of the gas will decrease. The graph that demonstrates Boyle's Law is curved as indicated by choice e).

As temperature increases, so does the volume of a gas.

As temperature increases, so does the pressure of a gas.

14 – 17 *Answer: (eacd)*
Tyndall Effect: The light scattering by particles in a colloid or particles in a fine suspension solution.
Brownian movement: The random motion of particles suspended in a fluid resulting from their collision
Phenolphthalein reaction: pink color in basic solution
Hydrogen bonding in water creates stronger than normal surface tension.

18 – 21 *Answer: (daec)*
Any mercury-filled thermometer will reveal the silver-gray color. Also note that mercury is a metal that is in the liquid state.

Potassium permanganate is a purple salt that forms a purple solution.

Sodium salts, when burned, will turn a flame a bright yellow color.

Besides its terrible choking odor, chlorine gas is famous for its green color.

22 – 25 *Answer: (cabd)*
The alkali metals react with water to form hydroxides and release hydrogen.

The noble gases are the least reactive because of their completed outer orbital.

The halogen family contains the colored gases fluorine and chlorine at room temperatures, the reddish liquid bromine, and solid purple iodine.

Si and Ge in the carbon group are metalloids.

SAT Chemistry Subject Test No. 10 Answer to Part C

26. *Answer: (c)*
$2 \times 12 + 5 + 16 + 1 = 46$

27. *Answer: (b)*
sp^3 has one unshared paired of electrons.

28. *Answer: (b)*
An alkaline earth metal is found in Group 2 of the periodic table. This means that it will have two valence electrons and form an ion with a charge of 2+. When it reacts with oxygen's ionic charge of 2-, the two ions will combine in a 1 : 1 ratio.

29. *Answer: (a)*
The Nernst equation enables the determination of cell potential under non-standard conditions. It relates the measured cell potential to the reaction quotient and allows the accurate determination of equilibrium constants (including solubility constants).

30. *Answer: (a)*
$A + B \rightarrow 2C \quad \Delta H = +150\ kcal$
$C \rightarrow 2D + 2E \ \Delta H = -450\ kcal$
$F \rightarrow 4D + 4E \ \Delta H = +725\ kcal$
$A + B \rightarrow F \ \Delta H = 1(+150) + 2(-450) - (725) = -1475\ kcal$

31. *Answer: (e)*
Ethane is a hydrocarbon with all single bonds. This means that the two carbon atoms will both be sp3 hybridized.

32. *Answer: (d)*
$CH_4 + O_2 \rightarrow CO_2 + H_2O$

33. *Answer: (c)*
An increase in temperature will increase the amount of heat, which is one of the reactants. Because a reactant was added, more products will be made.

34. *Answer: (c)*
The oxidation potential is the opposite of the standard reduction potential of Cu^{+2}.

35. *Answer: (d)*
$Na^+ + e^- \rightarrow Na \quad E^o = -2.71$
$2H^+ + 2e^- \rightarrow H_2 \quad E^o = 0$

36. *Answer: (b)*
HF is a weak acid and will also act like a weak electrolyte. The other substances are strong acids, strong bases, or water-soluble salts.

37. *Answer: (c)*
$H_2SO_4 + 2NaOH \rightarrow Na_2SO_4 + 2H_2O$
$98\ g\ H_2SO_4 = 1\ mole\ H_2SO_4$
$40\ g\ NaOH = 1\ mole\ NaOH$
NaOH is the limiting reactant
$Na_2SO_4 : NaOH = 1 : 2$
$= \frac{x}{23 \times 2 + 32 + 4 \times 16} : 1$
$x = \frac{23 \times 2 + 32 + 4 \times 64}{2} = 71\ g$

38. *Answer: (d)*
The alkaline earth metals, which have two valence electrons, will have the biggest ionization energy increase from I_2 to I_3.

39. *Answer: (d)*
Graphite can absorb many neutrons that make graphite a good control material of nuclear fission reactions.

40. *Answer: (c)*
A weak acid and its salt can be prepared as a buffer solution.

41. *Answer: (e)*
$\frac{P_1V_1}{T_1} = \frac{P_2V_2}{T_2}$
$\frac{750 \times 10}{20 + 273} = \frac{760 \times V_2}{273}$
$V_2 = 10 \times (750/760) \times (273/293)$

42. *Answer: (a)*
2 moles Na : 820 = 0.5 moles of Na : x
$x = 205.0\ kJ$

43. *Answer: (e)*
$2NaClO_3(s) \rightarrow 2NaCl + 3O_2$
$\Delta H_{rxn} = \frac{2 \times (-98.2) + 0 - 2(-85.7)}{2} = -12.5\ Kcal$

44. *Answer: (c)*
In the same Ksp expression, the compound with smaller Ksp will precipitate first. Therefore, SrF_2 will precipitate first. I and II are true. Continuing to add NaF to increase the concentration of F^- will both precipitate SrF_2 and BaF_2.

45. *Answer: (b)*
The burette is the most precise piece of glassware listed. Because a burette is narrow, the meniscus will be prominent and of importance.

46. *Answer: (c)*
Main group elements' valence electrons are those electrons in the outermost energy level of s and p subshells.

47. *Answer: (c)*
To calculate the amount of acid needed, use the titration formula: $M_1V_1 = M_2V_2$ *=(1.0)(30.0)=* $(1.5 \times V_2)$. *Solve to find that the volume of acid is 20.0 mL.*

48. *Answer: (b)*
Fe_2S_3 *is insoluble in water.*

49. *Answer: (b)*
Continuing to remove the product will let the reaction complete.

50. *Answer: (a)*
Electrolysis a process by which an electric current is used to drive non-spontaneous redox reactions.

51. *Answer: (a)*
6.02×10^{23} *atoms of diatomic molecules = 0.5 moles of gas* $= \frac{22.4}{2} = 11.2$ *L*

52. *Answer: (c)*
The collision theory describes the relationship between reaction rates and the frequency of molecular collisions and the orientation at which compounds collide.

53. *Answer: (c)*
The universal gas law constant in units of J mol^{-1} K^{-1} *is needed.*

54. *Answer: (c)*
All of these statements are correct except for choice c), which should be "The empirical formula of $C_6H_{12}O_6$ *is* CH_2O*" instead.*

55. *Answer: (a)*
Propane has the formula of C_3H_8.

56. *Answer: (c)*
At 2nd equivalence point: $pH = \frac{pK2 + pK3}{2} = 9.78$

57. *Answer: (b)*
$n=3$
$l = 2$
$m_s = -1$
$Spin = -\frac{1}{2}$
The quantum number above represents $3d^7$, *which is the last electron configuration of Co.*

58. *Answer: (e)*
If an infinite amount of water was added to the solution, all the compound would dissociate completely.

59. *Answer: (d)*
Litmus will be blue and phenolphthalein will be pink in a basic solution. The concentration of hydroxide ions should also be greater than the concentration of hydronium ions.

60. *Answer: (c)*
Entropy: Gas > Liquid > Solid

61. *Answer: (c)*
Raoult's law: the partial vapor pressure of each component of an ideal mixture of liquids is equal to the vapor pressure of the pure component multiplied by its mole fraction in the mixture.

62. *Answer: (c)*
The lower the activation energy, the easier to break chemical bonds, therefore the faster the chemical reactions are.

63. *Answer: (d)*
Polar dissolves in polar, and $CH_3(CH_2)_4CH_3$ *is non-polar.*

64. *Answer: (e)*
All three masses given are equivalent to 1 mole of the compounds in question. Because the 1 mole samples are all dissolved to make 1 liter of solution, each solution is 1 molar.

65. *Answer: (a)*
A beta particle has -1 atomic number. Therefore, the emission of a beta particle results in a new element with the atomic number increased by 1.

66. *Answer: (e)*
CaO and FeO are bases in solutions.
$SO_3 + H_2O = H_2SO_4$
$CO_2 + H_2O \rightarrow H_2CO_3$
$N_2O_5 + H_2O \rightarrow 2HNO_3$

67. *Answer: (d)*
Phosphine: PH_3
$2 \times 6.02 \times 10^{23} = 1.204 \times 10^{24}$

68. *Answer: (b)*
Magnetism is a physical property.
Freezing is a physical change.

69. *Answer: (c)*

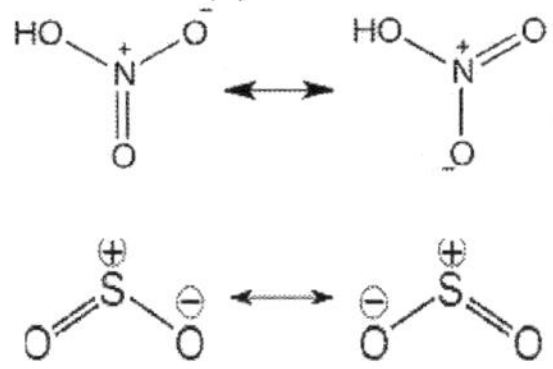

70. *Answer: (d)*
Raoult's law of partial vapor pressure requires an ideal solution to be accurate.

Index

END NOTE

You have now worked through the practice tests and read countless explanations. You are well-prepared and ready to take the test.

Thank you for choosing this book. I know you will face the test with confidence and grace. **Good luck, may the chemistry be with you**!

Dr. Jang, New Jersey, December 2015.

STAY TUNED FOR MORE BOOKS BY DR. JANG!

Dr. Jang's SAT 800 Series:

Dr. Jang's SAT 800 Math Workbook (2013, co-authored with Tiffany Jang)
Dr. Jang's SAT 800 Math Subject Test Level 2 (co-authored with Tiffany Jang)
Dr. Jang's SAT 800 Chemistry Subject Test (2015)
Dr. Jang's SAT 800 Physics Subject Test (2016)

Dr. Jang's AP 5 Series:

Dr. Jang's AP 5 Calculus AB/BC Workbook
Dr. Jang's AP 5 Physics 1 & 2 Workbook
Dr. Jang's AP 5 Physics C: Mechanics Workbook
Dr. Jang's AP 5 Physics C: Electricity and Magnetism Workbook
Dr. Jang's AP 5 Chemistry Workbook

Check Out More Services on Our Website:

www.DrJang800.com

The Goals of Dr. Jang's Books:

~For students:
To help you study based on your skill level.

~For teachers:
To help you plan lessons based on students' needs.

"Giving instruction based on each student's characteristics and ability will achieve the best educational results."

~ *Confucius*

29501457R00270

Made in the USA
San Bernardino, CA
14 March 2019